Anti-Communism in Britain During the Early Cold War

New Historical Perspectives is a book series for early career scholars within the UK and the Republic of Ireland. Books in the series are overseen by an expert editorial board to ensure the highest standards of peer-reviewed scholarship. Commissioning and editing is undertaken by the Royal Historical Society, and the series is published under the imprint of the Institute of Historical Research by the University of London Press.

The series is supported by the Economic History Society and the Past and Present Society.

Series co-editors: Professor Elizabeth Hurren (University of Leicester) and Professor Heather Shore (Manchester Metropolitan University)

Founding co-editors: Simon Newman (University of Glasgow) and Penny Summerfield (University of Manchester)

Editorial board: Professor Charlotte Alston (Northumbria University); Professor David Andress (University of Portsmouth); Dr Christopher Bahl (Durham University); Dr Milinda Banerjee (University of St Andrews); Dr Robert Barnes (York St John University); Dr Karin Bowie (University of Glasgow); Professor Catherine Clarke (Institute of Historical Research, University of London); Professor Neil Fleming (University of Worcester); Professor Ian Forrest (University of Oxford); Dr Emma Gallon (University of London Press); Professor Leigh Gardner (London School of Economics); Dr Sarah Longair (University of Lincoln); Dr Charlotte Wildman (University of Manchester); Dr Nick Witham (University College London)

Recently published

The Glasgow Sugar Aristocracy: Scotland and Caribbean Slavery, 1775–1838, by Stephen Mullen (November 2022)

The Poets Laureate of the Long Eighteenth Century, 1668–1813: Courting the Public, by Leo Shipp (August 2022)

Anti-Communism in Britain During the Early Cold War

A Very British Witch Hunt

Matthew Gerth

Available to purchase in print or download
for free at https://www.sas.ac.uk/publications

First published 2023 by
University of London Press
Senate House, Malet Street, London WC1E 7HU

© Matthew Gerth 2023

The right of Matthew Gerth to be identified as
author of this Work has been asserted by him/her
in accordance with sections 77 and 78 of the
Copyright, Designs and Patents Act 1988.

This book is published under a Creative Commons
Attribution-NonCommercial-NoDerivatives 4.0
International (CC BY-NC-ND 4.0) license.

Please note that third-party material reproduced here may
not be published under the same license as the rest of this
book. If you would like to reuse any third-party material
not covered by the book's Creative Commons license, you
will need to obtain permission from the copyright holder.

A CIP catalogue record for this book is
available from The British Library.

ISBN 978-1-914477-34-8 (hardback edition)
ISBN 978-1-914477-35-5 (paperback edition)
ISBN 978-1-914477-36-2 (.epub edition)
ISBN 978-1-914477-38-6 (.pdf edition)

DOI 10.14296/giub4814

Cover image: *It Seems We've Got Company (iStock/DjoleRad)*

Cover design by University of London Press.
Book design by Nigel French.
Text set by Westchester Publishing Services in
Meta Serif and Meta, designed by Erik Spiekermann.

For my parents, Arthur and Brenda Gerth

The Communist Party is at war. It is at
war with the rest of society, it is at war
with non-communist socialism, it is
at war with religion. It is at war with
tolerance and compromise.

Marxism teaches that man is a product
of his environment but that man is
capable of changing his environment
and thus changing himself.

Anything that hastens that change
is justifiable.

Anything.

And if the communist wants the
change badly enough he will do
anything.

—Bob Darke, *The Communist
Technique in Britain* (1952)

Communism seems to be the great
bogey in the Western hemisphere.
I cannot help feeling that a somewhat
exaggerated view is taken of the
whole thing.

—Guy Liddell, diary entry,
19 March 1945

Contents

Acknowledgements		ix
List of abbreviations		xi
	Introduction	1
1.	British McCarthyism	19
2.	Labour Party: the enemy within and without	57
3.	The Conservatives and the red menace	107
4.	Pressure groups: agents of influence	147
5.	The trade union movement: a fifth column?	189
	Conclusion	233
	Bibliography	241
	Index	259

Acknowledgements

Many special people have contributed their time and effort to make this book possible. I wish to thank first and foremost Paul Corthorn for his continuing guidance and supervision of my PhD at Queen's University Belfast. As both a mentor and friend, he has aided and encouraged me more than anyone else.

I am also indebted to the wise counsels of Alexander Titov, Kieran Connell, Richard Toye and Dianne Kirby. All have been nothing but generous with their advice, support and assistance during the writing process and far beyond.

Equally, my appreciation goes to my friends and colleagues who unwaveringly supported and backed me during this endeavour. These include Connel McKeown, Jessica Simonds, Samuel Beckton, Rebecca Kerr, Massimiliano Nastri, Oscar Holiday, Alexei Gavriel, Dominik Hamm, Bechara Karam, Charlie Freeland and Ryan McLean.

I have been afforded the great opportunity to publish this book within New Historical Perspectives by the University of London Press and the Royal Historical Society. This allowed me the guidance and assistance of a number of great historians. These are Heather Shore, Charlotte Alston, Ben Harker and Matthew Grant. I am grateful to all of them. No doubt their expert guidance and suggestions made this book better than it would otherwise have been. In addition, I owe a large amount of gratitude to Emma Gallon and Megan Garry-Evans from the University of London Press alongside Rosie Stewart at River Editorial.

Finally, I would like to thank the archivists and staff at The National Archives at Kew; the Modern Records Centre at the University of Warwick; People's History Museum Archive in Manchester; Lambeth Palace Library; Churchill Archives Centre in Cambridge; Public Record Office of Northern Ireland; Liddell Hart Military Archives in Kings College; and Weston Library in Oxford. Again, without their assistance this book would not have been possible.

List of abbreviations

AFL	American Federation of Labor
BBC	British Broadcasting Company
BHL	British Housewives' League
BLEF	British League for European Freedom
CAPRiM	Corporate Asset Protection and Risk Management
CCF	Congress of Cultural Freedom
CIA	Central Intelligence Agency
CIO	Congress of Industrial Organizations
CLP	constituency Labour Party
CPGB	Communist Party of Great Britain
CSCA	Civil Service Clerical Association
CYL	Communist Youth League
FBI	Federal Bureau of Investigation
FO	Foreign Office
GPO	General Post Office
GRU	Soviet military intelligence
HUAC	House Un-American Activities Committee
ICFTU	International Confederation of Free Trade Unions
ILP	Independent Labour Party
IRD	Information Research Department
IRIS	Industrial Research and Information Services Ltd
JBS	John Birch Society
JIC	Joint Intelligence Committee
KGB	Soviet Committee for State Security
LEL	League of Empire Loyalists
MI5	Security Service, British domestic security service

MI6	Secret Intelligence Service, British foreign intelligence service (SIS)
MP	Member of Parliament
MRA	Moral Rearmament Movement
NATO	North Atlantic Treaty Organization
NAWCS	National Association of Women Civil Servants
NCB	National Coal Board
NEC	National Executive Committee (Labour Party)
NKVD	People's Commissariat for Internal Affairs, interior ministry of the Soviet Union
NUJ	National Union of Journalists
NUM	National Union of Mineworkers
PLP	Parliamentary Labour Party
SIS	Secret Intelligence Service, British foreign intelligence service (MI6)
SOE	Special Operations Executive
TCA	The Consulting Association
TGWU	Transport and General Workers' Union
TNA	The National Archives
TUC	Trades Union Congress
UK	United Kingdom
UN	United Nations
US	United States of America
VTsSPS	Soviet All-Union Central Council of Trade Unions
WASP	White Anglo-Saxon Protestant
WFTU	World Federation of Trade Unions
WPC	World Peace Council
YCL	Young Communist League

Introduction

The British witch-hunt seemed pretty 'civilised'. That does not mean that it may not have been as effective – even more effective from the government's point of view ... we set out not to make martyrs whereas McCarthy made them left, right, and centre.[1]

—Douglas Hyde, former news editor for the *Daily Worker*

The decade after the Second World War saw the rise of anti-communism in the political sphere and governmental institutions of the United Kingdom (UK). In the grip of the emerging Cold War, the fight against domestic communism – in all its guises – fashioned into a broad consensus that took hold in mainstream politics. It formed through the concerted efforts of the Labour and Conservative parties, governmental institutions and pressure groups, and as a result of external influence from the United States (US). The consensus brought with it new counterinsurgency measures and a heightened sense of awareness over security matters. It also established an atmosphere of mistrust and paranoia. The era constituted a period when the British state – through mostly covert means – allied with non-governmental actors to battle against a number of its citizenry.

The times were strange indeed. When reviewing the rhetoric of the period, one comes to imagine proverbial barbarians ready to storm the gates of Westminster.[2] For some in government, the threat of a 'barbarian invasion' was not just a figure of speech. Records show that as early as 1946 the mandarins in Whitehall were actively preparing for a Soviet invasion of the British homeland. Files housed in The National Archives (TNA) in Kew detail a Joint Intelligence Committee directive for an in-depth topographical survey of the UK's coastline and beaches to be conducted post haste. The top-secret survey, working under the name 'Operation Sandstone', was then given to the US navy.[3] Leadership in both countries considered it of vital importance to assist in planning future American landings, which would be needed to liberate the UK from an impending Soviet occupation. Furthermore, in the minds of many in government, the barbarians had already breached the gates and were silently awaiting orders to strike.

Starting in 1948, MI5 quickly drew up plans to erect detention camps to house potential fifth columnists in the event of a national emergency.[4] First on the list were known members of the Communist Party of Great Britain (CPGB) and their suspected allies.[5] The government relied not only on topographical mapping and contingency plans to combat the menace. More proactive steps were also put in place, policies which strove to minimise and eliminate the perceived threat. For many, these measures did not go far enough. In both Houses of Westminster Palace, in demonstrations on the streets of London, in cabinet discussions, in trade union meetings and in printed publications, a warning arose that more was needed to safeguard the UK from a communist takeover. In corners of the political establishment there was a longing for McCarthyite solutions. Not all Britons viewed the excessive wave of red-hunting across the Atlantic as an entirely negative occurrence. A number of those in power strove to implement a version of their own which was palatable and acceptable to the political and societal makeup of the British nation.

Historiography

The above depiction runs contrary to the comforting and alluring traditional narrative of the era. This narrative suggests that while Americans were gripped in an exaggerated fear of communism, the level-headed British retained both their wits and their commitment to decency and fair play. 'Since the early days of the Cold War', historian Jennifer Luff maintained, 'observers have reproached American anti-communism by invoking the example of British moderation.'[6] Sociologists during the 1950s and 1960s were the first to make the comparison. University of Chicago professor Edward Shils argued that the lack of 'populist sentiment' in political life and the 'ruling classes' imposing a 'traditional sense of privacy' left British society immune to the frenzy of red-hunting infecting the US.[7] In 1964, Herbert Hyman of Columbia University maintained that in the UK the 'political exploitation of the communist issue, which could contribute to a climate of intolerance has been negligible', and argued that red-baiting during past election campaigns there was almost non-existent. The first historian to put forth this interpretation was David Caute who, in the late 1970s, lambasted the US for its 'anti-Communist hysteria' and its failure 'to sustain the authentically liberal values and standards of tolerance that persisted in Britain'.[8] Subsequently, a number of academics followed suit, arguing that a governmental overreaction towards domestic communism did not take place in the UK.[9] The proponents of this historical interpretation charge that, when equated with the excesses of American McCarthyism, the UK's response must be considered restrained and reasonable.

In sequent years, however, scholarship on the period has questioned the notion of the UK contemporaneously dodging its own red scare. As access to more documents became possible, researchers begun contesting the long-accepted version of events, subsequently arguing that a type of political repression indeed took place, but, because of a number of variables, one not as visible and high-profile as that contemporaneously erupting across the Atlantic. Perhaps the first historian to draw this conclusion was Dianne Kirby, who during the late 1980s began her PhD research questioning the established narrative.[10] Her work developed from the assertions of a number of left-academics who in the mid-1980s harshly repudiated Caute's claim.[11] Focusing on anti-communism repression in the Church of England, Kirby formulated the supposition that a type of 'British McCarthyism' did in fact exist.[12] The work of Rhodri Jeffrey-Jones also supports this view: Jeffrey-Jones wrote that 'taking a broad definition of McCarthyism, as is now standard practice ... it is evident that the phenomenon existed in Britain as well as in America'.[13]

Richard Thurlow drew similar conclusions, stating there existed a 'significant political paranoia, which developed into a kind of British McCarthyism'.[14] More recently, Luff refuted Caute's interpretation by contending the nation's 'liberal tradition' did not leave it immune from an exaggerated response to the so-called red menace.[15] The book *MI5, Cold War, and the Rule of Law* is the most significant and substantial revisionist work in this field of study to date. Viewing the events through a legal lens, the authors allege MI5 enacted gross abuses against civil liberties and argue 'the post-war focus on the Communist Party is not one that could easily be justified by the mandate with which MI5 was entrusted'.[16] They conclude that the security service violated the rule of law and exceeded its legal authority through its countersubversive activities. As the growing research in this revisionist movement has expanded, it is increasingly evident that, contrary to what many have attested, the UK did not escape 'an unwarranted obsession with communists and communism'.[17]

An obsession with communism is perhaps the best way to define the focus of this book. Unlike prior studies in the field, this monograph seeks to comprehensively demonstrate how domestic anti-communism exhibited itself in state policies, political rhetoric, party politics and the trade union movement of the UK of the early postwar years. Through an examination of how the phenomenon materialised and functioned in these facets of the body politic, we arrive at a more profound understanding of its impact on both the nation and its citizenry, alongside identifying the central architects of the anti-communism reaction. Taken as a whole, this response constituted an overreaction to the threat posed. Until recently, this response to the 'red menace' has attracted relatively little attention compared to the phenomenon of American McCarthyism. Throughout the years, numerous scholars have raised just such a point. In the 1980s, Reg Whitaker argued, 'There is no study of the domestic impact of the Cold War on British politics, as such; the picture has to be pieced together from fragmentary information from disparate sources.'[18] A decade later, Steve Parsons wrote:

> Anti-communism in Britain never reached the pathological heights that it did in the USA; no one was imprisoned because of their party membership; fear and hatred of communism were never used to measure one's patriotism and national identity. Yet a series of significant developments took place in post-war Britain – a domestic impact of the Cold War that has generally been passed over in silence.[19]

Closer to the present, Giora Goodman concurred with this assessment. She reasoned, 'the manifestations of domestic anti-communism in Britain during the early Cold War ... have received attention from historians but have not been fully explored'.[20] Karen Potter contended there is 'an incomplete accounting' of the 'manifestations of anti-communism in Britain during the Cold War years'.[21]

Anti-communism's manifestation in the UK of the early Cold War was not (nor should it be considered) a neatly mirrored version of the American experience. Because of the societal, governmental and institutional variances between the US and the UK, the British version transpired differently. Nevertheless, in the UK – just as in the US – the issue was politicised through the means of state repression, red-baiting and the 'othering' of fellow citizens. The handful of prior revisionist studies has identified segments within the religious and intelligence communities as the chief instigators for the more aggressive and disproportionate response. Yet neither these hierarchical men of the cloth nor the shadowy figures who lurked in the halls of the 'secret state' were the individuals seeking further oppressive measures to tackle the threat. When identifying the promoters of the British 'witch hunt', this book points to a subset of the nation's politicians – the representatives of the public good – as its driving catalyst, one primarily filled with those within the Labour Party. Yet while these elected overseers constituted the impetus of the fight against communism, the cause had many acolytes in the clergy, trade unions, civil service, police and security service. As we will see throughout the following pages, working as a collective, these individuals formed the consensus anti-communism that emerged from the era. Picking up where other academics have left off, this work provides a holistic account of anti-communism within British politics and government of the era.

Defining anti-communism

Since its inception, the political and economic ideology of classical Marxism has been met with fierce resistance. In a Hegelian move, an antithesis quickly formed to combat this new thesis. This counter-philosophy would manifest itself in diverse forms. Alongside an obsessive nature, it held two fixed tenets in its belief system – namely, that communism is a 'supreme and unqualified evil' and its followers seek to impose this evil on the entire world.[22] With this Manichaean viewpoint firmly in place, the opponents to communism went out to combat their nemesis. Through this confrontation, a new quasi-ideology – anti-communism – was created. Yet, anti-communism remains an elusive concept, since the term suffers from the imprecision of its meaning. In this work and many others, it signifies a type of creed or way of thinking.[23] Anti-communist is more than simply not being a communist – one must be actively opposed to communism and communists themselves. Anti-communism, as Moshe Lewin argued, 'is less a matter of research and more an ideology claiming to be a study':[24] one forged in both fiction and reality, a dangerous mixture, which had led to a form of psychosis in a number of its unhinged votaries. The crimes and abuses of communism are well documented.[25] Yet, anti-communists were unsatisfied in only fighting these real transgressions. A multitude of exaggerations, and sometimes outright fantasies, fuelled their ideology. They routinely practised mythmaking: myths of conspiracies, cultural and ethnic stereotypes, and civilisational clashes.[26] As philosopher Karl Popper pointed out, when conspiratorially minded individuals find themselves in positions of power, they often take on the perceived and imagined trappings of their enemies – thus imitating their foes.[27] Anti-communists often exemplified this type of governing approach when in authority.

Anti-communists of the time were didactic by nature. The rhetoric and methods of anti-communists developed from their belief system. In simplistic terms, they viewed their cause and themselves as a crusade and crusaders against an 'evil empire' and 'failed god'. Such thinking brought an intensity and urgency to their efforts, and in specific instances a willingness to transcend boundaries – both legal and ethical – when confronting their foe. Here it is worth recounting at length the commentary of sociologist Joel Kovel on the topic:

Because the moral logic of anticommunism had but two poles, it matched the Cold War geopolitical reality of a world divided into two hostile power blocs. Anticommunist statements of value were therefore drawn away from a simple negative assessment of communism and turned into a zero-sum game in which every demerit of the red East was automatically scored as an asset for the West. Thus bad became our good. Now once you enter this theological domain there is really no turning back. The morality of anticommunism drives toward a state of all-goodness defining our side of things, surrounded, indeed defined, by a force of all-badness: absolute evil, evil so great that anything – any violation of human rights, any crime, any war – is a priori justified.[28]

Alongside its moralistic nature, the ideology worked to buttress the status quo in non-communist countries. Thus, unlike its foil, it found tremendous success in the West. Anti-communism worked as a vanguard for the traditional social order.[29] Therefore, few governing elites found it objectionable, even as anti-communism penetrated societal and governmental institutions and shifted existing cultural attitudes. It quickly formed a cornerstone of national identity and the core belief system in numerous countries – nowhere more so than in the US and UK.[30] Federico Romero explained that domestic anti-communists within Western countries came from 'distinct political cultures' and were 'often engaged in fierce competition' between themselves for power and influence. However, during the early Cold War, they merged their different voices into 'a shared representation that structured public narratives and intellectual discourse no less than official propaganda'.[31]

Despite all these commonalities, the ideology manifested itself in different forms where it took root. As John Earl Hayes made clear, anti-communism 'needs to be understood in the context in which it has occurred'.[32] As this book demonstrates, in Cold War Britain the foundation of anti-communism rested on the following assertions:

- Communism was directly comparable and linked to fascism and Nazism.
- Communism constituted a conspiracy, not a political party or ideology.
- Communism functioned as a Soviet tool used to weaken the UK.
- Communism worked as a religion and those who followed it were willing to betray their country.

These core beliefs were what British anti-communism rested upon. They formed the driving motivators of the cause and consistently were found in the political rhetoric of the era and as stated justifications for governmental counterinsurgency measures. These assumptions also led to the politicisation of the anti-communist issue. The adopting of language casting communism as comparable to the despised ideologies of Nazism and fascism permitted the demonisation of the CPGB. The notion of a vast underlying conspiracy allowed for attacks on left-wing elements of society that challenged the ruling establishment. The charges that domestic communism was directed by a foreign power and that Marxists were more likely to betray the country gave sanction to the 'othering' of fellow Britons.

The explicit rejection of Marxism and Marxist political thought was another facet of British anti-communism that arose from the period. Conservatives denounced both, alongside a number in the Labour Party hierarchy. On various occasions, the Labour Party maintained it had no relation to Marxism and rejected any claim that it ever did. Several scholars have put forth a strong argument that Labour socialism and Marxist theory never held a close connection, even prior to the Cold War. Richard Toye argued that Marxist influence on Labour socialism existed, but its influence was quite limited.[33] Andrew Thorpe claimed that from its origin the Labour Party consistently preached a less radical version of socialism, which held more in common with 'German revisionism of the late nineteenth and early twentieth centuries than with classic Marxism'.[34] Stuart Macintyre suggested that by the 1920s there existed 'a distinct Labour socialist ideology' which functioned as a 'complete alternative' to Marxism.[35] Patrick Cosgrave, a one-time advisor to Margaret Thatcher, stated that while many 'assumed that Labour Party's socialism was Marxist in origin', the truth is it owed more to the creeds found in Methodism.[36] Labour's first prime minister, Ramsay MacDonald, viewed Karl Marx's methods as critical and destructive and argued against its revolutionary theories.[37] MacDonald declared Labour 'socialism marks the growth of society, not the uprising of a class'.[38]

By his own account, the party's second prime minister cared nothing for Marxist theory whatsoever. During a 1954 trip to the Soviet Union, Clement Attlee was asked by the British ambassador if he had ever 'read any of this Marx stuff'. Attlee stated he 'had read none of it, you know' and, in the recollections of Richard Crossman, cared more about finding out the most recent cricket scores from back home than discussing political theory.[39] Attlee's admission of not having read Marx by no means stopped him from disassociating the Labour Party from Marx's theories. In 1945, when responding to campaign attacks from Churchill, Attlee 'reminded' the prime minister that Labour socialism, unlike socialist parties on the continent, had no foundation in Marx. 'He [Churchill] has forgotten',

Attlee stated, 'that socialist theory was developed in Britain long before Karl Marx.'[40] Years later, during an interview with a reporter from an American magazine, he stressed: 'our system which has little to do with Marxism sprang from religious origins'.[41] Attlee was not alone in his lack of interest in and hostility towards Marx's theories. Foreign Secretary Ernest Bevin once retorted to his Soviet counterpart that 'members of the House of Lords are the only people in England who have the time to read Karl Marx'.[42] A number of lords on the Labour benches would have disagreed with Bevin's tongue-in-cheek assessment. They had no time for Marx either. Addressing a May Day rally in 1951, the minister of civil aviation – soon to be promoted to first lord of the admiralty – Lord Pakenham pointed out that any socialist party basing itself on Marxism was wrong, since true socialists believed not only in equality but also in the individualist value of every single person.[43] 'Speaking for myself', he would later say in the Lords, 'we have no use for Marxism whatever on these benches.'[44] During a speech on industrial relations in 1955, Labour peer Lord Amwell made clear he was 'not a Marxist; I do not agree with either his economics or his philosophy'. Amwell told his fellow lords he did 'not expect modern socialists to understand or accept Marx's theory. Not even those who call themselves Marxists have ever read his works except at second hand in bits and slogans'.[45] On behalf of the entire Labour Party, its chairman Morgan Phillips called Marxism a 'historically aberrant tendency in the development of British socialism' and argued Labour's version of socialism contradicts 'Marxism at almost every point'.[46] Phillips went on to denounce the theory unequivocally: 'Our rejection of Marxism as a philosophy has not made us any less revolutionary than those who claim to be his official spiritual descendants today and who would impose a new tyranny on the people of the world.'[47] By the early 1950s, a final break had occurred between Marxist theory and Labour socialist thinking, if one ever truly existed.[48] In *The Future of Socialism* (1956) – a book labelled one of the most important treatises on social democracy written in the UK – Anthony Crosland denounced Marxism as an irrelevant set of ideas.[49] 'In my view', Crosland wrote, 'Marx has little or nothing to offer the contemporary socialist, either in respect of practical policy, or of the correct analysis of our society, or even of the right conceptual tools or framework.'[50]

Inside the ranks of the Conservative Party, the distinction between democratic socialism and Marxist-Leninist totalitarianism was quite blurred – certainly on purpose when it was time for campaigning in general elections. Conservatives contended that any sort of post-capitalist society would eventually lead to the erosions of individual liberty and the death of democratic institutions. In more campaign-friendly terms, basically, socialism leads to communism. Alongside the two major political parties, the Church of England took a dim view of the political concept of Marxism. The leading article in a 1949 issue of the *York Diocesan Leaflet* decried the 'Marxian Attack on Religion'.[51] Archbishop Geoffrey Fisher argued that 'the premises of Marxian materialism' were 'irreconcilable' to Western Christian civilisation.[52] Oddly, Fisher professed to despise Marxism more than the theory of communism. He reasoned that 'Marxist communism rests upon principles which are not compatible with the Christian philosophy but communism can be detached from these principles and, to some extent, can be made compatible with Christian ideas'.[53] The Catholic Church was also antagonistic to the theory. The *Catholic Standard* put its thoughts on the topic quite succinctly in 1955: 'Marxism and religion can't co-exist.'[54] 'We have to take a stand for Christian doctrine founded on the Ten Commandments', the Archbishop of Birmingham proclaimed at a rally in 1952. He told the audience that to do so, 'We must take a stand, for example, against Marxism.'[55] From 1945 to 1956, the term 'Marxism' in the politics of the UK – as it did during the American red scare – held the same negative connotations as communism. This was especially, if not also surprisingly, the case within the ranks of the Labour Party leadership.

Alongside the explicit rejection of Marxist theory by the ruling political establishment, another major tenet of anti-communism was a strong anti-Soviet sentiment. Again, this resonated because of a fear of a fifth column working for a hostile foreign power.[56] In the possibility of an all-out war with the Soviet Union, it was suspected that some Britons would side against crown and country and underhandedly fight for the opposing side. The anti-communists considered the 'battle' against domestic communism as the 'home front' and a vital part of the Cold War, so by logical extension part of the fight against the Soviet Union. The anti-communists thought the hearts and minds of Britons at home needed to be won against communism or the Western defences against the East might dissipate and eventually fail.[57] This mentality of securing the home front echoed the same efforts made against the external enemy of Nazism during the Second World War. Such a mindset of danger from an 'enemy from within' was not only manifest inside political institutions but seeped into the overall culture as well. Tony Shaw wrote that a simple trip to the neighbourhood cinema could give such an impression: 'Cinema-goers were constantly reminded of the need to be on the look-out for political "deviants" masquerading as ordinary citizens ... implying that the Cold War was as much an international civil war as an inter-state conflict.'[58] Here, American influence takes a large amount of credit. Between 1948 and the early 1960s, Hollywood produced over 100 films in which the struggle against the evils of communism was an overt theme; nearly every one ran in British movie houses.[59]

Background and narrative overview

Dread over communism existed long before the Cold War. Both governmental and private attempts to combat it can be traced back to the 1917 Russian Revolution. To many in the Western world, the bloody execution of Tsar Nicholas II and his entire family marked a grave warning sign for their prospective futures if the threat of revolution could spread from the borders of the once-mighty Russian Empire. 'We are running a race with Bolshevism', warned Woodrow Wilson in March 1919, 'and the world is on fire.'[60] In the context of the times, few saw Wilson's declaration as mere hyperbole. The spring of 1919 saw Soviet republics declared in Hungary and Bavaria. The leader of the newly established Russian-based Communist International (or Comintern), Grigori Zinoviev, promised that this marked only the start, and estimated that 'within a year all [of] Europe will be communist'.[61]

Observers in the UK took the matter seriously; anxiety over a Russian-style upheaval crept into the public mindset. A 1919 protest by the Scottish Trade Union Congress quickly turned into a citywide general strike, which resulted in clashes between workers and police. The Battle of George Square, as it became known, appeared to many as the opening shots of a nationwide revolution. The secretary of state for Scotland called the strikers a 'Bolshevist uprising' and ordered onto the streets of Glasgow an army of 10,000 soldiers equipped with machine guns and tanks.[62] The fear of red insurrection endured. The reaction to a January 1926 radio programme called *Broadcasting from the Barricades* is evidence of its lingering into the mid-1920s. The twelve-minute broadcast aired on the British Broadcasting Company (BBC), claiming to be a live news bulletin covering a revolutionary mob rampaging the streets of London. The realistic 'news reports' stated that the rioters had blown up the Savoy Hotel and used trench mortars to topple Big Ben. It turned out to be all just a hoax – satirical in nature – perpetrated in jest by a Catholic priest who wrote detective novels named Frank Knox. The reaction it engendered was no laughing matter. Listeners from across the country were convinced that London lay in ruins. Relatives of guests staying in the Savoy Hotel urgently phoned the establishment to check on their loved ones. Through diplomatic channels, the Irish Free State made inquiries to find out whether the House of Commons had been destroyed.[63] This reaction proved quite similar to the scare induced in the US by Orson Welles's updated version of H.G. Wells's *War of the Worlds* twelve years later. The radio pranks of both Welles and Knox aroused in their audiences a dread of a potential future. In the US it was a growing concern over affairs in Europe and in the UK the likelihood of a communist-inspired uprising.[64]

For its part, MI5 considered the ability of the Soviet Union to inspire and instigate subversive activities more a direct threat than Soviet-sponsored espionage. It feared most of all a communist-inspired mutiny inside the British armed services.[65] A 1931 seamen's strike in the Atlantic Fleet docked at Invergordon contributed to the belief that a full-on rebellion was possible. Although the quickly ended dispute at Invergordon was not deemed red-inspired, the cabinet was told that communists 'had sent their best agents' to infiltrate navy ports to sow rebellion.[66] The resulting actions saw two CPGB members charged and imprisoned for mutiny and hundreds of seamen purged from the navy.[67] Another key target for MI5 were working-class communists. They were put under surveillance and were subject to arrests for their political beliefs – not in engaging in espionage activities. After a 1921 raid on the CPGB headquarters, the police arrested Albert Inkpin for printing seditious literature.[68] A visiting communist organiser from the US was sentenced to a month in jail for possessing a list of party members in Manchester. In 1931, Bernard Moore, a communist candidate for parliament in a Birmingham constituency, was arrested for being a 'disturber of the peace'.[69] The 1926 General Strike brought with it a large number of detained and arrested communists. Indeed, for MI5, communism constituted a problem bubbling up from the bottom of society.

Neither the intelligence community nor right-wing elements of the governing establishment trusted the Labour Party to combat communism. From the start of the first Labour government in 1923, MI6 withheld covert intelligence and foreign communication intercepts from its elected ministers. The agency determined these vital secrets were not safe in the hands of such potential security risks. The decision by Prime Minister Ramsay MacDonald to accord *de jure* recognition to the Soviet Union only strengthened this mistrust. So too did Labour's decision to halt the prosecution of J.R. Campbell, a communist journalist charged with attempting to subvert the armed services. The dropping of charges against Campbell resulted in a vote of no confidence in the House of Commons and the 1924 General Election campaign.[70] The election brought relations between British intelligence and the Labour Party to a new low. The matter turned on the publication of the so-called Zinoviev Letter. With only days to go before the October election, the *Daily Mail* detailed the contents of a letter purportedly sent from the Moscow headquarters of the Comintern to the CPGB. The letter, supposedly signed by Comintern leader Zinoviev, stated that a Labour victory would greatly benefit the Soviet cause. The Zinoviev Letter confirmed the suspicions of many Britons that the Labour Party was soft regarding its willingness to fight communism.[71] Doubts arose that the document ever existed, and its supposed contents were thought to be fabricated by MI6 to embarrass Labour and ensure its electoral defeat. Conservatives would go on to win the election by a wide margin, with many in Labour blaming it on the forged Zinoviev Letter.[72] Conclusive evidence never surfaced that MI6 had a hand in orchestrating the affair, though many in Labour Party circles still believed it did. Historian Keith Jeffrey reached the same conclusion: 'right-wing elements, with the connivance of allies in the security and intelligence services, deliberately used the letter – and perhaps even manufactured it – to ensure a Labour defeat'.[73]

By the late 1930s, the perceived threat from communism and Soviet agitation diminished considerably. Governmental counterinsurgency activities remained predominantly focused on the armed forces, the trade unions and the CPGB.[74] Yet, the anti-communist spirit had dampened after the nation weathered the storms of the 1926 General Strike, and the 1934 unemployment marches, without either spiralling into full-blown Marxist revolutions. In addition, many in the UK found Stalin's Soviet Union less menacing – because of its emphasis on socialism in one nation rather than international revolution. The situation had changed so much that in 1938 Head of MI5 Vernon Kell boasted to his French counterpart that 'Soviet activity in England is non-existent, in terms of both intelligence and political subversion.'[75] In terms of communist subversion, Kell was mostly correct. Historian Peter Clarke attested there was zero likelihood of a red takeover of the UK during the interwar years. Clarke wrote:

> The spectre of Bolshevism in Britain was mainly just that: a phantasm. The Communist Party of Great Britain, set up in 1920, was tiny; and the fact that it took its orders from Moscow was not so much sinister as inhibiting ... the security forces naturally had a professional interest in providing spine-chilling reports on ... examples of subversion. Though the significance of activities was largely in inflating the red menace, for theatrical effect and political advantage.[76]

In retrospect, the anti-communism of the interwar period was largely driven by the threat of revolution and subversion, not that of espionage or conspiracy. It was a period when right-wing politicians and intelligence agencies were the primary purveyors of anti-communism in government policies.

Mirroring the changing politics of the time, the advent of the Cold War and the rise of the Labour Party to power brought a new and heightened brand of anti-communism in the years following the Second World War. The quasi-ideology reached its pinnacle during this postwar era, as communism replaced Nazism and fascism as the dominant enemy of the state and the citizenry it governed. As East–West tensions worsened, communism became increasingly unacceptable. Under the premiership of Clement Attlee, a consensus on how to deal with the threat emerged. The ruling Labour Party set the direction and generated the degree of intensity of the domestic fight against communism. This constituted a startling shift from the interwar times. Shortly after taking power, evidence of Labour's aggressive anti-communism appeared. Less than a year into office, its leadership targeted communists for fomenting domestic disruptions in the new postwar climate and began implementing new counterinsurgency and counterintelligence measures. Although Labour spearheaded and initiated this transformation, it continued under the subsequent ruling Conservative governments. Under the guidance of both parties, the government systematically put in place unprecedented measures to combat and curb communist influence. It sought to purge and prohibit communists from government jobs; halt their inclusion inside the democratic process; limit their ability to travel; wiretap and put under surveillance a number of its citizenry; question the patriotism and loyalty of all individuals with communist affiliations; and secretly indoctrinate the British population into holding a more anti-communist worldview. Direct pressure from the US government contributed to heightened security measures and increased anti-communist policies in the British government, but contemporaneously the British public's negative reaction to the excesses of the American witch hunts moderated and shifted these measures to forge a less overt and more shadowy response. As this book seeks to show, what transpired came to be a very British witch hunt.

Chapter structure

The first chapter of this book examines extreme anti-communism which arose in the political discourse of the times. It describes the efforts of two of the most dogged and prolific anti-communists of the era – former Foreign Office (FO) diplomat Robert Vansittart, who sat in the House of Lords as an independent, and Sir Waldron Smithers, a maverick Tory member of the House of Commons. This duo represents the quintessential McCarthyite anti-communist reaction, thus disproving such methods were absent in British politics. The thematic core of the chapter regards the use of political repression – as opposed to state – and explores the type of illiberal anti-communism that is conventionally considered a uniquely American phenomenon. An accounting of the motives and techniques used by these individuals and others gives credence to the argument that 'British McCarthyism' did exist and operated in quite the same manner as its American namesake.

Chapter 2 focuses on Labour anti-communism during the Attlee government. While in power, Labour crafted a form of consensus anti-communism which functioned as governmental policy; the chapter examines Clement Attlee's efforts to eliminate supposed crypto-communists from the Parliamentary Labour Party (PLP). The prime minister employed MI5 to seek evidence to justify these removals. Next, the issue of security vetting is covered extensively. Ordered by the Labour government, and implemented by MI5, this is perhaps the most recognisable manifestation of domestic anti-communism of the early Cold War. Colloquially called 'the purge', the vetting process sought to remove communists and other potential subvariants from sectors of government service. The fact the purge only applied to several government departments is often championed as evidence of governmental restraint. However, its limited scope had very little to do with protecting civil liberties and personal freedom, owing more to the logistic impossibility of vetting the entire civil service. Also evidenced is MI5's concern that the government allowed the purge to expand beyond its original mandate. The lukewarm public reception to the initial announcement of vetting procedures convinced Attlee to stealthily enact subsequent anti-communist measures with no future announcements. Included here is an examination of the employment of visa and immigration restrictions to halt communist influence and the establishment of the Information Research Department and the Committee on Communism (Home). The existence of these two governmental entities was classified as top secret; though both conducted domestic operations that affected the British citizenry, the public was kept in the dark.

Chapter 3 is dedicated to the Conservative Party and its dealings with anti-communism. It first covers the use of electoral red-baiting by the party during the 1945 and 1950 General Election campaigns. In both instances, the Conservatives sought explicitly to link the ideology of socialism to that of the reviled communism. Detailed next are the non-governmental investigations conducted by the Central Office of the party into communist activities. These efforts by the party's leadership amounted to an unofficial and non-governmental witch hunt. Included as well is an in-depth analysis of the Philby affair of 1955. Rightfully suspected of being the 'third man' who aided in the escape of Guy Burgess and Donald Maclean, Philby was publicly cleared on the floor of the House of Commons by Harold Macmillan. While Philby is considered the crown prince of British traitors, his exoneration has received very little attention in the various monographs and biographies which depict his exploits. Yet the Philby affair exposes a rift in the anti-communism consensus of the period.

Chapter 4 investigates the activities of the anti-communist pressure groups operating during the era. A robust anti-communism movement functioned inside the British political sphere that existed outside the party and governmental structures. The individual examinations of these pressure groups identify a number of key parties pushing the anti-communist agenda. These organisations both worked within the political framework of the UK and as private organisations cooperated with and garnered covert assistance from government agencies. The chapter examines how British officials aided these groups in their anti-communist activities and how these organisations provided interested parties with the means to influence their agendas through undisclosed means.

Finally, Chapter 5 deals with the trade union movement and industrial unrest. Communists and their opponents alike regarded the best chance – short of a Soviet invasion – for a communist takeover to succeed as resting on control of organised labour. For both sides, it was a battle that needed to be won. The chapter explains the context of the conflict and outlines the methods used to counter communism by trade unionism leaders; it examines state participation in the matter, alongside how the Conservative and Labour governments dealt with industrial unrest. The chapter strongly argues that a governmental consensus formed clandestinely to fight communism in trade unions, since any overt attempts would prove counterproductive. While in power, both Labour and the Conservatives stuck to this strategy. However, the two political parties in government demonstrated a total deviation in their attitudes towards industrial action and unofficial strikes. Despite convincing evidence provided to him by MI5 refuting the charges, Attlee and members of his cabinet accused communists of engaging in sabotage and blamed them as chief instigators of a number of high-profile strikes. Conversely, after returning to Downing Street, the Conservatives rarely made such unsubstantiated allegations – instead, they accepted the assessments of the intelligence community (MI5, Special Branch, and so on) as facts.

Notes

1. D. Hyde, *I Believed* (London, 1951), p. 99.

2. Young Citizens Challenge to Communism, *Communism: The Enemy Within Our Gates* (London, 1949).

3. Over 1,300 files pertaining to Operation Sandstone are housed in The National Archives in Kew, categorised under the subheading ADM 326.

4. These plans, released to the public in 2005, scheduled the use of the Isle of Wight as well as Ascot and Epsom racecourses as internment facilities if a war with the Soviet Union appeared imminent. See TNA KV 4/251.

5. Guy Liddell's diary, entry 27 July 1951 (henceforth Liddell diary, date). The Liddell diaries are housed in the following files at TNA: KV 4/185–KV 4/196 (1939–45) and KV 4/466–KV 4/475 (1945–53). Codenamed 'Wallflowers', they were considered so sensitive that MI5 kept them locked away in a safe. Liddell's wartime diaries were released in 2002 and his Cold War musings were not declassified until 2012.

6. J. Luff, 'Covert and overt operations: Interwar political policing in the United States and the United Kingdom', *American Historical Review*, 122 (2017): 727–57, at p. 734.

7. See ch. 2, sect. iv, 'The British pattern: The bulwark of privacy', in E. Shils, *The Torment of Secrecy* (Chicago, 1956).

8. D. Caute, *The Great Fear* (New York, 1978), p. 20.

9. G. Goodman, 'The British government and the challenge of McCarthyism in the early Cold War', *Journal of Cold War Studies*, 12 (2010): 62–97, at pp. 63–5; P. Hennessy and G. Brownfeld, 'Britain's Cold War security purge: The origins of positive vetting', *Historical Journal*, 25.4 (1982): 965–74, at p. 970.

10. D. Kirby, 'The Anglican Church in the period of the Cold War 1945–55' (unpublished Hull University PhD thesis, 1990).

11. See *Socialist Register 1984: The Uses of Anti-Communism*, ed. R. Miliband, J. Saville and M. Libman (London, 1984).

12. D. Kirby, 'Ecclesiastical McCarthyism: Cold War repression in the Church of England', *Contemporary British History*, 19 (2005): 187–203, at pp. 187–8.

13. R. Jeffreys-Jones, *We Know All About You* (Oxford, 2017), p. 126.

14. R. Thurlow, *Secret State* (Oxford, 1994), p. 217.

15. Luff, 'Covert and overt operations', p. 734.

16. K. Ewing, J. Mahoney and A. Moretta, *MI5, Cold War, and the Rule of Law* (Oxford, 2020), p. 458.

17. S. Haseler, *The Tragedy of Labour* (Oxford, 1980), p. 75.

18. R. Whitaker, 'Fighting the Cold War on the home front: America, Britain, Australia and Canada', in *Uses of Anti-Communism*, p. 33.

19. S. Parsons, 'British McCarthyism and the intellectuals', in *Labour's Promised Land? Culture and Society in Labour Britain 1945–51*, ed. J. Fyrth (London, 1995), 224–45, at p. 240.

20. Goodman, 'Challenge of McCarthyism', p. 63.

21. K. Potter, 'British McCarthyism', in *North American Spies*, ed. R. Jeffreys-Jones and A. Lownie (London, 2013), 167–83, at p. 167.

22. R. Milliband and M. Liebman, 'Reflections on anti-communism', in *So Register 1984: The Uses of Anti-Communism*, ed. R. Miliband and M Liebman (London, 1984), 1–22, at p. 2.

23. J. Fleming, *The Anti-Communist Manifestos* (New York, 2009), p. 15; S. Anderson, *The Quiet Americans: Four CIA Spies at the Dawn of the Cold War* (New York, 2020), see preface; M. Holzman, *The Language of Anti-Communism* (Briarcliff Manor, 2017), p. 2.

24. M. Lewin, *The Soviet Century* (New York, 2005), p. 474.

25. See *The Black Book of Communism: Crimes, Terror, Repression*, ed. S. Courtois (Cambridge, MA, 1997).

26. J. Fayet, 'Reflections on writing the history of anti-communism', *Twentieth Century Communism*, 6 (2014): 8–21, at p. 14.

27. R. Brotherton, *Suspicious Minds* (London, 2015), pp. 217–18.

28. J. Kovel, *Red Hunting in the Promise Land* (London, 1994), p. 9.

29. Fayet, 'Reflections on writing', p. 14.

30. S. Tate, *A Special Relationship?* (Manchester, 2012), p. 47.

31. F. Romero, 'Cold War anti-communism and the impact of communism on the West', in *The Cambridge History of the Cold War*, ed. N. Naimark, S. Pons and S. Quinn-Judge (Cambridge, 2017), p. 299.

32. J. Haynes, *Red Scare or Red Menace* (Chicago, 1996), p. 3.

33. R. Toye, *The Labour Party and the Planned Economy, 1931–1951* (Woodbridge, 2003), p. 112.

34. A. Thorpe, *A History of the British Labour Party* (London, 1997), p. 310.

35. S. Macintyre, *A Proletarian Science* (Cambridge, 1980), p. 65.

36. P. Cosgrave, *The Strange Death of Socialist Britain* (London, 1992), p. 26.

37. G. Foote, *The Labour Party's Political Thought* (London, 1997), p. 59.

38. R. Moore, *The Emergence of the Labour Party 1880–1924* (London, 1978), p. 118.

39. R. Crossman, *The Backbench Diaries*, ed. J. Morgan (London, 1981), pp. 342–3.

40. K. Harris, *Attlee* (London, 1982), pp. 256–7.

41. *Birmingham Daily Gazette*, 2 February 1950, p. 1.

42. Quoted by Lord Pakenham, Hansard, House of Lords debates (henceforth HL), vol. 572, c. 866 (22 May 1996).

43. *Bucks Herald*, 11 May 1951, p. 7.

44. Hansard, HL, vol. 182, c. 147 (29 April 1953).

45. Hansard, HL, vol. 193, c. 671 (13 July 1955).

46. *Western Morning News*, 10 June 1950, p. 4.

47. *Daily Herald*, 31 July 1950, p. 4.

48. S. Haseler, *The Gaitskellites* (London, 1969), p. 82.

49. V. Allen, *The Russians Are Coming* (Shipley, 1987), p. 30.

50. A. Crosland, *The Future of Socialism* (London, 1956), pp. 20–1.

51. *York Diocesan Leaflet*, no. 254, August 1949, p. 3.

52. Geoffrey Fisher to Charles Smith, 22 October 1948, Geoffrey Fisher Papers (henceforth Fisher) vol. 41, Lambeth Palace Library.

53. Fisher to Peggy Mitchell, 31 March 1948, Fisher vol. 53.

54. *The Standard Catholic*, 18 November 1955, p. 6.

55. *Guardian*, 13 October 1952, p. 10.

56. Romero, 'Cold War anti-communism', p. 305.

57. A. Deighton, 'Britain and Cold War, 1945–1955', in *The Cambridge History of the Cold War* vol. 2, ed. M. Leffler and O. Westad (Cambridge, 2017), 112–32, at p. 113.

58. T. Shaw, *British Cinema and the Cold War* (London, 2001), pp. 45–6.

59. Shaw, *British Cinema*, p. 4.

60. A. Read, *The World on Fire* (London, 2008), p. 160.

61. C. Andrew, *The Defence of the Realm* (London, 2009), p. 111.

62. J. Jenkinson, *Black 1919* (Liverpool, 2008), p. 42.

63. K. Lacey, 'Assassination, insurrection and alien invasion: Interwar wireless scares in cross-national comparison', in *War of the Worlds to Social Media*, ed. E. Hayes, K. Battles and W. Hilton-Morrow (New York, 2013), 57–82, at pp. 72–3.

64. J. Barber, 'The *War of the Worlds* broadcast: Fake news or engaging storytelling?', in *Radio's Second Century*, ed. J. Hendrick (Newark, 2020), 96–118, at p. 102.

65. C. Andrew, *Secret Service* (London, 1985), pp. 359–61.

66. Austen Chamberlin to cabinet, 21 September 1931, TNA CAB 23/90B.

67. Luff, 'Covert and overt operations', p. 744.

68. *Pall Mall Gazette*, 9 May 1921, p. 4.

69. *Western Daily Press*, 22 October 1931, p. 10.

70. T. Phillips, *The Secret Twenties* (London, 2017), p. 176.

71. C. Andrew, 'The British Secret Service and Anglo-Soviet relations in the 1920s part i: From the trade negotiations to the Zinoviev letter', *Historical Journal*, 20 (1977): 673–706, at p. 700.

72. See G. Bennett, *The Zinoviev Letter: The Conspiracy That Never Dies* (Oxford, 2018).

73. K. Jeffery, *MI6* (London, 2010), p. 216.

74. S. Twigge, E. Hampshire and G. Macklin, *British Intelligence* (Kew, 2008), p. 29.

75. Andrew, *The Defence of the Realm*, p. 185.

76. P. Clarke, *Hope and Glory* (London, 2004), p. 106.

Chapter 1

British McCarthyism

Look round. You see floods, torrents, train accidents, two feet of snow in Jerusalem. Something tremendous is happening. Britain again will have to lead the world as she did in two world wars. As she saved the world from the dictatorship of Hitler so she will save the world from communism.[1]

—Waldron Smithers

After all, they are among those unable to defend themselves against communist intrigue and deceit unless people like myself stand up for them. After all, we are fighting for our lives. The substance of this motion is that we must not mention names. Was there ever such rubbish? You cannot possibly fight a cold war that way. You cannot possibly make a political omelette without breaking some bad eggs.[2]

—Lord Vansittart

The Cold War produced a form of political repression and societal paranoia in many countries which often infected governmental and civic institutions. In the UK and the US, anti-communism rumbled like thunder over the political atmosphere as international tensions rose between East and West. Charges of red infiltration were levelled fast and furious by a number of politicians. These men of zeal dedicated their lives to the crusade against Marxism-Leninism and did much to amplify the supposed threat the ideology engendered. In their hunt to root out the menace, they targeted governmental ministers, teachers, journalists and even clergymen. No one was above suspicion. Although the general public did not rush to support their efforts, their charges and allegations impacted governmental and societal attitudes. They heightened the level of suspicion and paranoia in politics.

This chapter explores the concept of British McCarthyism primarily through the red-hunting careers of two politicians. It uses the efforts of Lord Vansittart and Sir Waldron Smithers to examine how a type of McCarthyite repression functioned in the nation. Both men urged an extreme national reaction to communism. They called for an all-out war to halt the 'red menace' – neither wished for anything less. Although no public *auto-da-fé* resulted from their actions, they left in their wake a path of damning attacks and red-baiting allegations which heightened the level of political anxiety over the communist issue. Tangible evidence of this is shown throughout the chapter. It first looks at the earliest form of 'Vansittartism' propagated against the Germans during the Second World War, soon to shift after the fighting stopped, not in form, but in target, towards communism. This new version of Vansittartism took on a very bellicose and anti-Labour form, as the rhetoric of Vansittart, and a unique type of 'journalist' named Kenneth de Courcy, shows. It examines the repressive rhetoric used by Vansittart, paying close attention to his famed 28 May 1950 speech in the House of Lords and the national reaction it elicited. The next section details both Vansittart's specific criticism of the Church of England's response to communism and in more general terms the Anglican and Catholic anti-communism of the early Cold War period. It then turns to the career of Smithers and both his involvement in the public red-baiting of Minister of War John Strachey and his efforts to garner a governmental investigation of the BBC.

Vansittartism

Robert Vansittart fancied himself as a British Cassandra of the twentieth century. Like the character from the Greek legend, he warned of impending threats, but most refused to take heed.[3] However, many of his contemporaries viewed him quite differently. They called him the British Joseph McCarthy and mockingly labelled him 'VanWitchhunt'. In 1902, Vansittart joined the FO at the age of twenty-one. After numerous diplomatic and governmental posts, he attained the position of permanent undersecretary of state for foreign affairs in 1930.[4] Shortly after the rise of Hitler, Vansittart began an unsuccessful attempt to warn against the dangers of Nazism to his FO superiors. His strong opposition to appeasement policies led to him being stripped of his position by Neville Chamberlain in 1938. Vansittart officially retired from the FO in 1941, and the same year Winston Churchill raised him to the peerage as Baron Vansittart of Denham. A marked shift occurred in Vansittart after he left the FO in failure. Friends and colleagues noted the change. While visiting 'Van' (as his intimate friends called him) during the war, journalist Malcolm Muggeridge described his host as 'an aggrieved man' with 'a deep underneath of real conceit'. Muggeridge found it difficult to understand this, since 'he was head of his profession, received every honour, was given a peerage, married a rich and lovely wife and is now a national figure'. He guessed that a 'wounded conceit' was the cause of Vansittart's 'bitterness'.[5] Muggeridge did not catch Vansittart on a bad day; in years to come others saw the same general sense of acrimony in the lord. After having lunch with Vansittart in May 1948, Harold Nicolson described his dining companion as gloomy over world affairs and with a bitter disposition. Nicolson deduced Vansittart's mood came from a 'disappointment in his own career' and a sense of grievance over failed ambitions.[6] This personal bitterness and anger were not limited to Vansittart's private interactions. A 1949 profile piece appearing in the *Observer* described how when Vansittart expressed his political views he showed 'an intensity of passion which he is not always able to control ... And there is little in the language of invective that Lord Vansittart will not use to release the pent-up fury that boils within him'. When sparring with political opponents, the article stated he resembled 'a ferocious tiger, driven by uncontrollable emotion to rend his victim in pieces'.[7]

This change in temperament was perhaps only more evident after leaving government employment. Years earlier, John Colville surmised that 'hatred and harsh words are the methods which he prescribes' in dealing with perceived enemies.[8] Focusing on his time running the FO, historian John Ferris maintained that Vansittart often circulated reports against his opponents, withheld information that damaged himself and used allusions to secret sources to bolster his authority.[9]

A lifelong opponent and critic of what he termed Prussian militarism, Vansittart spent much of the interwar period and the entire span of the Second World War warning against the evils of Germany. It obsessed him to the point that both a number of his contemporaries and later historians argued he was a vehement Germanophobe.[10] When reviewing Vansittart's writings of the time, the charge is hard to dispute. In 1941, Vansittart published a book titled *Black Record: Germans Past and Present* in which he argued that the Germanic race and culture were as responsible for the current war as were the Nazi Party and Hitler. He wrote that the history of the Germans could be summated in a three-word quote from the Roman Tacitus – 'they hate peace'.[11] Vansittart claimed 'for generations Germany has been trying to annex not only the earth but the heavens'.[12] During the war, he argued for the harshest terms towards Germany in any future postwar settlement. In 1942, he declared in the Lords that 'this time the world will not allow any government to weaken from the pledge to exact the punishment of German butchers as a condition of peace'.[13] Writing in a 1944 article, he described the Germans as a duplicitous people who always blamed their woes on 'a man, a clique, a class, but not we'. For this duplicity, Vansittart continued, he despised them, and 'what I despise I cannot trust'.[14] After the failed 20 July attempt to kill Hitler, he refused to give the plotters any credit. He claimed that their motive was only to quickly 'wind up' the failing war to have a 'fresh run at it a third time'.[15]

From these wartime contributions of Vansittart the concept of 'Vansittartism' emerged. The term, used by critics, was meant to denounce those who pressed for postwar destruction of the German state and held its citizens collectively accountable for the sins of the Nazi regime.[16] The anti-Vansittartists were mostly left-leaning in their politics (pacifists, Labour MPs, and so on), with a prominent number being members of the clergy.[17] However, the divide over opposition to Vansittartism did not break down along partisan lines – a large number of Labour politicians had no issue with such an uncompromising anti-German position.[18] A key argument against Vansittartism was that such vicious attacks against the German people and pledges of a forthcoming Carthaginian peace only served to undermine the war effort, since it strengthened the resolve of Germans to fight on. Even the Nazi leadership were in agreement with Vansittart's domestic critics on that assessment. Joseph Goebbels once quipped that somewhere in Germany after the war they should erect a monument to him engraved with the words 'to the Englishman who rendered the greatest service to the German cause'. The chief Nazi propagandist also gleefully wished for 'Vansittart [to] carry on', since 'he is merely supplying grist for our propaganda mill'.[19]

Because of its negative connotations, few in the UK classified themselves as 'Vansittartists' or self-identified with the concept – except Vansittart himself, who appropriated the term to fit his purpose. In *Lessons of My Life* (1943), he wrote:

> I must clear the ground by explaining very briefly what Vansittartism is and what it is not. I did not invent the word. My opponents did. I should not have been vain enough to credit myself with a doctrine. They did that; and I hasten to assure them that they are mistaken. It is not a doctrine: it is common sense, based on professional knowledge.[20]

For Vansittart, the defeat of Nazism at the end of the Second World War did little to dampen his distrust of the Germans. For him, 8 May 1945 did not spark a road to Damascus moment on the 'German question'. The record suggests such a moment never came. In 1946, he asserted the Germans remained unrepentant and that 75 per cent of them were 'still Nazis at heart'.[21] A year later he stated that 'the democratisation of Germany is a difficult, if not impossible, task'.[22] In 1950, Vansittart remained 'sure that the German danger will return'.[23] However, the postwar era did mark a turning point for Vansittart; it shifted his focus towards what he soon came to consider an even more diabolical enemy. As he did with German militarism, he endeavoured tirelessly through the coming years to warn his fellow countrymen of the 'red menace' of communism. Norman Rose eloquently wrote in his biography of Vansittart, 'Like a latter-day Cincinnatus, he returned from his estates to save his countrymen from new dangers.'[24]

All-out war

Unlike many of his cold warrior contemporaries, before the end of the Second World War Vansittart voiced little concern over the threat of communism. When working at the FO in the 1930s, he argued for the UK and France to ally formally with the Soviet Union. He considered this the only realistic prospect in deterring Nazi aggression.[25] During the war, Vansittart praised on numerous occasions the many sacrifices the Soviet Union had endured against the German war machine.[26] However, in the aftermath of Moscow's refusal to assist the Warsaw Uprising in August 1944, he gradually began to speak out against the UK's wartime ally.[27] Vansittart showed increased concern over the developing global situation and voiced his opinions frequently as international tensions rose again. His rhetoric soon soared against communism and the Soviet Union to the level of odium he had earlier displayed against Nazism and Germany. In *Events and Shadows* (1947), a book written warning of increased dangers of the Cold War, he contended that the objective of the 'Muscovites' was nothing less than the world-rule of communism.[28] He stressed that unlike the nationalist ideologies of Nazism and fascism, the creed of Marxist-Leninism held universal appeal to many around the world. The quasi-religious nature of it bred zealots who were willing to betray their country and use deceitful tactics in obtaining their goals. Communists of all nationalities worked in uniform fashion; they 'turn to Moscow as Moslems to Mecca'. Using charged language, he cautioned 'they are more convinced and convincing believers than Mahomed's invading sectarians a dozen centuries ago; also their creed is somewhat more concrete'. He surmised that, similar to Islam, communism worked as a 'primitive doctrine', only it used tanks instead of camels. Hence, the UK diligently needed to expose and root out its red fifth columnists to survive the coming onslaught, which it had failed to do so far.[29] In a 1947 hard-hitting debate broadcast by the BBC, R. Palme Dutt, chair of the CPGB, denounced such assertions as 'stale red scare and anti-Soviet calumnies'.[30] Dutt's biographer wrote that in the intense argument the communist 'ran rings around' the lord.[31] Almost assuredly, the loss of such a dispute did nothing to weaken Vansittart's resolve.

An irksome fact plagued Vansittart in his efforts – the inability of Britons to realise that a third world war had begun. It started 'considerably before the end of the second' and it needed winning; there was 'no room or reason for timidity'.[32] While the communists, 'who were always at war', understood the gravity of the situation, the West had yet to get to grips with the reality. To start winning the war, Vansittart argued Britons needed to fight back both at home and abroad against the enemy. Such was Vansittart's assessment of the Yangtze Incident. In April 1949, the forces of the Communist People's Liberation Army were on the verge of winning their long-fought struggle against the Nationalist Chinese government. The fall of China, for the West, was at hand. As the civil war raged, the admiralty ordered the frigate HMS *Amethyst* up the Yangtze River to assist in guarding the British Embassy in Nanjing. The *Amethyst* came under fire from communist artillery, and while attempting to evade the shelling, it ran aground. The incident resulted in the death of seventeen British sailors, including the ship's captain. Vansittart argued that for the 'ruthless murders' of British servicemen 'communism must be taught a sharp lesson'. He lamented that in earlier times such a transgression would have brought an open declaration of war by previous governments and that the RAF should have bombed the artillery batteries that molested the *Amethyst*. Yet such measures 'would have involved courage in high places, so nothing was done'. The incident proved 'communism is our open and implacable enemy', thus 'we should treat all communists and their pals accordingly'.[33] This included those in the UK. Prior to the attack on the *Amethyst*, and for too long, the 'British public has been patient with the communist conspiracy'. 'All over the country let British communists be called to account' for the murderous assault on the *Amethyst*, he urged. It was the only way to show them 'it's an ugly game' and 'not worth the candle'.[34] Although Vansittart's statements never openly called for violence towards British communists, they bordered on the edge of the edge. Such bellicose and provocative rhetoric did not go unnoticed. Labour MP Konni Zilliacus denounced Vansittart for using the 'tragic incident' as a casus belli for war with China and 'inciting a pogrom against communists and socialists in Britain'.[35]

Vansittart did not hold a monopoly on such combative language. Another Briton preached the need for an alternative measure than just bombing a single artillery battery on the Yangtze or formally declaring war on Red China. To end the threat of international communism, tougher stuff was required. Kenneth de Courcy, a journalist and editor of his own newsletter, *Intelligence Digest* (domestic circulation around 70,000 in 1950), caused numerous heads to spin in Whitehall when he advocated for a pre-emptive atomic attack on the Soviet Union in 1950. De Courcy, a would-be spymaster and want-to-be kingmaker, had long been a thorn in the side of the British government. By his own admission, Churchill came very close to locking up the self-described committed patriot and ardent anti-communist during the Second World War.[36] Since then, the FO, MI5 and Downing Street had sought ways to impede de Courcy's journalistic efforts as well. All were concerned about the hyperbolic and sensationalist new stories that appeared in *Intelligence Digest*, alongside de Courcy's uncanny ability to glean sensitive intelligence from a wide range of governmental and international sources. In many ways, the 'de Courcy issue' plagued and consumed government officials more than other pressing concerns. However, the matter proved delicate. The well-connected de Courcy had several Conservative backbenchers in Westminster at his beck and call. However, the need to muzzle him was even more apparent in 1949 when de Courcy became the first to report the initial test of an atomic bomb by the Soviet Union.[37] His revelation of Russia going nuclear scooped all news outlets, and, as described in the US's paper of record, the *New York Times*, de Courcy had published 'long before the United States, Britain and Canada jointly announced it'.[38] De Courcy's stock in certain intelligence circles soared – especially those in Washington. He used his newly amplified influence to scaremonger the Atlantic world over the threat from the 'Soviet Marxist aggressive empire' and to denounce the UK's 'socialist government' for its unwillingness to stand up both at home and abroad to communism.[39] 'The public have not been told that in twenty-four months from now the Russians will be in a position to launch "A" [atomic] and "H" [hydrogen] bombs from the latest type of submarines against all our maritime cities', de Courcy claimed. The only possible safeguard to stop such a Soviet attack, he argued, came from 'the threat of retaliation', one which 'we do not yet possess'.[40] Yet the Americans did.

Perhaps, for that reason, de Courcy embarked on a lecture tour across North America in 1950. On 6 April, to a packed house in Toronto's Massey Hall, he warned his Canadian audience that war with the Soviet Union was likely in two years and presently 'Russia could wipe out maritime facilities of the democracies in a week if it attacked'. The well-attended assembly garnered a significant amount of press attention. In its coverage of his address, Canada's paper of record, *The Globe and Mail*, described de Courcy as the 'top man in a personal spy system' supported by his 'extremely wealthy' magazine.[41] Indeed, such talk gave credence to his alarmist views to the newspaper's readership. In the past, such talk had allowed de Courcy to glean intelligence from unsuspecting British officials both in the UK and abroad. Cognisant of such abilities, Foreign Secretary Ernest Bevin had drafted a secret, and unofficial, advisory to embassies and consuls specifically pertaining to de Courcy only eight days prior to his lecture in Toronto. In the memo, Bevin describes de Courcy as 'a man of considerable drive and ability' who is 'violently anti-Soviet' and who 'believes that the Catholic faith of General Franco is the surest bulwark against Soviet domination of Europe'.[42] While Bevin praised de Courcy as 'an able journalist', he admonished his reporting, since de Courcy 'makes little or no attempt to check the accuracy of his information and is quite undiscriminating in the methods which he employs to obtain it'. 'Mr. de Courcy might again, as he has done in the past, constitute a serious embarrassment to His Majesty's Government or official circles, in this country or abroad', the memo concluded. Thus, 'He should not, therefore, be given any special facilities during his travels.'

Surely, if de Courcy discovered the existence of the FO warning regarding him, he would have considered it a plot by the Labour government to silence him – which, in all fairness, it was. It had little effect in stopping de Courcy, and regardless of the memo, several British officials considered both the man and his speeches as valuable assets. Reporting on de Courcy's time on the lecture circuit in Canada, the UK trade commissioner in Montreal stated the general impression he got of de Courcy's visit was it 'had given people a better understanding of the imminence of danger from Russia'.[43] The deputy undersecretary for Commonwealth relations J.J. Saville Garner wrote he 'heard privately ... Mr. de Courcy had electrified his Canadian audience into a real understanding of the communist menace'.[44] The department head of the information office at Commonwealth relations found it perplexing that the FO were so against de Courcy's 'violently anti-Soviet' activities: 'I would have thought that at any rate, [they were] something to be thankful for.' He went on to ponder whether de Courcy's support for Franco might turn out to be the correct stance to take, since 'it is anybody's guess' and 'perhaps it will work!'[45] Garner speculated that the FO's animosity towards de Courcy – 'an enterprising journalist who has built up some reputation' – came from his attitude 'during the war against Hitler, when his violent antagonism to communism led him into very doubtful views about Germany'. Garner disagreed with the FO holding such a grudge; de Courcy's 'violent' anti-communism was what was needed, 'since the situation is very different today and I do not see that there is any need to treat him as sinister'.[46]

Regardless of how various mandarins felt on the matter, de Courcy continued issuing his hyperbolic warnings of impending doom for the West. However, he soon changed tactics. In his new estimation, the threats of reprising atomic attacks were no longer sufficient in halting the impending world war, which he warned was just on the global horizon. De Courcy shifted his earlier stance of retaliation to one of an immediate attack on the Soviet Union. It stood as the only solution, since it decapitated the head of the international communist conspiracy. In a November 1950 speech delivered at the Executives' Club in Chicago, de Courcy put the argument in these terms:

> We are not fighting Red China. They do not want to fight us at all. We are not fighting North Korea ... You are fighting a single inspiration from the Kremlin. All their equipment comes from Russia. All the general staff direction comes from Russia. All the organization comes from Russia. The boys being killed in Korea were killed by communist bullets with Russian artillery and they are facing an army supported and inspired by the Russian general staff. The Russians have fired the first shot in the Third World War.[47]

The longer the 'Atlantic System' waited, he surmised, the stronger its mortal enemy, 'Marxist imperialism', grew. 'Are we to fool about the periphery when the decision lies in our grasp by striking a very deadly, fatal blow at the guts of the Russian Empire?', he rhetorically asked the audience. De Courcy recommended that the US immediately attack with its atomic capabilities the main oil-producing areas in the Soviet Union to neutralise the threat or it faced losing the Cold War.[48] All-out war constituted the only way for the West to survive.

Such talk caused fear back home in London; de Courcy proved, oddly enough, 'an anti-communist menace' promoting a war which would likely result in the deaths of countless millions and leave the UK in ruins. The palpable threat of his words came from information originating from the British embassy in Washington reporting 'that de Courcy is being taken seriously in some quarters in the US defence department'; indeed, quite high quarters. Through a contact the embassy discovered that the assistant to the secretary of defense for international security affairs, Major General James Burns, was 'warmly' recommending both 'the [Intelligence] Digest, as well as Mr. de Courcy' to colleagues. In addition, on one occasion, when de Courcy visited Washington, he had dinner with Burns's superior secretary of defense, Louis Johnson, 'who was considerably impressed' with the British journalist.[49] In 1952, Anthony Eden reported to MI5 the news that Johnson's soon-to-be replacement, John Foster Dulles, 'was in close touch with de Courcy'.[50] The British government would continue to keep a close watch on de Courcy for the forthcoming years until multiple convictions of fraud placed him in Wormwood Scrubs.

Putting de Courcy's longing for nuclear war aside, the failures of the government were becoming more the focal point of Vansittart's anti-communist rhetoric as the 1950s approached. The Yangtze Incident and the seeming refusal of Attlee and Labour to enact more robust counterinsurgency measures were factors for the lord's attitudinal shift. He concluded that, in theory, governments must do more, since the only 'effective action that can be taken against communism' came from state power.[51] While he had earlier praised Attlee and other Labour leaders for their 'courageous anti-communist utterances', he became disillusioned by their apparent unwillingness to follow them up: 'we need not words, but anti-communist action'. In 1949, Vansittart accused the Soviets of operating a spy ring through the London embassies of the Soviet Union and its Eastern European allies. He also charged that international friendship societies (the Anglo-Rumanian Society, the Anglo-Bulgarian Club, the Hungarian Club and the Hungarian Association) acted as Soviet fronts and hubs for espionage activities.[52] He pressed the government to deport Soviet diplomats en masse and close all such friendship associations. Stoking his fury, Labour refused to do either.[53] Vansittart came to see the Attlee government and the Labour Party as inadequate agents for winning the Cold War. His attacks on communism were then often tinted with an anti-socialist narrative. He started stressing that the 'British left' needed to realise that 'communism had always used' socialism as a 'stalking-horse' in rising to power.[54] 'Too many socialists in all Western countries' were politically too close to 'communism to conceive the deadly danger which they promote'. Many socialists were 'either fellow-travellers or they have not sufficient sense to come in out of the rain'. Vansittart campaigned that 'vigorous resistance to communism' was 'the acid test of party politicians' and Labour had failed to pass it.[55] Thus, during the 1950 and 1951 General Elections, Vansittart lobbied against the Attlee government.[56] In 1955 he warned that 'grave dangers faced us' if Labour was returned to power.[57] Alongside his anti-Soviet stance, de Courcy took a hard line against domestic communism as well. He cosied up to Vansittart and wholeheartedly supported the lord's charges against governmental failures to halt the red infiltration throughout British institutions.[58]

By 1950, Vansittartism had crept back into the political consciousness of the nation, albeit directed at a new enemy: the scourge of international communism. Vansittart, in language reminiscent of the 1930s, warned that guilty men were turning a blind eye to the threat at hand and appeasers roamed the halls of British institutions foolishly seeking an unrealistic peace. For men like de Courcy and Vansittart, the times called for aggressive action, not lasting coexistence. The 'Russians' and the 'Red Chinese' were desperately in need of a virtuous bombing and domestic communists a lesson that they had chosen the wrong side in a very 'ugly game'.

Lord VanWitchhunt

The apotheosis of Vansittart's anti-communist campaign came in the form of an eighty-minute address he gave in the House of Lords on 29 March 1950. The speech solidified his image as one of the UK's most dedicated cold warriors but also presented him with the dubious honour of being labelled the British McCarthy.[59] It consisted of an onslaught of charges and accusations, which even keen observers of the time could have easily confused with the utterances of the most die-hard American McCarthyite. 'What this country needs is a good shaking up', stressed Vansittart, 'and if it cannot take that, it must take the consequences – and they will be bitter.' Vansittart did not hold back; he claimed that communist fifth columnists had infested the majority of the political and civil institutions of the country. These included the Church of England, the civil service, the FO, the armed forces, the universities, the BBC, the trade unions, the British Legion, the Joint Industrial Council (known as the Whitley Council) and even the planning offices for the Festival of Britain. As Joseph McCarthy had done less than two months before in Wheeling, West Virginia, Vansittart claimed to possess a list of known communists working inside the government. Vansittart's list included the names of sixteen employees of the Department of Inland Revenue.[60] He maintained he knew the identities of communists inside other government departments as well, including the War Office and the ministries of food, health and education. Although he refused to name them, he maintained that communists had no place inside the civil service on any level and thus they needed removing. This included those at the BBC. 'Passing to another infected field', Vansittart accused the government of employing 2,000 communists as teachers who used 'a dozen different ways of inculcating communism' to the youth of the nation.[61] He concluded his speech by arguing that the UK needed to put its own house in order against the evil and motioned: 'That attention be called to the extent of communist infiltration into the public service and other important branches of public life in this country; and to resolve that continuous and resolute precautions are necessary for public security.'[62]

The immediate reaction to Vansittart's speech inside the chamber ranged from enthusiasm to cautious opposition. Rising directly after

Vansittart's remarks, Lord Milverton agreed that 'We cannot tolerate enemies within our gates' and went on to argue that there 'is no room in the world for communism and freedom and one or the other must eventually win'. He urged that a step in the right direction was for the censorship of the *Daily Worker*. Shortly afterwards, Viscount Swinton contributed to the dread generated by Vansittart's more bellicose statements by adding that actions by the Soviet Union were tantamount to war. Praising J. Edgar Hoover and calling it a 'pleasure' to have worked closely with him during the Second World War, Swinton also stated that he sympathised with the need for secrecy that the Federal Bureau of Investigation (FBI) required to work under. Swinton added that communism stood as a threat unlike any the UK had since encountered because of its insidious and hidden nature. It is not easy to discount these supportive statements as insignificant or of minor consequence by little-known lords. Both Lord Milverton, a former colonial governor of Gambia, Fiji, Jamaica and Nigeria, and Lord Swinton – previously president of the board of trade, secretary of state for the colonies and later secretary of state for air – were accomplished and respected politicians in their own right. Speaking from the Labour benches, the lord chancellor Viscount Jowitt gave a tepid response:

> First of all, I must be careful what I say; and, secondly, I feel we have to avoid the traditional dangers of Scylla and Charybdis. I do not want to convey to your lordships that this is not a serious matter, or that there is any justification for complacency, because I do not think there is. On the other hand, I do not want to convey to the public at large, and to our friends overseas in particular, the idea that we are riddled with communism.[63]

After recommending a minor adjustment to the wording of Vansittart's motion, Jowitt put the question to a vote which the lords unanimously passed.

Coming only weeks after similar charges made by McCarthy in the US, Vansittart's speech garnered international news. Cognisant of the adverse British reaction McCarthy received, Vansittart had attempted to distance himself from the perception that he sought to follow in the senator's footsteps. In his opening remarks, he denounced the US politician by saying his charges held 'nothing in common with the shy-making ballyhoo of Senator McCarthy'.[64] For many journalists it appeared this was not the case; a number of newspapers across the globe readily made the easy comparison between the two. After the speech, headlines announced 'Witch-Hunting Fever Is on in Britain' and reporters dubbed its author 'Lord VanWitchhunt'.[65] 'We would hate to see Lord Vansittart becoming another Senator McCarthy', the *Guardian* worried, since 'when one gets the anti-red fever it is hard to check it.'[66] Not surprisingly, the harshest condemnation of the speech in the UK came on the pages of the *Daily Worker* – it labelled the lord a vulgar liar.[67] *Tribune* magazine, a mouthpiece for the Labour left, took a harsh line against the speech as well. 'It has been clear for some months', it wrote, 'that there is a vociferous section in this country determined to begin a witch-hunt' and that no better example existed of the fact than 'the ravings' of Vansittart.[68] Commentators remarked that a new form of Vansittartism had arisen.[69]

Politically speaking, no disapproval came from the Labour government. Embroiled in its own efforts against communism, it did not denounce Vansittart or refute his claims to the public. However, political condemnation for Vansittart came, led by the Labour peer Lord Stansgate – father of Anthony Benn. On 5 April, Stansgate announced his intention to introduce in the Lords a motion to censure Vansittart. He claimed that Vansittart 'without due regard to their truth or falsehood' made serious allegations against the character and conduct of specific persons or groups who, because of parliamentary privilege, had no opportunity to defend themselves. The announcement proved controversial since such an unusual and extreme step held no recent precedent.[70] However, the likelihood of such a motion passing was not remote. A key point of Stansgate was that on 29 March Vansittart had directly criticised a sitting member of the Lords, the bishop of Branford, as being a communist. Such an attack on one of their own did not sit well with many in the chamber – especially since the bishop claimed the charge untrue, and that his accuser had used 'a misrepresentation of fact and a revision of my words' in the case against him.[71] The threat of censure did not sway Vansittart; he wrote to Stansgate that he looked forward to the debate over the matter and 'shall have the greatest pleasure in saying what I think of it'.[72] He got the opportunity on 2 May when the lords put the matter to debate.

For their showdown, Stansgate came well prepared. Viewing Stansgate as their prime defender, a number of the accused groups and individuals provided evidence to him of their innocence prior to the debate. The general secretary for the Festival of Britain told Stansgate that no one under his employment was distributing Marxist literature, as Vansittart claimed. An 'exhaustive enquiry' discovered the existence of a single communist pamphlet which had been delivered in the post to the Festival Office and ended up in the rubbish bin.[73] Stansgate received a similar letter from the deputy director of the Bureau of Current Affairs which argued that Vansittart's claim that it employed a communist on its staff was simply untrue.[74] In defence of his motion during the lords' debate, Stansgate cited these sources in asserting Vansittart 'did not use due care' when making his earlier accusations. Speaking in turn after Stansgate were the accused bishop of Branford and Lord Simon – the general director of the BBC. Both were highly critical of Vansittart and charged that his earlier speech contained gross inaccuracies.[75]

When given the opportunity to defend himself, Vansittart remained unrepentant and defiant. He labelled Stansgate 'my adversary' and a fellow traveller on the 'red train of thought'. 'The substance of the motion is that we must not mention names', he scoffed; 'you cannot possibly fight a cold war that way.' A third world war had begun, the accused argued, and 'we are fighting for our lives'. He ended the speech in the role of the aggrieved victim: 'Why should I give up the last good morsel of life merely to be insulted as I have been today?'[76] Then he added he had not expected thanks for his efforts but did not expect the lords to subject him to such terrible treatment. In a visual act of contempt, he took a physical copy of the motion against him and crumpled it up.[77]

Speaking on behalf of the government, the leader of the House of Lords, Viscount Addison, quickly sought to defuse the heated situation. He voiced his support for Vansittart's resolution passed on 29 March and stressed that both he and the government took the threat of domestic communism seriously. He paid tribute to Vansittart for raising public awareness of the issue but stressed the government was not as ineffective in dealing with it as Vansittart maintained. He then employed a little-used procedure to shut down debate and quash the motion without it coming to a vote. Supporting him in this decision was Lord Salisbury, the Conservative leader of the Lords. Despite vigorous protests from Stansgate, the matter of the question was settled, at least in the halls of the British upper chamber.

Spiritual warfare – religious anti-communism

Although Vansittart accused a litany of British institutions of communist penetration in his 29 March address, the one he attacked the most vigorously was the Church of England. When he named communists individually, the majority were Church clergymen. Alongside the bishop of Branford, Vansittart labelled the infamous Hewlett Johnson, the dean of Canterbury, as a communist. By then, Johnson had long been a lightning-rod for criticism for his pro-Soviet views and stated sympathies to the communist ideology; for these, his opponents labelled him the 'Red Dean'.[78] Johnson was continually irking the British government, since many foreigners confused him with the archbishop of Canterbury and thus believed the Church officially sanctioned his pro-communist activities.[79] Calls for the removal of Johnson from his post were quite frequent. Yet, according to the head of the Church, Archbishop Geoffrey

Fisher, he had no authority to do so, since Johnson never broke ecclesiastical or civil laws.[80] In order for Fisher to dismiss Johnson, an act of parliament was needed granting him the power to do so. Although the archbishop considered Johnson a 'fanatically minded person' who made 'outrageous statements', he did not think the matter worth pursuing, since 'his intolerable opinions carry no weight in this country now and do no harm'. Vansittart viciously disagreed; he called for the excommunication of the 'evil charlatan' Johnson. However, Vansittart's animosity towards Johnson paled in comparison to the contempt he held for a little-known priest named Gilbert Cope. Vansittart took issue with Cope for an earlier political tract he wrote titled *Christians in the Class Struggle*. The lord claimed Cope's pamphlet urged 'the liquidation' of opponents to Marxism. On 29 March, Vansittart denounced him as a 'murderous priest' and 'potential killer' and wondered aloud why Birmingham University, where Cope worked, had employed him.[81] By 1950, Vansittart's animus for clergymen like the bishop of Branford, Johnson and Cope was long held. Earlier, he denounced the three in a chapter of his appropriately titled book, *Bones of Contention* (1945). He wrote that he objected to these collections of 'Christians' who with 'episcopal backing should sponsor a policy of persecution, imprisonment and eventual slaughter, to suit their own material fancy'.[82]

Although a lifelong member of the Church of England, Vansittart did not hold the institution in high regard because it allowed such clergymen to hold ecclesiastical positions and because of its unwillingness to combat communism enthusiastically. The same went, he argued, for the rest of the Protestant denominations. They had all abandoned out of apathy the central spiritual struggle of the time; these churches 'were an army without discipline or generalship'.[83] The 'impertinent puritans' were unwilling to put 'their own house in order'; instead, they harboured 'communising priests' in eminent positions and a number of their clergy were spineless men who 'would sooner submit to communism than resist'. If the Church of England did not 'cleanse itself and play its part' against the red threat, then it 'will fade away'. Until all of 'protestantism realised that communism is its deadly and irreconcilable foe', the UK 'shall go on losing the Cold War, as we are doing now'.[84]

However, Vansittart stressed on various occasions that a constructive model to follow for these churches existed. He spoke of it with affection and longing. The saving grace for religious opposition to Marxism rested in the hands of the Catholic Church. In the struggle against communism, 'Catholics are better equipped than we are'.[85] He 'envied' them for seeing the fundamental incompatibility of communism to Christianity and 'knowing how to fight for existence'. In *Even Now*, Vansittart explained:

> The Catholic Church is in a better way owning to superior discipline. The Catholic record toward Hitler warrants some blushes, but toward Stalinism the performance is more virile; indeed the Catholic Church is the only well-organized body of resistance on earth; more organization seems needed. It may be true that protestantism, owning to its latitudes, is less a religion than a religious state of soul. The real reason, however, why it is not yet pulling its weight is that it cannot unite in seeing its own external dangers, and is disarmed by its own disarming charity.[86]

Vansittart had little use for 'disarming charity' or any such benign creeds. He saw them as weaknesses, 'which lead many churchmen and socialists still to look upon the communist as only some slightly erring brother, and which leads Liberals and Conservatives also to say in my astonished presence that some particularly bad fellow-traveller is "not a bad chap really at bottom, you know"'.[87] Ex-editor for the *Daily Worker* turned die-hard anti-communist, Douglas Hyde held quite similar sentiments. Hyde preached that the spread of communism was made possible by the spread of such 'wrong ideas, wrong values, wrong standards'. The ex-communist wrote that if a CPGB takeover of the UK occurred, several in the Church of England would work as 'stooge leaders' for the new regime. 'The world stands today at the cross roads and men and nations are having to choose between communism and Christianity', Hyde argued, 'and in practice, for men and nations, as events are proving, this means ... a choice between communism and the Catholic Church.'[88] In Hyde's judgement, only his religion could answer Marxism.[89] Hence, he considered the three million British Catholics as the nation's most potent defence against a communist takeover. Indeed, while Catholic anti-communism had always been strong, the Cold War only intensified it further. The Church considered the growing influence of the Soviet Union and its doctrine of 'godless communism' as a direct threat to both the spiritual and corporal holdings of Catholicism.

Not surprisingly, the archbishop of Canterbury found it difficult to see eye to eye with Vansittart and Hyde. During the debate over the censure motion, he conceded that a small number of priests in the Church of England and the 'free churches' held 'communist opinions' and defended their freedom in doing so. This by no means meant he felt sympathy towards communism. He vigorously opposed it and urged the British government and statesmen to 'take every possible political step to deliver us from the threat' it posed only short of outright war.[90] It was in fact 'their absolute duty', since communism 'is evil and its consequences are evil'.[91] Such anti-communist feelings resulted in a very pro-American sentiment throughout the Anglican hierarchy. Fisher denounced 'communist-inspired attempts' to belittle 'the remarkable help which the United States is giving us'.[92] A number in the Church viewed the continuation of US assistance under the Marshall Plan as crucial for the survival of the UK. Cyril Garbett, archbishop of York, argued that without it 'we could not resist Russia' and the UK would 'either be invaded by the Soviet Union or become another of her helpless satellites'.[93] Despite these cold warrior-type sentiments, Archbishop Fisher argued that the fight against 'political communism' should not be Anglicanism's primary concern. Vansittart labelled this sentiment a dereliction of the Church's duty – 'this is not leadership but abdication'.[94] Like Fisher, the local clergy were sceptical of adopting anti-communism at any price, even the more theologically conservative-minded ones. Reverend Arthur Burrell, vicar of St George's in Birmingham, warned his parishioners in 1955 that the Church does not:

> [S]mugly think that communism is the main source of danger. That kind of ideology I believe to be the sworn enemy of that way of life which we know as Christians in our hearts to be right. But the main indictment of our age and society ... is that the non-communist world believes it can fight communism only by violent fits of anti-communism.[95]

The 'surest answer' to the 'black threat of communist tyranny', stated Reverend Edward Ashford in 1950, at the height of the Korean War, was simply 'a great swelling-forth of pity and charity and religion in the hearts of non-communists'. He added: 'If the churches of England were filled each Sunday with God-fearing men and women that would be enough to turn the tide of human history away from the dreadful threat hanging over us.'[96] In stark comparison, British Catholics were not guided by such sanguine beliefs. The Catholic bishop of Leeds received international criticism when in 1954 he claimed France would not even fight to defend itself against a Soviet attack, since 'perhaps half of the Frenchmen have allegiance which is not to France' but the communist ideology.[97] Only a month earlier a crowd of over 3,000 packed into St Columb's Park in Londonderry to listen to the bishop of Derry urge 'all peoples in Northern Ireland' to take the threat from the 'red menace' seriously. 'Make no mistake about it', he warned, '[t]he aim of materialistic communism is to enslave man mentally, spiritually, and physically.'[98]

Fisher fundamentally rejected Vansittart's suggestion that Anglicans should follow the example of the Catholics. In 1949, the Vatican excommunicated, *ipso facto*, all its members who were communists or who aided and abetted communism. Fisher called this decision a 'tragedy', since it added a doctrine 'which had no foundation in scripture to its creed'.[99] The archbishop argued that Catholicism allowed no freedom of speech and 'in its own way [is] as totalitarian as communism'.[100] Indeed, a number in the Church of England argued that alongside its efforts in speaking out for the rights of Christians behind the Iron Curtain, it should likewise draw attention to the persecutions done to 'Christians' by Catholics in Spain and Latin America.[101] Conversely, Vansittart urged for the full integration of Catholic Spain into the Western defence apparatus or, he warned, the UK risked being at the mercy of the 'communist barbarians'.[102] Such was the similar view of many British Catholics, including, most notably, Labour MP and member of the faith John McGovern; they doggedly campaigned for the total restoration of diplomatic relations with the ostracised Franco regime.[103] While Vansittart lauded the uniformed and dogmatic way in which the Catholic Church opposed communism, Archbishop Fisher viewed these as a show of weakness in personal faith and a 'dangerous' appeal to authority – 'a weakling may run to the Church of Rome because he cannot trust himself [or] his own judgement'.[104] In January 1954 the *Belfast Newsletter* took umbrage at a forthcoming report by an Anglican Church assembly that stated that while 'the communists regard the Roman Catholic Church and its members as its main enemy', it must be noted that not 'everything' the Catholics 'do in opposition to the communists is necessarily good'.[105] Disagreements on the appropriate course of action against communism further increased friction between the two Christian faiths. Unlike the Anglicans, the Catholics were visibly unwilling to render the struggle against the red peril completely into Caesar's hands. 'The Vatican's struggle to assert the superiority of Christian values over Marxist communism is not confined to prayer alone', reported Robert Shearer in a 1949 article appearing in the *Western Mail*. 'Pen, radio, cinema and lecture tours' have all been 'utilised for many months past to weaken the strength of communism'.[106] A year later, the Church of England felt it wise to follow the Church of Rome a little way down this path, albeit not in such an overt manner.

Although publicly disputing the charges that it had not done enough to oppose communism, the Church of England secretly launched an initiative against it shortly after Vansittart's attack. The bishop of Chichester in a letter to the archbishop proposed the creation of a committee, 'whose existence would be unknown to the public', to discuss ways and means of opposing the falsehood of communism in England. The idea had come forth during an unofficial meeting of several clergymen and prominent lay members of the Church. They all agreed that the Church 'could take a wise and active part' in opening the eyes of their fellow countrymen to the dangers it presented. Those proposed for such a committee included

Harold Macmillan, Lord Salisbury, Ian Jacob of the BBC and the poet T.S. Eliot.[107] The archbishop supported and approved the committee's creation, provided that its existence 'remain[ed] confidential'. He conceded that no Church body was yet dedicated to giving 'special attention to the communist propaganda and the possible action and reaction from the side of the Church of England' and such a committee would rectify this shortfall. Noting the external pressure that had recently been brought to bear, Fisher added: 'Vansittart would say that it is quite time that we did something to purge our own ranks!'[108] After its establishment, the committee regularly received assistance and intelligence from the Information Research Department (IRD) of the FO to bolster its efforts in spreading anti-communist propaganda.[109] The Church of Scotland had already commissioned such a committee to combat communism, with similar ties to the IRD, in 1949.[110]

Waldron Smithers: the prophet of woe

Many might find it hard to believe that Waldron Smithers existed outside the pages of a novel or the Middle Ages. Like a mythical antagonist from a Charles Dickens book, he railed against the destitute and wished that the 'poor ignorant masses knew their place'. Although he longed for the 'Real Toryism' of the nineteenth century, Smithers viewed himself not as a Dickensian character but more as an Old Testament prophet – in the words of the *Daily Herald*, a 'prophet of woe' preaching the gospel of 'reaction'.[111] Although he followed in his wealthy father's footsteps and became a stockbroker, he had an earlier ambition to pursue his dream of being ordained in his beloved Church of England. Instead, Smithers transferred this religious zeal into zeal for electoral politics. After standing for and winning his father's old constituency in 1924, Smithers played the role of a lay bishop crusading for the UK to return to the Victorian values of the nation's golden age. His deep-dyed support for Stanley Baldwin's National government earned him a knighthood in 1934. It also garnered him national attention after he wrote a campaign song titled 'Stanley Boy', whose lyrics appeared on ten million leaflets and its tune on ten thousand gramophone records, both issued by the Conservative Central Office.

Unlike Vansittart, Smithers supported the appeasement policies of the Chamberlain government. He voted for the 1938 Munich agreement and supported Chamberlain against Churchill in 1940.[112] For Smithers, the threat to the UK came not from Nazism but communism. In 1938, he wrote that nothing demanded support more urgently than 'the efforts of those who are engaged in countering the work of communism', since it represented a 'fiercer and more brutal' enemy than that of the simple 'rule of tyrants'.[113] In a memorandum to the Home Office, Smithers praised 'Herr Hitler' for expelling communists from Germany, and in 1938 reminded Lord Londonderry that 'Jewish propaganda is always on the side of communism'.[114] 'There is no doubt that the communists are working with their usual subversive methods', he earlier wrote to Londonderry, warning the lord: 'It is not easy to estimate what progress they are making.'[115] Throughout the late 1930s and early 1940s, Smithers lobbied cabinet ministers and the Home Office to take a harsher tone towards the communist foe. He also attempted to create a 'Right Wing Book Club' to counteract the 'communist-controlled' Left Book Club.[116] During the period, he officially supported a host of private anti-communist organisations including the Economic League, Fund to Fight Communism, Anti-socialist and Anti-communist Union, and International Entente against the Third International.[117] By the end of the Second World War, as British politics turned to deal with Cold War affairs, Smithers had long established himself as a veteran in the war against the 'red menace'.

By 1945, many found it hard to take Smithers seriously.[118] One reason perhaps was that, as one contemporary delicately phrased it, he held the reputation of having a robust appetite for 'the consoling effects of alcohol'.[119] Or perhaps it was more likely that his beliefs were decidedly outside the political mainstream of the period. As a devoted follower of the free-market economics of Friedrich Hayek, Smithers routinely joined the Austrian-born economist in criticising any expansion of state control and opposing 'socialists of all parties'.[120] Smithers's defence of Hayek's theories made him a vocal critic not only of the ruling Labour government but also economic moderates within his own party. Seeking converts to their ideas, both Smithers and Hayek were eager to convert Churchill to their neoliberal theories.[121] However, Hayek's version of classical liberalism did not begin to rise inside Conservative circles until the late 1960s.[122] Often Smithers's foes only laughed at his reactionary and histrionic statements. When Smithers asked Attlee in the Commons to read an inflammatory pamphlet titled *British Socialism Is Destroying British Freedom* by Cecil Palmer, Attlee simply retorted he could not, since his time for reading fiction was quite limited.[123] During the 1950 election, the pro-Labour *Daily Herald* ran verbatim quotes of Smithers's speeches which they titled 'Blithers'. In 1947, Guy Liddell labelled him that 'silly old blimp' and another MI5 employee preceded the *Herald*, labelling him 'Sir Waldron Blithers'.[124] When Smithers introduced into the Commons a petition from Newfoundlanders opposing confederation, a Labour MP wryly asked him how many names on the list were communists.[125] When Smithers requested – hopefully in jest – that Churchill place a number of 'fellow travellers including members of this house and of the church' at the site of the UK's first atomic bomb test, former Labour minister George Isaacs said such a proposal would risk MPs being blown into 'Smithereens'.[126] Communist MP William Gallacher stated that if communists did not exist, then Smithers 'would be struck with vocal paralysis'.[127]

Despite being dismissed as a buffoon, Smithers's position in the Commons allowed his anti-communist attacks a wide audience. Because of the gravity of the topic, many of his questions and speeches could not simply be laughed off. No one retorted with wit or humour to his repeated calls for the UK to mirror the US by establishing a parliamentary committee – or conversely a Royal Commission – to investigate 'un-British activities'. The red-hunting reputation of the House Un-American Activities Committee (HUAC) in the UK was no laughing matter. When responding to Smithers's request, governmental ministers were cautious in their tone. Mindful of not upsetting certain American politicians, Herbert Morrison stated he could 'express no opinion as to its [HUAC's] suitability in the United States', but he did not believe such a similar 'method of procedure would be appropriate in Great Britain'.[128] Nor did many laugh when Smithers called for not only the executions of uncovered 'atomic spies' but also the public hanging of the 'Red Dean of Canterbury', Hewlett Johnson, for being a communist traitor.[129] Upon one memorable occasion in the Commons, he found himself thoroughly rebuked for his antagonist rhetoric. In the late evening of 27 June 1950, Smithers launched into a lengthy sermon-like speech on the perils of communism. In usual fashion, he labelled communism as the 'most momentous and awful menace with which mankind has ever been faced'.[130] He proceeded to frame the East–West international tensions as a 'spiritual war' and cited biblical scripture in denouncing the Labour government as 'wicked' for not vigorously fighting the threat. He then claimed 'that for America to give money to this government is to subsidise communism'. Smithers argued, in principle, that the Attlee government was comparable to the totalitarian rule of Stalin and Hitler. Labour MP George Wigg called Smithers's quoting of scripture in such a political manner something 'near to blasphemy'. 'There is a view held on this side of the house that the honourable gentleman is an amiable idiot', Wigg continued. 'I dissent from that view. I do not think he is amiable.' Home Office Undersecretary Geoffrey De Freitas questioned Smithers's devotion to democracy, saying his words rang of 'hatred and intolerance and generally display[ed] marked totalitarian tendencies'.[131] Geoffrey Bing wondered aloud whether the government should consider detaining Smithers, as it did with pro-Nazi MP Archibald Maule Ramsay during the Second World War.[132]

The Strachey controversy

Smithers's diatribes advocating public executions and classifying the government as a 'den of vipers' garnered attention, but little to no support – yet, not all of his red-baiting antics proved ineffective or seemed to many as outlandish. A reshuffling of the Labour government after the 1950 General Election brought increased fears of communists creeping into the halls of power. The move of John Strachey from the minister of food to the post of secretary for war was the catalyst. During the 1930s, a much more politically radical Strachey left the Labour Party to stand for MP as a pro-communist independent candidate. He also published a book titled *The Coming Struggle for Power* (1932) in which he wrote, 'The coming of communism can alone render our problems solvable.'[133] In 1935 he ran afoul of American authorities when, after conducting a lecture in a suburb of Chicago, he was arrested and later deported on the charge of seeking the violent overthrow of the US government. In the interwar period, it would have been hard to describe Strachey as anything less than a communist sympathiser or fellow traveller; he defended Stalin's purges and supported the formation of a Popular Front with the CPGB.[134] However, Strachey put all this aside in 1940 by denouncing communism and renouncing his earlier-held beliefs. Nonetheless, Smithers did not believe the conversion had been genuine and argued that Strachey remained untrustworthy. This time he had powerful allies; he was not alone in his suspicion.

The campaign against Strachey's appointment to secretary of war started in the broadsheets of the British press, specifically, those newspapers owned by publishing magnate and Conservative politician Lord Beaverbrook. On 2 March 1950, the *Evening Standard* carried a front-page story claiming Strachey 'remains an avowed communist' and 'has never publicly retracted his belief in communism'.[135] It stated the move to his new post was unwise, since it allowed him access to sensitive intelligence which could be compromised. Aware of the potentially damaging reaction such a charge carried, the Labour government quickly sought to refute it. In an unprecedented move, Downing Street issued a late-night press release mere hours after the accusations had hit the newsstands. It described the headlines as untrue and disgraceful, and maintained that 'Strachey was no communist.'[136] That same night Strachey also personally gave a statement in which he admitted that while it had 'always been public knowledge that I supported the communist doctrine in the years preced[ing] the last war ... I have never been a member of the Communist Party', and that he had renounced its policies in 1940.[137] These immediate repudiations did little to halt the red-baiting charge.

Beaverbrook did not relent; the *Evening Standard* refused to withdraw the accusation. Instead, the newspaper's editor, Herbert Gunn, and Beaverbrook conspired to find a smoking gun proving Strachey's communist affiliations. Gunn enlisted the help of John Baker White, a Conservative MP and Economic League official, and Douglas Hyde, an ex-communist turned vicious anti-communist, to discover proof that Strachey had in fact been a member of the CPGB.[138] Despite the failure to uncover anything new, Gunn promised Beaverbrook the 'investigation into Strachey would continue'. Beaverbrook and Gunn's zeal for attacking Strachey drew the worried attention of the National Union of Journalists (NUJ). The NUJ requested a report from the editorial board of the *Evening Standard* on whether union members employed by the newspaper were pressured to carry out 'unethical' work on the 'Strachey story'. Gunn refused to comply, arguing, 'the preparation of a news story was no business of the NUJ'.[139] An infuriated Strachey agreed the hits he was taking from the *Standard* were far below the belt. He went so far as to consult Attorney General Hartley Shawcross about suing the paper, and Gunn personally, for criminal libel. Shawcross talked him out of such a move, explaining no jury would convict on the charge, and the case could stretch on for months until it failed[140] – something the government surely wished to avoid.

The *Evening Standard*'s reporting on Strachey not only alarmed the NUJ but many in the US too. To its dismay, the British embassy in Washington reported to the FO: 'the Beaverbrook attack on the new secretary of state for war has attracted a good deal of attention here and the papers carry long reports from their London correspondents on the subject'. It worried that even 'pretty sensible and levelheaded' papers, such as the *Washington Post*, were covering the story, so the allegations could not 'altogether be disregarded'.[141] In mid-April the largest pictorial and news magazines in the US, respectively *Life* and *Time*, both owned by the ardent anti-communist and powerful magazine magnate Henry Luce, savaged Strachey. The editorial appearing in *Life* said it anticipated being told that the political attitudes of Strachey 'are none of America's business', but argued:

> To this we say in advance, nonsense. The Atlantic Pact is American business. The strength and security of Western Europe is American business. The attitudes, the capacities and innate loyalties, intellectual and political, of those who govern Western Europe are therefore of legitimate interest to Americans ... A Marxist of John Strachey's stripe has no business being British minister of war. It just won't do.[142]

Such stories, the British embassy warned, could have a lasting negative impact on Anglo-American cooperation in the matters of intelligence sharing if US officials deemed Strachey unreliable. Its apprehension over the subject proved more than credible. British contacts in Washington informed the government that Beaverbrook and Luce's attacks on Strachey's trustworthiness had garnered a powerful convert, that being Kenneth de Courcy's one-time lunching companion, Secretary of Defense Louis Johnson.

An international controversy erupted over the Strachey allegations after a North Atlantic Treaty Organization (NATO) conference held in Hague in early April. A report circulated by the *Associated Press* stated 'American officials' sought the removal of Strachey from his post and that during the conference the US had withheld intelligence secrets from the UK.[143] A follow-up article by the *New York Times* claimed an anonymous 'high United States official' stated that the US had clandestinely received the consent of British Defence Minister Emanuel Shinwell for withholding intelligence in the presence of Strachey.[144] The charges attracted significant press attention, since they gave the impression that the US was attempting to pressure the Attlee government to remove Strachey or otherwise face being denied vital intelligence.[145] The American and British governments officially denied anything like that had transpired at the Hague. Johnson, who had met privately with Shinwell during the conference, publicly labelled the story as nonsense. Yet the historical evidence cast doubt on Johnson's official denial. Herbert Gunn reported to Beaverbrook the anonymous source for the *New York Times* story was indeed actually Johnson, who remarked, off the record, that the attendance of Strachey at the conference 'forced the US to withhold all top naval and military secrets from Britain'.[146] Confirming Gunn's account were press sources of the British government which 'inferred very clearly that Johnson himself was the source of the original leakage in the Hague'. This came as no surprise to British officials who had already regarded Johnson as 'somewhat of a devious character'. They had been informed of Johnson's distrust of Strachey's political reliability. An FO contact in the US reported that when the charges first appeared in the Beaverbrook press, Johnson had confided to journalist Drew Pearson that 'he was damned if he would be told by anyone what information he should or should not give to British ministers and would act as he thought fit about passing on information to Mr. Shinwell and Mr. Strachey'.[147]

The FO was also privy to the fact that Johnson personally requested the State Department to conduct an inquiry into the past activities of Strachey and Shinwell. But for the FO, a key mystery over Johnson and the Hague conference remained. What exactly transpired during the meeting between Johnson and Shinwell? A memo addressed to the high-ranking diplomat Gladwyn Jebb stated the FO knew that Johnson had brought Strachey up with Shinwell, 'but in exactly what context and what Mr. Shinwell replied' remained unknown.[148] The FO requested the defence ministry to provide a summary of the meeting, yet no reply exists in the relevant FO files on the subject.[149] Both the statements attributed to Johnson and the seeming refusal of the defence ministry to provide a summary of the private meeting between Johnson and Shinwell hint to the likelihood that Johnson did attempt to pressure the British government into removing Strachey from his ministerial post. Ultimately, the FO decided the best response for the Washington embassy to take over the matter was 'to induce oblivion' on the 'Strachey controversy as rapidly as possible'.[150]

Taking the direct opposite approach of the FO on the whole affair was Waldron Smithers. He sought not to induce oblivion but to promote controversy. While Beaverbrook denounced Strachey in the press and Johnson worked against him in Washington, political opposition against the newly appointed minister of war galvanised around Smithers. In more accurate terms, Smithers constituted the entirety of the political opposition, since he was the only British politician who demanded the removal of Strachey from his post.[151] Even Lord Vansittart – who Smithers affectionately looked up to for giving him 'renewed hope and confidence' in their collective anti-communist struggles – refused to denounce Strachey publicly.[152] As usual, Smithers used his parliamentary position to make his attacks. In mid-March, alluding to the Strachey dispute, Smithers asked Attlee to explain what steps were being taken regarding ministerial appointments 'from a security point of view'. Refusing to take the bait, the prime minister replied he did not have to accept the implication of the question, since the responsibility of selecting governmental ministers rested solely in the position of the prime minister.[153] Thus he did not have to answer any questions posed by members of the Commons on the matter. Attlee's straightforward refusal to debate the appointment of Strachey did not deter Smithers. He decided to take the matter directly to the king by way of a public petition. Throughout April, Smithers gathered signatures calling for the Commons as a whole to recommend to the crown the removal of Strachey, and also Shinwell, from their posts, since 'both men showed earlier in their careers sympathies for communism'.[154] On 8 May 1950, to both cheers and boos, Smithers introduced onto the floor of the House the petition signed by over 18,000 Britons. While the petition garnered press coverage on both sides of the Atlantic, it provoked no official governmental action. After the petition, the controversy over Strachey began to fade. However, Smithers's attacks did not diminish; in June he went so far as to classify Strachey as 'a Marxist tumour' on the body politic.[155] Yet the moment had gone. The matter of Strachey's past was shortly to be overshadowed by the first shots of the Korean War later that summer.

Reds in the BBC?

Since 1946, Smithers had begun accusing the BBC of having a pro-communist slant. In a letter sent that year to BBC chairman Sir Allan Powell, he stated his discomfort when appearing on 'Brains Trust', a panel show, in which he criticised Soviet foreign policy. Smithers stated he felt he was in the 'presence of evil' and that a 'Russian agent' obviously wrote a question put to him.[156] Throughout the coming years he charged that the BBC promoted Marxist-Leninist propaganda. Once, Smithers went so far as to shout at BBC parliamentary reporter Roland Fox, calling him and the rest of the reporters employed by the BBC 'all a lot of commies'.[157] Smithers did more than shout; he urged for a governmental investigation into the matter.

Joining Smithers in his disdain for the BBC was Lord Vansittart. In fact, the key opening volley in Vansittart's contentious speech of 29 March 1950 focused on communist infiltration in what Vansittart dubbed the 'most potent weapon in the Cold War' – namely, the BBC. He claimed that allowing the continued employment of communists within the BBC hampered its ability to fight against Russian propaganda and permitted subversive elements of the population to indoctrinate the nation. These and other similar accusations appear to come directly from lengthy communications Vansittart had with a former employee of the BBC. In the months leading up to his speech, Vansittart and Smithers regularly conversed with Count Alexis Bobrinskoy, a White Russian emigre. Later a professional actor, whose credits included Alfred Hitchcock's *The Man Who Knew Too Much* (1956), in 1950 Bobrinskoy was a laid-off employee of the BBC with an axe to grind. Hired in September 1946 as a Russian translator and announcer for the international wing of the BBC, he was discharged in 1949. In his writings to Vansittart and Smithers, Bobrinskoy claimed the cause for his dismissal 'had a purely political background, whatever other reasons my chiefs may put forward'.[158] In his service report to the Broadcasting Committee of the BBC, Bobrinskoy stated that the sole justification for his firing laid in the summation by other members of the Russian section that he delivered the text in a 'counter-revolutionary, bourgeois voice' and such a 'perfectly senseless and unfounded statement has ruined my career at the BBC'.[159] Bobrinskoy reasoned that communist sympathies held by several employees at his former employer were affecting the editorial content of the broadcasts and slanting them towards a more pro-Soviet worldview. Bobrinskoy found a welcoming audience for convincing Vansittart and Smithers that a communist conspiracy existed deep within the BBC. It proved quite an easy task.

Unbeknownst to Smithers and Vansittart, the security service already had its own similar suspicions. In 1947, MI5 obtained a Home Office-issued warrant to look into the matter.[160] The agency wiretapped the phone lines of BBC employees, seeking evidence on those with 'communist connections'. The probe proved inconclusive. Although MI5 suspected three people working in the Eastern European Department were attempting 'to get their point of view across by wrapping it up with other information', they did not have enough evidence to act.[161] In 1952, MI5 returned to the hunt – this time to satisfy the persistent urgings of Smithers.

To Smithers's dismay, the overall governmental attitude towards domestic communism did not fundamentally alter with the return of a Conservative to Downing Street after the 1951 General Election. Like his predecessor, Winston Churchill refused Smithers's request to set up a Royal Commission to investigate communist activities in the UK and also his suggestion to outlaw wildcat strikes, which communists usually supported.[162] Such refusals are not surprising, since Churchill typically showed less concern over domestic communism than Attlee. However, the possibility of communists exerting their influence through the BBC stood as a notable exception. In 1950, Churchill became alarmed at the possibility after receiving a letter from an organisation headed by Lord Craigavon, the son of the first prime minister of Northern Ireland, called the Listeners' Association. Both Vansittart and Smithers were avid supporters of the organisation, whose raison d'être appeared to be exposing communism infiltration in the BBC. The letter to Churchill contained an attachment reproducing correspondences between the group and the BBC over the airing of a programme highly critical of Churchill titled 'The Soviet Point of View'. It documented how when the Listeners' Association asked why the programme was allowed to be aired, a BBC programme director replied that they had an 'editorial responsibility' to let all sides be heard. When pressed why several anti-communists were barred from expressing their opinion on the network, the programme director refused to comment.[163] Churchill forwarded a copy of the attachment to Herbert Morrison, asking him to investigate the issue; Morrison replied that he would take the matter up with the BBC directors.[164]

A parliamentary question by Smithers brought the issue back to Churchill's attention in 1952. He told the prime minister that reliable sources had provided him with evidence of subversive influences inside the BBC. Instead of merely dismissing Smithers, as usual, Churchill requested him to pass on what information he had dealing with the matter. Taking him up on the offer, Smithers persistently wrote Churchill requesting for an investigation. He provided the names of eight individuals who worked at the BBC who he claimed were using the institution to spread communist propaganda. These included A.W. Morrison, second in charge of the Overseas Department, and 'a Jew called Mr. Goldberg' who controlled the selections of BBC programmes. Smithers warned that 'we have traitors in our midst and although I should deplore suppression of free speech, they should be treated as traitors'.[165]

Churchill forwarded the claims to the Home Office and responded to Smithers, telling him he had 'all these matters in mind'.[166] The Home Office contacted MI5 over Smithers's allegations and administered an inquiry into the situation. They reported to Peter Oates, Churchill's principal private secretary, that MI5 held records on 147 BBC employees whom it determined were communists, communist sympathisers or suspected communists. An MI5 report to Oates provided notes to Downing Street on the individuals Smithers had named. After reviewing the situation, the security service concluded that communist influence in the BBC did 'not constitute a serious danger'; however, 'the position is carefully watched' and the security service was in 'constant touch with the BBC about communists in their employment'. It was reported that the security service secretly vetted employees and prospective employees for evidence of communist sympathies. In full compliance, the BBC submitted to MI5 a weekly average of twenty-four names of its workers for review. In turn, MI5 reviewed them and reported their findings to the BBC, though it lamented 'the corporation sometimes finds it difficult to rid itself of established staff known to be communists'.[167] Satisfied that MI5 had the matter well in hand, Churchill wrote to Smithers saying the situation was under control. Unbeknownst to Smithers, the public or the BBC employees under investigation, MI5 was already covertly addressing the situation.

Conclusion

Despite Vansittart's protestations to the contrary, Smithers and the lord sought a McCarthyite response. In searching for parallels in their own nation's history, some are easily found. Smithers's demand for an un-British activities committee eerily mirrors the times of Pitt the Elder and his establishment of the Grand Inquest of the Nation in 1742. Vansittart's call for attacks on the communist conspiracy infecting the UK reverberated like the charges of Titus Oates of a popish plot in 1678. 'Vansittartism', in its loosest definition, never took hold, nor did it ever come close to garnering the level of support McCarthyism gained in the US. To Smithers's chagrin, no British HUAC ever materialised. Despite the urgings of Vansittart, no pogroms against domestic communists arose. However, the two have strikingly similar parallels. Vansittart's assault on Protestantism for its perceived failure to combat communism directly correlates to the opinions voiced by J.B. Matthews, a long-time congressional investigator and confidant to McCarthy. In 1953, Matthews wrote that the 'largest single group supporting the communist apparatus in the United States today is composed of Protestant clergymen'.[168] The same is true of Smithers's accusations against Strachey and Shinwell. These attacks are comparable to McCarthy's statements questioning the loyalty of two US cabinet members Dean Acheson and George Marshall. However, what these men were able to achieve was a move by British institutions to a more anti-communist standpoint.

One institution in particular was the Church of England. While some could argue the decision by Fisher to form an official Church body to fight communism shortly after Vansittart made his remarks against the Church was mere coincidence, it seems highly unlikely, since Fisher explicitly mentions Vansittart when agreeing to its establishment. Also, Vansittart's criticisms of Anglicanism's 'soft' response and his praise for the Catholic 'hard' reaction to communism are telling. They speak to the broader theme of what part religion played in the anti-communist movement inside the UK. Much has been written on this subject, a good amount of it emphasising the prominent role religion played in the international struggle between the 'godless' East and Christian West. Religion certainly factored into the propaganda battle between the two, with the West's 'appropriating of Christianity' for its usage against the East, as Dianne Kirby argued.[169] Anti-communist literature and rhetoric played up maltreatments of fellow Christians behind the Iron Curtain and claimed that if communism came into power in the Atlantic world, churches and cathedrals would burn there. However, it must be noted that anti-communism worked as its own quasi-spirituality; it needed no prior religious faith to function. Although an Anglican, Vansittart rebuked the Church when it refused to fully embrace the anti-communist crusade to his liking. He did not stand as the only prominent politician whose belief in anti-communism trumped their faith in a higher power. Herbert Morrison – arguably the Labour Party's witchfinder general of communists – is famously quoted as saying he belonged to no religious denomination and 'socialism was [his] religion'.[170] Clement Attlee stated during an interview with Kenneth Harris that he did not believe in Christian 'mumbo jumbo' and regarded himself as a person 'incapable of [having a] religious experience'.[171] For the most part, Churchill was a committed secularist; only on the best occasions did he profess to be something akin to an 'optimistic agnostic'.[172] Even when religious beliefs did factor into the equation, they were generally not overriding. The perfect example might be Smithers. Although a devoted churchgoer, it is hard to believe that if he had lapsed in faith, Smithers would have expressed any less animosity to the red religion of communism. His calling for the public execution of his fellow Anglican Hewlett Johnson acutely supports such an argument. Shifting from personalities to institutions, the Church of England held a more tolerant acceptance of communism than the Labour government of the time – a reality that is evident when examining the anti-communist efforts put forth by Labour in the subsequent chapter. Conversely, when sticking solely to religious opposition to communism, a strong argument stands that the Moral Rearmament Movement, which is covered in detail in Chapter 4, clearly outshined the Church of England in the fight against domestic reds as well.

Returning to the efforts of the central figures, the establishment of a secret Anglican anti-communist committee is but one empirical example of their impact. Also of note are Smithers's roles in promoting covert investigations into the BBC and the international controversy over John Strachey. Nevertheless, Vansittart and Smithers's influence was less far-reaching than that of their American counterparts. Because of the uniform nature of the British government, they were unable to independently conduct investigations from within the Commons or the Lords as their anti-communist counterparts in the US were able to in the Senate and the House of Representatives. This did not mean they were entirely dismissed. Clandestinely, MI5 investigated Vansittart's unsubstantiated charges of governmental subversion, though without the fanfare of a public hearing as occurred in the US when McCarthy made similar allegations.[173] Vansittart's charge that communists infested higher education only produced one named casualty. After Vansittart's 28 March 1950 speech, the University of London suddenly dismissed lecturer Andrew Rothstein, a known communist; in response, the student union passed a resolution criticising his removal on 'political grounds'.[174] Although the Rothstein incident obviously does not represent a systemic removal of communists from academia, it does suggest a shifting of attitudes in the universities during the early Cold War. Curiously, that same year, MI5 began surreptitiously compiling a list of all communists working in both universities and colleges.[175] Official restrictions were placed on communists in the field of adult education; lecturers were proscribed from working as tutors in departments which provided educational services to the armed services.[176] After the attack on HMS *Amethyst*, the admiralty ordered the ousting of all communist members of staff from Pangbourne Nautical College.[177] Taking note of the era, historian Eric Hobsbawm stated that 'no known communists were appointed to university posts ... nor if already in teaching posts, were they promoted'.[178] Since communist professors and lecturers were quietly denied a future in academia, no outright purge was even necessary.

The type of red-hunting promoted by Vansittart and Smithers did not stop at the hallowed halls of academia. The central council of the John Lewis Partnership voted in place a ban on communists from working in its businesses.[179] The firm employed 12,000 workers and owned twenty department stores throughout the UK, including the prominent shopping venues of Peter Jones and John Barnes in London, alongside the nationwide Waitrose chain.[180] When Lord Stansgate questioned the move in the Lords, the chairman of the company, J. Spendan Lewis, admonished Stansgate for his troubles. In a personal letter to the lord, he argued it was 'very harmful indeed' to criticise or doubt the right of a private business from excluding employment to 'communists or for any other reason, such as a disinclination to worship golden calves or an inclination to play the part of Moses on a duodecimo or any other scale'.[181] Joining the effort to purge themselves of reds was the Boy Scouts Association. During the 1950s, a number of its young members were expelled for having communist affiliations.[182]

Although previous historians have contested the fact, like McCarthy and his followers in the US, the rantings and ravings of Vansittart and Smithers had a real impact on the political culture and governmental policies in the UK. However, the anti-communism preached by Vansittart and Smithers smacked of partisan attacks and right-wing fears – which limited its more general appeal. Alongside others like de Courcy, both viewed British socialism as only providing weak-kneed protection against the threat to the rise of Marxist totalitarianism inside the UK and the rest of the world. As is discussed in Chapter 4, Smithers and Vansittart, like the Conservative Party leadership, sought to associate Labourite ideas of democratic socialism and social democracy with the spread of undemocratic communism and the destruction of British liberty. Few in the UK found this link credible. Neither of these two proved a successful vessel in galvanising their brand of extreme anti-communism into a national movement. Neither the reactionary and alcoholic Smithers nor the retired and embittered Vansittart were able to sway the British populace to garner a national following as the young and media-savvy McCarthy did in the US.[183] However, as the following chapters show, a disproportionate anti-communist response within the UK did exist – yet not the type envisioned or pushed for by Vansittart and Smithers who promulgated a McCarthyite message. They represented the vocal extremes, not the shadowy consensus that ultimately formed to combat the 'red menace'.

Notes

1. *Daily Herald*, 15 February 1950, p. 7.

2. Hansard, HL, vol. 167, c. 29 (2 May 1950).

3. *Daily News* (New York), 25 August 1954, p. 35.

4. I. Colvin, *Vansittart in Office* (London, 1965), p. 19.

5. *Like It Was: The Diaries of Malcolm Muggeridge*, ed. J. Bright-Holmes (London, 1981), p. 256.

6. *Harold Nicolson Diaries 1945–1964*, ed. N. Nicolson (London, 2004), p. 308.

7. *Observer*, 13 March 1949, p. 7.

8. John Colville, *The Fringes of Power* (London, 1985), 398.

9. J. Ferris, 'Indulged in all too little? Vansittart, intelligence and appeasement', *Diplomacy and Statecraft*, 10 (1995): 122–75, at p. 128.

10. J. Charmley, *Chamberlain and the Lost Peace* (London, 1989), pp. 6–7.

11. R. Vansittart, *Black Record* (London, 1941), p. 20.

12. Vansittart, *Black Record*, p. 3.

13. *Western Daily Press*, 20 May 1942, p. 4.

14. *New Europe*, October 1944, p. 8.

15. Hansard, HL, vol. 133, c. 168 (26 September 1944).

16. M. Roi, *Alternative to Appeasement* (London, 1997), p. 10.

17. A. Goldman, 'Germans and Nazis: The controversy over "Vansittartism" in Britain during the Second World War', *Journal of Contemporary History*, 14 (1979): 155–91, at p. 156.

18. See I. Tombs, 'The victory of socialist "Vansittartism": Labour and the German question, 1941–5', *Twentieth Century British History*, 7 (1996): 287–309, at p. 287.

19. Goldman, 'Germans and Nazis', p. 167.

20. Vansittart, *Lessons of My Life* (London, 1943), p. 30.

21. *Nottingham Journal*, 17 April 1946, p. 1.

22. *Daily Worker*, 11 November 1947, p. 2.

23. Vansittart to John Percival, 2 January 1950, VNST II 1/36.

24. N. Rose, *Vansittart* (London, 1978), p. 278.

25. Roi, *Alternative*, p. 174.

26. Goldman, 'Germans and Nazis', p. 179.

27. N. Davies, *Rising '44* (London, 2003), p. 296.

28. Vansittart, *Events and Shadows* (London, 1947), p. 63.

29. Vansittart, *Events and Shadows*, p. 146.

30. *Daily Worker*, 11 November 1947, p. 6.

31. J. Callaghan, *Rajani Palme Dutt* (London, 1993), p. 234.

32. Vansittart to editor of *The Times*, 19 March 1948, VNST II 1–25.

33. *Everybody's*, 13 August 1949, p. 8.

34. *Everybody's*, 7 May 1949, pp. 2–3.

35. *Everybody's*, 21 May 1949, p. 3.

36. Winston Churchill, handwritten note, undated, document 349, Churchill Papers (henceforth CHUR) 2-67A-B, Churchill College, Cambridge.

37. *Intelligence Digest*, vol. 11, no. 10 (September 1949), p. 1.

38. *New York Times*, 8 January 1950, p. 19.

39. US State Department report sent to Walter Bedell Smith by W. Park Armstrong, 8 January 1951. Freedom of information request by the author.

40. *Western Mail*, 16 February 1950, p. 4.

41. *Globe and Mail*, 6 April 1950, p. 4.

42. 'Mr. Kenneth de Courcy and Intelligence Digest' by Ernest Bevin, 29 March 1950, TNA FO 115/4511.

43. J. Paterson to Godfrey Shannon, 7 August 1950, TNA DO 231/28.

44. File note by J.J. Saville Garner, 4 September 1950, TNA DO 231/28.

45. File note by Alec Joyce, 1 September 1950, TNA DO 231/28.

46. File note by J.J. Saville Garner, 4 September 1950, TNA DO 231/28.

47. *Vital Speeches of the Day*, vol. 25, no. 5 (1950), p. 137.

48. *Intelligence Digest*, vol. 16, no. 1 (1950), p. 5.

49. N.W.H. Gaydon to Mr. Stephens and Mr. Burrows, 22 May 1950, TNA FO 115/4511.

50. Liddell diary, 29 December 1952.

51. Vansittart to Waldron Smithers, 9 October 1949, VNST 1/36.

52. Vansittart to A.L. Kennedy, 31 January 1950, VNST 1/41; *Daily Mail*, 20 March 1949, p. 1.

53. *Guardian*, 10 March 1949, p. 5.

54. Vansittart, *Even Now* (London, 1949), p. 143.

55. *Daily Mail*, 24 January 1950, p. 4.

56. *Daily Mail*, 24 January 1950, p. 4; Vansittart to G.M. Lindsay, 28 December 1949, VNST II 1–35.

57. *Sunday Dispatch*, 1 May 1955.

58. C. Moran, *Classified* (Cambridge, 2013), pp. 117–19.

59. Rose, *Vansittart*, p. 280.

60. Hansard, HL, vol. 166, c. 627 (29 March 1950).

61. Hansard, HL, vol. 166, c. 613 (29 March 1950).

62. Hansard, HL, vol. 166, c. 631 (29 March 1950).

63. Hansard, HL, vol. 166, c. 649 (29 March 1950).

64. Hansard, HL, vol. 166, c. 608 (29 March 1950).

65. *Argus Melbourne*, 4 April 1950, p. 2, on the moniker 'VanWitchhunt' given to him by the *Reynolds News*. Vansittart scoffed, calling it 'the sort of jibe that I would have made at my prep. school on an off-day'.

66. *Guardian*, 31 March 1950, p. 6.

67. *Daily Worker*, 11 April 1950, p. 2.

68. *Tribune*, 7 April 1950, p. 3.

69. *New Statesman and Nation*, 19 August 1950.

70. *Birmingham Daily Gazette*, 5 April 1950, p. 1.

71. *Birmingham Daily Gazette*, 3 April 1950, p. 4.

72. Vansittart to Lord Stansgate, 4 April 1950, Papers of William Wedgwood Benn, 1st Viscount Stansgate (henceforth ST) ST 1/125, Westminster Parliamentary Archive.

73. Gerald Barry to Stansgate, 26 April 1950, ST 1/125.

74. Boris Ford to Stansgate, 26 April 1950, ST 1/125.

75. Hansard, HL, vol. 167, cc. 16–23 (2 May 1950).

76. Hansard, HL, vol. 167, c. 45 (2 May 1950).

77. *Northern Whig*, 3 May 1950, p. 1.

78. J. Butler, *The Red Dean of Canterbury* (London, 2011), pp. 242–4.

79. Kirby, 'Ecclesiastical McCarthyism', p. 190.

80. Geoffrey Fisher to Waldron Smithers, 22 March 1951, G 26 Papers of Council of Foreign Relations (henceforth CFR), Lambeth Palace Library.

81. *Daily Mail*, 30 March 1950, p. 1.

82. Vansittart, *Bones of Contention* (London, 1945) p. 122.

83. Vansittart to the editor of *Daily Telegraph*, 20 September 1950, VNST 1/42.

84. Vansittart, 'Christianity and Communism', 10 August 1949, VNST 1/37.

85. *Donegal News*, 30 July 1949, p. 3.

86. Vansittart, *Even Now*, p. 117.

87. Hansard, HL, vol. 166, c. 616 (29 March 1950).

88. D. Hyde, *The Answer to Communism* (London, 1949), p. 52.

89. *From Communism towards Catholicism*, pamphlet by Douglas Hyde, 1948.

90. Fisher to Canon Scrutton, 29 December 1955, Fisher vol. 154.

91. Archbishop's address to the Diocesan Conference, 12 July 1949, CFR G/61.

92. *York Diocesan Leaflet*, no. 254, August 1949, p. 3.

93. *Derry Journal*, 9 July 1954, p. 1.

94. Vansittart, 'Christ or Stalin?', reprint located in Fisher vol. 70.

95. Quoted in I. Jones, 'The clergy, Cold War and the mission of the local church: England ca. 1945–60', in *Religion and The Cold War*, ed. D. Kirby (London, 2002), 188–99, at p. 191.

96. I. Jones, 'The clergy', p. 195.

97. *Belfast Telegraph*, 25 November 1954, p. 5.

98. *Londonderry Sentinel*, 7 September 1954, p. 2.

99. Fisher to Eleanor Adlard, 21 August 1950, Fisher vol. 70.

100. Fisher to Lady Roberts, 12 April 1950, Fisher vol. 70.

101. Church Council on Foreign Relations meeting notes, 18 November 1949, CFR G 6/1.

102. *Daily Mail*, 29 March 1950, p. 4.

103. *Catholic Herald*, 14 July 1950, p. 8.

104. Fisher to Waldron Smithers, 2 April 1953, Fisher vol. 131.

105. *Belfast Newsletter*, 29 January 1954, p. 10.

106. *Western Mail*, 31 December 1949, p. 2.

107. Lord Bishop of Chichester to Fisher, 31 March 1950, CFR G 6/1.

108. Fisher to Bishop of Chichester, 3 April 1950, CFR G 6/1.

109. Kirby, 'Ecclesiastical McCarthyism', p. 190.

110. See E. McFarland and R. Johnston, 'The Church of Scotland's special commission on communism, 1949–1954: Tackling "Christianity's most serious competitor"', *Contemporary British History*, 23 (2009): 337–61.

111. *Daily Herald*, 18 May 1949, p. 2.

112. J.B. Wilson to K.J. Robertson, 1 June 1944, D/497, Beaverbrook Papers (henceforth BBK), Westminster Parliamentary Archive.

113. Smithers to Members of the Carlton Club, 1 December 1938, TNA HO 45/25476.

114. Memorandum by Waldron Smithers, undated, though likely written in 1938, TNA HO 45/25476; Smithers to Lord Londonderry, 22 December 1938, D3099/17/40, Papers of Lord Londonderry, Public Record Office of Northern Ireland (henceforth PRONI). Smithers's distrust of 'Jews' is also evident in a 1944 letter he wrote to Anthony Eden. See TNA FO 954/26B/352.

115. Smithers to Lord Londonderry, 25 April 1938, PRONI D3099/17/40.

116. Smithers to Lord Halifax, 24 November 1936, LH/1/59, Records of the Leader of the House of Lords, Westminster Parliamentary Archive.

117. Smithers to John Anderson, 15 March 1940, TNA HO 45/25476.

118. E.J. Robertson to J.B. Wilson, 23 June 1944, BBK/D/497.

119. J. Boyd-Carpenter, *Way of Life* (London, 1980), p. 79; A. Farrant and N. Tynan, 'Sir Waldron Smithers and the long walk to Finchley', *Economic Affairs*, 32 (2012): 43–7, at p. 44.

120. F. Hayek, *Hayek on Hayek*, ed. S. Kresge and L. Wenar (Chicago, 1994), p. 107.

121. R. Toye, *The Roar of the Lion* (Oxford, 2013), p. 211.

122. A. Farrant and N. Tynan, 'Sir Waldron Smithers and the muddle of the Tory middle', *Economic Affairs*, 32 (2012): 63–7, at p. 63; A. Farrant and N. Tynan, 'The control of engagement order: Attlee's road to serfdom?', in *F.A. Hayek and the Modern Economy*, ed. S. Peart and D. Levy (London, 2013), 157–80, at p. 159.

123. Hansard, House of Commons debates (henceforth HC), vol. 473, c. 1001 (4 April 1950).

124. Liddell diary, 24 October 1947.

125. Hansard, HC, vol. 462, c. 451 (2 March 1949).

126. *Daily Mail*, 11 July 1952, p. 2; Hansard, HC, vol. 503, c. 1517 (10 July 1952).

127. Hansard, HC, vol. 437, c. 252 (22 May 1947).

128. Hansard, HC, vol. 456, c. 502 (20 September 1948).

129. *Derby Daily Telegraph*, 7 March 1950, p. 1; *Daily Herald*, 10 December 1954, p. 7.

130. Hansard, HC, vol. 476, c. 2244 (27 June 1950).

131. Hansard, HC, vol. 476, c. 2252 (27 June 1950).

132. Hansard, HC, vol. 476, c. 2254 (27 June 1950).

133. J. Strachey, *The Coming Struggle for Power* (London, 1932), p. 357.

134. P. Corthorn, 'Labour, the Left, and the Stalinist purges of the late 1930s', *The Historical Journal*, 48.1 (2005): 179–207, at p. 202.

135. *New York Times*, 3 March 1950, p. 16.

136. *Sheffield Daily Telegraph*, 3 March 1950, p. 1.

137. *Western Morning News*, 4 March 1950, p. 1.

138. Herbert Gunn to Lord Beaverbrook, 17 March 1950, BBK/H/252.

139. Gunn to Beaverbrook, 28 April 1950, BBK/H/252.

140. H. Thomas, *John Strachey* (London, 1973), p. 260.

141. F.R. Hoyer Millar to Michael Wright, 4 April 1950, TNA FO 371/81635.

142. *Yorkshire Post and Leeds Intelligencer*, 15 April 1950, p. 1.

143. *New York Times*, 3 April 1950, p. 1.

144. *New York Times*, 6 April 1950, p. 27.

145. K. Young, 'Cold War insecurities and the curious case of John Strachey', *Intelligence and National Security*, 29 (2014): 901–25, at p. 910.

146. Herbert Gunn to Lord Beaverbrook, 6 April 1950, BBK/H/252.

147. F.R. Hoyer Millar to Michael Wright, 4 April 1950, TNA FO 371/81635.

148. E.M. Rose to Gladwyn Jebb, 28 April 1950, TNA FO 371/81635.

149. Gladwyn Jebb to William Elliot, 28 April 1950, TNA FO 371/81635.

150. File notes on file AU 10210/4, 4 May 1950, TNA FO 371/81635.

151. *New York Times*, 4 April 1950, p. 6.

152. Smithers to Vansittart, 27 November 1949, VNST II 1/36.

153. Hansard, HC, vol. 472, c. 37 (14 March 1950).

154. Hansard, HC, vol. 475, cc. 1–2 (8 May 1950).

155. *Daily Worker*, 7 July 1950, p. 4.

156. *Perth Daily News*, 27 July 1946, p. 6.

157. N. Robinson, *Live from Downing Street* (London, 2012), p. 112.

158. Alexis Bobrinskoy to Vansittart, 9 September 1949, VNST 1–39.

159. BBC Service Report on Bobrinskoy, VNST 1/39.

160. Liddell diary, 8 November 1947.

161. Liddell diary, 1 January 1948.

162. Hansard, HC, vol. 522, cc. 835–6 (19 January 1954); Hansard, HC, vol. 526, cc. 1784–5 (29 April 1954).

163. C.H. Rolleston to Winston Churchill, supplement to letter, 9 February 1949, CHUR 2/99 A-B.

164. Churchill to Herbert Morrison, 13 April 1950; Morrison to Churchill, 15 April 1950, CHUR 2/99 A-B.

165. Smithers to Churchill, 18 June 1952, TNA PREM 11/995.

166. Churchill to Smithers, 8 July 1952, TNA PREM 11/995.

167. R.J. Whitlock to P.G. Oates, 15 August 1952, TNA PREM 11/995.

168. *Reds and Our Churches*, pamphlet by J.B. Matthews, 1953.

169. Kirby, 'Ecclesiastical McCarthyism', p. 201.

170. *Forward*, 22 April 1916, p. 1.

171. 'The politics of faith', *Guardian*, 5 May 2010.

172. 'Optimistic agnostic' is how Churchill's last private secretary described his superior. A. Browne, *Long Sunset* (London, 1995), p. 204.

173. Liddell diary, 23 July 1951.

174. *Sunday Mirror*, 2 April 1950, p. 2.

175. Liddell diary, 1 December 1950.

176. See R. Fieldhouse, *Adult Education and the Cold War* (Leeds, 1985).

177. S. Parsons, 'British McCarthyism', p. 235.

178. E. Hobsbawm, *Interesting Times* (London, 2002), p. 182.

179. *Gazette of the John Lewis Partnership*, vol. 31, no. 14, 7 May 1949, p. 1.

180. *Daily Herald*, 26 April 1949, p. 1.

181. J. Spendan Lewis to Lord Stansgate, 14 May 1949, ST 1/125.

182. See S. Mills, 'Be prepared: Communism and the politics of scouting in 1950s Britain', *Contemporary British History*, 25 (2011): 429–50.

183. T. Doherty, *Cold War, Cool Medium* (New York, 2003), p. 16.

Chapter 2

Labour Party: the enemy within and without

I think we must accept the fact that the present rulers of Russia are committed to the belief that there is a natural conflict between the capitalist and the communist worlds. They believe that they have a mission to work for a communist world. But they would naturally prefer to achieve this by infiltration without an armed conflict.[1]

—Ernest Bevin

The British Labour Party and I myself have been vigorously opposing the Communist Party in this country ever since its formation – long before Senator McCarthy was ever heard of.[2]

—Clement Attlee

On 27 October 1948, Waldron Smithers asked Clement Attlee to form a parliamentary select committee to investigate un-British activities along similar lines to the notorious HUAC working in the US. Although present in the House of Commons, the prime minister refused to engage with the Conservative MP, allowing Herbert Morrison to field the question. Often a verbose speaker, Morrison limited his responses to 'No, sir'. Smithers persisted, urging that 'in view of the rapidly increasing menace of communist infiltration ... which is the root cause of most of the trouble in the world today', a coming 'showdown' with the Communist Party was necessary 'before it was too late'. Persisting as well, Morrison repeated 'No, sir' again. This brief encounter between radically different individuals is often cited to show how Clement Attlee's Labour government rejected the red-scaring allure then plaguing the American political landscape.

Often describing himself as the 'last real Tory in the House of Commons', Waldron Smithers embodied the typical vehemently anti-communist politician of the period. Those searching for the personification of a 'British McCarthy' characteristically cite Smithers or Lord Vansittart. Morrison is never mentioned as a candidate. Yet to classify Morrison – or many other members of the Labour leadership – as anything other than an anti-communist negates the meaning of the word.[3]

Perhaps the earliest instances of Labour's aggressive stance towards domestic communists took place over the issue of housing. Because of the devastation wrought by six years of German bombing, a shortage of housing plagued the postwar UK. Despite Labour promises to quickly alleviate the situation, the pace of progress did not match widespread expectations. In July 1946, around fifty displaced families took matters into their own hands and moved into abandoned army camps in Scunthorpe. Their novel idea spread like wildfire. Within a matter of weeks over 40,000 people had taken up vacancies in similar unused military facilities. Just as the government started to tackle the issue, squatters began occupying entire city blocks of abandoned flats. Attlee demanded stern action from his ministers and ordered no efforts should be made to parlay with the squatters. The Ministry of Works and police were ordered to guard all empty buildings in London, and the local councils were told to cut water and electricity to a number of illegally occupied flats. As the movement grew, the CPGB began aiding and in some instances leading and directing would-be squatters. The government's firm stance against them had driven the squatters to accept CPGB assistance – 'desperate people were looking to the party to find them homes'.[4] Home Secretary Chuter Ede received instructions to discover any future moves of communist support and to take proactive steps to prevent them. Following the direction coming from Labour, MI5 and Special Branch also began investigating CPGB involvement. Communist support for the squatters only further infuriated Attlee, though his attorney general counselled him against rash action. Hartley Shawcross advised him not to seek blanket prosecutions against the squatters since such a move threatened to turn the 'communist-supported movement' into a popular cause.[5]

The FO offered up another solution to the unpopular mess that framed the matter in an entirely different light. 'There is considerable capital to be made out of it', an FO report assessed, 'if the official line about these squatters is to regard them as dupes of the communist endeavour to use them for their own political ends', since the government could argue 'the first type of furnishing' installed in these buildings 'is the Iron Curtain'.[6] Soon afterwards Attlee's press secretary, Francis Williams, disseminated the agreed narrative to the press. Downing Street then issued a statement asserting that the government took 'a serious view' of squatting, and despite the CPGB having little to do with the earlier movements into abandoned camps, they labelled the entire matter as one 'instituted and organized by the Communist Party'. The press release also revealed that criminal proceedings against the 'communist instigators' were under consideration. Following up on the threat, on 14 September, in London, the police arrested five communist activists for conspiring to incite trespass of the peace.[7] Although the central issue which drove the squatting movement was the lack of available housing, Labour was able to successfully criticise it as a communist-instigated plot seeking to discredit the government. Attlee and Labour would employ similar red-baiting tactics in the field of industrial relations.

Labour government: the foundation of Cold War British anti-communism

By the waning months of 1945, Karl Marx's opening sentence of the *Communist Manifesto*, written almost 100 years earlier, still weighed heavily on the minds of many throughout the UK. The fear of the spectre of communism was not confined only to the Vansittarts and Smithers of the nation; it plagued and occupied the minds of those in the British security services, mandarins filling departments in Whitehall, the armed forces and the members of the newly formed Labour government.

Initially, for many communists, and the left-wing of the ruling party, this fear came as a shocking revelation. For a socialist government to display such anti-communist opinions and to go so far as to enact measures to suppress the ideology seemed against the basic premise the Labour Party stood for. The victory of Clement Attlee over Winston Churchill in the General Election of 1945 signalled that the British citizenry did not desire a return to normalcy, but a radical transformation of the status quo. With the release of the Beveridge Report – which read in parts more like a manifesto than a white paper – the battleground for the inevitable postwar electoral duel between the two main political parties was decided. After six years of sacrificing their 'blood, sweat and toil' against the Axis powers, the time had come for correcting societal ills and fostering a fairer nation. In this effort, the voting public turned to the party promising to create a more egalitarian society and seize the means of production for the good of building a 'New Jerusalem'. It did not shy away from campaigning on these goals. As its election manifesto stated: 'The Labour party is a socialist party, and proud of it. Its ultimate purpose at home is the establishment of the "Socialist Commonwealth of Great Britain".'[8] The manifesto did urge patience and cautioned that tearing down the old society would take time, declaring 'Socialism cannot come overnight, as the product of a week-end revolution.'[9] If further evidence was needed of how the Labour Party sought to govern, an observer needed only to listen to an excerpt from its official anthem, 'The Red Flag':

> Then raise the scarlet standard high,
> Within its shade we'll live and die,
> Though cowards flinch and traitors sneer,
> We'll keep the Red flag flying here.

> Look round, the Frenchman loves its blaze,
> The sturdy German chants its praise,
> In Moscow's vaults its hymns are sung
> Chicago swells the surging throng.

With words indicating a willingness to die for the socialist cause and talk of traitors and cowards, it held a revolutionary fervour that the British populace could not misconstrue. A verse of the song praised international solidary between workers in France, Germany, the US and Russia: a sentiment usually associated with Marx and his call to arms – namely, 'workers of the world unite'. As Labour took power on 1 August 1945, it did not appear that the song and its significance were a product of a bygone era. The government benches filled with 393 Labour MPs rose in one unified voice to sing it, marking the first time the song had been played in the halls of Westminster. The 'peaceful revolution', as Attlee designated his socialist government, had begun.

Classifying the Attlee government as a 'revolution' radically stretches the meaning of the word; it resulted in the formation of a welfare state and the nationalisation of only 20 per cent of the country's industry. Neither of these governmental policies were unique and in the postwar era were characteristic features of numerous industrialised nations.[10] While in power from 1945 to 1951, Labour never utilised public ownership as a means to control the economy.[11] As Richard Toye pointed out, 'Attlee government's policy in the 1940s was merely interventionism under the barest veneer of planning'.[12] By 1948 the Labour government was satisfied with accepting a mixed economy dominated by the private sector. Herbert Morrison even proposed limiting any further nationalisation.[13] A command economy never materialised – neither did a socialist commonwealth. Also, Attlee's UK did not transform into a hospitable society for fellow revolutionary comrades in the struggle for workers' rights. Especially not for members of the Communist Party, which had pledged to do its 'utmost to develop ... unity and to strengthen the organizations of the labour movement and their active support for the Labour government'.[14] The Labour Party did not wish to form a popular front or create a 'social democratic bridge' to reach out to the CPGB.[15] By 1945 Labour had been fighting for two decades against the CPGB's attempts to infiltrate the party – on direct orders from Moscow – thus its leaders were wary of any type of general communist 'mischief'.[16] Now in power, the party leadership had had enough. The men who filled the positions of prime minister (Clement Attlee), deputy prime minister (Herbert Morrison) and foreign minister (Ernest Bevin) were all devoted socialists but were by 1945 also committed anti-communists and some of the earliest cold warriors.[17] One might think the new realities of the Cold War changed these men, as they were professed democratic socialists and committed to social democracy in the years prior to the conflict. In the preceding years, after having ascended to power, they supported the right-wing authoritarian regimes of Iran, South Korea and Greece, showed devotion to the idea of empire and held to the basic tenets of capitalism. Not so: no dramatic shift had occurred. For underneath all the rhetoric of 'revolutions', the celebrated imagery of 'red flags' and the declared beliefs in a 'Socialist Commonwealth' lay a dominating sense of moderation and pragmatism within these Labour leaders dating back to the 1930s, which remained unaltered with the emergence of the Cold War. Although a party of the left, Labour showed 'as great an interest in defending the West and its traditions' as the Conservatives.[18] From the party's inception, it functioned, as historians have noted, as 'the most effective bulwark against reaction and revolution'. Andrew Thorpe argued that during the interwar period, Labour did more to block the rise of the extreme left than any other British institution.[19] Its leading figures, who came to power in 1945, had long been dedicated to halting both class warfare and any type of Marxist-inspired uprising and stopping a formal link to non-democratic leftist elements. Attlee's distrust of communism was deep-seated, going back to his time as deputy leader.[20] Nor was Morrison one of the enthusiasts in the Labour Party for the Soviet experiment; while initially pro-Soviet in his youth, he rapidly formed a base hatred for any ideology which did not safeguard constitutional procedures.[21] Putting ideas into deeds, in 1923 he proposed to the Labour National Executive that the party move against communists in the trade unions and the local parties.[22] In 1937, when general secretary of the Transport and General Workers' Union (TGWU), Bevin went so far as vowing to 'smash the trade unions' if they ever came under the influence of the Communist International.[23]

During the interwar period, despite Labour's consistent opposition to domestic communism and its stalwart commitment to the democratic process, a 'rising euphoria' existed in the party for the Soviet Union and its workers' paradise.[24] It formed a paradox and one of Labour's diverging perceptions of the Soviet Union and the CPGB. Labour viewed domestic communists as disrupters and would-be infiltrators, while they saw those in the Soviet Union as trailblazers for progress and freedom. Herbert Morrison notwithstanding, most in Labour held a soft spot in their hearts and minds for the Soviet experiment.[25] The party, as a whole, fondly looked East with a level of admiration for the economic and foreign policies of the newly formed state – which many still referred to as Russia. Stalin's anti-fascist stance in the mid-1930s appealed to many in Labour; especially welcomed by the party was his early support of the Republican cause in Spain.[26] This later proved to be a double-edged sword. When Soviet-backed communists in Spain began murdering their compatriots, a number on the British left saw their euphoria turn to horror. Both George Orwell and Arthur Koestler returned from Spain as emerging anti-communists.[27] A number in the Labour Party also soured to the concept of Stalinism. The show trials and purges ordered by the Soviet dictator gave many on the British left the impression that 1936 Moscow had somehow been transformed into revolutionary Paris gripped in the Reign of Terror.[28] Nevertheless, during the late 1930s the growing anti-Stalinist faction inside Labour remained circumspect in forcefully denouncing the Soviet abuses, since, by all appearances, they still rested in the minority. One of the most notable persons in this wing of the party was Clement Attlee, who, despite direct knowledge of the show trials, remained silent.[29] This was not so with Morrison, who openly attacked the central governing tenets of the Soviet Union. In a July 1936 article for the *Daily Herald*, he boldly – for the time – stated that 'the economic condition of the Russian workers is definitely inferior to that of our country and of most of the Western communities', then added that 'the [Soviet] political dictatorship is irksome, tyrannical, injurious to intellectual freedom and the speed of economic advancement'.[30] As the murderous purges continued into 1937, opposition rose inside the party. That year Attlee found the changing political situation safe enough to denounce Stalin's brand of totalitarianism. In *The Labour Party in Perspective* (1937), he wrote:

> It is inevitable that all dictatorships, whether of the left or the right, should be police-ridden states, with the invariable accompaniments of espionage, dilation, and terrorism. The insistence on the maintenance of democracy by the Labour Party against those who advocate dictatorships, whether on the Berlin or Moscow model, is found upon a deep conviction that any divergence from it involves loss of liberty. Liberty once surrendered is very hard to recapture.[31]

Joining in on the anti-Soviet shift within Labour was Ernest Bevin, who, in no uncertain terms, linked domestic communist agitation with the Soviet Union. Frustrated over continued CPGB attempts to infiltrate the TGWU and communists' efforts to force damaging strike actions, Bevin confronted the Soviet ambassador at a public reception in 1937. 'I have built up the Transport Union', he boasted, and then warned: 'and if you try to break it I'll fight you – and fight you to the death'.[32] Less than two years later, with the signing of the Molotov–Ribbentrop Pact in August 1939, the tide fully turned against pro-Sovietism in Labour. Directly after the end of the Second World War, Attlee, Morrison and Bevin – by then in the new anti-Soviet majority – did their very best to kill this sentiment within the party once and for all.

Not surprisingly, animosity towards communism in the Labour Party escalated with the Soviet–Nazi agreement. It remained high even after the invasion of the Soviet Union by Germany brought Churchill and Stalin into a willing partnership against the forces of fascism. Throughout the war Attlee and Morrison, although bitter rivals for party leadership, worked together against the CPGB. In 1941, Morrison banned the publishing of the *Daily Worker*.[33] He declared 'wicked and poisonous minds' were behind the CPGB and if the general public were privy to the knowledge he held as home secretary, they would never even think of voting for a candidate with such an association.[34] Joining in, Attlee called communists 'fools' who had 'surrendered their minds long ago' and maintained the CPGB worked as an untrustworthy puppet of the Soviet Union.[35] In 1943, the Labour Party National Executive rejected the CPGB's application for affiliation, insisting that communists were out of harmony with British objectives and were tied too closely to the foreign policy aims of the Soviet Union. In a ballot preceding this announcement at the forty-second annual convention the delegates – through a card vote – voted 1,951,000 to 712,000 against allowing affiliation.[36] During a speech at the convention, Morrison lambasted the CPGB and its leader, Harry Pollitt. Morrison said, 'The communists still believe in revolution by violence. They still believe that bloodshed is necessary.' He continued, 'The trouble with communists is that they have dual-purpose minds. They tell you one thing and mean another.'[37] Alongside his deputy, Attlee also held strong reservations about close or formal ties with the CPGB. These reservations appeared to arise now from not just an ideological basis but also a practical standpoint. Returning from the 1945 Potsdam conference, Attlee concluded 'there was no possibility of real Anglo-Soviet co-operation'.[38] He realised the future of both his party and the nation resided in fostering stronger ties with the US than with potential postwar collaboration with Stalin. Speaking specifically on the CPGB, he claimed it disregarded values required for a civil society. Three years after the 1943 conference – and a year after taking power – the party conference voted against affiliation with the CPGB again, this time in an overwhelming six to one majority.[39]

Furthermore, the conference passed by a vote of 2,413,000 to 667,000 to bar any political organisation not already affiliated with the party ineligible from ever receiving it. In a crowning speech before the vote, Herbert Morrison hinted that the financing of CPGB came from foreign sources and that many domestic communists were likely involved in espionage against the crown and empire. Morrison demanded the CPGB 'liquate itself' for the good of the nation.[40]

Although already firmly established, the anti-communist opinions of these party leaders increased as they entered into decision-making roles in the new government. Even more left-leaning members of Labour exhibited paranoia towards communist encroachment after entering government as well. Minister of Health Aneurin Bevan voiced the fear that the CPGB might gain control of hotels in London by blackmailing their managers, then forge them into centres for espionage.[41] In 1946 Harold Laski called the CPGB an authoritarian movement which sought to subvert all freedoms. He labelled its leaders disciplined conspirators seeking to destroy the Labour Party.[42] Contesting a 1948 parliamentary byelection for Labour, Harold Nicolson announced he would not abide any communist support: 'I do not want their beastly votes. I want British votes, not Russian votes.'[43] Minister of Food John Strachey blamed 'communist sabotage' when an ill-thought-through agricultural project in Africa failed to produce results.[44] In May 1950, as minister of war, in the most literal sense of the meaning, Strachey turned into a red-hunter. During a trip into the Malayan jungle, Strachey, with a rifle in hand, joined a Gurkha patrol as they pursued communist guerrillas.[45] While Attlee, Morrison and Bevin's attitudes towards communism remained consistent from the interwar period, Cold War realities indeed changed many in the party.

Factors contributing to this hardening against communism were internal battles with more left-wing members of the Labour Party; increased espionage activity sanctioned by the Soviet Union; external pressure from the US to heighten security procedures, especially concerning atomic energy; and early briefings from the British intelligence community. This last contributing element cannot be overstated. Prior to the Second World War, the Labour Party was wary and mistrustful of the intelligence services.[46] This enmity came from a long history of animosity dating back to the 1920s that included these agencies spying on prominent Labour leaders and a standing suspicion that MI5 was behind the forging of the Zinoviev Letter.[47] The Second World War brought a thawing of tensions between Labour and the security services, since Attlee in the post of deputy prime minister and Morrison as home secretary worked regularly with members of MI6 and MI5. In power, Labour's leadership frequently utilised MI5's resources for domestic surveillance and gathering lists of communists they wished to be investigated. On several instances, party members in government were more zealous in rooting out communists than the security services and Special Branch whose job it was to find these supposed security risks and potential traitors.

'Lost sheep' and crypto-communists

One of the earliest concerns of the new prime minister was the clandestine penetration of communists into the nation's parliament. Although in 1945 two communist MPs, Willie Gallacher and Phil Piratin, sat in the House of Commons, Attlee worried that many in his party held secret allegiances of similar kinds. Termed 'crypto-communists', these individuals supported the aims of the CPGB and were potential security risks because of their sympathies for the Soviet Union. Attlee considered this type of 'hidden' communist as a unique threat, stating, 'We have, therefore, to look at this attacking from within, and it is the duty of any government to take action. In addition to all these classes of professed fascists and communists, there are also the crypto-communists.'[48] Opponents, such as Attlee, of these crypto-communists viewed them as much more dangerous than their exposed confederates. These 'wolves in sheep's clothing' could damage the government by asking embarrassing questions of ministers. Such parliamentary questions promoted the Soviet Union as the true version of a socialist state and argued for the UK's alignment with the Eastern bloc instead of the 'aggressive superpower' the US.[49] These crypto-communists in parliament were only suspected in the Labour Party. Famed writer George Orwell described and denounced these types of Labour MPs in 1947: 'There is, for instance, a whole group of MPs in the British parliament ... who are commonly nicknamed "the cryptos". They have undoubtedly done a great deal of mischief, especially in confusing public opinion about the nature of the puppet regimes in eastern Europe.'[50] By not identifying themselves as communists, statements by these Labour members of the Commons reached a larger audience and initially could not be dismissed as pure communist propaganda. For evidence of these crypto-communists, Attlee turned to the once Labour-despised intelligence community for assistance. He specifically sought the help of Guy Liddell, the deputy chief of MI5 and head of counter-espionage. In a meeting between the two on 19 November 1946, Attlee, 'huddled up and looking exhausted', expressed to the intelligence officer that he considered himself personally responsible to the nation and the government to see that secret communists 'did not get into positions where they might constitute a danger to the state'.[51]

The day prior to his meeting with Liddell, a rebellion within his party gave Attlee a more urgent motive for hunting hidden communists inside parliament. In October, the prime minister had received a letter signed by twenty-one Labour MPs who urged Attlee to reconsider aligning with the US against the Soviet Union. What resulted from this letter was a proposed King's Speech amendment written by Richard Crossman. The motion, supported by seventy-two Labour members of parliament, sought 'a democratic and constructive alternative to the otherwise inevitable conflict between American capitalism and Soviet communism'.[52] If the motion was carried in the Commons, it effectively meant the immediate resignation of the government, since such an amendment constituted a censure motion. Therefore, this rebellion of the left-wing of the party did not only stand as a symbolic gesture. With veiled attacks against Attlee and Bevin, Crossman, arguing for his amendment, lambasted what he termed the ideology of anti-communism. He stated, 'anti-communism is as destructive of true democracy and of socialism as is communism, and one of the jobs of a Labour government ... is to fight the battle not only against the communist ideology, but against the anti-communist ideology'.[53] When the vote came on the passage of the amendment, it was overwhelmingly rejected by a tally of 353 to 0. Ultimately, not a single member of the house voted against the government, but what distressed Attlee was the 100 abstentions on the government's side of the aisle. Included in this total were five parliamentary private secretaries. Many in the Labour Party did not only see these abstainers as rebels – which is what the mainstream British press dubbed them – but also as something far worse. Attlee called Crossman part of the 'lunatic fringe'.[54] Tom O'Brien, Labour MP for West Nottingham and member of the general council of the Trades Union Congress (TUC), speaking of these fellow party members, said:

> They stand condemned as moral assassins ... They behave, I am sorry to say, like a contemptible coterie of Comintern lickspittles and degrade democratic politics beyond measure. Some of the signatories of the amendment are political softies who do not realise that they are playing the game of the 'Harry Pollittbureau'.[55]

Evident in O'Brien's rhetoric was his feelings that many Labour MPs were unwitting dupes of Harry Pollitt, general secretary of the CPGB. But in the subtext, he implied that some of these 'assassins' were playing the 'game' of the communists. O'Brien was not the only party leader with such suspicions. General Secretary of the Labour Party Morgan Phillips collected and held files on pro-Soviet MPs that he termed 'Lost Sheep(s)'.

A stalwart anti-communist, Phillips maintained, 'In Britain the Communist Party is more a conspiracy than a party.'[56] In his estimation, these 'Lost Sheep' were individuals who used their position and prestige to support communistic policies rather than those of traditional Labour.[57] During a Commons speech in October 1946, Attlee lambasted one such MP, John Platts-Mills, by declaring that Platts-Mills's speech, which had been critical of the government's foreign policy the previous day, 'was in fact not much more than a reproduction of the ordinary propaganda stuff of the Communist Party'.[58] Not content in shaming these 'Lost Sheep', Attlee sought to expel them from the ranks of the Labour Party and ultimately from the halls of government.

One day prior to his 19 November discussion with Attlee, Liddell held another mystifying meeting – this time with Secretary of State for War Frederick Bellenger. It involved a request from the prime minister for information on the wartime activities of a Labour MP named Geoffrey Bing.[59] Bellenger produced for Liddell a message from Attlee suggesting that Bing had given away military secrets to communists and inquired if Bing held current membership in the Communist Party. The note from the prime minister troubled the deputy director general of MI5 since it directly involved a minister in this type of delicate inquiry. In previous private meetings, Attlee stated to Liddell that 'he wanted to deal with matters of this kind personally'. Liddell voiced his concerns to Bellenger that the security service's 'aim and object was to remain entirely non-party in all these matters and to avoid any suggestion that the department was a Gestapo'.[60] It is unclear if he expressed this distress to Attlee. However, on the same day as his meeting with the prime minister, Liddell provided Bellenger with information about Bing's communist activities and the recommendation that he be considered a security risk; Bellenger 'seemed quite satisfied with this assurance'. The whole affair of Bing bothered Liddell. In his official report he wrote:

> It had always been the policy of our office to keep entirely clear of politics, and this particular case seemed to be a border-line one. We might be open to the criticism that we were using our records for the purpose of conducting a heresy hunt within the Labour Party, although it seemed to me in this instance that we were covered by the fact that BING, until a few days ago, had been one of the whips, and in that sense a person who was given certain access to government information.[61]

Adding credence to Liddell's fears that the security service was involved in a witch hunt for the Labour Party was the fact that Bing, a member of the Labourite rebels opposing Attlee's foreign policy, had just resigned his position of whip on 2 November, embarrassing the party. A year later in the Commons he was highly critical of Bellenger's position on vetting for the Army Educational Service.[62] Bing accused Bellenger of wishing to remove communists from Army Education Corps.[63] Regardless of Liddell's reservations, MI5 would keep a very close tab on Bing for years to come. He was considered by the agency as one of its most vicious domestic opponents. In 1947, famed spymaster Maxwell Knight reported that Bing's proposed amendment for a Northern Ireland bill that suspended the Ulster Special Powers Act was nothing more than a 'communist tactic'.[64] During the spring of that year, Knight and other MI5 officers anticipated and feared that 'crypto-communist members of parliament, backed by the two official communist members, were seeking an opportunity for launching an attack on MI5'.[65] A top-secret internal report stated, 'The principal instigator of the attack will be Geoffrey BING.'[66] The attack never occurred, but this did little to allay the concerns that secret communists in the House of Commons were the enemy not only of the current Labour government but the security service as well.

In May 1947, per the agreement made in their meeting in November, Liddell delivered to Attlee the names of John Platts-Mills, Lester Hutchinson, Leah Manning and Elizabeth Braddock as probable crypto-communists in the House of Commons. Liddell wrote:

> I thereupon gave him the names of PLATTS-MILLS, HUTCHINSON, MANNING and Mrs. BRADDOCK. He was not surprised to hear about HUTCHINSON, and had already taken for granted that PLATTS-MILLS was a C.P. member. He was, however, considerably shaken to hear of Leah MANNING and Mrs. BRADDOCK. He then volunteered the information to me that he thought DODDS was C.P. member; that SWINGLER probably was, and that D.N. PRITT almost certainly was.[67]

Volunteering names to the list created by Liddell, Attlee included Norman Dodds, Stephen Swingler and Denis Pritt.[68] However, these were not the only Labour MPs to be targeted or classified as crypto-communists. In an internal MI5 report, Charles Smith and Donald Bruce were also named as such.[69] Morgan Phillips's list of 'Lost Sheep' held numerous other names, including Konni Zilliacus and Leslie Solley.[70] In what was an embarrassing moment for Guy Liddell, Herbert Morrison sought to compile his own personal list of crypto-communists from information held by MI5. In February 1949, Morrison asked Liddell for a list of 'fellow travellers' so he could personally 'smoke them out' of the Labour Party. Liddell 'dodged' the request and by doing so did not relay the information that

Attlee already had such a list but had for whatever reason decided not to tell Morrison about its existence.[71]

Although Attlee estimated he did not have enough evidence on or provocation by these crypto-communists and 'Lost Sheep' to expel them from the Labour Party, this promptly changed. The next year Attlee and his Labour government found themselves – as they did during the King's Speech amendment of the previous year – tested by members of the far-left in the party. In 1948, thirty-seven Labour MPs sent Pietro Nenni, leader of the Italian Socialist Party, a telegram supporting his efforts in the forthcoming Italian General Election.[72] Nenni was in an alliance with the Italian communists, a coalition that was deemed unacceptable by the Labour Party leadership. The policy of Labour's National Executive Committee (NEC) was to withhold support from any socialists in Europe who opened the door to communist infiltration. Also, the NEC had earlier sent a message of good wishes to the Socialist Unity Party, a splinter group refusing to ally with the communists. Dubbed the 'Nenni Telegram affair', the matter sent shockwaves through the halls of Westminster.

Labour MPs whose names were listed on the telegram denied either signing such a document or lent their support under the pretext of misunderstanding its final content. Conservatives in the Commons called for a subcommittee to investigate the charges of adding names of MPs to the telegram without their prior consent. Alongside Waldron Smithers, both Anthony Eden and Winston Churchill agreed that hearings were needed to sort out the situation. Herbert Morrison refused partisan calls for parliamentary hearings, arguing that only Labour MPs were involved in the telegram so it should be a party matter, but assured Smithers, and the rest of the Commons, it would be 'dealt with effectively'.[73] In the mind of the prime minister the matter was quite clear. Attlee labelled the signers of the telegram 'active instigators' who knew exactly what they were doing. 'They wanted to sabotage the foreign policy of the government they were returned to support', he argued during a May Day rally in Plymouth. 'They wanted to see Italy go the way of Romania and Czechoslovakia.'[74] Even the left-leaning *Tribune* called the telegram 'an act of sabotage' which only assisted the communists. In a front-page story on the matter, the magazine stated that the correct place for a number of Labour MPs – who preferred a 'Communist victory in Europe' – was in the CPGB, which had 'also dedicated itself to the aim of destroying the Labour government and disrupting the labour movement'.[75] Prior to Attlee's blanket denunciation of the signers, the NEC did conduct hearings into the issue. They were tantamount to an ideological purge, which resulted in the expelling of the central author of the controversial document, John Platts-Mills, from the Labour Party on 28 April 1948. Other expulsions were threatened, though never materialised. Attlee and the NEC hoped that the example they made with Platts-Mills would halt other left-wing rebels from refusing the party line. They were not successful.

A letter published in the 30 October 1948 edition of *New Statesman and Nation* made this obvious to the party leadership. Written by Konni Zilliacus and entitled 'The Labour Party's Dilemma', it stated that the British Labour Party could not be both against communists in Europe and for the workers of the continent. Zilliacus specified: 'To be anti-communist on the continent therefore ... means coming down on the side of the capitalists against the workers. Up to now the leadership of the Labour party has resolved the dilemma by sacrificing the workers of Europe to its anti-communist fanaticism'.[76] From his election to parliament in 1945, Zilliacus was a vocal critic of his party's foreign policy and a constant thorn in the side of the Labour government. Hatred towards Zilliacus ran deep in the party. Replying to a letter from Zilliacus denouncing Labour's foreign policy, Attlee personally admonished him for his 'astonishing lack of understanding of the facts'.[77] Hugh Gaitskell classified him as a member of the 'lunatic fringe' and a 'pseudo-communist'.[78] Herbert Morrison labelled him 'a man who seemingly finds it much easier to consider that the Russians and Yugoslavs can be right than to admit that the British are ever right'.[79]

In response to the letter, former Chancellor of the Exchequer Hugh Dalton wrote to Morgan Phillips, 'I feel we cannot, much longer, avoid dealing with the author, as we did with Platts-Mills.' In his typed note to the general secretary, Dalton scrawled: 'Have we got a dossier on him?'[80] Collected in Phillips's 'Lost Sheep' file, the party did; a 'private and confidential' report on Zilliacus gave the following assessment:

> Over the last three years, Zilliacus' speeches and writings have for the most part taken the form of violent attacks on the Labour government's foreign policy. He is recognised in Cominform literature as the leading British exponent of 'left-wing social democracy', i.e. those socialists whose substantial agreement with Cominform policies must ultimately lead them into complete agreement with the communists.[81]

While Labour leaders were seeking to force Zilliacus out, other party members were contemplating something a bit more extreme for another 'Lost Sheep'. In April 1949, Christopher Mayhew, undersecretary of state at the FO, pushed for Leslie Solley's prosecution. Mayhew called Solley 'a particularly unpleasant fellow travelling Labour MP'.[82] The attempted charge came from Solley allegedly working as an intermediary between the Romanian government and a British newspaper. To the dismay of Mayhew and Bevin, the FO legal advisors assessed the evidence against Solley as not sufficient for a legal case.

The 1949 House of Commons vote to join NATO was the next catalyst which brought the removal of three additional 'Lost Sheep' from the Labour Party, including Zilliacus – who was already on thin ice with Transport House. Only six Labour MPs voted against signing the NATO treaty; of these, three were shortly removed from the party ranks. Konni Zilliacus, Leslie Solley and Lester Hutchinson, all considered pro-Soviet in their politics and who consistently opposed the Atlanticist foreign policy of Attlee and Bevin, were expelled. Joining Platts-Mills and Denis Pritt, who was removed from the party in 1940 for his support of the Soviet Union during the Winter War, these five MPs formed the Labour Independent Group.[83] Without sheltering and support from the official Labour Party, all of these MPs lost their seats in the 1950 General Election. Zilliacus reapplied to join the Labour Party in 1951, but before his readmission in 1952, Herbert Morrison, then foreign secretary, ordered MI5 to provide him with a report on Zilliacus's activities and communism connections.[84] In addition to those who were officially expelled, a large number of others whose names appeared on lists as suspected communists found themselves out of the Commons as well. These included Leah Manning, Stephen Swingler and Donald Bruce. Alongside these so-called crypto-communists, the two 'official' members of the Communist Party – Willie Gallacher and Phil Piratin – were not returned to their seats. Reflecting on their defeats in a speech after the election, Morrison crowed over their 1950 campaign losses:

> The fellow-travellers, and the plain honest-to-goodness mugs, also badly failed. Their leaders were trounced at the polls even where they had previously deluded the local electorate into putting them into the House of Commons on false pretences. The voters woke up and the whole gang of them went out with a bump. The Communist party and their friends, and all the fellow-travellers and the innocents who have lapped up the communist doctrine and communist propaganda, should stop and consider the meaning of this dramatic event.[85]

After the 1951 General Election, with Labour out of power, Attlee's goal to purge the House of Commons of pro-Soviet and communist MPs lost official governmental support. The communists in the Labour Party issue turned to a strictly in-house affair. With the battle for control of the party waging between the Gaitskellites and the Bevanites, accusations of communist infiltration rotated from the House of Commons to the rank-and-file members of Labour. Although no attempts were made to smear

Aneurin Bevan as an out-and-out communist or fellow traveller, questions were raised about his supporters in the party and his judgement when it came to dealing with the 'red menace'. In a series of articles commissioned for the *Daily Herald*, Labour MP Elizabeth 'Bessie' Braddock wrote of the 'The Great Communist Plot' and how the CPGB was actively influencing constituency Labour Parties (CLPs). 'I am astonished at the number of leading Labour people who still treat this menace with indifference', Braddock admonished. 'The communist who works inside the Labour party is a factor with whom we now have to reckon.'[86] Joining her in voicing concern was Hugh Gaitskell, former chancellor of the exchequer and future Labour Party leader. During a speech at Stalybridge, after the 1952 Labour Party conference, Gaitskell agreed with Braddock and stated that the CPGB had adopted the new tactic of ordering its members and supporters to infiltrate Labour. Reflecting on the annual conference, Gaitskell recounted being told 'that about one-sixth of the constituency party delegates appeared to be communists or communist inspired'. 'This figure may well be too high', he admitted, 'but if it should be one in ten or even one in twenty, it is a most shocking state of affairs into which the National Executive should look at once.'[87] The issue did turn more openly bipartisan in 1953 when Conservative MP Tufton Beamish published an open letter to Herbert Morrison urging him to purge the communistic Bevanites from the Labour Party for the national good.[88]

The party leadership concerns over communism infiltration declined – except for baseless accusations of one lone Labour MP – and did not arise again until the 1960s. In fact, during the late 1950s, the attention of the Labour general secretary turned from rooting out communists within the Labour ranks towards silencing a McCarthyite inside his own party. By 1958, Morgan Phillips's 'Lost Sheep' file stopped centring on supposed crypto-communists and instead was filled with reports and complaints about John McGovern, a troublesome Labour MP and paranoid anti-communist from Scotland. Alongside being absent for numerous votes (he missed ten three-line whips during the 1957–8 session) and having subpar attendance in the Commons, McGovern worried Transport House because of his wild accusations levelled at the ranks of the PLP.[89] He had earlier caused consternation for the NEC during the 1955 General Election, after which he was blamed for the defeat of a Liverpool city councillor then running as a Labour candidate in the Scotstoun constituency. During the campaign, McGovern accused the candidate of having close connections to the 'revolutionary' Communist Party.[90] By 1958, McGovern, actively neglecting his parliamentary duties, travelled extensively, promoting the virtues of the Moral Rearmament Movement throughout Europe and the US. When questioned about his absence due to these activities, McGovern stated, 'it was his destiny to spread the beliefs of Moral Rearmament'.[91] During these speaking engagements, he labelled the Labour Party as a home for both active communists and would-be traitors. In April 1959, at a speech given in Los Angeles, McGovern remarked that of the 286 members of the PLP, twenty-six were 'either undercover communists or fellow-travellers' and that seventy-five members, 'if democracy were losing the struggle tomorrow, would throw off their democratic mask and join the communist world'.[92] At a press conference in Berlin weeks later, he ominously stated, 'There are dark forces in the party I represent', and recalculated his figures by charging that twenty-six Labour MPs were outright communists and seventy others were fellow travellers.[93] With the party no longer in government, accusations of crypto-communists inside the PLP were considered a potential election issue that could prohibit a Labour return to power. They created the impression that a vote for Labour could potentially bring secret communists into the British government. Morgan Phillips responded by asking publicly for McGovern to name names and questioned why he had not reported such allegations formally at past meetings of the PLP. Phillips accused him of having no evidence to back up such charges and told him to withdraw them at once.[94] McGovern refused, writing to Phillips that 'I have never made false statements even about my political enemies, I shall never withdraw this statement ... The weakness of your letter is that it shows no desire to effect a cure but rather to continue the cancer.'[95] Given McGovern's advanced age (seventy-two) and his declaration that he would not stand at the next general election, Phillips and the party allowed the matter to rest. No formal action was taken. Ultimately, McGovern left Labour, claiming it was too sympathetic to communism; during the 1964 General Election, he threw his support behind the Conservatives.[96]

The later episode of McGovern notwithstanding, was this early fear of crypto-communists during the Attlee government justified? The prime minister's apprehensions were not as far-fetched as they sounded. During the autumn of 1948 MI5 discreetly informed the prime minister that Wilfred Vernon (then a sitting Labour MP) had willingly passed secrets to the Soviets in the late 1930s.[97] Even the members of the CPGB appraised the two MPs of their party elected in 1945 as a low estimation of their real strength in the House of Commons. Douglas Hyde, a former editor for the *Daily Worker*, wrote in his autobiography:

> On the morning that the election results began to come through we [the CPGB] got a series of surprises. The first was the sweeping Labour gains, second was the communist defeats, third was the

realisation that among the Labour men returned were a number of our own party members who had slipped in almost unnoticed as it were ... By the time the list was complete we knew that we had a least eight or nine 'cryptos' in the House of Commons in addition to our two publicly-acknowledged MPs.[98]

If these numbers were either inflated or conservative, the fact remained the same: the Labour government's alarm over hidden communists inside the House of Commons brought forth tangible actions against such a fear. These crypto-communists and 'Lost Sheep' were effectively viewed as fifth columnists attempting to subvert the Western alliance that Attlee and Bevin sought to forge. Through aiding the Crossman rebellion, the sending of the Nenni telegram and refusing to vote for NATO, they displayed their 'true colours'. Attlee expressed this sentiment seamlessly in a speech denouncing them to a meeting of the TUC in 1946. 'We cannot afford to run risks', he argued. Warning further, he said: 'There is a small but vociferous section in this country that seek on every occasion to attack the policy of this government and which seems resolved to declare that, whatever is done, Britain is wrong.'[99] By utilising the service of MI5 to inform on, survey and uncover these risks and through the party apparatus of Labour, Attlee sought to purge certain members of the House of Commons for holding and displaying communist sympathies.

The purge: negative and positive vetting

Vetting is generally defined as investigating someone thoroughly, especially in order to ensure that they are suitable for a job requiring secrecy, loyalty or trustworthiness. The British government utilised two systems of vetting during the early Cold War period. These processes were 'positive' – vetting which was overt such as interviewing subjects and having them fill out questionnaires – and 'negative', which was done in secret or unbeknownst to the individual being examined. Although procedures were in place prior to 1945, a series of public scandals pushed the narrative that these were not effective and needed to be overhauled. The Igor Gouzenko defection, the discovery of the spying activities of Klaus Fuchs and the disappearance of two highly placed civil servants, Donald Maclean and Guy Burgess, forced the government to admit that a problem existed in defending the secrets of the realm. The Maclean and Burgess defections, though still undiscovered, were reported at the time to have caused 'disturbance in the public mind at home' and would probably 'have embarrassing results on our relations with the United States'.[100] If self-motivation of the British state to revise security measures was not enough, added pressure to increase vetting came from the US. The singular goal, often stated but at other times cloaked in more diplomatic wording, for increased vetting directly after the Second World War was to stymie – if not eliminate entirely – disloyal communists who were subject to disclose information to the Soviet Union. The factors contributing to this set goal cannot all be chalked up to hysteria. To the chagrin of the British government, there were numerous Soviet moles and security risks employed in the civil service and other sections of the nation's governmental infrastructure.

During the Second World War, under the premiership of Winston Churchill, communist infiltration and concerns that current vetting practices for sensitive positions were inadequate were apparent in the halls of government. In 1943, a national organiser of the Communist Party, Douglas Frank Springhall, stood trial and was sentenced to seven years' imprisonment. Springhall obtained classified information for the Soviets from a clerk in the air ministry and a staff officer in Special Operations Executive (SOE); both of these sources of Springhall had communist affiliations. A month after Springhall's conviction, Duff Cooper, then chairman of the cabinet committee on security, relayed to Churchill that even though the CPGB denied knowledge of Springhall's activities, 'in fact the party machine is regularly used for espionage and that this had continued since the conviction of Springhall'.[101] Cooper went further in his warning, arguing that 'it may fairly be stated that any member of the Communist Party should be regarded as a potential agent'. Home Secretary Herbert Morrison agreed with Cooper's assessment. Morrison wrote to the prime minister, 'There is a special danger in employing on secret work persons who are members or adherents of the Communist Party.' In his assessment, 'experience has shown that people who are otherwise reliable and honourable are untrustworthy when there is a conflict between their obligations to the [Communist] party and their duty as public servants or as loyal citizens'.[102] Labour and Conservative members of Churchill's National government agreed that domestic communists and the Soviet Union both posed threats to the UK's internal security – even while both of these 'threats' were officially allied with the UK against the Axis powers.

In the discussions on how to officially deal with this danger, changes to the governmental vetting were suggested. MI5 reported that the 'case of Springhall gives an excellent opportunity for formulating and implementing a uniform policy' concerning vetting communists. David Clarke, head of the department responsible for monitoring the CPGB, reported that the spy ring orchestrated by Springhall revealed the dangers of employing such individuals, and 'in the future there can be no good reason for underestimating those risks'.[103] With the haphazard procedures then in place, in certain instances initial vetting was not conducted until after employment had already begun or, even worse, did not occur at all. Since there was no general policy concerning employing communists by the British government, positive vetting could not be widely used and attempts to control communist individuals already employed had their limitations. Clarke identified fifty-seven communists who had access to classified information. Such a situation had occurred since none of the various departments in which these communists were employed had coherent vetting protocols.[104] The recommendation of MI5 was for the implementation of a universal vetting system for all security-related departments and a transfer of communists presently working in these areas to other posts. Morrison's solution to the problem was a drastic public relations effort. He pushed for openly charging the CPGB of disloyalty against the crown through its organising espionage for a foreign state. The prime minister, alongside Chancellor of the Exchequer John Anderson, strongly disagreed with this latter tactic and dismissed the notion of issuing such a statement.[105]

Deciding against implementing any new forms of vetting, Churchill instead set up a secret tribunal – termed the Inter-Departmental Security Committee or simply 'The Panel' – to determine on a case-by-case basis the communists in government. The Panel consisted of members of the Security Executive, a ministerial body whose duties were 'to consider questions relating to defence against the "fifth column" and initiate action'. Instituted in May 1940, the Security Executive had no executive powers. Its mandate stated that direct 'action will not be taken' but only 'through the appropriate departments'.[106] Churchill also applied this limited directive to The Panel in its role in determining threats of communists in government. When deemed necessary, its function was to hold hearings on individuals MI5 suspected of spying or engaging in other subversive activities, then give a recommendation to the head of the department in which the communist being examined worked. In the opinion of MI5, instituting another ministerial advisory committee was not a 'satisfactory method' of tackling the issue at hand.[107] Churchill's answer to the Springhall affair did not change the vetting procedures in any way, nor did it prohibit communists from entering sensitive departments in the future. In 1955 a Privy Counsellors' investigation created to review governmental vetting agreed with this assessment, stating:

Our present system really only began in 1948. Before then there was nothing like a systematic system for checking by departments against the Security Service records of the names of the staff employed by them on secret work ... Secondly, before 1948, when a communist was discovered, all a department could do was to transfer him to non-secret or less secret work, if it could do this without rousing the man's suspicions. They could do nothing openly because there was no mandate to treat communists as unfit to be employed on secret work.[108]

The Panel that Churchill created did not officially meet until 1944. In the view of MI5, it was 'unworkable' and did nothing to strengthen vetting procedures, since it only reviewed cases of individuals already employed and under suspicion.[109] Within a year, a far more damaging espionage case of Alan Nunn May placed severe pressure on the government to revise and restructure its vetting procedures towards communists. Musing on this newer episode, Roger Hollis wrote, 'as this case must surely make it abundantly manifest to the government something will have to be done about communists in government departments and in other secret employment'.[110] Whereas Churchill, in Hollis's opinion, did not find significant evidence to change government vetting in regards to communist infiltration, the postwar Labour government agreed with Hollis's assessment for several diplomatic and political reasons.

In 1945, the defection of a cypher clerk working at the Soviet embassy in Canada named Igor Gouzenko brought revelations that the Soviet military intelligence (GRU) was operating a major spy ring. One of the participants named by Gouzenko was Alan Nunn May, a British citizen and nuclear scientist. Nunn May had been sent to Canada in 1943 to work on Anglo-Canadian research for the atomic bomb.[111] Gouzenko labelled Nunn May as a source of passing highly sensitive intelligence to the Soviet Union. MI5 responded by placing Nunn May under surveillance and monitoring his phone calls. Eventually, he simply confessed having given samples of uranium and reports on atomic research to an unnamed individual, but refused to label his actions as treasonous.[112] The discovery of Nunn May's espionage activities was a lot more upsetting than those of Springhall for two key reasons. First, the passing on of atomic secrets by Nunn May to the Soviet Union caused grave concerns for the overall security of the UK. Seeing the devastation wrought by the atomic bombings on Japan forced the British government to realise that a hostile country – such as the Soviet Union – with such weaponry was an existential threat. No longer could the UK count on the ocean surrounding it to safeguard it from total destruction. The second reason was the negative response towards the British from the only atomic-wielding nation in existence – the US. The exposure by Gouzenko of Nunn May made many in the US question the security apparatus of their British allies. Although British manpower and knowledge contributed to the invention of the atomic bomb, the US still held strict control over the nuclear technology needed to manufacture them. Sharing this vital information was a top priority of the FO and British military. The exposure of Nunn May put in question future exchanges of atomic secrets to the UK from the US. The British ambassador to the US, Roger Makins, expressed this frustration in a top-secret telegram, stating: 'In regards to the Canadian espionage case ... the question of security of the US information has once more been brought prominently to the fore ... I need not emphasize the effect which all this is likely to have on the question of the exchange of information with ourselves.' Summing up the British government's position even more bluntly, he ended his top-secret message with: 'US reluctance to give us what we want is bound to be greatly increased.'[113] As Makin predicted, the Gouzenko affair strengthened the resolve of the Truman administration to protect the American atomic monopoly. US politicians estimated safeguards were necessary to halt the spread of sensitive information to foreign powers – even established allies such as the UK. On 1 August 1946, three months after Nunn May's sentencing to ten years in prison for violating the Official Secrets Act 1911, Harry Truman signed into law the McMahon Act (officially entitled the Atomic Energy Act of 1946). A key proviso in the new law prohibited the sharing of atomic secrets with any foreign nation – this greatly distressed Attlee. Earlier in the year, when speaking with Averell Harriman, the US ambassador, he conveyed the opinion that until nuclear energy came under the control of the United Nations (UN), the US should simply give the UK atomic bombs, or at the very least provide the data needed for the production of atomic energy.[114] The McMahon Act and the Americans' perception that the security procedures of their 'British cousins' were inadequate gave Attlee no alternative but to order the building of an independent British atomic weapons programme.

With the defection of Nunn May and his arrest, the game effectively changed in how communist subversion was viewed in the postwar period. A report sent from MI5 to the air ministry describes the transformation of the 'red menace':

> The main risk to be feared from the Communist Party in the pre-war period was on unrest in the industrial sphere and in the armed forces of the Crown, leading possibly to political strikes and even to revolutionary outbreaks. The higher social status of the present membership has brought a new danger to the fore as the scientists

and professional workers, who are now in the party ranks, have access to far more secret information than had the pre-war membership. The danger of leakage of information to the Soviet Union is thus very much greater than it was previously.[115]

As a covert member of the Communist Party, Nunn May completely met the above threat assessment and thus gave the British government a substantial reason to start profiling such individuals as security risks.[116] A Joint Intelligence Committee (JIC) report dated 18 November 1946 added further credence to increasing the vetting of communists.[117] Entitled 'Spread of Communism Throughout the World and the Extent of Its Direction from Moscow', it estimated that to would-be communist spies it mattered little if Russia was an ally with the UK, as was the case during the Springhall affair, or an enemy. The report argued that communists disregarded this differentiation since their allegiance was only to the party and the foreign power the party served.

In early January 1947, Attlee formed the Cabinet Committee on Subversive Activities (GEN 183).[118] The main purpose of this committee was to review vetting procedures in government and industries dealing with secretive information. Ostensibly it was formed to keep any kind of destabilising human elements outside of government, including fascists. Its targets quickly became only suspected communists and the CPGB members. A report by the working party of the main committee (GEN 168) stated that after reviewing 'the various organizations or groups which might provide the breeding grounds of subversive activities either now or in the future, we are satisfied that, of those, the communists' organization is the only one to which serious attention needs to be given'.[119] On 11 February, during the first meeting of GEN 168, it was agreed that, since they did not constitute a risk, 'the activities of movements of the extreme right could be left out of the account'.[120] Although future vetting forms and government pronouncements would include the dual threats of fascists and communists, it was evident from the start that unofficially to Whitehall and Downing Street the communists constituted the only viable danger. The main reason for focusing on communist subversion came from the belief of many in government that the Soviet Union was engaging in a 'campaign against this country'.[121] A memo from the FO to MI5 the previous year already expressed this mindset. Harold Caccia, future permanent undersecretary of state, wrote, 'Another question that occurs to me is the lessons to be learnt about the steps which Russians are likely to take to penetrate our own governmental organizations.'[122]

Throughout Whitehall, the need for heightened security measures was readily apparent by 1947. The current vetting procedures were solely reliant on the records of the security service. MI5 typically only had records on applicants if they held public membership in the CPGB or were a known fellow traveller. Such was the case for John Strachey, who was a communist sympathiser in the 1930s.[123] The red-baiting likes of Waldron Smithers and Lord Beaverbrook were not the only ones who were apprehensive of this particular cabinet member; MI5 kept tabs on Strachey until 1950. This method of surveillance only identified known communists and 'Russian sympathisers'. It left undetected covert members of the CPGB – like Alan Nunn May – and so-called drawing-room communists. This posed a major problem to the members of the working committee of GEN 183. They ascertained that the CPGB actively discouraged some potential members from joining, since it believed that certain individuals, with a hidden allegiance, could infiltrate sensitive positions in government departments. Another concern GEN 183 faced was that, with CPGB membership not illegal, prohibiting persons of that legitimate political party from government service remained a questionable issue. These dual threats of known CPGB members and their covert allies were considered a serious risk, thus an overhaul of the entire vetting process was endorsed:

> The range of information which would be of interest to the communist organization is wide. First and foremost come military secrets, including scientific development such as atomic research, radar, etc. and industrial intelligence bearing on our war potential. But this does not by any means exhaust the vulnerable area: information may be sought about government policy or intentions in almost any field, either by the Russian government or by the Communist Party at home, and the leakage of economic or purely industrial information may be no less serious. If effective countermeasures are to be taken, they must, therefore, cover a wide field.[124]

In determining how to deal with known communists, it was decided that individuals who adhere to a Marxist-Leninist ideology held divided loyalties – which might in certain scenarios turn to active disloyalty. Civil servants needed undivided allegiance to the state, so barring known communists from government service appeared necessary. Although not all communists could be considered disloyal or Soviet agents, 'there is no way of separating the sheep from the goats, at least until the damage has been done or suspicion is aroused'. Because of logistical restraints, it was calculated that 'to debar communist[s] from all employment' was impractical, though not immoral.[125] The governmental branches in which they were to be excluded were: the Cabinet Office, service departments, the Ministry of Defence, the FO, the Home Office, departments of scientific and industrial research, and the Control Office.

Negative vetting – meaning investigations of individuals who were in such governmental fields or potential prospects had their backgrounds screened – was the recommendation of the full subversive activities committee to the prime minister. Minister of Defence A.V. Alexander had reservations on procedure practicalities that GEN 168 endorsed, but he expressed to Attlee 'on security grounds it is arguable that we ought to go further'.[126] The prime minister's response had little equivocal terminology attached to it. He wrote back to Alexander, 'I agree. We cannot afford to take risks here, and the general public will support us.' Emphasising the red threat, but also politically covering himself, he ended the letter with, 'Action should be taken in regard to fascists as well as communists although the former are feeble.'[127] The instituting of Attlee's 'purge procedures' were purely an anti-communist response, even though few individuals in government wished to describe it as such, in fear of negative connotations this would invoke with the general public.

On 15 March 1948, in the House of Commons, Attlee publicly announced the introduction of governmental vetting. In his opening statement he defended this action by stating Communist Party membership or associating with it calls into question the loyalty of individuals to the UK. Therefore, communists were banned from governmental positions whose nature was 'vital to the security of the state'. When questioned on how far the purge would extend, Attlee replied it would 'extend everywhere where important secret matters have to be covered'.[128] Communist MP William Gallacher sarcastically mocked Attlee during the announcement. In an ironic gesture, Gallacher started singing 'The Red Flag', which caused an uproar in the Commons.[129] One of the bitterest indictments of the new security procedures came from a member of Attlee's own party. John Platts-Mills, the 'Lost Sheep' who a month later would be expelled from the Labour Party, asked: 'In view of the prime minister's beginning of a purge of communists, is there any reason why he should not go on to Jews and socialists?' Attlee matter-of-factly responded, 'because Jews and socialists have a loyalty to this country'. Then he added, 'that is not so with many communists, and some fellow travellers'.[130]

The divided response to Attlee's announcement brought about a parliamentary debate on what many press headlines were already terming the 'Communist Purge'. Notwithstanding the criticism from the two CPGB members, in the Commons, pushback against the purge announcement came mostly from within the Labour Party. Standing in opposition to the new measures, Labour MP Harold Davies stated, 'We are being driven hysterically to believe that Britain is in danger from communists and fellow travellers.' Davies added, 'I will fight to the last against this. This is demand for unnatural power, a witch hunting campaign, a claim for power which will rot the socialist party.'[131] Davies proposed a motion backed by forty-one additional Labour MPs that condemned Attlee's statement and argued, 'it constitutes a departure from the principles of democracy and civil liberty'.[132] Unlike with Labour, broad support for Attlee's announcement came from the Conservative Party in Westminster. However, some Conservative MPs did attempt to use the occasion to jab at Labour. Charles Mott-Radclyffe, the Conservative MP representing Windsor, while strongly supportive of the purge, attempted to use the debate over it as a platform to accuse John Strachey, then minister of food, of being 'tempted to embrace the hammer and sickle'.[133]

Even though deeply involved with drafting the framework for the procedures, the security service had a negative reaction to Attlee's announcement of them. 'None of us liked it', Liddell stated in his diary, 'as it created the impression that [MI5] had been bungling for years and that the Labour government were now going to see our activities were supervised.' After listening to Attlee's words, Liddell wrote that it gave the direct impression that the security service was effectively now the 'whipping boy' for the previous failures. 'The whole tone of the speech gives the impression that appalling stupiditys [sic] have been committed by the security authorities in the past.'[134]

As with the Labour Party, the various trade unions who represented civil servants reacted in a mixed way to the recent security measures. Speaking in support of the new vetting procedures, Independent MP and parliamentary secretary for the Civil Service Clerical Association (CSCA) William Brown stated, 'The communist objective, the communist method, and the communist morality make them dangerous to any existing society, and that society is entitled to take measures for its own defence.'[135] Brown attested during the Commons debate that the CSCA, a union representing civil servants, would support the anti-communist measures as well. This proved not to be the case. CSCA General Secretary L.C. White declared that Attlee's new policy was a serious and dangerous step which would lead government employees to lie and cover up their political affiliations. Backing the prime minister's decision was the National Association of Women Civil Servants (NAWCS). Its general secretary expressed concerns over interference with the freedom of the individual, arguing it was potentially dangerous but agreeing that considering the dangers of the present day, 'full measures' must be taken. Resistance in the overall trade union movement remained minimal. A conference of the TUC, which included leaders representing nearly 200 trade unions, rejected a motion calling for the repeal of the government's security measures by a card vote of 134,640 to 73,819.[136] However, a later vote at the TUC annual meeting in September on a motion criticising the fact that union officers were prohibited from representing accused civil servants was much closer.[137] The consensus of both the Labour Party and the trade unions was a shaky and qualified yes to Attlee's new security procedures. Yet public talk of witch hunts and the possibility of an emerging police state worried many. Cognisant of such concerns and nervous about the reputation of the security service, Liddell pointed out to Attlee 'that in the minds of the press and the public we [MI5] appear as a bunch of irresponsible autocrats who, without authority, were empowered to victimise civil servants'. The prime minister showed no sympathy over the agency's image, saying such a matter 'was to some extent unavoidable'.[138] Nevertheless, when government actions were taken in the future, none were so publicised.

Once established, the purge procedures functioned through questioning workers regarding communist affiliations and confronting them with accusations. The information gathered for the formal employee interview came mostly from the security service, although the suspect would not be privy to the evidence assembled against them; MI5 worried that sources could be compromised otherwise.[139] Then a determination was made if the individual needed transferring to another governmental department or dismissed outright from their position. While the suspect had the right to appeal this decision, they were not allowed to have representation present from their civil service union. Concerns from MI5 about the procedures increased shortly after they were instituted. The massive pool of civil servants needing vetting totalled 300,000, with an additional 50,000 being added annually.[140] The sheer logistics of reviewing numerous files and searching for potential suspects strained the resources of MI5.[141] The vetting of so many individuals stretched the agency to its 'utmost limit'. In June, Roger Hollis lamented that it was placing an 'intolerable burden upon the Security Service'.[142] Hollis, MI5's chief representative on the Committee on Positive Vetting, begged for the number of people requiring vetting to be kept as low as possible.[143] Thus the major contributing factor of limiting the purge to only sections of the civil service was not a political decision but more a practical one.[144] Simply put, MI5 did not have the resources to monitor communists throughout the entire civil service. Also, this now routine vetting forced limited resources away from investigating espionage cases that MI5's leadership deemed far more threatening.

Adding to the security service's consternation was the scope of the vetting; the purge 'seems to be extending itself outside the prime minister's ruling'.[145] Overzealous department heads were taking the initiative in hunting for communists without MI5's involvement. This eagerness extended to members of Attlee's own cabinet. When speaking to Solly Zuckerman – prominent scientist and later chief scientific advisor to

Harold Wilson – Herbert Morrison bluntly asked him if 'you [are] by not any chance fooling around with these communists?' In a later meeting with Liddell to discuss Zuckerman's possible CPGB membership, Morrison 'was seriously perturbed' when Liddell stated there was not sufficient evidence to purge Zuckerman from his current position.[146] In Whitehall, as MI5 feared, a 'purge atmosphere' took hold in certain departments. Such concerns were at the highest levels of the agency; as early as February 1949, Director General of MI5 Percy Sillitoe confessed to his deputy 'that he was concerned about the purge' which 'might be going too far'.[147] A geographical region not affected by the purge was Northern Ireland. Inspector-General of the Royal Ulster Constabulary Richard Pim relayed to MI5 that since 'very few civil servants were members of the Communist Party', the new vetting procedures had not been extended there.[148]

Not surprisingly, alongside MI5 officers, the CPGB leadership held grave concerns over the new purge atmosphere. They adopted a bunker mentality and prepared for the worst. The party began destroying its records, registration forms and membership lists with names of party members working in the civil service, the General Post Office (GPO) and government factories.[149] Although seemingly a paranoid response, this practice was in retrospect a wise decision. A solution introduced by Sillitoe to elevate the massive workload of the security service was the concept of vetting 'from the outside'. Sillitoe boasted that MI5 held 'an almost full list of the membership (numbering 40,000)' of the CPGB, including details of 'age, sex and employment' in addition to 'a virtually complete list ... about 3,500' of members in the Communist Youth League (CYL). With this wealth of information, it could quickly cross-check these lists for potential suspects in the civil service.[150] In response to the new government vetting process the CPGB carried out its own 'strict review of membership' to identify informers. It worked from the assumption that all telephone lines at CPGB locations were tapped by MI5, so all calls likely to reveal names and addresses of party members were ordered to be made from outside telephones. The general mood was one of 'depression and of [the] feeling that the party had lost the initiative'.[151]

Ann George, private secretary to Education Minister George Tomlinson, became the first person officially purged under the new procedures. In April, the permanent secretary of her department gave Tomlinson a letter stating she had twenty-four hours to answer formally whether she was a communist. She refused to either admit to or deny the charge.[152] The episode reminded many Britons of the American experience of HUAC and the dreaded term 'witch hunt'. The case of E.J. Hick, a clerical officer who had worked in the air ministry since 1939, also generated negative press attention for the vetting process. Congruent with his post in the ministry, he held the position of president of the CSCA – the trade union of civil servants that denounced the new vetting procedures. Even though Hick's CPGB membership was commonly known for numerous years, he was forced on leave from his job in June. In September, the purge removed Dr Cabot Seton Bull, a leading atomic research scientist working at Harwell Laboratory (known officially as the Atomic Energy Research Establishment), from his position. Bull had already resigned his CPGB party membership before entering government work. In a move that did little to aid Bull's case, CPGB General Secretary Harry Pollitt claimed he did not know anything about Bull.[153] To many Britons, this blanket denial was just a form of communists protecting one of their most valuable agents. The purge moved to the FO in January 1949, when a clerical officer employed in the archive department was suspended from her job for her CPGB membership.[154]

In October, the *New York Times* reported that a London-based comedienne found the 'Communist Purge' no laughing matter.[155] Beryl Lund, a member of the left-wing Unity Theatre in north London, who also worked as a junior clerical post in the Ministry of Supply, was removed from her post after she was accused of associating with communists. The move seemed suspicious to some, since the play Lund was currently acting in at the Unity Theatre criticised the purge. The production, entitled 'What's Left?', which ran over 100 performances during the summer of 1948, mirrored the concern of many of the populace about the perceived red-baiting and the strict anti-communist stance of the Labour government. Cynics viewed the decision to 'purge' her as being politically motivated. Afterwards, Lund stated she found it difficult to appeal against her suspension when she knew neither the charges against her nor the evidence supporting them. Ultimately, after being placed in a 'dead-end job', she migrated to Italy. Even with the publicising of these high-profile cases, for sheer numbers the purge was disappointing to the likes of rabid right-wing anti-communists such as Waldron Smithers. When questioned by Smithers in January 1949, Attlee conceded that only seventeen cases had gone to the appeals tribunal. Six other cases were considered proven since the suspects elected not to appeal and ten more were currently under review.[156] From the political left and right anxieties over the purging placed the new vetting procedures under the piercing spotlight of public scrutiny that the government neither appreciated nor expected.

In addition to the civil service, the need to 'purge' communists from particular industrial sectors was agreed upon as well. By 1949, MI5 had 'for some time been anxious' about the security risks that private firms engaging with classified information created. Herbert Morrison agreed with this assessment, arguing that the 'present methods of excluding untrustworthy persons from secret government work were not sufficient'.[157] Defence Minister A.V. Alexander concurred, arguing that communists employed in the private sector were 'as dangerous as the employment of persons of doubtful loyalty in government departments', since contractors had access to government secrets. Despite these urgings to expand the purge, apprehension remained after the negative reaction that accompanied the announcement of civil service vetting. Warnings about how to proceed were numerous. Norman Brook counselled Attlee that this expansion of the purging procedures brought 'substantial risks of a political outcry' and recommended to the prime minister 'to move rather cautiously and not to give the Security Service a free rein in hounding out suspects'.[158] A GEN 168 committee meeting report mirrored this unease. 'There must be no question of a witch-hunt which could be represented as a move to "purge" all communists from work on government contracts.'[159] While the need to conceal the purge's expansion was duly noted and generally accepted, the existing situation was estimated as grossly insufficient and thus needed changing, despite the political risks. As the process stood, MI5's only course of action when presented with a security risk in the private sector was to attempt to convince the firm employing the suspect to move them to a less sensitive position which did not involve governmental secrets.[160] A new measure needed enacting since this was not always possible. In 1949, the cabinet agreed that the minister of supply and the Admiralty – the ministries most private firms contracted by the government reported to – now had the right to 'require' firms to 'exclude undesirable persons' from secret governmental work.[161] Unlike with the announced civil service vetting protocols, there was no appeal process for individuals targeted for dismissal. It was likely this, combined with the dread of the probable political fallout of increasing the purge from civil servants to private governmental contractors, that kept Attlee from publicly announcing this expansion of security vetting. Currently the number of employees removed through this 'industrial purge' is still undisclosed by the British government.

Despite criticism from various corners – trade unions, MI5, Labour Party members and the public at large – the need to introduce even more vetting became apparent in the latter half of 1949. To Western cold warriors, the communist threat exponentially grew that year with the news of the Soviet Union obtaining the atomic bomb and the success of the Chinese Communist Revolution. Remarking on the latter, Liddell called the revelation that an 'existential threat' to the UK now controlled the destructive power of the atom 'the event of the year'.[162] In terms of the timing, both British and American experts wrongly estimated that the Soviet Union was at least two more years away from gaining nuclear capability. A likely reason to many in London and Washington for this rapid technological advancement by the Soviet Union was the discovery of communist agents who had previously worked on or close to the Manhattan project. A German-born naturalised British citizen named Klaus Fuchs soon made headlines in just such a case. A theoretical physicist stationed at Los Alamos Laboratory during the Second World War, Fuchs fell under suspicion of the FBI and MI5 in September 1949. Through information from a top-secret counterintelligence project, codenamed Venona, it came to light that he passed atomic secrets to the Soviets. After tracking and watching Fuchs during November and December, MI5 picked him up for questioning and obtained a confession from him in January 1950. With his arrest came alarmed calls from both sides of the Atlantic to tighten security and vetting procedures. Evidence suggested that the security service had ignored earlier warning signs regarding Fuchs's loyalty. MI5 files showed that on two occasions during the 1930s sources identified him as a communist – but both were disregarded.[163] The political ramifications were terrible; the arrest of Fuchs showed that a lapse of British security aided the Soviet atomic bomb programme.

The susceptibility of communists to Soviet recruitment was now a foregone conclusion. Future British Ambassador to the Soviet Union Geoffrey Harrison, then stationed in Moscow as counsellor, warned MI5, stating 'Russia's two weapons [are] the Red Army and communism, but for the time being ... she preferred to use the latter'.[164] In the security service's opinion, the Soviet Union was effectually waging war against the British state through fifth columnists, only until it saw fit to send in the Red Army. US intelligence agents and Washington policymakers agreed with this assessment. They went 'so far to suggest that American secrets should not be developed in Britain, as she might well be overrun before the Americans could come to her assistance'.[165] Liddell noted if war with the Soviets did come, 'the Americans are taking the somewhat irritating attitude that we [the UK] may well be blotted out in the first few hours'.[166]

Despite the potential public outcry, stricter measures were needed to halt the flow of sensitive information into the eager hands of the Soviet intelligence services. In April 1950, GEN 183 established the Committee for Positive Vetting. Chaired by John Winnifrith, its purpose was to initiate a system where individuals were asked either through forms or personal interviews if they were currently or previously connected to communist organisations. This did not alter the basic policy of removing communists from their positions, which went untouched from its enactment in 1948; what expanded were the methods for detecting suspects.[167] Contrasted with negative vetting, where doubt was usually established before an investigation was officially sanctioned, with positive vetting everyone in a department or section was forced to undergo the process – even, ironically, Winnifrith himself.[168] Cabinet Secretary Norman Brook described the process of positive vetting to Attlee as 'primarily a change of attitudes and methods' in checking the reliability of individuals. While the purge procedures instituted a sweep through the files of Special Branch and MI5 for damaging information on employees, positive vetting involved active investigations of all individuals in a targeted governmental department. This method mirrored those practised by the US government, which pressured the British to adopt a similar security formula.

In fact, US pressure was the strongest force pushing the UK to adopt stricter vetting procedures, especially in the field of atomic power after the discovery of Fuchs.[169] Exacerbating the American calls was the news in September 1950 of the defection of Bruno Pontecorvo, a colleague of Fuchs, and later the next year of the unexplained disappearances of Guy Burgess and Donald Maclean.[170] From 1950 to 1951 this external pressure was omnipresent during the deliberations in Whitehall over positive vetting. In June 1951, after strong urgings from Washington, representatives from the US, the UK and Canada held a tripartite conference on atomic energy security. The summit's main focus was to set stronger safeguards on nuclear secrets held by the three nations. Since the British government sought assistance from the Americans in the field of nuclear technology, it sought to placate them as much as possible. The report on the conference recommendations passed on to GEN 183 from Winnifrith's committee stressed the importance of complying with American wishes in terms of security. It stressed that vetting needed to specifically target communists to satisfy their ally:

> We want the American atomic secrets and we won't get them unless they modify the McMahon Act. Officials have already offered the procedure now proposed and nothing short of that offer and the direct question to the candidate about communist associations is from the Americans' point of view a sine qua non [essential condition] will secure their co-operation. It is fair to add that, even if we confirm the offer, there is no guarantee that the McMahon Act will be modified and that we will get their atomic secrets.[171]

In October 1950 Winnifrith's committee recommended the new procedure to the full cabinet, arguing it reinforced 'the duty of the public service to take all reasonable steps to check the reliability of persons holding vital posts'. However, it stated the process would not be infallible; since 'these enquiries may reveal open association with communism, they will fail to detect the really dangerous crypto-communists'.[172] The security service shared this opinion. MI5 agreed in principle that communists in many areas of government needed exposing and removal. Yet its major concern rested again in the logistical strain the proposed positive vetting procedures would impose on the agency. MI5 feared that it left few resources for the 'hunt' of secret communists and deep-cover Soviet agents that vetting processes were unlikely to uncover. To alleviate this burden, a GEN 183 meeting chaired by Attlee agreed that departments could seek the assistance of 'local police' in investigating and vetting if MI5 did not have the resources needed to 'reach a certain conclusion' on an individual.[173]

Alongside the strain on the already overworked security service, another stumbling block to positive vetting came in the form of the aforementioned fear of the people's reaction. A constant worry that kept arising when reviewing the recommendations made at the tripartite conference was that the British populace would not accept them. The recommendations were for instituting the methods used in the US, which already had negative connotations after the execution of the Rosenbergs. If announced publicly, the government would undoubtedly face criticism. Since communism was legal and 'there are many people who still believe – or say they believe – that adherence to the communist creed is not incompatible with the loyalty to their own country', the measures would be viewed as an 'un-British inquisition' against specific individuals for holding private beliefs.[174] The solution to this dilemma agreed upon by GEN 183 and Attlee was the same as in regards to the industrial purge. The British government did not announce the new measures.

The defeat of Labour in the 1951 General Election left it for Winston Churchill's Conservative government to implement positive vetting. The transition of power did little initially to undermine the vetting process. By 1955, the total number of civil servants known or suspected to be communists and assessed by MI5 as security risks totalled 3,400 – with a third of those working as postal employees.[175] The number of dismissals from government positions of the purge procedures in 1948 until the mid-1950s was 124,[176] though some have suspected the number of communists purged was substantially higher.[177] In comparison 2,700 were discharged under similar procedures in the US between 1947 and 1956.[178]

The singular target of the vetting procedures installed in the UK during the early Cold War period was communists. Early in the process the British government attempted to claim these measures were put in place to halt all subversives from having access to secret information and policy-making political posts. However, in private discussions, it was revealed that it considered the only viable threat as coming from those individuals who were associated with communist ideology. In pinpointing reasons for dismissing, transferring or refusing posts in government, the main consideration that effected the decision was if a person held affiliations with communism. Even though thousands of Britons were members of the CPGB, and while communists served in the House of Commons, the British policy towards individuals with this political viewpoint was that all were potential traitors and fifth columnists lying in wait. The key considerations restraining the vetting process and the purge had more to do with matters of public support and logistics than with concern for the working rights of accused communists. In the eyes of the British establishment, these 'would-be traitors' had already chosen the wrong side in an ideological war.

Restrictions of visas for communists and fellow travellers

In 1952, Attorney General James P. McGranery gave notice to the press that he was revoking Charlie Chaplin's right to re-entry to the US.[179] McGranery ordered the Immigration and Naturalization Service to determine whether the famous actor should be refused travel rights in the US for being subversive. Called to testify in front of HUAC during its investigation regarding Hollywood, in 1947 Chaplin had emphatically denied being a communist and holding any such affiliations with the Communist Party. McGranery's order caused an uproar across the UK since Chaplin was a British subject. Alongside concerns centred on Chaplin's case, the Internal Security Act of 1950 (commonly known as the McCarran Act) was denounced throughout the British Isles.[180] The law authorised US consular officers to bar foreigners from entering the US on the mere suspicion that they may be sympathetic towards the communist cause. Despite the adverse reaction to these American measures from inside the UK, comparable methods were carried out in the UK as well. Less famous but similar incidences to that of Chaplin occurred in the UK. In 1954, the UK refused to extend a work permit for an American psychologist employed at the University of Birmingham. The reason British authorities gave was that in the US he was wanted for questioning on his alleged membership in the Communist Party.[181] Although pressure from the US contributed to this case, it is only one example of communist political affiliations being used to determine if individuals were allowed entry into the UK. Although this particular case occurred under a Conservative government, the precedent for such measures began under Labour. In the early Cold War period, like the US, the Attlee government also barred entry to communists and suspected fellow travellers, but in a more ad-hoc fashion. Unlike in the US, no new laws were passed to codify these restrictions on communists. The reason for this difference was not that the British government worried less about communists but that it held no such need for new legislation to bar undesirables. In the UK, the Aliens Restriction Act of 1914, enacted during the First World War but extended in 1919, gave complete power over foreigners' rights to visit and be admitted to the home secretary.

Curiously, as in the realm of vetting, members of the Labour government were more passionate in seeing the deportations of suspected communist agitators than was the security service. In 1947, Attlee personally sought the deportation of Frank Piazza, a waiter who was dismissed from service for a dispute over whose responsibility it was to carry dirty dishes back to the kitchen. Piazza's firing caused around 700 of the catering-staff employed at the Savoy Hotel, where he had worked, to go on strike. The timing of the strike happened to coincide with the wedding of the future Queen Elizabeth. Attlee viewed this as not a simple coincidence but more a communist plot to disrupt the royal nuptials. Since Piazza was an Italian emigrant, Attlee asked the deputy director of MI5 why he had not already been deported as an 'undesirable alien'. Guy Liddell had to remind the prime minister that it was not the policy of the Home Office to halt the naturalisation process for members of the Communist Party.[182]

An underlining security concern, which held a foreign policy dimension for the British government, was the efforts and underlying objectives of the World Peace Council (WPC) and its affiliated front organisations. Founded indirectly by the Soviet Union, in 1950 the WPC was the centrepiece of a Soviet-sponsored attempt to generate a worldwide 'peace movement' whose dual missions were for 'building up the image of the USSR as the champion for peace while subverting the military preparedness of the NATO through manipulation of the latent desire for peace among these populations'.[183] Alongside the WPC, the government classified numerous other 'peace' groups as thinly veiled communist fronts. Concerned that the messages of these organisations could potentially resonate in a large segment of the British population, Attlee sought ways to hinder the peace movement in any possible way, short of banning their functions and declaring them illegal. To stymie involvement and partition in the peace campaign, the government used the informal measure of denying entry visas to foreign attendees and guests of the WPC and other associated organisations. The WPC announced its intention to hold in Sheffield the second annual World Peace Festival in 1950. In response to this announcement, the cabinet agreed with the suggestion of Foreign Secretary Ernest Bevin to 'do everything possible to cripple the conference'. Giving a widely publicised speech on the upcoming festival at the Foreign Press Association on 1 November, Attlee articulated the government's position in the strongest of terms:

Of course the communists say that this conference is not organized by them. Communist activities generally are camouflaged in this country, they usually get a few respectable but misguided people to provide the sheep's clothing ... We shall not deny admission to people who in good faith may wish to attend this conference, but we are not willing to throw wide our doors to those who seek to come here to subvert our institutions, to seduce our fellow-citizens from their natural allegiance and their daily duties and to make propaganda for those who call us cannibals and warmongers.[184]

Asked why he did not simply ban the upcoming WPC event, Attlee maintained that the government did not have the legal right to do so. When a question on this topic was raised in the Commons, Home Secretary James Chuter Ede agreed with Attlee's legal assessment. The law as it stood did not allow the banning of such an organised event. However, when the international delegates arrived in Dover, forty of the sixty-five delegates and their staff were turned back and refused entry into the UK based on the fact they might be 'detrimental to internal security'.[185] British authorities also denied visas to all the members of the committee running the conference. However, in a Machiavellian move the government allowed a small number of festival delegates entry so it would not appear its decisions were politically motivated.[186] Effectively the Attlee government banned the meeting through the roundabout but already established process of visa control. With little recourse, the planned Sheffield Festival was moved to Warsaw. Reacting to this, the British Peace Committee organised a thousand-person protest in Trafalgar Square.[187] In the House of Commons, questions were raised about the issue concerning human rights, yet the press and the general public showed little interest in the entire situation.

Official Committee on Communism (Home) and the IRD

The negative response to the purge procedures did not dampen the anti-communist spirit in the Labour government. The year 1951 saw the establishment of a new committee to coordinate government efforts to 'combat communist activities in the United Kingdom'.[188] Sparking its formation was fear that domestic communists would attempt to halt British economic recovery and even damage the rearmament efforts which followed the start of the Korean War in June 1950.[189] Entitled the Official Committee on Communism (Home) and more commonly known as the Brook Committee, its objectives, as listed in its founding guidelines, were:

To focus all available intelligence about communist activities in the United Kingdom, and to recommend to ministers what action can properly be taken to counter such activities.

To give any necessary guidance on administrative and policy questions to the briefing group of Information Officers handling anti-communist information material for use in the United Kingdom.

To co-ordinate any anti-communist activities in this country which may be approved by ministers (apart from normal information activities undertaken by the group mentioned in paragraph (b) above).[190]

The committee was a mirror image of two other committees established in 1949, the Official Committee on Communism (Overseas) and the Ministerial Committee on Communism, both established to organise anti-communist activities overseas by the Labour government in December 1949. Initially, ministers rejected the establishment of a solely domestic anti-communist committee, 'on the ground that so long as the British Communist Party remains a legal political organization the government cannot undertake officially an action to discredit it'.[191] By the end of 1950, with the increase of international tensions, the Ministerial Committee changed its mind on the need for, and also on the legality of, such a committee for safeguarding the home front from the communist threat. The memorandum defending the creation of the Brook Committee stated:

Communism is a world-wide force directed from the centre in the interests of Russian imperialism and we cannot treat communism in the United Kingdom as a democratic political issue detached from the main Soviet threat to our existence. It is part and parcel of that threat, and there are a number of manifestations of communist activity in the United Kingdom which are in the nature of a conspiracy organized against our national survival ... It is because the activities of communism in this field have not only been intensified in recent months but have shown signs of achieving some success, and because in the present situation the consequences of their achieving even greater success would be so grave, that we bring this subject again to the attention of the ministers.[192]

The Brook Committee's initial targets of investigation for communist infiltration were 'four particularly important' subsections of the population – the armed forces, industrial workers, education and scientists. Despite the initial reluctance to set up the committee, it proved quite popular around the halls of government. Prior to the committee's first meeting, Norman Brook had already received a request by the air ministry to investigate a Soviet radio monitoring station in Middlesex that 'represents an unacceptable risk to the security of our air defence arrangements'.[193] Brook was also offered assistance from the FO with regards to anti-communist propaganda and activities that might prove 'applicable in the home field', alongside 'suggestions about the official machinery that may be required at home'.[194]

The committee worked closely with an entity set inside the FO with the unassuming name of the Information Research Department. Sanctioned by Ernest Bevin and created and headed by Labour MP and FO undersecretary Christopher Mayhew in 1948, the IRD's purpose was to conduct an 'ideological offensive against Stalinism'.[195] A protégé of Bevin, Mayhew was a driving force of Labourite anti-communism. Elected to parliament in 1945, he lost his seat in the 1950 General Election. With the death of Bevin in 1951, Mayhew won the byelection to fill his seat. In a message supporting Mayhew, Attlee praised his selection and maintained that Mayhew would uphold the assertion that the 'Labour government's determined policy of co-operation in defence of liberty and the raising of general world standards is the only effective answer to communism'.[196] Indeed, Mayhew was the epitome of the cold warrior archetype, something that did not go unnoticed by his fellow party members. During a meeting of the PLP, a left-wing MP attacked Mayhew for 'seeing reds under the bed'.[197] Initially, the IRD focused on exporting anti-communist propaganda to foreign audiences. By the 1950s, it sought to manipulate public opinion inside the UK as well. As Mayhew describes, 'At home, our service was offered to, and accepted by, large numbers of selected MPs, journalists, trade union leaders and others.'[198] After the creation of the Brook Committee, both organs sought to synergise and coordinate their efforts in propaganda efforts in the UK. While the IRD and the Brook Committee worked to influence the worldviews of Britons, both sought to hide this mission from the general public. As pointed out previously, after the ill-fated reception of the negative vetting protocols, government officials feared a backlash if new anti-communist measures were brought to light. This was the case with regards to the Brook Committee, whose mere existence was highly classified. The committee remained 'top secret' even after the downgrading of the Overseas Committee to 'secret'.

Fielding a staff of experts on the Soviet Union and Marxist-Leninist ideology, the IRD compiled large numbers of facts and figures on the negative components of communism and human rights violations of the Soviet Union. Historian Robert Conquest found employment early in his career as one such staffer.[199] In one of its earliest domestic endeavours, the IRD, through the contribution of Conquest and others, produced a series of 'Speaker's Notes' that were offered to 'anti-Stalinist' MPs and government ministers. These contained facts and talking points which were anti-communist in nature or countered general communist arguments.[200] In addition to this inter-government information initiative, the IRD reached out to the leadership of the country's trade unions. Its members kept frequent contact with Herbert Tracey, the TUC publicity director. Via Tracey, Christopher Mayhew arranged 'for the dissemination inside the Labour movement at home of anti-communist propaganda, which we are producing for overseas consumption'.[201] Historian Andrew Defty attests that the FO had few reservations about directing anti-communist propaganda inside the UK. Defty wrote that in the postwar period 'there was a growing concern in Whitehall about the depth of pro-Soviet sentiment in Britain', thus justifying IRD conducting internal operations.[202] In September 1951 the IRD expanded their domestic activities, opening an official 'home desk' to focus solely on shifting public opinion in the UK.

One curious anecdote involving the IRD is the reception and retention of what is now generally termed 'Orwell's List'. In 1949, Eric Blair, commonly known by his pen name George Orwell, forwarded a list of thirty-eight writers whom he classified as crypto-communists to a friend, Celia Kirwin, working at the IRD.[203] Initially, Kirwin, the assistant of Robert Conquest, visited Orwell while he lay ill in a sanatorium in Gloucestershire. During their discussion, she asked him for possible contacts among Orwell's circle that might prove useful for the IRD. Instead, he later wrote back to Kirwin offering to provide a list of names of individuals whom the department should avoid. Orwell stated these individuals were untrustworthy and should not be employed by the government and were especially not fit for working with the IRD. Subsequently, in another project, the IRD funded and promoted foreign-language editions of Orwell's *Animal Farm*. Domestically, the IRD created their own publishing house entitled Ampersand – which over the span of three decades published twenty books. The department also dealt with more established publishers to reach larger audiences.[204]

Contacts between the IRD and the Brook Committee were quite frequent. Members in both sought to find new ways to spread the anti-communist message throughout the UK. In a curious proposal, they sought to use satire as a tool to disseminate their political message. During a 1952 meeting of the committee, J.W. Nichollis of the FO recommended approaching either popular comedian Jimmy Edwards or someone similar with 'a view of introducing anti-communist themes into their programmes on the BBC'. Although the idea garnered serious consideration inside the committee, it rejected it since 'there was a danger that the use of the BBC for this purpose might eventually be traced back to the committee'.[205] However, one proposal that was enacted was the dissemination of anti-communist literature and pamphlets inside the various trade unions.

Although the committee frequently met during the first two years of its existence, by late 1952, after the Conservatives took power, it began to lose steam, and many in Whitehall questioned its actual relevance. During this time, its own chairman, Norman Brook, wrote that while the committee 'has reviewed a fairly wide field of possible anti-communist activities in the United Kingdom the positive results of all this have not been spectacular'.[206] While it would only meet twice in 1953, the Brook Committee did escape the fate of the Ministerial Committee on Communism, which the new Conservative government disbanded after coming to power. When the Brook Committee convened again on 1 December 1954 it focused on communist involvement in the London dock strikes. After discussing the strike and the security service's assessment of it, the overall consensus of the committee was that although communists were actively involved in the industrial action, they played no role in its instigation and 'the fact that the communists took part in the dock strike made very little difference'. Regarding future activities of the committee, Brook suggested since 'there seemed to be no increase in the communist menace', he saw no reason to continue regular meetings 'except when they were required for a particular purpose'.[207] In 1960 the minister of defence and the chiefs of staff viewed the Brook Committee as having lost its usefulness. They relayed to Brook that there was little reason for them to be represented on the committee and only wished to attend if 'communist attempts to penetrate the armed forces' were on the agenda.[208]

The Official Committee on Communism (Home) continued until the late 1960s, yet it had not conducted a meeting since 1962. In 1969, it was formally reconstituted as the Official Committee on Subversion at Home.[209] The height of the Brook Committee's influence lasted only two years, from 1951 to 1952. Afterwards, though it continued to send out frequent reports on communist activities in the UK, it did not pursue anti-communist actions and was effectively overshadowed by the domestic activities of the IRD. As solely a propaganda instrument, the IRD's more defined goal led to it achieving not only more tangible results but also a more lasting impact on the anti-communist agenda in the UK. After Labour was voted out of power in 1951, the IRD continued its activities under the successive Conservative governments. With the change of government, John Peck, a former wartime private secretary to Churchill, took over the reins of the IRD. The IRD's operations did not halt until 1977 when Harold Wilson ordered it dismantled – even then, it still had over 100 journalists on nearly every national newspaper using its material, knowingly or not.[210] Ever the cold warrior Mayhew unsuccessfully lobbied Margaret Thatcher to restart the department in 1980. He called the Wilson government's 'suppression' of the department 'an outrage' and 'part of Labour's softness towards communists, which has done so much damage to the country'.[211]

However, the closing of the IRD did not mark the end of government-sponsored propaganda. In 2007, as a response to the 'war on terror' and during Gordon Brown's premiership, the Home Office christened a new department entitled the Research, Information and Communications Unit (RICU). Its founding goal was to shift the beliefs of young British Muslims to a more pro-Western – and thus acceptable – mindset.[212] Brown called the battle against Islamic extremism 'the same cultural war that had to be fought against communism from the 1940s and 50s onwards'. He made the comparison after reading *Who Paid the Piper?* (1999) by Frances Saunders.[213] The book documented how the CIA used covert methods to promote anti-communism through cultural and literary means. Observers have noted the RICU has since functioned as a new IRD.[214]

Conclusion

After taking power in 1945, the Labour government systematically put in place measures to combat and curb communist influence. It sought to purge and prohibit communists from government jobs; halt their inclusion inside the democratic process; limit their ability to travel; wiretap and put under surveillance many of its own citizenry; question the patriotism and loyalty of all individuals with communist affiliations; and sought to secretly indoctrinate the British population into holding a more anti-communist viewpoint. If examining these activities solely on their own qualities, they form a narrative that describes a national government at war with a specific political ideology and willing to use a variety of measures to either disrupt or eradicate its influence inside the nation. However, when compared to the US governmental responses to communism during the same period, the British narrative is drowned out by the vastness and excesses of the American reaction. During the American red scare, the US government banned the Communist Party, jailed individuals for subversive activities, investigated the entertainment industry and purged public educators. No such 'witch hunts' occurred in the UK. No new laws or regulations were passed against the Communist Party and, to the lament of Waldron Smithers, neither did parliament set up a committee on un-British activities. If Attlee and his government sought to fight communism just as did their US counterparts, why did these events not occur in the UK? The answer filters down to worries over public opinion and that no additional legislative measures were necessary in the British form of government.

The legality of the CPGB made it difficult to enact direct procedures against it in the eyes of the average citizen. Established in 1920 and having representation in parliament gave the party credibility that worked against the government's attempts to marginalise and suppress it. As shown by the discussions inside the cabinet, and various correspondences between departments, this legitimacy did lessen the drive of the government to seek ways to attack and hinder this political party or harass its members. Another factor which prohibited Labour was the overwhelming negative impression Britons held of the American red scare.

A less opportunistic motive shaped the anti-communist activities of Whitehall and Westminster. When Smithers requested that Morrison set up a parliamentary un-British activities committee, Morrison responded with a one-word answer: 'no'. Shortly afterwards the Labour government covertly established the 'top-secret' Brook Committee that not only investigated communists but also actively worked against them. In 1948, when Attlee arrived in the House of Commons, he came to announce the new purge procedures, not to call for a parliamentary vote to establish them. Thus the purge became a reality without any statutory authority.[215] Subsequently, Attlee and Churchill expanded the protocols through executive orders to include private corporations and introduced positive vetting upon governmental departments without any public proclamation. With regards to restricting certain communists and fellow travellers' entry into the UK, again the process did not need legislative oversight but only the order of the home secretary for any individual to be barred. When Ernest Bevin ordered the creation of the IRD and Christopher Mayhew directed it to indoctrinate the British public against communism, again they needed only the permission of the sitting prime minister – Clement Attlee. The absence of new anti-communist laws and statutes by the British government during this period should not be misconstrued as a sign of tolerance towards communism.

Notes

1. Ernest Bevin to Clement Attlee, 9 January 1947, TNA FO 800/476.

2. *Chicago Daily Tribune*, 15 May 1953, p. 5.

3. Francis Beckett wrote: 'Morrison had been in the forefront of the battle to keep communists out of the Labour Party, becoming known as Labour's witchfinder-general.' F. Beckett, *Clem Attlee* (London, 1997), p. 303.

4. J. Hinton, 'Self-help and socialism: The squatters' movement of 1946', *History Workshop*, 25 (1988): 100–26, at p. 101.

5. Hartley Shawcross to Clement Attlee, 16 September 1946, TNA PREM 8/227.

6. Beckett, *Attlee*, p. 256.

7. *The Times*, 16 September 1946, p. 5; *The Times*, 5 October 1946, p. 2.

8. C. Barnett, *The Lost Victory* (London, 1995), p. 212.

9. *Let Us Face the Future* by Labour Party Executive Committee.

10. T. Burridge, *Clement Attlee* (London, 1985), p. 200.

11. K. Laybourn, *The Rise of Socialism in Britain* (Stroud, 1997), p. 141.

12. Toye, *Labour Party and Planning*, p. 5.

13. J. Wood, 'A "third way"? The Labour left, democratic socialism and the Cold War', in *Labour's Promised Land?*, ed. J. Fyrth (London, 1995), 73–87, at p. 75.

14. K. Laybourn and D. Murphy, *Under the Red Flag* (Stroud, 1999), p. 122.

15. P. Taylor, *Britain and the Cold War* (London, 1990), p. 63.

16. P Corthorn, *In the Shadow of the Dictators* (London, 2006), pp. 213–14; P. Corthorn, 'Labour, the left, and the Stalinist purges of the late 1930s', *The Historical Journal*, 48.1 (2005): 179–207, at p. 183.

17. D. Lomas, *Intelligence, Security and the Attlee Governments, 1945–51: An Uneasy Relationship?* (Manchester, 2016), p. 46.

18. Haseler, *Tragedy of Labour*, p. 25.

19. A. Thrope, '"The only effective bulwark against reaction and revolution": Labour and the frustration of the extreme left', in *The Failure of Political Extremism in Interwar Britain*, ed. A. Thorpe (Exeter, 1988), 11–28, at pp. 27–8.

20. J. Swift, *Labour in Crisis* (New York, 2001), p. 87.

21. Toye, *Labour Party and the Planned*, p. 57; B. Donoughue and G. Jones, *Herbert Morrison* (London, 1973), pp. 112–13.

22. H. Harmer, *The Longman Companion to the Labour Party, 1900–1998* (London, 1999), p. 165.

23. Ernest Bevin to G.D.H. Cole, 27 January 1937, Papers of Ernest Bevin, MSS.126/EB/X/44, Modern Records Centre (henceforth MRC), Warwick University.

24. B. Jones, *The Russia Complex* (Manchester, 1977), p. 23.

25. Corthorn, 'Labour, the left, and the Stalinist purges', p. 180.

26. Jones, *Russia Complex*, p. 24.

27. Both men later went on to author world-renowned novels denouncing the Soviet experiment: Orwell with *Animal Farm* and Koestler with *Darkness at Noon*. Western anti-communists used the two books extensively as propaganda tools during the ensuing Cold War.

28. Corthorn, 'Labour, the left, and the Stalinist purges', p. 206.

29. Corthorn, 'Labour, the left, and the Stalinist purges', p. 187.

30. *Daily Herald*, 6 July 1936, p. 10.

31. C. Attlee, *The Labour Party in Perspective* (London, 1937), pp. 150–1.

32. Quoted in F. William, *Ernest Bevin* (London, 1952), p. 203.

33. War Cabinet conclusions, 21 July 1941, TNA CAB 65/19/8.

34. *Derby Daily Telegraph*, 16 June 1943, p. 8.

35. *Daily Mirror*, 15 January 1940, p. 3; *Daily Herald*, 21 February 1940, p. 6.

36. *Birmingham Daily Gazette*, 17 June 1943, p. 1.

37. *New York Times*, 17 June 1943, p. 3.

38. K. Harris, *Attlee* (London, 1982), p. 267.

39. *Labour Party Annual Report 1946*, p. 174.

40. *Birmingham Daily Gazette*, 13 June 1946, p. 2.

41. Cabinet minutes of Norman Brook, 17 November 1947, TNA CAB 195/5/66.

42. Harold Laski, *The Secret Battalion* (London, 1946).

43. Nicolson, *Diaries and Letters*, p. 130.

44. Liddell diary, 21 January 1946.

45. *Gloucester Citizen*, 31 May 1950, p. 12.

46. R. Aldrich, 'Secret intelligence for a post-war world: Reshaping the British intelligence community, 1944–51', in *British Intelligence Strategy and the Cold War, 1945–51*, ed. R. Aldrich (London, 1992), 14–49, at p. 33.

47. C. Attlee, *As It Happened* (London, 1954), p. 64.

48. Hansard, HC, vol. 448, c. 3420 (25 March 1948).

49. D. Lilleker, *Against the Cold War* (London, 2004), p. 87.

50. G. Orwell, 'Burnham's view of the contemporary world struggle', *New Leader*, 29 March 1947 in *The Collected Essays, Journalism and Letters of George Orwell*, ed. S. Orwell and I. Angus (London, 1970), 313–25, at p. 32.

51. Liddell diary, 19 November 1949.

52. Hansard, HC, vol. 430, c. 526 (18 November 1946).

53. Hansard, HC, vol. 430, c. 526 (18 November 1946).

54. Jones, *Russia Complex*, p. 121.

55. *Scotsman*, 18 November 1946, p. 5.

56. *Daily Herald*, 28 June 1947, p. 1.

57. C. Andrew, *The Defence of the Realm* (London, 2009), p. 411.

58. Hansard, HC, vol. 427, c. 1675 (23 October 1946).

59. MI5 report on Bing, 19 November 1946, TNA KV 2/3812.

60. Liddell diary, 18 November 1946.

61. MI5 report on Bing, 19 November 1946, TNA KV 2/381.

62. MI5 report on Bing, 28 February 1947, TNA KV 2/3812.

63. Hansard, HC, vol. 433, c. 1645 (21 February 1947).

64. Maxwell Knight to Dick White, 9 May 1947, TNA KV 2/3812.

65. 'Attack on M.I.5.' sent to Dick White, 6 March 1947, TNA KV 2/3812; Maxwell Knight to Dick White, 28 March 1947, TNA KV 2/3812.

66. 'Attack on M.I.5.' sent to Dick White, 6 March 1947, TNA KV 2/3812.

67. Note by Guy Liddell, 21 May 1947, TNA KV 2/3812.

68. Pritt was already on the radar of MI5 as a potential communist subvert and it held extensive files on him dating back to 1932. See TNA KV 2/1062; KV 2/1063; KV 2/1064.

69. 'Attack on M.I.5.' sent to Dick White, 6 March 1947, TNA KV 2/3812.

70. 'Lost Sheep' file, box 4, Papers of Morgan Phillip, Labour Party Archive (henceforth (LPA), People's History Museum, Manchester.

71. Liddell diary, 21 February 1946.

72. *Daily Herald*, 17 April 1948, p. 1.

73. *Daily Worker*, 20 April 1948, p. 1.

74. *Western Morning News*, 3 May 1948, p. 2.

75. *Tribune*, 23 April 1948, p. 2.

76. *The New Statesman and Nation*, 30 October 1948, p. 372.

77. Clement Attlee to Konni Zilliacus, 17 February 1946, MS Attlee dep. 31, Papers of Clement Attlee, Bodleian Library University of Oxford (henceforth MS Attlee).

78. *The Diary of Hugh Gaitskell*, ed. P. Williams (London, 1983), p. 453.

79. H. Morrison, *An Autobiography* (London, 1960), p. 322.

80. Hugh Dalton to Morgan Phillips, 1 November 1948, LPA, General Secretary's Papers (henceforth GS), 'Lost Sheep' file.

81. 'Mr. K Zilliaous. M.P.', LPA/GS, 'Lost Sheep' file.

82. Christopher Mayhew to Ernest Bevin, 19 April 1949, Mayhew 4/1/2, Papers of Christopher Mayhew, King's College London (henceforth Mayhew).

83. *Belfast Newsletter*, 21 June 1949, p. 5.

84. Liddell diary, 27 March 1951.

85. Speech by Morrison, issued by the Labour Party, 24 March 1950, LPA/LID/Anticommunist Propaganda 1949.

86. *Daily Herald*, 28 August 1952, p. 4.

87. *Daily Mirror*, 6 October 1952, p. 1.

88. 'The Trojan Horse: An Open Letter from Mr. Tufton Beamish to Mr. Herbert Morrison', pamphlet by Tufton Beamish, 1953.

89. Herbert Bowden to John McGovern, 15 May 1958, LPA/GS, 'Lost Sheep' file; Morgan Phillips to E. Alcock, 9 March 1959, LPA/GS, 'Lost Sheep' file.

90. *The Times*, 25 June 1955, p. 11.

91. Report signed by W.S. Marshall, 15 June 1958, LPA/GS, 'Lost Sheep' file.

92. *Salisbury Times*, 17 April 1959, p. 3.

93. *Canberra Times*, 30 May 1959, p. 3.

94. Morgan Phillips to John McGovern, 29 May 1959, LPA/GS, 'Lost Sheep' file.

95. *The Times*, 15 June 1959, p. 6; McGovern to Phillips, 11 June 1959, LPA/GS, 'Lost Sheep' file.

96. P. Corthorn, 'Cold War politics in Britain and the contested legacy of the Spanish Civil War', *European History Quarterly*, 44 (2014): 678–702, at p. 684.

97. D. Lomas, 'Labour ministers, intelligence and domestic anti-communism, 1945–1951', *Journal of Intelligence History*, 12 (2013): 113–33, at p. 118.

98. Hyde, *I Believed*, p. 212.

99. *Derby Daily Telegraph*, 24 October 1946, p. 12.

100. Memo by William Strang, 10 July 1951 in Annex A Report of Security Conference of Privy Counsellors, 30 November 1955, TNA CAB 134/1325.

101. Duff Cooper to Winston Churchill, 31 October 1943, TNA KV 4/251.

102. Herbert Morrison to Winston Churchill, 9 November 1943, TNA KV 4/251.

103. 'Communists engaged on secret work', by David Clarke, 21 October 1943, TNA KV 4/251.

104. C. Andrew, *The Defence of the Realm* (London, 2009), p. 279.

105. John Anderson to Herbert Morrison, 12 November 1943, TNA KV 4/251; Winston Churchill to Morrison, 13 November 1943, TNA KV 4/251.

106. Neville Chamberlin, 'Home Defence (Security) Executive', 27 May 1940, TNA CAB 66/8/2.

107. David Petrie to Alexander Maxwell, 29 December 1943, TNA KV 4/251.

108. Security Conference of Privy Counsellors 'Personnel Security Arrangements in the Civil Service', 6 December 1955, TNA CAB 134/1325.

109. Roger Hollis to D.B., 17 April 1947, TNA KV 4/251. In the same memo, Hollis stated that The Panel was effectively dead and that its chairman, Herbert Creedy, destroyed his papers regarding it.

110. R.H. Hollis to D.G., 1 October 1945, TNA KV 4/251.

111. Statement of Alan Nunn May, 15 February 1946, TNA KV 2/2212/4.

112. Statement of Alan Nunn May, 20 February 1946, TNA KV 2/2212/3.

113. JSM Washington to Cabinet Office, 21 February 1946, TNA CAB 126/303.

114. A. Goldberg, 'The atomic origins of the British nuclear deterrent', *International Affairs*, 20 (1964): 409–29, at p. 413.

115. Noel Stephen Paynter to John Oliver Archer, 21 March 1946, TNA KV 4/251.

116. Security service file, 'Alan Nunn May', undated, TNA KV 2/2209.

117. 'Spread of communism throughout the world and the extent of its direction from Moscow', JIC report, 18 November 1946, TNA CAB 81/134.

118. Minutes of 'Ad hoc ministerial meeting', 6 January 1947, TNA CAB 130/16.

119. Ministerial Committee on Subversive Activities, 'The employment of civil servants', 1 May 1947, TNA CAB 130/17.

120. Minutes of Working Party of Subversive Movements, 11 February 1947, TNA CAB 130/17.

121. Working Party on Subversive Movements, 'The nature and purpose of Soviet policy', 25 March 1947, TNA CAB 130/17.

122. Harold Caccia to Roger Hollis, 11 May 1946, TNA KV 4/251.

123. P. Corthorn, *In the Shadow of the Dictators* (London, 2006), p. 64.

124. Ministerial Committee on Subversive Activities, 'The employment of civil servants', 1 May 1947, TNA CAB 130/17.

125. Ministerial Committee on Subversive Activities, 'The employment of civil servants', 1 May 1947, TNA CAB 130/17.

126. A.V. Alexander to Clement Attlee, 20 December 1947, TNA PREM 8/946.

127. Clement Attlee to A.V. Alexander, 21 December 1947, TNA PREM 8/496.

128. Hansard, HC, vol. 448, cc. 1704–5 (15 March 1948).

129. *Western Morning News*, 16 March 1948, p. 3.

130. Hansard, HC, vol. 448, c. 1705 (15 March 1948).

131. *Lincolnshire Echo*, 25 March 1948, p. 1.

132. *Aberdeen Press and Journal*, 18 March 1948, p. 1.

133. Hansard, HC, vol. 448, c. 3396 (25 March 1948).

134. Liddell diary, 22 March 1948.

135. Hansard, HC, vol. 448, c. 3407 (25 March 1948).

136. *Falkirk Herald*, 31 March 1948, p. 7.

137. The tally of the card vote defeating the motion was 3,841,000 to 3,461,000.

138. Quoted from MI5 archives in Andrew, *Defence of the Realm*, p. 384.

139. Liddell diary, 19 March 1948.

140. M. Jago, *Clement Attlee* (London, 2017), p. 300.

141. Liddell diary, 7 April 1948; R. Aldrich, *GCHQ* (London, 2010), p. 368.

142. C. Andrew, *The Defence of the Realm* (London, 2009), p. 385.

143. C. Pincher, *Treachery Betrayals, Blunders and Cover-Ups* (London, 2011), p. 368.

144. R. Aldrich, *The Hidden Hand* (London, 2001), p. 118.

145. Liddell diary, 12 May 1948.

146. Liddell diary, 2 December 1948.

147. Liddell diary, 22 February 1949.

148. Liddell diary, 30 July 1948.

149. Liddell diary, 16 April 1948.

150. Minutes of Cabinet Committee on Subversive Activities meeting, 5 April 1950, TNA CAB 130/20.

151. Liddell diary, 16 April 1948.

152. *New York Times*, 24 April 1948, p. 7.

153. *New York Times*, 7 September 1948, p. 10.

154. Christopher Mayhew to Clement Attlee, 4 April 1949, Mayhew 4/1/2.

155. *New York Times*, 6 October 1948, p. 4.

156. Hansard, HC, vol. 460, cc. 556–7 (24 January 1949).

157. Minutes of Cabinet Committee on Subversive Activities meeting, 30 March 1949, TNA CAB 130/20.

158. Norman Brook to Clement Attlee, 7 December 1949, TNA PREM 8/946.

159. Minutes of Cabinet Committee on Subversive Activities meeting, 9 March 1949, TNA CAB 130/20.

160. C. Andrew, *The Defence of the Realm* (London, 2009), p. 385.

161. Minutes of Cabinet Committee on Subversive Activities meeting, 30 March 1949, TNA CAB 130/20.

162. Jago, *Attlee*, p. 301.

163. T. Bower, *The Perfect English Spy* (London, 1995), p. 93.

164. Liddell diary, 25 November 1949, TNA KV 4/471.

165. Liddell speculated that 'if war was coming in the next five years it was more likely to occur through subversion and infiltration'. Liddell diary, 24 October 1947.

166. Liddell diary, 24 September 1948.

167. Security Conference of Privy Counsellors, 'Personnel Security Arrangements in the Civil Service', 6 December 1955, TNA CAB 134/1325.

168. Peter Hennessy interview with Winnifrith, 31 July 1982.

169. C. Andrew, *The Defence of the Realm* (London, 2009), p. 393.

170. S. Turchetti, *The Pontecorvo Affair* (Chicago, IL, 2012), pp. 138–9.

171. Committee on Positive Vetting, 'Atomic Energy Security', 15 August 1951, TNA CAB 130/20.

172. Committee on Positive Vetting report, 27 October 1950, TNA CAB 130/20.

173. Minutes of Committee on Positive Vetting meeting, 13 November 1950, TNA CAB 130/20.

174. Committee on Positive Vetting report, 'Atomic energy security', 15 August 1951, TNA CAB 130/20.

175. Security Conference of Privy Counsellors, 'The role of the security service in personnel security', 7 December 1955, TNA CAB 134/1325.

176. Aldrich, *Hidden Hand*, p. 427.

177. K. Ewing, J. Mahoney and A. Moretta, *MI5, Cold War, and the Rule of Law* (Oxford, 2020), p. 259. The book estimated it could be as high as 11,447.

178. D. Caute, *The Great Fear* (New York, 1978), p. 275.

179. *New York Times*, 20 September 1952, p. 1.

180. *Londonderry Sentinel*, 8 November 1952, p. 2.

181. G. Goodman, '"Who is anti-American?" The British left and the United States, 1945–1956' (unpublished University College London PhD thesis, 1996), p. 251.

182. Liddell diary, 18 November 1947.

183. W. Ullrich, 'Preventing "peace": The British government and the second world peace congress', *Cold War History*, 11 (2011): 341–62, at p. 344.

184. *Belfast Newsletter*, 2 November 1950, p. 5.

185. *Dundee Courier*, 11 November 1950, p. 3.

186. Ullrich, 'Preventing peace', p. 355.

187. *Western Daily Press*, 20 November 1950, p. 1.

188. Memorandum by Pierson Dixon, 23 June 1951, TNA CAB 134/2.

189. Lomas, *Uneasy Relationship*, p. 186.

190. Official Committee on Communism (Home), Constitution and Terms of Reference of the Committee by Norman Brook, 7 June 1951, TNA CAB 21/4371.

191. 'Communism in the United Kingdom' by the Official Committee on Communism (Home), 16 December 1950, TNA, CAB 134/2.

192. 'Communism in the United Kingdom' by the Official Committee on Communism (Home), 16 December 1950, TNA, CAB 134/2.

193. Arthur Sanders to Norman Brook, 30 May 1951, TNA CAB 21/4371.

194. Pierson Dixon to Norman Brook, 5 May 1951, TNA CAB 21/4371.

195. C. Mayhew, *Time to Explain* (London, 1987), p. 108.

196. Clement Attlee to Christopher Mayhew, 14 June 1951, MS Attlee 121.

197. Christopher Mayhew to the editor of *The Times*, 20 February 1976, Mayhew 4/1/2.

198. Mayhew, *Time to Explain*, pp. 111–12.

199. For an example of Conquest's work for the IRD, see 'Communist trials: The technique of confession', in TNA FO 1110/335.

200. Christopher Mayhew to C.P.A. Warner, 21 January 1949, Mayhew 4/1/1; Wilford, 'Secret Cold War', p. 360.

201. Quoted in H. Wilford, 'The Information Research Department: Britain's secret Cold War weapon revealed', *Review of International Studies*, 24 (1998): 353–69, at p. 363.

202. A. Defty, *Britain, America and Anti-Communist Propaganda 1945–53* (London, 2004), p. 249.

203. For a copy of the list, see George Orwell to Celia Kirwan, 6 April 1949, TNA FO 1110/191.

204. Aldrich, *Hidden Hand*, p. 459.

205. Official Committee on Communism (Home) minutes, 24 March 1952, TNA CAB 134/737.

206. 'Possible anti-communist activities at home: View of the chiefs of staff', 14 October 1952, TNA 134/737.

207. Official Committee on Communism (Home) minutes, 1 December 1954, TNA CAB 134/739.

208. N.K. Reeve to D.R.J. Stephen, 11 March 1960, TNA CAB 21/4371.

209. David Heaton to Burke Trend, 2 January 1969, TNA CAB 165/432.

210. 'Rear window Cold War: The British ministry of propaganda', *Independent*, 26 February 1995.

211. Christopher Wilson to Margaret Thatcher, 8 February 1980, Mayhew 4/1/2.

212. 'UK government running "covert" propaganda campaign to stop Muslims joining Isis', *Independent*, 2 May 2016.

213. K. Payne, 'Winning the battle of ideas: Propaganda, ideology, and terror', *Studies in Conflict and Terrorism*, 32 (2009): 109–28, at pp. 109, 117.

214. A. Kundnani, *The Muslims Are Coming!* (New York, 2014), p. 164.

215. K. Ewing, J. Mahoney and A. Moretta, *MI5, Cold War, and the Rule of Law* (Oxford, 2020), p. 231.

Chapter 3

The Conservatives and the red menace

Communism today suppresses all freedom of worship and every other freedom wherever it can seize power. Communism is ruthless in its methods and worldwide activities. We in Britain have a special responsibility to guide and keep the world in the true path of freedom.[1]

—Anthony Eden

I very much doubt whether it is the communists in this country who are the root of all our troubles. They certainly have a large measure of assistance from fellow-travellers and others who give sympathetic aid to their views.[2]

—Winston Churchill

The return of the Conservatives to power in 1951 came at the height of the red scare in the US. In the US, Harry Truman and his allies fought almost daily charges of Joseph McCarthy and his compatriots. The McCarthyites claimed that numerous American institutions were filled with communist traitors and the president's administration was selling the nation out to both domestic and foreign enemies. At home, across the Atlantic, rumours of the fate of two highly placed civil servants, Donald Maclean and Guy Burgess, swept through the halls of Westminster and onto the front pages of the daily newspapers. Public speculations of communist agents fleeing with the nation's secrets were becoming more and more common. Concurrently for both countries, the novelty of the emerging Cold War had turned back into the familiarity of a hot one. In Korea, British and American soldiers fought the communist ideology not with words, but with bullets. 'The contrast between the East and West, between communism and democracy, between evil and Christianity, is approaching its climax', Field Marshal Bernard Montgomery warned the government in December 1951.[3] Nevertheless, under the premierships of Winston Churchill, and his handpicked successor Anthony Eden, domestic anti-communism did not widely deviate, at least directionally, from the path adopted by the preceding Labour government. Historian Richard Thurlow stressed 'it was the Labour, the "people's party", rather than the traditional Conservative's Blimpish views on communism that can more justifiably be compared to some of the more sinister aspects of McCarthyism'.[4] As Labour's leadership crossed to the opposition benches, their policies on governmental vetting, visa restrictions and calming domestic opposition to the Korean War were left to the Conservatives for implementation and/or continuation. To the surprise of few, the Churchill and Eden governments took up the mantle in enacting these initiatives and defending their need to the British populace. For his part, the increasingly frail Churchill relied on the committed anti-communist Cabinet Secretary Norman Brook for guidance on security matters, thus cementing previous policies enacted under Brook's direction to continue unabated.[5] The shining example of the continuation of these anti-communist measures was the Privy Counsellors' report commissioned by Eden defending the vetting procedures commissioned by the previous Labour government. From an ideological standpoint, the Conservatives, being the party of the right, held no sympathy for the communistic left.[6] Yet they did little to strengthen the campaign against it. In fact, in particular instances, they damaged the anti-communist efforts of the nation. During its time outside of government, 1945–51, the Conservative Party emphasised its anti-communist and pro-American stances when compared to other British political parties. But after the 1951 election, long-held mores regarding class injured the anti-communist credentials of the Conservatives.

Because of the circumstances and events of the age, the Attlee government found itself confronting the 'red menace' and sought to create measures to combat it. Conversely, the Churchill and Eden governments were obliged to navigate the events unleashed by the fears and anxieties this battle fostered. How ruling members of the Conservative government reacted to these demands for investigations particularly underlines the engrained views of social hierarchy that held sway inside the party. Many in the Conservative leadership still viewed the danger from communism originating from the faceless masses, not from the upper-class elite. This blind spot was evident in their response to investigating the aftermath of the Maclean and Burgess affair.

The first section of this chapter explores Conservative anti-communism as a campaign issue. In the 1945 and 1950 General Elections, the party sought to draw a link between socialism and communism for electoral advantage. Because of the stalwart anti-communist credentials of the Labour Party, neither time was the tactic successful. Also included here are efforts by the party to combat communism through independent means. Unbeknownst to the Conservatives, these measures mirrored those already being enacted by the Labour government – such as a committee to investigate domestic communism and inquiries into supposed red activities. The chapter then tracks how anti-communist measures enacted and proposed by the Labour government were continued by the subsequent Conservative administrations of Churchill and Eden with little alteration. It then delves into the theme of class and societal privilege and how these affected the search for Soviet agents inside the British government. When it came to hunting communists, in this specific instance, the issue of class and status blinded the Conservatives more than the protection of civil liberties. Despite evidence pointing to the existence of further communist penetration inside the British government, no action was taken to open an investigation into the matter. Meanwhile, Labour in opposition called for rooting out 'communists in government', while the Conservatives decried the call as a proposed 'witch hunt'. Here the Labour 'witch hunters' were proven correct.

Socialism equals communism

From 1945 until 1951, the Labour Party determined how the state dealt with domestic communism. Fundamentally, the Conservative leadership agreed with the anti-communist agenda the Attlee government put forth. However, like in the US, where influential Republicans charged the Democratic administration with being woefully negligent in combating the 'red menace', the Conservatives made similar charges. On 5 March 1946, speaking from the heartland of the US, Winston Churchill cemented his credentials as a cold warrior of the utmost calibre. In the now famous 'Sinews of Peace' speech, while highlighting the explicit dangers of a totalitarian Soviet Union and decrying the iniquities of communist ideology, Churchill warned of the external threat that the adherents of Marxist-Leninist philosophy posed.[7] For many Churchillian supporters, on both sides of the Atlantic, up until the present day, this speech encapsulates the heart of the emerging struggle between East and West of the initial postwar period.[8] Yet, only a year earlier, he delivered a radio broadcast that champions of Churchill's legacy are less likely to cite or emphasise. In this 4 June 1945 transmission, which Churchill used to open the Conservative General Election campaign, he attempted to highlight the perils of another adversary to the British people. In the wartime prime minister's words, this enemy to British freedom was not a foreign threat, as it had been for the last seven years or would be again in his speech from a small town in Missouri, but one much closer to home, and of a domestic nature. It was the potential electoral success of the Labour Party. More specifically, Churchill denounced the socialist political ideology promoted by former members of his coalition government, who were now members of an opposition party. Although the Conservative leader did not openly use the term 'communism', the direct implication of voting for the Labour Party remained crystal clear. Not mincing words, Churchill declared, 'I must tell you that a socialist policy is abhorrent to the British ideas of freedom ... there can be no doubt that socialism is inseparably inter-woven with totalitarianism and the abject worship of the states.' Further adding to this sentiment, he stated, 'No socialist government conducting the entire life and industry of the country could afford to allow, free, sharp or violently-worded expressions of public discontent. They would have to fall back on some form of Gestapo.'[9] The implicit meaning of the broadcast boiled down to the suggestion that voting for a Labour government would bring the UK one step closer to a communist-style dictatorship. As the political fallout from the speech showed, few British citizens found this accusation credible. Churchill's personal physician noted in his diary the speech 'had not gone down well with anybody' and that 'no one agreed with the line that Winston had taken'.[10] For his part, Attlee dismissed it as a 'secondhand version' of the academic views of the free-market econo-mist Friedrich Hayek.[11] Although considered by most contemporaries and historians as a political misstep, Churchill never regretted or repudiated the speech, and only lamented that he should have omitted the word 'Gestapo' and substituted in its place the NKVD – the Soviet equivalent.[12] Dubbed Churchill's 'Gestapo speech' or 'crazy broadcast', this incident is one of the first highly publicised cases of political red-baiting from the Anglo-American world during the early Cold War period.

Although Conservative attacks continued to occur, they paled next to the charges batted about across the Atlantic. After his infamous 'Gestapo broadcast', Churchill and other party leaders were more cautious in their charges. Very rarely did they directly charge specific Labour pol-iticians. What transpired instead was an attempt to link the ideology of socialism to the eventuality of a communist takeover, forgoing any specific attacks on Labour itself. The associating of communism with one's political opponents was not solely a Conservative tactic. In 1948, Herbert Morrison classified communism as a right-wing ideology more in line with Conservative ways of thinking: 'I have never admitted, and I admit less and less, that the communists are on the left. They are on the right.'[13] The same year, Attlee stated at a May Day rally in Plymouth that 'there can be no greater mistake than to imagine that the Communist Party is a party of the left ... the communists are extreme reactionaries'.[14] Conservatives found it increasingly difficult to criticise the Labour Party when its leadership were aggressively purging its own elected MPs accused of communist sympathies. In fact, Churchill praised Labour after its 1946 decision barring communists from the party, stating he agreed 'with every word' of Attlee's attacks on the CPGB. In 1947, during a Commons debate over conscription, he vowed to support the Labour government 'on all occasions when they are challenged by the crypto-communists and pacifists and other trends of left-wing opinion, which they have exploited to the full in bygone days, and which they now very naturally and healthily resent'.[15] As the Cold War increasingly took hold, Labour's anti-communist credentials were becoming impossible for the Conservatives to dispute. An unofficial endorsement of Labour's anti-communism came in March 1950 from Sir Paul Dukes, an ex-spy and expert on Soviet affairs. Dukes proclaimed that the Kremlin despised Attlee and Labour, whom the Soviets classified as renegades, far more than Churchill and the Conservatives.[16] Dukes's assertion carried weight since he was the most successful MI6 agent to operate in the Soviet Union during the interwar period and a celebrity for his endeavours. Sources closer to the heart of the Conservative Party agreed that Labour's war on communism was genuine. Marjorie Maxse, in an inter-party memo to the general director, gave her assurance of Labour's commitment to the cause. Maxse, chief organisation officer of the party, reminded her superior, 'Transport House, as you know, is dealing very energetically with any suspected communist sympathisers'.[17] 'Nothing could be more unfair, or for that matter shortsighted', Conservative MP Oliver Lyttelton wrote to Churchill in 1949, 'than to pretend that the present socialist government is other than a bitter enemy of communism.'[18] By all accounts, Churchill and the Conservative leadership could find little to criticise in Labour's efforts combating communism. In 1946, Harold Macmillan went so far as to praise Herbert Morrison publicly for his stalwart anti-communism.[19] Despite praising Labour in their efforts, the Conservative Party, seemingly for political reasons, still elected to focus on the perceived ideological connection between socialism and communism.

'We are resolutely opposed to the communist way of life', Attlee affirmed during a 1948 Commons debate on foreign affairs. He continued, 'I am quite sure that Mr. Stalin is enough of a realist to appreciate the complete failure during the difficult interwar years of the communist creed to make any effective advance in this country.' The prime minister suggested 'he should give up that idea that somehow or other this country is going to turn to communism'.[20] Churchill and his followers did not dispute Attlee's sincerity or choose to endorse stricter measures for combating Marxist-Leninism in the UK. In fact, the only suggested policy the Conservative Party recommended at their 1948 party conference was a more intensive campaign to publicise communist subversion – the same aim as Christopher Mayhew's recently created IRD. In July the same year, the party formed a Committee on Communist and Fascist Activities whose objective was to report to the Conservative Executive Committee on the political aims and tactics of these subversive groups and also recommend methods of combating them. It was eerily similar to the Committee on Communism (Home), which the Labour government formed four years later. In its preliminary report the Conservative Committee on Communist and Fascist Activities conceded some credit to their political opponents and admonished their fellow party members for their inaction:

> In the past the Conservative Party has been remiss in not issuing well-informed specifically anti-communist literature. While maintaining the outward appearances and practices of a legal political organization, the Communist Party is a conspiracy. Until recently the leaders of the socialist party were more ready to recognise that fact than the leaders of the other political parties, though they have proven themselves incapable of dealing with the conspiracy so recognised ... The ignorance of the nature and extent of the danger is almost as widespread among Conservatives as among members of other parties.[21]

The simplistic answer of the committee to right these past wrongs was the hiring of a 'full-time expert on communism whose special task should be the study of the conspiracy from the national and international aspect'. In turn, it 'condemned absolutely' the idea which some Conservatives had supported of a governmental outlawing of the Communist Party, arguing: 'The effect of banning communism would be to ban anti-communism which would be a bad thing.'[22] Shortly after its formation, the committee ceased to exist. Its duties of researching and reporting on the subject of communism for the party were turned over to the Conservative Research Department, though in its short lifespan it did have an impact on the party's campaign strategy. The committee voiced support for the anti-communist actions of the Labour administration, but suggested 'that a socialist government increases the danger and conspiratorial power of communism' by reasoning 'the socialist preaching of the class war creates the condition upon which communism thrives'.[23]

This supposition, of socialism leading to communism, was a mainstay of Conservative rhetoric against the Labour Party, despite the overwhelming evidence of Labour's support for anti-communist measures. 'Communism is only socialism ruthlessly and vigorously applied by revolutionary instead of legal methods', Harold Macmillan publicly stated in 1949, 'hard instead of soft, red instead of pink.'[24] The same year, Conservative MP Alan Gomme-Duncan stated:

> People say the great danger today is communism and I am convinced they are right. The immediate danger in Great Britain, however, is not the Communist Party, but the nursery in which communists are bred – the socialist party. Let us attack the nursery and the plant will wither. That is what we have got to go for hammer and tongs.[25]

Only a few months earlier, Anthony Eden surmised that while 'many socialists in this country are convinced, stout-hearted opponents of communism and yet to others, it must seem that communism is the only logical conclusion to full state socialism'.[26] During a speech in February 1950, voicing the same sentiment, Churchill warned his audience: 'The British socialists do not appreciate clearly enough that socialism is a preliminary state to communism and communism is the accomplishment of socialism.'[27] Speaking to an American audience the previous year, he warned of how easily communism could take hold:

> [A] church of communist adepts whose missionaries are in every country as a fifth column, in your country, ours, everywhere, and so on within every country is a fifth column ... with a feeling that they may be running a risk, but if their gamble comes off they will be the masters of the whole land in which they are a minority at the present time. They will be the Quislings with power to rule and dominate all the rest of their fellow countrymen.[28]

The timing of these attacks in 1949 and 1950 is telling. With a General Election approaching, the tone of the Conservatives turned from praising the anti-communist credentials of the Labour Party to claiming it sought democratic socialism, not a 'third-way' brand of social democracy. Hence Labour's brand of socialism was just a harbinger of and gateway to a Marxist dictatorship. The baseless charges by leading Conservative politicians were an orchestrated campaign conceived by the party to win votes, not to protect the nation from the 'red menace'.

In January 1949, Mark Chapman-Walker, chief publicity officer of the Conservative Party, presented to Director General Stephen Pierssene a propaganda plan for the likelihood of a 1950 General Election. The plan consisted of three themes which the party would emphasise through posters, newspapers articles, speeches and radio broadcasts. The themes were (a) state control versus the individual, (b) constructive conservatism and (c) a Conservative government for security. Under the subheading for security, Chapman-Walker wrote:

> This again must be a constructive theme. The defence of the West against communism, and the defence of British institutions against communism at home, cannot be considered apart from imperial policy and an adequate defence policy. The socialists are not an effective force against communism – on the contrary, they provide the 'culture' in which this germ best develops – and their pre-war record shows them to be incapable of taking the necessary measures for Imperial defence. The Conservative Party, on the other hand, is the national party; at a time of crisis the nation turns to the Tories.[29]

The leadership of the Conservative Party accepted Chapman-Walker's plan. This 'constructive' campaign linking the Labour Party to the likelihood of a communist police state was a coordinated effort. Party candidates mentioned the theme of socialism as a stepping-stone to communism in 32 per cent of their pre-election addresses.[30] Official campaign posters outlined the theme in no uncertain terms; they read: 'Thought for to-day: Socialism leads to Communism'. In addition to attacking Labour, the Conservatives specifically targeted the seats of the supposed crypto-communists which Labour had expelled: D.N. Pritt, John Platts-Mills, L.J. Solly and Lester Hutchinson.[31]

How Labour and many on the pro-Labour left countered red-baiting was not in disparaging the Conservatives' use of the tactic, but instead arguing their charges were predicated on a groundless assumption. Attlee, Morrison and others exerted little effort in denouncing the Conservatives for their accusations. Instead, they chose to defend two central tenets of British socialism as effective tools against the 'red menace'. They contrasted both democratic socialism and social democracy with the evils of communism. In an editorial denouncing Conservative attempts at red-baiting during the gear-up to the 1950 General Election, the pro-Labour *Socialist Commentary* condemned the 'deliberate confusing of socialism and communism' by Churchill in a recent speech. The magazine called it a dishonest and mischievous tactic. However, the majority of the article addressed the matter by arguing against communism, and pointing out how democratic socialism existed as its 'complete and irreconcilable antithesis'. The confusion of Churchill, and many 'within the labour movement itself', the article maintained, was that they believed that communists and socialists were working towards the same aims – the overthrow of capitalism – but only by different means. Such was not the case. The central takeaway of the editorial was quite simple: communism lacked the fundamental concept of human dignity – Labour socialism did not. It surmised, 'the corner-stone of [Labour's] programme has been this respect for the dignity of all human beings', but through 'communist collectivisation', the Soviet government 'had ridden roughshod over every facet of human dignity'.[32] In a later issue, the magazine maintained that such a difference between British socialism and Soviet communism did not come from the misappropriation of Marxist ideals, but from fundamental flaws ingrained into that theory. 'Marxism was never a guide for the techniques of government', Lucjan Blit, a regular contributor to the *Socialist Commentary*, conceded in the December 1950 issue of the magazine, yet added, 'but neither is it a guide in any respect for the advance of social democracy.'[33] In the same speech in which he denounced them as reactionaries, Attlee condemned communists for their prior attempts 'everywhere ... to undermine and destroy the parties of social democracy'.[34] In 1950, Ian Mikardo, a member of Labour's NEC and a future party chairman, stated his party's obsession in shoring up its anti-communist credentials was ironically playing into the hands of their opponents – both the communists and the Conservatives. Mikardo contended:

> If a Labour leader can deliver a long and pungent speech of which every sentence is about communism, and which doesn't, by so much as a word, make any mention of conservatism, that tells you where the real danger lies in the present situation and at the next election ... Just as Soviet imperialism seeks to overthrow social democracy by diverting us into military expenditure and away from our positive task of work rehabilitation, so British communism achieves its only victory in diverting the Labour Party into negative anti-communism and away from our positive social and economic programme.[35]

The Conservative effort against Labour in 1950 fell short. The election results saw Labour holding onto power, but with a decreased majority. For their part, Labour termed their returned majority as actually a victory against communism. In their electoral campaign, they sought to define a Conservative victory as an outcome wished for by the CPGB. A Labour flier entitled *What Is the Communist After?* claimed 'communists would let the Tories in. It's an old communist trick. In pre-Hitler Germany they worked with the Nazis to bring down a socialist government'.[36] Speaking after the election, Herbert Morrison called the results a 'verdict of the British people on the communists and their hangers-on'. Morrison went on:

> This verdict was utterly clear and may prove of historic importance. Far from being weakened by this election the authority of the British government in world affairs has been strengthened by the

electorate's clear-cut rejection of communism and of anyone who has any truck with communism. Those who have sought to weaken us and to strengthen anti-democratic influences abroad on vital matters of world affairs are out. The communists put their maximum effort into this campaign ... [But] for every one British voter who supported them there were over 300 who voted anti-communist.[37]

Both the Labour and Conservative Parties' efforts against communism continued, but in the forthcoming 1951 General Election the Conservatives chose not to revive their anti-communist attacks against Labour. Their attempts to red-bait did not produce for their party any electoral advantage. Ultimately, it only resulted in Labour displaying more vigour in its rhetoric against their mutual enemy – namely, the communists.

Central Office witch hunt

Like the Labour Party, the Conservatives considered, but to a lesser extent, the threat of communist infiltration in general society as a serious matter – so much so that they conducted their own inquiries into the subject. While the Labour government instituted a formal investigative body – the Committee for Communism (Home) – the Conservatives used party connections. The Central Office requested party associations and constituency offices on the local level to 'send all information about communist activities' to it, since it had a 'special section dealing with this'.[38] Working – in the same respects as an intelligence agency – Conservative Party members not only conducted inquiries ordered by the Central Office, they also infiltrated and surveilled CPGB meetings.[39] Directing these ongoings was Marjorie Maxse. As a former MI6 section chief of staff during the Second World War, Maxse was ably fitted for such a mission.[40] What she discovered attests more to the heightened paranoia over communism than to any type of grand conspiracy conducted by the CPGB. The cases she examined ranged from the trivial to the farcical.

In 1949, former MP and then-candidate Irene Ward wrote to Maxse, detailing her concern over communist membership in the National Union of Seamen. Ward recounted how a 'reliable family' told her that as much as 30 per cent of the union were communists. She urged that the party needed to sort out the situation. After looking into the matter, Maxse discovered the number of communist members in the union to be 'nearer to 3% than 30%', and its leadership was, in fact, very anti-communist.[41] The same year the Central Office eyed the British Legion with suspicion, claiming communists were attempting to take over the organisation and 'have succeeded in obtaining office in local branches and being elected delegates to national conferences'. An inter-party memo addressed to Maxse claimed communists sought to establish a federation of 'ex-servicemen to use in connection with their bogus peace campaigns'.[42] Alarmed by the prospect, Maxse contacted the British Legion. Answering on behalf of the Legion was its president Ian Fraser – a Conservative Party member and MP. 'I must say that I have seen very little evidence that they [communists] use the British Legion in order to spread communism', Fraser responded. Defending a number of the Legion's communist members, he argued: 'some of these men are genuinely proud of their army service and work for the British Legion voluntarily because they like to serve in this way'. Nevertheless, he did reassure her that 'We are constantly watching the matter, however.'[43]

Some of the other cases the Central Office dealt with were of a much more dubious nature. One involved an accusation by a worried party member in Glasgow that communists were using evangelists for propaganda purposes. Instead of dismissing the bizarre allegation outright, the Central Office suggested that the local Scottish association send an 'observer' to one of the evangelists' gatherings and report back findings.[44] After having 'thoroughly investigated' the charge, the secretary of the Scottish Unionist Association reported: 'there is no substance whatever in it'. 'I know Mr. Thomson personally', the secretary added about the party member who made the accusation. 'He would like all communists to be exterminated. As a matter of fact, he is the type of Unionist who makes socialists and communists.'[45] An even odder complaint involved Blackwell Booksellers. A member of the South Shields Conservative Association claimed the company distributed communist propaganda through its book deliveries.[46] The party member stated he received a parcel of books from Blackwell wrapped in a copy of a communist broadsheet. The Central Office determined 'it would appear that a packer employed ... is inserting communist propaganda in books sent out'. A Central Office agent contacted Blackwell over the matter. Replying on behalf of the company was Basil Blackwell, the chairman and the son of its founder. It is not hard to imagine from Blackwell's response that he probably found the affair quite amusing:

> The facts are, we get scores of publishers' parcels every day, and the wrapping of these, very often consisting of unsold sheets of books, is put within handy reach of the packers who whip it up indiscriminately to make the lining of the parcels. It is not impossible that a

Labour minister might get from us a parcel protected inside by odd sheets of *The Right Road for Britain*. Imperial Caesar, dead and turned to clay, as you will remember, may serve to plug a vent-hole; and, in reverse, the bloody nonsense of the communist may serve to protect an honest book from damage.[47]

Maxse considered Blackwell's answer 'quite reasonable' but cautioned that the matter still needed watching.[48] Another incident arose when the local Golders Green chapter of the CPGB proposed adding a speed limit on a dangerous road. In 1951, the general director of the Unionist Party in Scotland reported members of the British Correspondence Chess Association were using chess move communications to spread communist propaganda. All such reports were taken seriously and investigated.

One unsettling level of extrajudicial oversight the party wielded was the collection of private information on individual members of the CPGB, which they used in attempts to hinder their livelihood. In particular incidents the Central Office investigated persons who were informed on by party members as potential troublemakers. One telling example dealt with the chief engineer at Ford Company's Works in Dagenham. His brother, a Conservative, reported the engineer as a likely saboteur. After collecting his home address, work history and political affiliations, the Central Office concluded that 'no action is called by us'.[49] The possibility of measures being taken against a member of the public is quite telling in its own right. In September 1950, fears arose concerning communists on the faculty of a Trent Park Training College indoctrinating students. Finding a 'remedy' to the problem was discussed among the various Conservatives in the Central Office.

After its narrow victory in the 1951 General Election, the Conservative Party sought to bolster its anti-communist propaganda and tapered off its private hunt for communist threats in society. A year earlier on 4 July 1950, the party established an office committee entitled 'Party Literature on Communism', which appeared to have succeeded the Committee on Communist and Fascist Activities. Its sole purpose was to 'govern [the] production of the party's literature on the subject of communism'.[50] In September 1951, the Conservative Political Centre published a thirty-seven-page pamphlet entitled *Communism in Great Britain*, which accused Marxism and its followers of a litany of evils.[51] George E. Christ, the editor of the Conservative *Weekly News Letter* and former chief publicity officer of the Conservative Central Office, argued that with the party back in power it needed to shift its propaganda focus against Labour onto communism. Commenting on the party's need for an updated strategy, he wrote:

Until now I have not been very much interested in anti-communist propaganda. I felt that our job was to get the socialist government out, and that we ought to concentrate on them. Communists were an embarrassment to the socialist government, and we could rely on Transport House doing the job for us. Now that we are in power the situation has changed. On political questions we can expect the communists and socialists to be more or less allies, while in the field of direct action troubles fermented by the communists will very much embarrass the Conservative government, and will be secretly welcomed by the socialist opposition.[52]

The cause of the anti-communist measures of the party shifting towards propaganda, rather than more direct involvement, occurred in 1951. Marjorie Maxse retired this year from her post in the party. After her departure, the reportage of party investigations tapered off. Her successor in dealing with communism activities was Sylvia Sackville, the vice-chairwoman of the party and wife to David Maxwell Fyfe. Unlike the ex-MI6 officer Maxse, Sackville showed little enthusiasm for the cloak-and-dagger-type investigations conducted by her predecessor. Alongside with the change of personnel, the status of the party as a whole changed. The October 1951 General Election brought the Conservatives back into government and with this the power to investigate any type of communist activity through official means. No longer were the party's private investigations necessary. Any concerns could now go directly to the Cabinet Level Committee on Communism (Home) which continued to function under the new government.

Policy continuation from Labour

The defeat of Labour in the 1951 General Election left it for the Conservative government of Winston Churchill to implement positive vetting. As mentioned previously, the transition of power did little initially to undermine the vetting process. However, when further details emerged regarding the missing diplomats Donald Maclean and Guy Burgess, this forced the Conservatives to contemplate adding even more security measures. Despite how 'distasteful' they found vetting, pressure from the US gave them little choice. In his authorised history of MI5, Christopher Andrew stated 'the main pressure for extending positive vetting ... came from the United States, whose concerns about weaknesses in British security were strengthened by the defection of Burgess and Maclean'.[53] The two main factors pushing the Churchill government to expand the vetting procedures were pressure from the US and the initial stages of the programmes which were already put into place by the preceding Labour administration. Regardless of British reservations about vetting, Churchill needed to press forward. In January 1952, he announced the expansion of positive vetting. Despite logistical issues, MI5 were instructed to 'operate the PM's purge to the utmost of [its] ability'.[54] The FO took a dim view of the effectiveness of these new measures: 'Positive vetting, while the best safe-guard so far devised, will not necessarily reveal the skilful and dedicated communist agent.' Nevertheless, after the Maclean and Burgess affair, the ministry grudgingly admitted: 'The Russians are known to be very anxious to penetrate the Foreign Office now.'[55] The question shortly arose of whether this new extended vetting should include cabinet ministers. Churchill baulked at the suggestion, unlike Attlee, who confessed later in life that he felt such a measure was more than justified.[56]

Another example of how the American way of thinking influenced the British security apparatus was when a proposal arose about granting MI5 policing powers like those held by the FBI in the US. With the flight of the two high-profile civil servants, the danger of future suspects also fleeing was considered substantial. Therefore, it was thought that the security service should have the ability to detain individuals deemed flight risks. In August 1952, the new home secretary, David Maxwell Fyfe, organised a committee to examine such a proposal.[57] Headed by Norman Brook, the committee drafted a parliamentary bill legalising the detention of persons suspected of violating the Official Secrets Act. Brook argued the measure would give 'political advantage' in escaping 'American criticism' over past failures of the British government concerning security-related affairs. The proposal did not move forward. This was not because of concerns based on civil liberties but the ever-present concern of public outrage to such a new law. The government feared the potential of 'damaging criticism' if it applied such 'cat and mouse' procedures to such persons who had not yet 'any criminal charge against them'.[58]

Heightened tensions over security matters brought another delicate issue to the fore of the government under the Conservatives. By the 1950s, across the Atlantic, anti-communist campaigners were explicitly linking homosexuality with an engrained proclivity for communist subversion and Soviet sympathies. Thus, gay and lesbian people employed by the US government were perceived as threats. In 1953, through an executive order, President Eisenhower officially legalised the termination of homosexual people's employment for being security risks; the new law caused hundreds of State Department employees to lose their jobs and sparked thousands of firings of individuals throughout other sectors of the federal government. This moral panic over LGBT employees and their purging from governmental jobs is now known as the 'lavender scare'.

Such a fear manifested in the UK as well, stoked by governmental attempts to placate American sensibilities over the matter. In 1951, MI5's head of departmental security produced a list of justifications for the vetting of homosexual people in public service. He generalised these into the following claims which he surmised homosexual people typically held:

(a) Maladjusted to the social environment and may therefore be of an unstable character;
(b) they stick together and are backward in giving information even though it is their duty to do so;
(c) in so far as their activities are felonious they are at least in theory open to blackmail by a hostile intelligence agency.[59]

The following year, Foreign Secretary Anthony Eden approved a statement of general principles to deal with what FO mandarins colloquially called 'the homosexual problem'.[60] These guidelines stated that when evidence of 'guilt is clear' and where it is evident that the offender 'has brought public discredit' on the FO, the individual would be 'dealt with' under 'disciplinary regulations'. This meant probable dismissal from their position. If 'guilt is confessed or otherwise clearly established', but had not been brought to the public's attention, then the policy stated it was best 'to warn the officer that if any further case of homosexual practices comes to notice he will have to leave the service'. Mere 'gossip among colleagues ... sufficient to arouse suspicion of homosexual practices' was grounds for a full investigation into an individual. If such 'stories persist' – true or not – the directive stated the usefulness of the accused needed to be considered 'diminished' and any 'future appointments will naturally have to be carefully considered'.[61] The measures would almost certainly have been more draconian if Robert Vansittart still reigned as permanent secretary at the ministry. Vansittart wrote that alongside communism and *Deutschtum* (Germanness), he held an 'illiberal' abhorrence for homosexuality as well.[62]

In 1955, the political flap over the Maclean and Burgess defections forced Eden, now prime minister, to appoint a committee of Privy Counsellors to review security procedures, which produced a white paper in 1956. Part of the vetting protocols which the committee considered with 'special care' was the question of homosexuality. As in the US, some of its members explicitly linked sexual orientation with the question of loyalty. Lord Jowitt suggested that those accused individuals who displayed 'character defects' should be more thoroughly investigated for communist tendencies 'to decide whether the two different facets can properly be regarded as having a cumulative effect'.[63] The FO advised the committee that thus far it did not think it 'appropriate to lay down any hard and fast rules' and dealt with allegations on a case-by-case basis. The lack of a formal policy did not mean the FO did not take the matter seriously. It labelled 'practising homosexuals' as 'serious security risks' because of their being liable to blackmail, thus 'any members of the service suspected of indulging such tendencies' were 'carefully watched'.[64] The deliberations of the Privy Counsellors showed that they were opposed to homosexual people in the FO for a much more trivial reason than national security. The committee stated with regards to homosexual people:

> The security risk arising from the possibility of blackmail was not so important as the fact that the individual might be the subject of scandal when posted abroad, and that foreigners, particularly Americans, would not trust him if he were known to be, or suspected to be, homosexual.[65]

As was often the case on matters of security, the driving motivation for the banning of homosexual people from FO posts came from a desire to placate the US. Fears born and bred in the US again governed British official policy. In the final report, the probation against homosexuality was judicially worded. It was listed with a number of other 'character defects' such as drunkenness, addiction to drugs and 'other forms of loose living' which may 'affect a man's reliability'.[66]

The Privy Counsellors on the committee were much less circumspect when addressing the dangers posed by other elements. They assessed that 'today the chief security risk is that presented by communism'. 'The risk is not confined to members of the Communist Party', stated their report, 'but extends to sympathisers with communism.' The white paper gauged that governmental security protocols already in place were adequate, but more effort was required to implement them more effectively: 'We are dismayed to find what a small proportion of positive vetting which needs to be done has so far been carried out.' Also, it recommended that the primary responsibility of the vetting procedures was 'to identify the members of the British Communist Party, to be informed of its activities and to identify that wider body of those who are both sympathetic to communism, or susceptible to communist pressure', since these 'present a danger to security'.[67] In defending the established procedures, the report shielded the government's 'right to continue the practice of tilting the balance in favour of offering greater protection to the security of the state rather than in the direction of safeguarding the rights of the individual'.[68]

After the announcement of the Privy Counsellors' report on security, opposition to vetting rose enough to affect mainstream politics. Speaking of the white paper's recommendation of supporting the protection of the state over civil liberties, a Labour MP stated: 'What appals me about this is that this sentence might very well have been written by Senator McCarthy.'[69] In October 1956, at the 55th Annual Conference of the Labour Party held in Blackpool, an amendment was introduced to a document entitled 'Personal Freedom'. It held a five-point plan intended to protect subjects of vetting:

1. Rules governing employment on security-work should be approved by the parliament and made known to every person engaged upon it.
2. No person should be removed from his employment on a mendacious charge.
3. Every person suspected of being a security risk shall be advised in writing of the charges against him.
4. A right of appeal to three high court judges who, sitting in camera, shall examine the security officers who brought the charge.
5. This court, if it has evidence of misconduct in the administration of security organizations, shall report the matter, through the Lord Chancellor, to the Privy Council.[70]

The plan was the brainchild of a new pressure group called the Campaign for the Limitation of Secret Police Powers. Labour MPs Benn Levy and Will Griffiths headed the campaign and its sponsoring council included Aneurin Bevan, Michael Foot and Kingsley Martin. The group formed over the issue of John Lang, a solicitor who was dismissed from private employment because of his marriage to a former member of the Communist Party. The *Spectator* wrote: 'Lang's case may yet turn out to have been the last straw on the patient back of public opinion.'[71] This did not prove to be the case. Despite the campaign for governmental reform of the purge and vetting protocols, governmental and industrial vetting procedures against communists and other leftists stayed firmly in place. Since the mid-1950s the use of positive and negative vetting have remained routine procedures that those working or seeking employment in sectors of the civil service and the intelligence and military branches have had to endure. These security regulations are now considered a necessary evil – effectively, they are now a sign of the times – and few today argue that the continuation of these measures is unwarranted.

In 1952, the Conservative government also standardised the unofficial ban on foreigners wishing to attend any functions or conferences associated with the WPC or what was then being identified as the 'world peace movement'. Instead of the ad-hoc admissions policy under Labour, the new home secretary, David Maxwell Fyfe, took a zero-tolerance position on the issue. After taking office, he had to consider the admission of non-Britons to an upcoming meeting of the World Federation of Scientific Workers and a Youth Peace Festival – both events were closely tied to the peace movement supported by the Soviet Union. The tactic Maxwell Fyfe took for this blanket omission policy rested not on regarding these potential visitors as a 'direct danger to security or to industrial peace' or asking 'were there any grounds peculiar to individual delegates for excluding them?' He concluded that allowing any foreigners to participate in peace movement activities on British soil would weaken efforts by the FO to expose the movement as an instrument for Soviet policy and 'mislead people in this country'.[72] However, the new procedure did allow for foreign communists to attend meetings organised by CPGB, as long as the event did not develop into a large international gathering. In 1954, the Home Office refused all foreigners who attempted to attend a conference hosted by 'Teachers for Peace'. Unaware of this decree, many teachers who arrived at various airports and seaports were immediately turned away and denied entry. A seventy-six-year-old delegate from Germany who came for the conference was detained in the airport detention block and had his cell patrolled by armed guards. When questioned about why these teachers were barred from entry, the Home Office stated they did not need to give specific reasons.[73] This policy laid out by the home secretary remained in place for subsequent years.

The Philby affair

While analysing the anti-communist responses in the UK and the US, Herbert Hyman identified a key feature that separated the two cultures. 'At the popular level', posed the Columbia University professor, 'it may be in the area of deference, not tolerance, that we will find one key to the puzzle of the political tolerance that emerged in England in the fifties.'[74] Although the Conservatives supported Attlee's purge procedures, they, like many others, viewed official vetting as somehow un-British and unpleasant. Prior to the Cold War, recruitment to the civil service involved a relaxed process of personal contacts, privilege and school ties – effectively an 'old boys' network.[75] Class, cultural capital and deference to prestigious educational institutions played a larger role in attaining a position in the security services and government jobs than ideology, discretion and political reliability. This notion permeated throughout the British political landscape, often blinding inquiries into individuals and making ministers wary of implementing strong vetting processes.[76] A sense that a person's societal position or pedigree could determine their loyalty did not entirely leave the British mindset during the early Cold War period. The blinding power of class and privilege affected the judgement of many whose occupation was to root out security risks. Even when evidence of irregularities and purported espionage mounted up against certain government officials, they were considered by many of their peers as 'hav[ing] been given an unfair shake'. This prejudice existed outside the Conservative Party, but it had less of a hold inside Labour ranks, a fact that rankled some. Writing in his diary in 1946, Duff Cooper lamented that 'the lack of the old school tie may prove the undoing of the Labour Party and so finally of our governmental system'.[77] Unbeknownst to Cooper, forthcoming events pertaining to the Cambridge spy ring proved the opposite opinion better suited the facts.

Evident during Labour's years in power, this deference to class persisted throughout the 1950s. Conservatives did not diverge from the anti-communist measures and policies constructed under Attlee. Yet they could not fathom that the ranks of the British establishment could possibly be a breeding ground for communist-motivated treason. However, by the time the Conservatives regained power in 1951, the proof that this worldview rested on false premises was increasingly evident. The embarrassment and shock after the disappearance of Donald Maclean and Guy Burgess shifted the attitudes of many in the British establishment, but not all. Although the defection of these highly placed government officials happened on Labour's watch, the Conservatives refused to investigate the matter further openly. Both in Transport House and Washington, DC, talk of an attempted Tory cover-up and whitewashing of the affair circulated.[78] Unlike in the US, where the Republicans targeted Alger Hiss, the archetypical Ivy League-educated member of the political elite, the Conservatives and the British establishment shielded the upper-class Cambridge graduate Kim Philby in 1955.

The 1955 public debate over Philby is the quintessential example of Conservative deference to position and class overshadowing security concerns; a point which scholars have yet to make. Although the life and times of the infamous spy have been well recounted, the 1955 Commons debate is one key event of his life that rarely receives the attention it deserves. Even with the copious amounts of published works on Philby, it is still quite an unexamined turning point in contemporary British history. The affair both contextualises how one aspect of class worked in the framework of anti-communism of the era and sets the stage for a growing paranoia that more Philbys – namely, undetected traitors in high places – were in government working for a much redder and less free UK; such paranoia lasted deep into the final decades of the Cold War. The affair held all the hallmarks of a would-be McCarthyite moment, typified by an accuser flinging reckless accusations of treason and communist subversion. While the atmosphere and circumstances appeared straight out of a meeting of the HUAC in Washington, DC, it occurred in the House of Commons. Marcus Lipton, Labour MP for Brixton, accused the government of whitewashing and refusing to investigate thoroughly the charges that the 'third man' tipping off the flight of Burgess and Maclean was Kim Philby.[79] On 7 November 1955, he demanded a full and public investigation into communist penetration of the civil and security services. Charged with making slanderous statements against Philby, Lipton was viciously attacked for his seemingly outrageous accusations. No attack was more stinging than that by Richard Brooman-White, Conservative MP from Rutherglen. He stated in a heated debate with Lipton that:

> After listening to the hon. and gallant member [Lipton], one is at least quite clear where he stands on that. He is in favour of acting on suspicion, of smearing on suspicion, by directing public suspicion on to an individual [Philby] against whom nothing at all has been proved. We must leave it to his own conscience to straighten out what that may cost in personal suffering to the wife, children and friends of the person involved.[80]

These very poignant words rang false once the details of the Philby case became publicly known. Brooman-White's defence of Philby did not only come from a sense of fair play but a personal motivation as well. Philby obtained a wartime position with the MI6 through the direct intervention of Brooman-White. Philby recounted that a friend, Tomás Harris, had placed a call to Brooman-White and 'the old-boy network began to operate'.[81] In combination with allegiances from the so-called old boy network, Philby found an ally in Harold Macmillan, who in the same debate recounted that 'no evidence has been found to show that he [Philby] was responsible for warning Burgess or Maclean'. Going even further in his defence, the foreign secretary stated that 'while in government service [Philby] carried out his duties ably and conscientiously. I have no reason to conclude that Mr. Philby has at any time betrayed the interests of this country'.[82] During his defence of the accused, Macmillan mentioned both Philby's education at Cambridge and his position as first secretary at the British embassy in Washington, DC. Macmillan later wrote that with regards to the Philby affair, his chief concern was the protection of individual rights. Such a motivation rings disingenuous.[83]

Cover-up and whitewashing

The events leading up to the abovementioned confrontation paint an enlightening portrait. Since Burgess and Maclean's vanishings, rumours had circulated regarding their loyalties and current whereabouts. From the start, the FO decided the entire affair needed concealing and 'publicity should be avoided as long as possible'. This cover-up extended to the UK's closest ally. Although pressured by the American State Department for answers over the disappearances, FO mandarins 'decided that we should not take the State Department into our confidence' and that they should actively 'limit US governmental knowledge of the affair'.[84] Despite the enduring intrigue and the potential for scandal, the Conservative government showed little concern over the case of the missing diplomats. The prime minister's personal secretary, John Colville, recounting Winston Churchill's attitude of the ongoing saga, wrote:

> I don't think he was much interested in the case of Burgess and Maclean. In fact I had to press him to ask the cabinet office to provide a note on the incident. I think he merely wrote them off as being decadent young men, corrupted by drink and homosexuality ... He certainly did not look upon it as an indication of widespread communist infiltration – and I doubt if he had ever heard of Philby.[85]

The aged Churchill's interest in domestic intelligence ebbed and flowed. On occasions, MI5 felt they were humouring a confused old man rather than dealing with the national leader. At times, his concerns for state security were less grounded than MI5 would have liked. During the summer of 1952, Churchill requested Dick White to investigate the problem of UFOs.[86]

In April 1955, KGB defector Vladimir Petrov confirmed both men were currently residing in Moscow after travelling there on their own accord.[87] The press and parliamentary attention rapidly returned to the now five-year-old mystery. In response, the British government attempted to discredit Petrov, calling his information nothing more than hearsay. It marked an odd turn, since it represented one of the only times a Western government had sought to discredit a Soviet defector – a task more likely attempted by the KGB.[88] The government's attempt to question Petrov's revelation failed. The public now knew that the two diplomats were communist spies. But the question remained: how did they know to flee on the same day that Foreign Secretary Herbert Morrison ordered the arrest and questioning of Maclean? All eyes turned to the current Conservative foreign secretary Harold Macmillan for answers. In late April, he was first questioned by Marcus Lipton, the MP who later forced Macmillan to defend Philby publicly. On the floor of the Commons, Marcus Lipton asked about the ongoing investigation into the disappearances. The foreign secretary replied that he needed more time to consider the situation. Adding to the tension, and further embarrassing Macmillan, Lipton's Labour colleague, Jean Mann suggested 'asking the Russians if they know anything about Burgess and Maclean'.[89] She then made a not-so-veiled reference to the possibility of more traitors existing: 'if they would like any more like Burgess and Maclean they have just to ask us and we will send them over'.[90] Macmillan wisely chose not to respond.

Lipton and Mann were both correct. Many in British intelligence had already drawn the same conclusion: that someone strategically placed in government service had tipped off Burgess and Maclean. Another mole existed who had told the two that the time had come for them to exit the stage post haste. An MI5 report sent to the FO in January 1952 stated: 'There is no room for doubt that it was as a result of a leakage of information that Burgess and Maclean disappeared from this country on 25 May 1951'.[91] On MI5's list of suspects for this 'third man', Kim Philby ranked number one. Yet certain government authorities were less willing to accept the fact. Philby's chief accuser was Helenus Milmo, the man MI5 selected to interview him in 1951 regarding the disappearances. After interrogating Philby and reviewing the facts of the case, Milmo, an experienced barrister and former MI5 employee, reported: 'I find myself unable to avoid the conclusion that Philby is and has for many years been a Soviet agent and that he is directly and deliberately responsible for the leakage which in fact occurred.' But deference and personal ties clouded the already muddled situation. MI6, Philby's employer, refuted Milmo's assessment and responded: 'We feel that the case against Philby is not proved and moreover is capable of a less sinister interpretation than is implied by the bare evidence.'[92] Despite MI6 backing their man, Philby was forced to resign. Tim Milne, an MI6 agent and close friend of Philby, claimed the chief reason for Philby's departure was 'simply to preserve good relations with the Americans', and if not for that, Philby would have been allowed to stay.[93] After the defections of Burgess and Maclean, CIA Director Walter Bedell Smith requested that William Harvey, the CIA station chief in Berlin, who knew Philby personally, write up his views on Philby's potential involvement. Harvey unequivocally denounced Philby as a Soviet spy.[94] Smith sent a letter to MI6's Director General Stewart Menzies stating Philby, by no means, should return to Washington, DC.[95] Shortly afterwards, Philby found himself unemployed.

In the spring of 1952, a year after his resignation from MI6, Philby lunched with his former boss, Menzies. Recounting the meeting with Guy Liddell, Menzies, despite the mounting evidence, told the MI5 deputy general that he believed Philby innocent. Suspicious of Philby, Liddell advised his superior not to allow personal connections to impact his judgement. Liddell had 'come to the conclusion that the only thing in cases of this kind, where one knew an individual fairly intimately, was to sink one's personal views ... otherwise one was liable to get misled'.[96]

Wise guidance for any intelligence officer, but not advice Liddell himself consistently practised. His close friendship with Guy Burgess had all but shattered any chance for further career advancement.[97] Yet this earlier damning association did not stop Liddell from meeting frequently and discussing intelligence and state matters with his close friend Anthony Blunt.[98] During their friendship, Blunt passed on a wealth of secrets he garnered from the British agent to his Soviet handlers. Like Philby, whom Liddell distrusted, a fog of suspicion also hung over Blunt. In July 1952, only months after giving his warning to Menzies, an MI5 informant suggested to Liddell that Blunt 'was a far more active communist' during his time at Cambridge than had previously been disclosed. Instead of turning his suspicion on to his friend, Liddell doubted the informant, a former communist, who Liddell classified as 'a hot anti-communist'. He argued that people who go through such a political conversion are 'inclined in self-justification to exaggerate things'. Liddell conceded that Blunt 'dabbled in communism' but maintained that his friend was never a communist; he only cared for 'artistic matters' and held no real interest in politics. Blinded by personal connections and class prejudices, both Liddell and Menzies refused to believe their friends were capable of treachery. To this point, the day after Liddell received the accusations against Blunt, the deputy director of MI5 did not order the surveillance of this still undetected communist spy. Instead, Liddell dined out with Blunt at the Travellers Club – the most exclusive gentlemen's club in London – and discussed security matters.[99]

On 19 September 1955, a spokesman for the FO conceded for the first official time that Donald Maclean and Guy Burgess were long-term agents of the Soviet Union. That same week the Eden government released a white paper on the investigation. The anonymous author of the unsigned paper was Graham Mitchell, then in charge of MI5's counterintelligence branch. Almost everyone outside of the FO found the explanations within it unconvincing, incomplete and even misleading. The paper claimed that grounds did not exist to doubt Maclean's loyalty and no proof existed he was a past member of the Communist Party. Both assertions were false. The white paper then contradicted itself by claiming that MI5 held doubts about Maclean and Burgess and was 'on their track' but had 'insufficient evidence' to stop them from leaving or formally arresting the two. These statements challenged the claim British authorities requested the French government to 'intercept' and detain Maclean shortly after his disappearance. If the British authorities had no legal power to stop Maclean in England, then why would they in France?[100] For many, the white paper was more of a whitewash. Summing up this sentiment was none other than the persistent Marcus Lipton: 'This disappointing White Paper adds nothing at all to what everyone already knows.' Cleverly voicing contempt in a populist manner, Lipton added, 'There are two kinds of intelligence, the intelligence of the average citizens and the intelligence of the Foreign Office. The White Paper is an insult to both.'[101] The consensus among the press and the general public was that the official report raised more queries than it answered. For those outside of government following the case, one question stuck out more than any others. The question appeared in stark black and white on the front page of the *Western Mail* – 'DID THIRD MAN WARN BURGESS AND MACLEAN?'[102] In an attempt to alleviate the frustration and resolve lingering questions, the Conservative government immediately announced that a public debate regarding the white paper was forthcoming. It was a foregone conclusion to everyone that Harold Macmillan was the man who would be in the eye of the storm.

Writing to the cabinet prior to the debate, Macmillan's concerns focused solely on how to defuse the issue over both the white paper and the revelations of the two now not-so-missing diplomats. He conceded, 'there are certain questions which have been pushed hard especially by the press, which have to be answered' and his task 'will not be very easy' in defending the government's handling of the Burgess and Maclean affair. His primary concern was halting any calls for an official parliamentary investigation. The foreign secretary argued that such an open inquiry into the affair was 'dangerous' since 'nothing could be worse than a lot of muckraking and innuendo'. He then likened the prospect of any public investigation into the espionage charges to messy divorce cases which made daily headlines. Macmillan desired to leave the whole affair untouched. He recommended shifting the focus of any forthcoming inquiry 'not into the past but into the future'. He maintained the primary advantage for this was that 'the public will feel that something is being enquired into'.[103] Nowhere in the memorandum did Macmillan voice concern over the prospect of a 'third man' or show any willingness to speak on the topic. He personally considered the affair over 'Burgess and Maclean, a perennial and sordid topic. It takes up a lot of time and we get nowhere. I shall be glad when the debate is over'.[104] It is evident that Macmillan never even considered conducting a thorough investigation for any more communist agents.

Macmillan exonerates Philby

On 25 October 1955, six days after the delivery of the memorandum, Marcus Lipton interrupted Macmillan's sanguine plans to focus the coming debate on the future while leaving the past untouched. Shielded by the armour of parliamentary privilege, Lipton named Philby as the 'dubious third man'. In a leading question directed at Eden, he accused the prime minister of covering up Philby's treasonous activities; Lipton claimed the prime minister was attempting to stifle any debate over the whole affair. Pressed to respond, Macmillan, replying for the prime minister and the Conservative government, promised an upcoming opportunity to debate the issue.[105] Macmillan faced a choice. The mysterious 'third man' now had a human face. Questions about such a contentious charge against Philby could not go unanswered. To condemn Philby – or even to plead ignorance, as he had done in the past – would further embarrass the FO and darken the reputations of a number of civil servants and intelligence officers who earlier promoted and later defended their friend and former colleague. Macmillan ventured down the opposite path, seeking to protect one of his own, both occupationally and socially. He was certainly not the first to venture along this road for Kim Philby. While investigating Philby in 1952, MI5 received a list of six acquaintances he knew from university. Five out of the six, they discovered, had 'communist traces'. However, it was determined it 'would not be possible to interrogate these individuals without it being apparent' to them that Philby was under 'considerable suspicion'. The risk, if they spoke out about this suspicion, was too high for the simple reason that it would embarrass Philby's former employer.[106]

To no avail, the head of MI5, Dick White, pleaded with Macmillan to reject both his instincts and the advice of his ministry to clear Philby.[107] Agreeing with White, former Chairman of the JIC and ambassador to the Soviet Union and France Patrick Reilly called Macmillan's conduct regarding Philby a grievous error.[108] Macmillan, and to a lesser extent Eden, were not the only Conservatives who proclaimed the innocence of Philby. Even before he defended Philby during the 7 November Commons debate, Richard Brooman-White had tirelessly laboured in the protection of the communist agent. The right-wing anti-communist MP played a role in having the initial investigation of Philby officially terminated. At the request of Macmillan's private secretary John Wyndham, Brooman-White authored a brief for the foreign secretary on the case. Wyndham considered Philby's friend a respectable candidate since Brooman-White had been in the Secret Intelligence Service (SIS) and recognised the political subtleties of the whole affair. The brief he produced for Macmillan led profoundly in the favour of his friend's innocence.[109] After Philby's resignation from the SIS, the Conservative MP used his contacts to procure a job for his friend in the field of journalism.[110] As a cover for his MI6 activities, the agency persuaded the *Observer* and the *Economist* to hire Philby as a foreign correspondent.

Alongside Macmillan's publicly exonerating Philby, the Commons debate over the Maclean and Burgess white paper emphasised the stark differences between the Labour and Conservative Parties in regard to their attitudes to the entire sordid affair. Because of the circumstance that a Labour government was in power during the defections of the two Soviet agents, the debate was framed as a non-partisan matter. As customary standards mandated, Macmillan as current foreign secretary gave a statement and answered questions regarding the issue at hand, but joining him in this task from across the aisle was Herbert Morrison, the foreign secretary in office when Maclean and Burgess disappeared. Although speaking on the same topic, the tone and substance of the two men's speeches were starkly different.

In addition to defending Philby, Macmillan cast doubt on the entire notion of a 'third man', praised the FO, underscored the recently introduced new vetting procedures and emphasised – as he had planned – the future. Recounting the event in his memoirs, Macmillan framed the debate as a towering contest between those who championed civil liberties versus those who wished for a curtaining of them in the name of security. Although his fellow MPs assembled in the Commons to hear the government's explanation over the worst case of espionage in the nation's history, in recounting the atmosphere and the mindset of his colleagues, Macmillan described an assembly of competing ideologies. 'Members seemed divided between those who would be prepared to give the executive far more drastic powers', Macmillan argued, 'and those who preferred to run some risk in order to maintain the older traditions of the British system of law and equity'.[111] It took no guesswork on the part of his readership to determine the side the author championed. If his account is believed, Macmillan's responsibility and task were not to answer credible questions about past failures of the FO and to shed light on the defection of two government officials. He fashioned his duty as one to prohibit 'Morrison from turning this into a party matter' and refuting Morrison's calls for 'a general inquiry into the Foreign Office and the system of security'.[112] If Macmillan's own gallant attempt to halt the erosion of freedom was on his mind when he wrote his memoirs, he had a less lofty concern when travelling to the Commons on that day. While in a car going to the debate, he remarked to his assistant private secretary: 'I hope the opposition doesn't know that Maclean's brother Alan is employed by my family's publishing company.'[113] If he had any lingering doubts about exonerating Philby, these were absent as well. Mulling over the debate in his private diary, Macmillan viewed it as a personal success. 'Altogether a great relief that this is over', he wrote on the day and then added, without a hint of irony, 'My speech is said to be the best I have ever made.'[114]

Unlike Macmillan, his predecessor was not content to look only to the future or frame the debate as one of high principles. A man of humble origins and a political fighter, Morrison used the Commons discussion as a platform to defend his record as foreign minister and to continue his fervent battle with communism. Contrasting with Macmillan, who spurned even saying the word, Morrison took the opportunity to denounce the ideology and its disciples. He classified the very existence of communism as a security problem, since it stripped away loyalty to the nation and created enemy agents from the ranks of the British citizenry. 'It is sometimes said that communism is a religion', Morrison remarked. 'I do not think that is fair to religion. I think that in some ways it is a disease.' Lingering on the topic of communism, he challenged the notion that the upper class of society was immune to this particular disease:

> [T]he new situation of a voluntary act of service in the interests of a foreign power against one's own country is a very serious matter for security in all sorts of ways. Let no one think that this aspect is confined to the working classes: I do not think that anyone does think so. In fact, the cases with which we are concerned are not of that character. There have been some working-class cases, but the funny thing about the middle and upper classes, the well-to-do class, is that if they go wrong in this fashion they are, if anything, worse than other people. It is so. They begin by revolting against their families and they may finish up by secretly revolting against the state. That is rather curious.[115]

Touching on points which his predecessor refused to comment on, the former foreign minister criticised the protection and the deference given to those accused from an elitist and privileged background. Referring to Macmillan's earlier words, he retorted, 'I am not quite as satisfied as he is with things as they are.' Morrison reminded his audience that Maclean and Burgess were both communists during their time at the prestigious Cambridge University. He maintained that while this fact on its own was not enough to mistrust an individual, it should be a contributing factor in assessing an individual's loyalty – 'all sorts of things happen at the universities ... abnormal ideas are evolved'. Emphasising his working-class background, he added, 'I am a product of the elementary schools, and I am not ashamed of the fact.' Alongside class and privilege, Morrison attacked another facet of exclusivity which shielded the two communist agents from detection. Morrison condemned the 'old boy network' which perpetuated the employment of the erratic and alcoholic Burgess:

> In my judgment, in the case of Burgess ... a severe reprimand was not good enough. I think that in both of these cases they should, for those offences, have been dismissed. I think that in the Civil Service as a whole – whether it is more so in the Foreign Office I do not know – there is a tendency, if an officer falls down on his job or is guilty of an offence which is somewhat serious, to say, 'He is an old colleague. Can we not do something about it to prevent him from being fired?' ... I think that a little sacking now and again would not do any harm. It would do some harm to the men concerned but it might do a lot of good to the rest of the service.[116]

Concerning the issue of 'the third man', Morrison – contradicting Macmillan – assessed that such an individual existed, and had thus so far evaded detection. He put forth the case that the evidence that at least one more Soviet mole remained was too damning to discount. Originating from a self-interested motivation, Morrison furthermore sought to absolve himself of any blame for the defections occurring under his ministerial watch. He ended his speech by demanding from the Conservative government a full investigation. 'The country will not be satisfied without an inquiry of some sort, covering an adequate field', he asserted, 'for our country has a right to know that adequate action is being taken arising out of an experience which is disturbing and worrying to us all.'

Although Macmillan and his fellow Conservatives defended the integrity of the FO, many on the other side of the chamber did not follow this line. Joining Morrison's condemnation of the underwriting factors of class and governmental privilege which had allowed the now evident communist subversion to take place were several of his fellow Labour MPs. Frank Tomney accused Macmillan of conspiring with members of the FO to attempt a cover-up 'to protect somebody from the follies of misjudgement, mismanagement and neglect'. He claimed that an independent inquiry was the only way to reassure the public and to prepare the nation to face the looming threat. 'We have moved on into another world populated by opponents of a cunning and vicious nature', warned Tomney, 'into a world of communism whose methods and policies, and the way in which they must be fought, do not yet seem to be fully understood in some circles in Whitehall.'[117] Addressing the prime minister directly, Labour MP Alfred Robens accused the FO of covering up for its employees and argued that the public did not believe denials to the contrary coming from either political party. Speaking of the FO, John Cordeaux said although the ministry held a reputation 'of having too many receptions and cocktail parties' and 'being staffed by too many old school ties', he contended none of its critics would ever imagine it 'harboured traitors' until now. Cordeaux added that the FO still might be doing so. Speaking to the heart of the privilege issue, Alfred Robens, the MP representing Blyth, remarked:

> Another interesting thing is that while these men were protected and excuses were made for their drunkenness and perversions, ordinary working men who had communist affiliations were kicked out of their jobs almost at a moment's notice. Does this mean that there is one law for a communist sympathiser from Bermondsey and another for a communist sympathiser from Cambridge University?[118]

Although Labour MPs clamoured for a full investigation into the possibility of a 'third man' and the conduct that allowed for Burgess and Maclean to stay undetected in governmental service for such an extended period, the Conservative government refused to bend. It determined that the whole affair was better off left alone.

The day after the parliamentary debate, all eyes were on Kim Philby, who had scheduled a press conference for that morning. Charming and cocksure, Philby played the part of an innocent man proved vindicated. Although Lipton sought to indict Philby as a traitor, he had the reverse effect. With Macmillan publicly proclaiming his innocence, the Soviet spy revelled in his time in the public spotlight. 'I have never been a communist', protested Philby, then wryly added with a grin, 'The last time I spoke to a communist, knowing he was one, was in 1934.' When reporters directly asked if he was the so-called third man, he gave a direct no. Left with no choice, Lipton took back his accusation. Showing bitterness over the incident later, Lipton accused members of both parties of attempting to silence him: 'I was shouted down in the House ... Their instinct was to protect him.'[119] In Washington, DC, the news was received with fury and also bewilderment.[120] But if lingering doubts regarding Philby's loyalty existed in the upper ranks of MI5, none showed with his former employers at SIS or the FO. After his exoneration in the Commons, MI6 re-employed Philby and the FO requested the *Observer* to hire him as their correspondent for the Middle East.[121] He would go undetected until British intelligence finally received conclusive indication of his betrayal in 1962. Even then, he eluded them by following his earlier confederates in escaping to the Soviet Union. It is still debated how much Macmillan knew about the evidence mounting against Philby. The chances he was unaware of the warning signs over Philby are quite slim. Others in the Conservative government of the time indicated such knowledge, even if they had their doubts about its validity. In a 1952 meeting with Guy Liddell, Home Secretary David Maxwell Fyfe inquired 'whether we were still keeping an eye on Philby'. Liddell stated in the affirmative.[122]

'The establishment' versus anti-communism

In September 1955, an article appeared in the *Spectator*, a Conservative-leaning magazine, which popularised a term now defined as 'a social group exercising power generally, or within a given field or institution, by virtue of its traditional superiority'. Penned by Henry Fairlie, the article predicted the forthcoming cover-up by the Conservative government in the Commons debate over Philby. Writing on the government, he stated, 'their answers would almost certainly [be] unsatisfactory'. Fairlie excoriated the FO as well. 'Somewhere near the heart of the pattern of social relationships which so powerfully controls the exercise of power in this country is the Foreign Office', he maintained. Fairlie argued, 'No one whose job it was to be interested in the Burgess-Maclean affair from the very beginning will forget the subtle but powerful pressures which were brought to bear by those who belonged to the same stratum as the two missing men.'[123] He ended the piece by stating this was simply how 'the establishment' worked. It may be thought appropriate that the phrase 'the establishment' came into the vernacular in an article decrying the governmental whitewashing of the Maclean and Burgess investigation.

The question can be asked why the blame resides with the Conservatives more than their Labour opponents. As Duff Cooper lamented in 1946, Labour politicians did not cling tightly to the 'old school tie' or have a long-established loyalty to the mandarins of the FO or the upper echelons of the intelligence services. Lingering animosities between Labour and these governmental departments were not forgotten. For many a Labour politician, when they viewed the FO and the intelligence services they still saw the 'guilty men' who supported appeasement and were instigators of the Zinoviev Letter. Alan Bullock writes: 'The Foreign Office was a powerful symbol for many members of the Labour Party of all they had objected to in the traditional foreign policy.'[124] Feelings of mistrust worked both ways. When Attlee appointed Percy Sillitoe, an outsider and former policeman, to head MI5, many insiders considered it a deliberate slight against their agency. After taking office in 1945, the first priority of Foreign Secretary Ernest Bevin was the implementation of the 1943 Foreign Service Act, which curbed elitism in the diplomatic service. It was a reform many in the FO thought unnecessary and a political decision to satisfy Labour's backbenches. Evidence shows an atmosphere of

THE CONSERVATIVES AND THE RED MENACE   137

lingering wariness impacted the whole affair. Despite a cloud of suspicion falling upon Philby immediately after the disappearance of Maclean and Burgess, Herbert Morrison was never informed of Philby's likely involvement or of the financial settlement Philby received after he resigned from MI6.[125] On 27 September 1955, while having lunch with Attlee, Richard Crossman asked the Labour leader what he termed 'the 64-dollar question'. Did anyone from the security services bring to him the matter of security concerns about Maclean or Burgess before they disappeared? Attlee replied they kept him completely in the dark: 'I knew nothing whatsoever.' Crossman asked Attlee if he agreed that a special tribunal should be appointed, to which Attlee grunted his approval. The former prime minister added: 'If I'd been at the Foreign Office I'd have been more brutal when that sort of thing was discovered. I am more brutal than people imagine.'[126] When it came to rooting out communists, as the record of their time in government proved, both Attlee and Morrison had the capacity of fierceness – if not also brutality. Past incidences show that neither men let deference to traditions stop them from originating hunts for communists inside the Labour Party or the civil service. It is almost certain that if Attlee (or Morrison as his successor) had been in Downing Street in the autumn of 1955, Philby's fate would have taken a decidedly different turn.

The parliamentary affair over Philby showcases the ingrained preference in the UK for maintaining systemic deference to privilege and class. This led to an environment where segments of society sought to preserve the status quo by covering up irregularities and discounting warning signs of members of the British 'establishment'. From 1951 to 1956, the Conservative Party in government defended this traditional social order by refusing to investigate the FO and effectively exonerating a communist traitor. Even when pressured by the likes of Morrison and Lipton, alongside Fleet Street, the Conservatives chose to cleave to the time-honoured notion that class defined an individual more than political beliefs. They were not alone in these suppositions.

During a 1954 interview with a US magazine, when answering the question of if the British government was as concerned about communists as its American counterpart, Home Secretary David Maxwell Fyfe summoned up the Conservative position:

> Well I should say there is the concern, only we think, in our country, that the best method of dealing with them is to know who they are, have complete records about them, know what you're going to defend and keep them out of it, but try not to drive them underground and don't make them look more important than they are. We

are quite concerned with the problems of the communists, and – if I may, I hope I'm not deviating too much – remember that the great answer to communism, as an ideology and in part as a faith, is that we have a better faith.[127]

As Maxwell Fyfe maintained, the Conservatives did view the Cold War as a contest of ideologies, but they failed to envisage that the enemy had infiltrated the ruling class. Nor did they grasp the danger that came from such a threat. No one epitomised this point more than Macmillan. He essentially viewed the infiltration of communist spies as little more than a public relations concern. In a BBC interview later in life, he said such things as espionage and defection were 'not very important ... it's all rather exaggerated'.[128] Macmillan's official biographer stressed his blasé approach to security matters showed 'an insensitivity to the fundamental demoralization that unresolved fear of traitors in their midst could cause in government departments, let alone among the public at large'.[129] Writing on such a blind spot that Macmillan never grasped, David Caute cautioned, 'One Philby or Fuchs can do as much for Russia as fifty communist MPs.'[130] This proved accurate. By Soviet estimates, Burgess, Maclean and Philby provided over 20,000 pages filled with secrets during their treasonous careers.[131] Patrick Reilly was correct in saying that Macmillan's 'generous words' regarding Philby had a tangible impact. After the 'whitewash', MI5 refused to make any resources available further to investigate him, which frustrated those in the agency who correctly suspected his treason.[132]

Conclusion

In a similar manner to Clement Attlee's time in office, powerful extraneous forces affecting their decision-making compelled his Conservative successors. Akin to the Labour Party, the Conservatives viewed the Soviet Union, and its principal domestic agent the CPGB, as the foremost enemies of the nation. In the 1950 and 1951 General Elections, the CPGB were decimated at the polls. Although the Conservatives still considered domestic communists a potential 'threat', this peril had decreased publicly. Yet for political purposes they sought unsuccessfully to attack Labour with a negative anti-socialism agenda, which included linking it with communism – in hindsight, such efforts rang decidedly false.[133] When in power, both Churchill and Eden broadly accepted Labour's creation of a welfare state and its commitment to full employment, and kept the same approach to managing the economy along what David Carlton termed 'corporatist' lines.[134] No 'radical assault' or attempts to roll back

Labour 'socialism' occurred after the return of the Conservatives to power. In terms of domestic policy, the 1951 victory marked the least transformative shift between governments of one party to another until 1997.[135] Far from reversing the tide of socialism, which he vigorously denounced in campaign speeches, Churchill legitimised it.[136] Although Churchill held reservations over this new consensus-driven style of governing, the more left-leaning Eden did not. Prior to and during the Second World War, Eden showed disdain for the Conservative Party and its more right-wing supporters. He contemplated joining Labour and gave serious consideration to forming a new party consisting of left-wing Conservatives and right-wing members of Labour.[137] He envisioned the only opposition to this new postwar coalition would be the communists.[138] When Eden succeeded Churchill, he offered 'platitudes about favouring a property-owning democracy', but kept the postwar consensus firmly in place.[139]

Unlike the Labour leaders – Herbert Morrison, Morgan Phillips, Clement Attlee and Ernest Bevin – the Conservative leadership of Anthony Eden, Winston Churchill and David Maxwell Fyfe viewed the 'communist menace' from a different perspective. Because of their philosophical make-up, these men disdained Marxism and were as dedicated to the cause of anti-communism as their Labour contemporaries. However, for these Conservatives, the nature of the communist threat to the UK varied from that of their main political opponents. The Labour leadership – prior to and during their time in power – confronted communists and fellow travellers in both their party and the affiliated trade union movement. This anxiety over crypto-communists in the House of Commons and the battle with communistic influence in unions forged, and later strengthened, for Labour leaders the belief that the communist ideology had not just fostered international and political rivals. It both rested at the heart of and functioned as an insidious conspiracy. The Conservatives rejected this notion; they refused to categorise domestic communism as such.[140] During their time in office, Morrison and Attlee railed against the supposed covert actions of the CPGB and their supporters. The same was not the case for the Conservatives. After taking power, Churchill conceded in early 1952 there was little feasibility in arguing that the reds were the 'root of all our troubles'.[141] The Conservatives gauged the threat of domestic communism by the influence the CPGB exerted at the ballot box. The fiery denunciations of communists by ministers, so common during the Attlee government, were non-existent after Churchill returned to the premiership. Attlee's two successors viewed the face of the Marxist-Leninist danger much differently than him.

Before the Second World War, in both the US and UK, the lower classes were routinely suspected of communist sympathies. Yet in the US, the panic of communism morphed into one which feared the betrayal of the upper class. Leading this shift of targets were politicians such as Joseph McCarthy and Richard Nixon. The same transition did not occur in the UK. One reason was the rejection of populism by the Conservative Party. The second was that the Conservative Party sought to uphold the traditional elements of society and class.[142] Unlike with Alger Hiss and Harry Dexter White, where the Republicans attacked the establishment and the elitism that created these men, in the UK the Conservatives protected their own.

The 1955 exoneration of Philby and the whitewashing of the affair brought with it a backlash. After Philby's eventual 1963 defection became public – compounded by the uncovering of the double agent of George Blake in 1961 – 'mole-hunting' became one of the nation's unofficial pastimes. The failure to unmask the likes of Blake and Philby sooner opened the floodgates in the minds of many, leading to the suspicions of communist spies to deluge the national psyche. Despite Labour's renewed calls for a more thorough investigation of communist penetration inside government, Harold Macmillan, now prime minister, again refused. Hence, little was done to alleviate the growing problem. Whitehall continued to conceal the extent to which Soviet agents had penetrated its institutions. These included refusals to publicise the discovery of both Anthony Blunt and John Cairncross – other members of the Cambridge spy ring – alongside the discovery of the treachery of others, such as Melita Norwood. After the cover-ups of these spies became public, official denials could no longer be trusted. Thus, anyone and everyone was under suspicion. During the 1970s and 1980s the names of those accused routinely made the headlines.[143] The list of those accused was long and illustrious; class and privilege no longer protected those who were now falling under suspicion. Those accused of being a communist agent included Guy Liddell, Roger Hollis, Lord Rothschild, Lord Mountbatten, Graham Mitchell and even Prime Minister Harold Wilson.

To the internationally minded Churchill and a lesser extent his protégé Eden, the perils of communism came from the opposite side of the Iron Curtain and not from the boroughs of East London or the banks of the River Clyde. One of the first concerns of Attlee after gaining the premiership was rooting out communists from his backbenches. Conversely, after regaining power Churchill worried about the lack of sufficient troops in the UK to defend the country against a possible Soviet invasion. In the atomic age, it was baffling for his generals when he ordered the revival of the Home Guard to compensate.[144] Churchill viewed the Soviet Union as an existential threat to the West. Despite his decision to revive the anachronistic Home Guard, Churchill was still well aware of the atomic age and its destructive potential. 'Europe would have been communized and London would have been under bombardment some time ago', he maintained, 'but for the deterrent of the atomic bomb in the hands of the United States.'[145] If the recollections of Senator Styles Bridges are believed, then Churchill privately held a bellicose solution to the external communist threat. Bridges recounted to the FBI a conversation he had with Churchill in late December 1947 in which the Conservative leader advocated a pre-emptive atomic strike to decapitate the Soviet leadership, followed by all-out war with the Soviet Union.[146] Less than horrified by the suggestion, Styles, a future McCarthy loyalist, readily agreed with Churchill and wished for his country to quickly attack. With Churchill leading the Conservatives, the emphasis of fighting communism was directed to the international level. However, by 1951, as the Conservative Party returned to government, core anti-communist tendencies existed in British society. Just as they refused to overturn established policies of Labour in other areas of domestic affairs, the Conservatives allowed the anti-communist directives to stay in place. These formed another facet of the postwar consensus.

Notes

1. A. Eden, *Days for Decision* (London, 1950), p. 126.

2. Hansard, HC, vol. 496, c. 703 (25 February 1952).

3. Bernard Montgomery to Oliver Lyttelton, 27 December 1951, TNA PREM 11/121.

4. R. Thurlow, *The Secret State* (Oxford, 1994), p. 309.

5. R. Aldrich and R. Cormac, *The Black Door* (London, 2016), p. 161.

6. M. Kandiah, 'The Conservative Party and the early Cold War: Construction of "New Conservatism"', in *Cold War Britain, 1954–1964*, ed. M. Hopkins, M. Kandiah and G. Staerack (New York, 2003), 30–8, at p. 30.

7. R. Toye, *Churchill's Empire* (London, 2010), p. 267.

8. See P. White, *Our Supreme Task: How Winston Churchill's Iron Curtain Speech Defined the Cold War Alliance* (New York, 2012).

9. *Victory: War Speeches by the Right Hon. Winston Churchill*, ed. Charles Eade (London, 1946), pp. 88–9.

10. L. Moran, *Churchill: Taken from the Diaries of Lord Moran* (Boston, MA, 1966), p. 271.

11. C. Attlee, *Purpose and Policy* (London, 1947), p. 7.

12. R. Toye, 'Winston Churchill's "crazy broadcast": Party, nation, and the 1945 Gestapo speech', *Journal of British Studies*, 49 (2010): 655–80, at p. 655; R. Cockett, *Thinking the Unthinkable* (London, 1995), p. 94.

13. Herbert Morrison speech, issued by the Labour Party, 11 January 1948, LPA/LID/Anti-communist propaganda 1948.

14. *Western Morning News*, 3 May 1948, p. 2.

15. Hansard, HC, vol. 435, cc. 1688–9 (31 March 1947).

16. *Hull Daily Mail*, 18 March 1950, p. 3.

17. Marjorie Maxse to General Director, 22 December 1950, Oxford, Bodleian Library, Conservative Party Archive (henceforth CPA): CCO 4/4/36.

18. Oliver Lyttelton to Winston Churchill, 4 March 1949, CHAN II/4/5, Churchill College, Cambridge.

19. 'Is Mr. Morrison a socialist?', 18 October 1946, MS Macmillan 379, Papers of Harold Macmillan, Bodleian Library, Oxford.

20. Hansard, HC, vol. 446, c. 619 (23 January 1948).

21. Report by Committee on Communist and Fascist Activities, 8 July 1948, CPA: NUA 6/2/5.

22. Report of Committee on Communist and Fascist Activities, undated, CPA: NUA 6/2/5.

23. Report by the Committee on Communist and Fascist Activities, 8 July 1948, CPA: NUA 6/2/5.

24. *Hartlepool Northern Daily Mail*, 11 March 1949, p. 6.

25. *Fife Free Press*, 3 December 1949, p. 5.

26. *Yorkshire Evening Post*, 2 June 1949, p. 7.

27. *Western Morning News*, 16 February 1950, p. 1.

28. W. Churchill, *In the Balance* (New York, 1952), text of speech given on 25 March 1950.

THE CONSERVATIVES AND THE RED MENACE   143

29. T.F. Lindsay to Henry Hopkinson, 4 February 1949, CPA: CDR D-2-5.

30. H.G. Nicholas, *The British General Election of 1950* (London, 1951), p. 222.

31. Charles Gill, 'Fellow travellers', 18 January 1950, CPA: CCO 4/3/38.

32. *Socialist Commentary*, September 1949, pp. 205–6; *Socialist Commentary*, April 1956, p. 4.

33. *Socialist Commentary*, December 1950, p. 286.

34. *Western Morning News*, 3 May 1948, p. 2.

35. *Tribune*, 3 November 1950, p. 7.

36. *What Is the Communist After?*, Labour Party leaflet, LPA/LID/Anti-communist Propaganda 1950.

37. Speech by Herbert Morrison, issued by the Labour Party, 24 March 1950, LPA/LID/Anti-communist Propaganda 1949.

38. Marjorie Maxse to Robert Short, 24 July 1950, CPA: CCO 4/3/38.

39. Numerous detailed reports on communists meeting are in CPA: CCO 4/4/36.

40. Irene Ward to Marjorie Maxse, 1 June 1949, CPA: CCO 4/3/38.

41. Charles Gill to Marjorie Maxse, 3 June 1949, CPA: CCO 4/3/38.

42. Charles Gill to Marjorie Maxse, 12 July 1949, CPA: CCO 3/3/28.

43. Ian Fraser to Marjorie Maxse, 29 July 1949, CPA: CCO 3/3/28.

44. Charles Gill to Marjorie Maxse, 18 October 1949, CPA: CCO 4/3/38.

45. J. Cranna to Colonel Blair, 1 December 1949, CPA: CCO 4/3/38.

46. J.C.D. Dodds to Brigadier Clarke, 4 April 1950, CPA: CCO 4/3/38.

47. Homan to Marjorie Maxse, 8 May 1950, CPA: CCO 4/3/38.

48. Marjorie Maxse to Homan, 9 May 1950, CPA: CCO 4/3/38.

49. Charles Gill to Marjorie Maxse, 29 September 1950, CPA: CCO 4/4/36.

50. General Director to Heads of Departments, 'Party Literature on Communism', 4 July 1950, CPA: CCO 4/3/30.

51. 'Communism in Great Britain: A short history of the British Communist Party', by H.A. Taylor, CPA: PUB/24.

52. George Christ to D. Spencer, 16 November 1951, CPA: CCO 4/4/36.

53. C. Andrew, *The Defence of the Realm* (London, 2009), p. 393.

54. Liddell diary, 16 December 1952.

55. 'The possibility of present Soviet penetration of the Foreign Service', November 1955, TNA 158/133.

56. Andrew, *Defence of the Realm*, p. 294.

57. David Maxwell Fyfe to Winston Churchill, 2 August 1952, TNA PREM 11/999.

58. Cabinet report by Committee on Restriction on Travel of Security Suspects, 2 April 1953, TNA PREM 11/999.

59. Quoted from Security Service Archives in Andrew, *Defence of Realm*, p. 398.

60. A.J. de la Mare, cover letter to FO report on Maclean and Burgess, undated, TNA FCO 158/177.

61. 'Policy towards homosexuality in the Foreign Service', TNA FCO 158/177.

62. Vansittart, *The Mist Procession* (London, 1958), p. 413.

63. Report by Lord Jowitt, 28 December 1955, TNA CAB 134/1325.

64. Foreign Office to Security Conference of Privy Counsellors, 30 November 1955, TNA CAB 134/1325.

65. Meeting conclusions of Security Conference of Privy Councillors, 12 December 1955, TNA CAB 134/1325.

66. Security Conference of Privy Councillors, 'Report of the Conference', 7 January 1956, TNA CAB 134/1325.

67. Security Conference of Privy Councillors, 'Report of the Conference', 7 January 1956, TNA CAB 134/1325.

68. Statement on the Findings of the Conference of Privy Councillors on Security Volume 9715 of Cmd. (HM Stationery Office, 1956).

69. J. Mahoney, 'Constitutionalism, the rule of law, and the Cold War', in *The Legal Protection of Human Rights: Sceptical Essays*, ed. T. Campbell, K. Ewing and A. Tomkins (Oxford, 2011), 127–47, at p. 141.

70. *The Secret Police and You*, pamphlet published by The Campaign for the Limitation of Secret Police Powers, 1956.

71. *Spectator*, 13 July 1956, p. 7.

72. J. Mahoney, 'Civil liberties in Britain during the Cold War: The role of the central government', *The American Journal of Legal History*, 30 (1989): 53–100, at p. 72.

73. *Dundee Courier*, 29 December 1953, p. 5.

74. H. Hyman, 'England and America: Climates of tolerance and intolerance', in *The Radical Right*, ed. Daniel Bell (New York, 1962), 269–306, at p. 334.

75. M. Hollingsworth and R. Norton-Taylor, *Blacklist* (London, 1988), p. 25.

76. B. Porter, *Plots and Paranoia* (London, 1989), p. 186.

77. *Duff Cooper Diaries, 1915–1951*, ed. J. Norwich (London, 2005), p. 143.

78. R. Davenport-Hines, *Enemies Within: Communists, the Cambridge Spies and the Making of Modern Britain* (London, 2018), p. 562.

79. K. Philby, *My Secret War* (London, 1968), pp. 193–4.

80. Hansard, HC, vol. 545, cc. 1497–8 (7 November 1955).

81. Philby, *Secret War*, p. 37.

82. Hansard, HC, vol. 545, c. 1497 (7 November 1955).

83. For Macmillan's brief account, see H. Macmillan, *Tides of Fortune* (London, 1969), pp. 683–6.

84. Arthur de la Mare to Donald Maitland, 6 November 1955, TNA FCO 158/177.

85. Quoted in A. Boyle, *The Climate of Treason* (London, 1979), p. 394.

86. Aldrich and Cormac, *Black Door*, p. 168.

87. See V. and E. Petrov, *Empire of Fear* (London, 1956), pp. 271–6.

88. S. Kerr, 'British Cold War defectors: The versatile durable toys of propagandists', in *British Intelligence Strategy and the Cold War, 1945–51*, ed. R. Aldrich (London, 1992), 110–39, at p. 123.

89. On 2 November Macmillan did ask Soviet Foreign Minister Vyacheslav Molotov for help with the location of Maclean and Burgess. His inquiry was expressed as a joke, further evidence that Macmillan did not treat the investigation seriously. *Macmillan Diaries: The Cabinet Years*, ed. P. Catterall (London, 2003), p. 502.

90. Hansard, HC, vol. 540, cc. 909–10 (27 April 1955).

THE CONSERVATIVES AND THE RED MENACE   145

91. 'Notes on the early stages of the Philby case', prepared for Macmillan after Philby's defection in 1963. TNA PREM 11/4457.

92. 'Notes on the early stages of the Philby case', TNA PREM 11/4457.

93. T. Milne, *Kim Philby* (London, 2014), p. 172.

94. N. West, *Cold War Spymaster* (Barnsley, 2018), p. 165; T. Weiner, *Legacy of Ashes* (New York, 2007), pp. 255–6.

95. N. West, *The Circus* (New York, 1983), p. 63.

96. Liddell diary, 1 April 1952.

97. M. Carter, *Anthony Blunt* (London, 2001), p. 356; Philby, *Secret War*, p. 69.

98. Carter, *Blunt*, p. 285.

99. Liddell diary, 7 and 8 July 1952.

100. For a full text of the white paper and a list of its many known errors, see appendix 1 in N. West, *Mole-Hunt* (London, 1987).

101. *Northern Whig*, 24 September 1955, p. 1.

102. *Western Mail*, 24 September 1955, p. 1.

103. Cabinet Memorandum by Harold Macmillan, 19 October 1955, TNA CAB 129/78.

104. *Macmillan Diaries: The Cabinet Years*, p. 493.

105. P. Knightley, *Philby* (London, 1988), p. 194.

106. Liddell diary, 6 February 1952.

107. Bower, *English Spy*, p. 157.

108. A. Glees, *The Secrets of the Service* (London, 1987), p. 364.

109. Knightley, *Philby*, p. 195.

110. Boyle, *Treason*, p. 397.

111. Macmillan, *Tides of Fortunes,* p. 682.

112. Macmillan, *Tides of Fortunes*, pp. 682–3.

113. Bower, *English Spy*, p. 157.

114. *Macmillan Diaries, The Cabinet Years*, p. 503.

115. Hansard, HC, vol. 545, cc. 1509–10 (7 November 1955).

116. Hansard, HC, vol. 545, c. 1516 (7 November 1955).

117. Hansard, HC, vol. 545, c. 1456 (7 November 1955).

118. Hansard, HC, vol. 545, cc. 1598–9 (7 November 1955).

119. Quoted in Knightley, *Philby*, pp. 96–197.

120. Bower, *English Spy*, p. 158.

121. E. Harrison, *The Young Kim Philby* (Exeter, 2012), p. 182.

122. Liddell diary, 24 November 1952.

123. *Spectator*, 23 September 1955, p. 5.

124. A. Bullock, *Ernest Bevin: Foreign Secretary* (London, 1983), p. 72.

125. B. Donoughue and G. Jones, *Herbert Morrison* (London, 1973), p. 496.

126. Diary transcript, p. 219, Papers of Richard Crossman, MSS 154-8-18, MRC.

127. *U.S. News and World Report*, 15 October 1954, p. 87.

128. D. Thorpe, *Supermac* (London, 2010), p. 310.

129. A. Horne, *Macmillan 1894–1956* (London, 1988), p. 366.

130. D. Caute, *Fellow-Travellers* (London, 1977), p. 305.

131. V. Mitrokhin and C. Andrew, *The Mitrokhin Archives* (London, 1999), p. 209.

132. C. Pincher, *Their Trade Is Treachery* (London, 1981), p. 27.

133. P. Addison, *Churchill on the Home Front* (London, 1992), p. 387.

134. D. Carlton, 'Anthony Eden, 1955–1957', in *From New Jerusalem to New Labour*, ed. V. Bogdanor (London, 2010), 42–59, at p. 44.

135. V. Bogdanor, 'Winston Churchill, 1951–1955', in *From New Jerusalem to New Labour*, ed. V. Bogdanor (London, 2010), 23–41, at p. 30.

136. Bogdanor, 'Winston Churchill, 1951–1955', p. 26.

137. D. Dutton, *Anthony Eden* (London, 1996), p. 251.

138. D. Carlton, *Anthony Eden* (London, 1981), p. 185.

139. Carlton, 'Anthony Eden, 1955–1957', p. 44.

140. *U.S. News and World Report*, 15 October 1954, p. 88.

141. Hansard, HC, vol. 496, c. 703 (25 February 1952).

142. On the topic of populism, Richard Thurlow wrote: 'The Conservatives' ingrained dislike of populism and suspicion of American culture and values meant they were loath to imitate the practices of American anti-communist politics, no matter how much they sympathised with the sentiments behind it.' R. Thurlow, *Secret State* (Oxford, 1994), p. 309.

143. *Observer*, 15 March 1987, p. 13.

144. A. Seldon, *Churchill's Indian Summer* (London, 1981), p. 296.

145. Quoted in M. Gilbert, *Winston S. Churchill: Never Despair* (London, 1988), p. 566.

146. D. Milton Ladd to J. Edgar Hoover, 5 December 1947, FBI archival files, 'Winston Churchill part 3'.

Chapter 4

Pressure groups: agents of influence

Those who complacently treat these activities as mere nuisances should be reminded that every communist is an active or potential traitor ... But why do nothing? Why not join the democratic, non-party, anti-communist organization Common Cause?[1]

—Common Cause flyer

Now, when everybody is talking about communism they are on to that. There are large numbers of people belonging to the MRA [Moral Rearmament Movement] in the country; if they were really effective I think their influence might be considerable.[2]

—Lord Woolton, Conservative Party chairman

Pressure groups are entities that seek to influence governmental policies and public opinion but do not typically put forth candidates for elections or function as a political party. Pressure groups, or outside organisations, played a prominent role in the anti-communist activities affecting the domestic politics of the British state. They sought to combat communism in a myriad of ways: influencing political parties, altering government policies and transforming society. For the majority of these groups, the primary, if not only, objective was opposing Marxist-Leninist ideology and the Communist Party. The power and sway these anti-communist groups wielded disproportionality reflected the supposed threat of both. Communism had little popular support and virtually no prospects of gaining political power. In the 1945 General Election, the CPGB only garnered two seats in the House of Commons and accumulated less than 1 per cent of the national vote. Yet, effectively these anti-communist organisations ran a full-time propaganda campaign against communism.

Thus, the significant number of such anti-communist outside organisations and their influential nature is quite telling.

All the pressure groups examined in this chapter publicly claimed to have the same objective – first curbing and ultimately eliminating communism from the British Isles. But when scratching the surface, their motives were less uniform and more nuanced. The Manichaean battle against communism these organisations waged is only part of the narrative. The underlying intentions and functions of these groups paint a larger picture. They expose less apparent societal and international motivators of anti-communism in the UK. As this chapter makes clear, this cadre of factors included governmental, economic and foreign beneficiaries. These various interests, working through separate anti-communist organisations, for their own individual reasons, attempted to transform the UK into a less tolerant society. They were not entirely unsuccessful.

These groups' interactions and relationships with political parties and governmental institutions reveal the lengths, and also the limits, to which the British establishment was willing to go to in order to propagate anti-communism. In several instances these measures included covert collusion between members of the British government and a number of these private organisations. Often these relationships were mutually beneficial, which included intelligence sharing, propaganda formation and trade union infiltration. However, as will be shown, often the interactions were less reciprocally welcomed.

This chapter examines how the most noteworthy of these organisations functioned and their effect on the political climate of the period. It first looks at two groups, both individually impactful, whose efforts display a consistent trend of attempts to fight communism in the political sphere from a non-party level. These were the British Housewives' League (BHL) and the League of Empire Loyalists (LEL). The groups received little support from the British establishment but both were highly visible. However, the primary focus of this chapter is on the three most influential anti-communist organisations. These were Common Cause, the Economic League and the Moral Rearmament Movement (MRA). An analysis of each shows various facets of British anti-communism. All also highlight linkages between the three pressure groups with the British government, alongside the Labour and Conservative Parties.

The section on Common Cause gives a concrete example presenting how US political support and financial funds were funnelled to bolster and promote British anti-communism. In past research on covert US attempts 'to harden' anti-communist UK public opinion, the exploits of Common Cause are rarely mentioned. The previous works covering the topic mostly focus on CIA covert support of the Congress of Cultural Freedom (CCF) and the funding of its anti-communist and pro-American magazine *Encounter*.[3] Sponsorship by the British and American intelligence services for the CCF came to light in the 1960s; since then, these links have been thoroughly examined. The section on Common Cause offers to this existing historiography an explanation for the US desire to foster a more anti-communist UK. It argues that the US sought to stymie anti-British sentiment in the American public. It did this by attempting to influence the British populace into taking a harder anti-communist stance – something it believed the US citizenry would find more favourable.

Another facet of British anti-communism which historians have scrutinised is the religious dimension of the Cold War. Again, here a substantial amount of scholarly work is available regarding British churches and their anti-communist stance and activities. However, an unexamined part of this subset of Cold War research is the efforts of the MRA. The MRA conducted the largest and most controversial anti-communist campaign based on religious grounds in the UK during the early Cold War period. Yet academics focusing on the era have not covered its operations or impact. Like Common Cause, the theme of American involvement in British affairs is also relevant when reviewing the MRA. Both the movement's leader and a substantial amount of its financial backing originated from the US. Its ulterior motives are also of interest; the movement's anti-communist crusade was a means to a larger end. The MRA viewed communism as a useful enemy and anti-communism as a path to worldwide acceptance for the group's quasi-religious views. Its leadership surmised the fight against communism would lead the world into the hands of the MRA, after which the group sought to form its 'own utopian alternative'.[4]

The history of the Economic League highlights the point that anti-communist organisations did not all originate during the Cold War. The league formed shortly after the Russian Revolution, in 1919, and continued to function until shortly after the fall of the Soviet Union. It stood as a British staple for over seventy years. Funded primarily by corporations, the group existed as a political wing for managerial and capital interests which were naturally concerned by the threat of a Marxist economy taking hold in the UK. Like the other anti-communist organisations covered in this chapter, the league produced anti-communist propaganda, attempted to influence trade unions and lobbied the government and the two major political parties to take a stronger stance against communism. However, it functioned in another way, which set it apart from these other outside organisations. The Economic League also operated as a private vetting unit for businesses. A 1942 MI5 report classified the Economic League as 'an industrial espionage organization for its members'.[5] It gathered names of employees and recommended their dismissal if the league identified them as communists. Existing academic literature is available on the Economic League, yet it is primarily focused on two periods of its existence – either its interwar activities or its operations under the Thatcher years.[6] Very little is available addressing its early Cold War operations.

An interweaving theme prevails throughout the narratives of all three of these organisations. It is one of covert governmental assistance aiding these groups in fighting communism. The Economic League, Common Cause and the MRA all received varying degrees of support from both the Labour and Conservative governments during the late 1940s and into the 1950s.

The 'battle' of Albert Hall

Unlike the extreme right during the interwar era, opposition to communism throughout the postwar period was more political than a violent affair. A battle of Cable Street-like event never marked the robust rise of private anti-communist efforts. The closest that one can find is an odd confrontation which took place in and around Albert Hall during the summer of 1947. In June, the BHL elected to hold a rally to demand action from the Labour government. Founded three years prior by Irene Lovelock, 'a simple housewife', as she loved to profess, the league objectives were 'to free the housewife from the controls which hamper her efficiency in running the home'. The BHL stressed 'the women in the home, the nation's real chancellors of the exchequer and ministers of ways and means, should have a voice'.[7] The BHL began as a protest against continued food rationing but quickly turned into a right-wing pressure group, which at its height could boast a membership of 100,000. A decidedly free-market and pro-capitalist enterprise, the BHL fought for less governmental regulation and against future nationalisation.

Although it claimed to be a non-party organisation, it is safe to classify the BHL as an anti-socialist body. While its ranks of supporters did include Labour Party members, the group's leadership was decidedly pro-Conservative. In 1948, Dorothy Crisp, the group's newly appointed chairwoman, covertly lobbied the head of the Conservative Party, Lord Woolton, to provide funding for the league. She even bizarrely offered to resign her chairwomanship of the league and afterwards send messages to each member asking them to join the Conservative Party. It appeared Crisp saw the BHL as her own personal vehicle, which she sought to use for entry into Conservative circles and eventually the House of Commons.[8] Wisely, Woolton refused both of Crisp's requests, reminding her they 'would be a repudiation of the fact that you and I have both stated publicly that there never has been any connection between the British Housewives'

League and the Conservative Party'.[9] Woolton's words were technically true. However, in early 1948 the Conservative Central Office considered an amalgamation of the BHL with the Women's United Front, a similar organisation that Lord Woolton aided in its creation as a Conservative front.[10] The plan did not go forward.

Although Crisp's request for funds, and her offer of turning its membership into an auxiliary for the Conservatives, never reached the public, Labour politicians still considered the BHL as a hostile organisation. Manny Shinwell labelled its members 'maid servants of the Tory party' and Stanford Cripps called the league 'a political instrument encouraged and misdirected by our opponents'.[11] Regardless of describing itself as a non-partisan group, clandestine connections with the Conservative Party were not its only violation of such a pledge: it regularly and publicly attacked the CPGB and its guiding tenets.

Although not the league's sole raison d'être, it still openly functioned as an anti-communist organisation. In 1947, a resolution passed by the group's Kettering branch un-equivalently stated, 'We the members of the British Housewives' League view with exceedingly grave concern the present communistic activities and we will whenever possible help to stamp it out.'[12] Speaking at league rallies were the likes of Waldron Smithers, who talked on such themes as 'materialism of communism and false prophets'.[13] Attacks on perceived communist encroachment often appeared in the organisation's newsletter *Housewives Today*. 'Everyone who understands anything at all knows that communism is the enemy, we are fighting communism', read one article in its May/June 1948 edition. It recommended 'a purge from the school staffs' of all CPGB members so 'our children could be saved from the subversive influence of communism in schools'.[14] Despite its attempts to associate with the Conservatives, this did not stop the league from attacking members of the party. A *Housewives Today* news piece appearing in its January 1951 edition, titled 'Our Stand against Communism, Mr. Eden ought to know better', condemned a remark by Anthony Eden for supposedly subscribing to a communist viewpoint. An article in the same issue claimed that both parties were permitting 'the undermining of the family' by quasi-communist notions which were 'having a most pernicious effect' on society.[15]

It is doubtful the BHL shifted the opinions of many regarding communism. As Marjorie Maxse rightfully asserted, BHL, and a number of similar groups, preached almost solely to the converted. However, the league did make headlines when it engaged in the aforementioned 'battle' of Albert Hall. On 6 June 1947, over 7,000 of its supporters packed into the hall for a demonstration demanding the resignation of Labour ministers John Strachey and Manny Shinwell. The attendees' energy levels were piqued since many were still feeling the rush of storming Westminster Palace to demonstrate against the two ministers only a day before.[16] Not surprisingly, the selection of the night's speakers again tested the group's claim of being non-partisan. Alongside Dorothy Crisp, the principal speaker was Conservative frontbencher David Maxwell Fyfe.[17]

Shortly after the rally got underway, over 100 shouting protestors jumped up, unfurling banners denouncing the league and its attacks against the government. From the upper balconies of the hall, CPGB members showered down on the audience buckets of water and hundreds of leaflets titled: 'Don't be misled by the Housewives League'. The flyers depicted three well-dressed members of the BHL addressing a street meeting. The caption of the image stated: 'Never mind the label on the packet. The stuff inside is a Tory.'[18] Chaos erupted with rally attendees physically engaging with the communist demonstrators; the scene became one of women tearing hair and kicking. A male protestor attempted to charge the stage, but a number from the female audience halted his advance by attacking him with their umbrellas.[19] The brawl soon spilled onto the streets. Mounted police and many patrolmen were dispatched to break up the disturbance.[20] Despite their best efforts, sporadic fighting continued into the night. The evening ended with the battered umbrella man formally arrested and several CPGB members escorted away in police cars.[21]

The league did its best to garner as much publicity as possible from the fracas. A regional organiser of the group claimed that far from harming the BHL, the communist attack 'put it on the map'.[22] A BHL member stated she never considered Marxism as a threat, but after the trouble at Albert Hall, her eyes were open to the 'communist menace'.[23] Lovelock used the incident as a selling point for the BHL, claiming it proved the group was fostering a more anti-communist nation:

> For at least a year now we have given warning of the danger of communism. It was obvious, in the efforts made at the Albert Hall last June to wreck our meeting, that we were feared as a bulwark against this insidious threat to individual freedom. At first, when we said we stood against communism we were told it was a bogey with no power in England. Now we find many to support our view. It has been the same with much we are fighting for. Things we have said for months are trotted out by others as new and original. But we are making an impression, even if we do not get the credit.[24]

The Albert Hall scuffle proved the high watermark of the BHL. No more battles with the CPGB erupted. Over the following years, it steadily haemorrhaged members and with them political relevance. Only a few months after attempting to hand over the BHL to the Conservative Party, Dorothy Crisp resigned as chairwoman in a cloud of scandal. The BHL continued to exist until 2000, but by 1951 it had lost most of its relevance in the public sphere.

The League of Empire Loyalists: an assault from the right

Unlike the Labour Party, the Conservatives never found it necessary to purge their ranks of supposed crypto-communists. Yet they were plagued instead with attempts by far-right extremists seeking to infiltrate their membership. In almost all instances these extremists promoted their cause under the guise of anti-communism. The most disruptive threat from the right came in the form of an organisation founded in 1954, the LEL. This reactionary pressure group was the brainchild of a former leading member of the British Union of Fascists named A.K. Chesterton – cousin of the famed Catholic apologist G.K. Chesterton.[25]

The members of the LEL rallied around the banner of preserving the British Empire. Yet historian Mark Pitchford argued the fear of encroaching communism both domestically and throughout the colonies was the key factor in its emergence.[26] It proved popular within several demographics such as returning expatriates, colonial veterans and retired military officers.[27] Although Chesterton and a number in the leadership held past associations with Oswald Mosley's British Union of Fascists, the LEL appealed to traditional right-wingers. Its brand of politics was more reactionary than revolutionary.[28] By 1955, the LEL started garnering support, to some degree, inside the Conservative Party. Many in the party found this worrisome. From its initial emergence, the Central Office considered the LEL a menace to party operations. They were not proven wrong. Through a steady campaign of literature and public speeches, the LEL criticised the Conservative leadership for both betraying the empire and appeasing communists. Not satisfied only to denounce the Conservatives through its printed literature, the group routinely personally protested its leadership. A constant irritation for Conservative functions and meetings during the period were hecklers of the LEL. From 1955–6, these centred on the most obvious of choices, Anthony Eden. As the leader of the Conservative Party and prime minister, the group considered him the man most responsible for the rotting of the empire. The LEL heckled Eden when he spoke in public and often protested at 10 Downing Street.[29] The most infamous incident occurred during a state visit by Soviet leaders Nikolai Bulganin and Nikita Khrushchev. LEL members confronted Eden as he met the two foreign dignitaries inside Victoria Station. The LEL supporters shouted that Eden had just shaken hands with murderers and the Soviet leaders had come to make the British people into slaves.[30] It resulted in the arrest of two LEL officials and caused a minor international stir.[31]

Seemingly oblivious to the anger they generated, the LEL resented their hostile treatment by Conservatives. An LEL member demanded to know from Quintin Hogg why his party tolerated 'treachery in high places by communists and secret communists and fellow-travellers' but ejected from its meetings and events the 'Loyal Britishers' of the LEL.[32] Its author found no sympathy from its recipient; in his memoirs, Quintin Hogg described the LEL as 'the sworn enemies' of the Conservative Party.[33]

Setting the LEL apart from other British anti-communist organisations of the period was its decidedly anti-American standpoint. Such a stance is discernible through the editorial content of the group's newsletter *Candour*. In the editions of *Candour*, the organisation argued that US anti-imperialism, working in conjunction with Soviet communism, was stripping the empire away from the British people:

> Apart from driving the communists out of South Korea, United States policy has done nothing to discourage, and much to encourage, growth of the communist empire, whereas its attack on the British world system has been sustained and amazingly successful. If we are to survive it is imperative that our people be made to understand this unpalatable but undeniable truth.[34]

Such anti-American diatribes rose to a fever pitch in 1956 but did not necessarily hurt the group's recruitment efforts. In the disastrous aftermath of the Suez crisis – caused in part by threatened US intercession against the UK – a number of Conservative members, now mistrustful and wary of American foreign policy, were more respectful towards the league.

The LEL's Americaphobic stance did not prohibit it from having glaring similarities with a US organisation founded only four years later. The conspiratorial theories and reactionary politics of the LEL were analogous to those of the US John Birch Society (JBS). Like the LEL did to the Conservatives, the JBS situated itself on the right of the Republican Party and campaigned that communistic-controlled international interests sought to destroy the US through covert methods. In a striking parallel to the LEL, the reactionary JBS caused much more consternation for the right than the left that it detested. The JBS made wild claims such as accusing President Dwight Eisenhower and Chief Justice of the Supreme Court Earl Warren of being communist agents. Another commonality the two shared was an aggressive hostility towards the UN. The leadership and members of both the JBS and LEL campaigned for their respective nations to withdraw forthwith from it. In 1955, only minutes after Minister of Defence Selwyn Lloyd officiated over the raising and flying of the UN flag in

Trafalgar Square, LEL members tore it down while chanting 'Britain first' and 'stand by the Empire'.[35] The LEL as well took a firm stance against UK integration within Europe, calling any move towards continental federation an attempt to enact communism. Chesterton labelled the creation of a common market as 'an avowedly communist concept' and nothing other than slightly 'disguised European communist states'.[36]

The LEL continued to harass the Conservatives long after the resignation of their primary target, Anthony Eden. If anything, rancour increased due to the decolonisation policies of Eden's successor, Harold Macmillan. To put it mildly, the LEL membership were not sympathetic towards talks of 'Winds of Change'. The group's apotheosis of publicity-seeking antics occurred when it invaded the annual Conservative Party conference at Blackpool in late October 1958.[37] In what *The Times* termed 'excessive violence amounting to brutality', the Conservatives ejected LEL members as they interrupted the conference.[38] The violent methods used by the Conservatives to expel the league garnered extensive coverage in the press. By the early 1960s, the LEL's escapades were less frequent; its membership dropped dramatically (from a height of 3,000 to around 300 in 1961) and the group struggled with financial troubles.[39] In 1967, the remnants of the LEL disbanded to help form the National Front.[40]

Common Cause – an American front?

Common Cause was first and foremost an American invention. It formed in 1947 solely as a vehicle to combat domestic communism. It crossed the Atlantic when its leader, Natalie Payne, appealed to Unionist MP Malcolm Douglas-Hamilton to undertake the formation of a similar organisation in the UK. Intrigued by the prospect, he travelled to the US on a fact-finding mission to look into the group. Accompanying him was a man named C.A. Smith, who held the reputation of being somewhat of a maverick in and around the British ultra-left. Smith, and not Douglas-Hamilton, would arise as the driving figure behind Common Cause (UK). A Labour man during the 1920s, Smith stood unsuccessfully as a parliamentary candidate for the party in the 1924 and 1929 elections. By the 1930s, he had deserted Labour and converted to Trotskyism. In 1933, he met with Leon Trotsky and soon afterwards vocally supported the Fourth International. The rising influence of the Trotskyist movement inside of the Independent Labour Party (ILP) in the late 1930s allowed Smith to take over the leadership of the party in 1939. Smith's support of the war effort caused him to break with the ILP. Shortly afterwards he joined the Common Wealth Party, where he took up the post of its research officer.

As with the ILP, Smith soon took over the leadership of the Common Wealth Party. Again, Smith's position as Common Wealth Party chairman proved short-lived. The onset of increased international tensions with the Soviet Union turned Smith into a fervent anti-communist. After failing to steer the Common Wealth Party in this political direction, he resigned from the party in 1948.[41]

In November 1951 Smith and Douglas-Hamilton, accompanied by John Brown (former general secretary of the Iron and Steels Trades Confirmation), contacted prospective members for a British Common Cause. Shortly afterwards in January 1952, Common Cause (UK) began to function. The trio had been successful in their recruitment efforts and had found many influential supporters for the new enterprise. The organisation released a list of its governing council. It included well-known persons from both the Conservative and Labour Parties, alongside several prominent trade union leaders. The inclusion of John Brown, by Douglas-Hamilton and Smith, helps explain a large amount of trade union support early on. Prior to his participation in Common Cause, Brown had formed a short-lived but similar organisation, directed primarily at combating communism in trade unions. It went by the colourful name of Freedom First and had closely worked with the IRD to spread anti-communist propaganda.[42] The creation of Common Cause took up the mantle in the fight from Freedom First. It also brought about a diminishing domestic role of another anti-communist group called the British League for European Freedom (BLEF). The duchess of Atoll, a founding member of BLEF and a Common Cause supporter, stated with the start of Common Cause the BLEF put less emphasis on 'purely political work'.[43] The BLEF and its sister organisation the Scottish League for European Freedom were both heavily involved with MI6-sponsored exile operations behind the Iron Curtain. Although the two groups did function inside the UK, their domestic anti-communist activities were quite limited.

Like its American counterpart, Common Cause (UK) declared its main aim was 'to expose the Communist party as a treacherous conspiracy serving a foreign totalitarian dictatorship whose global imperialism threatens freedom everywhere'.[44] As with other anti-communist pressure groups of the period, Common Cause advertised itself as a non-partisan organisation which welcomed members from any political party – except, of course, the CPGB. In a letter to the Labour Party chairman, C.A. Smith emphasised this non-partisan nature by declaring, 'I myself [am] a life-long unswerving socialist.'[45] However, Smith's questionable affiliations did not put the Conservative Party off the organisation. The concern which arose in the Central Office was the prospect that Labour 'will use it [Common Cause] as an instrument to show how anti-communist they are and that it will eventually become a socialist organization on an anti-communist basis'.[46] This worry lessened. A later Central Office report on the group classified it as 'a genuine all-party anti-communist organization' but still cautioned 'it is too early to say whether they are working on the right lines'. The memo advised that 'too many' similar organisations had 'preached only to the converted'.[47] In the early days directly after Common Cause announced its formation, what struck the Central Office as odd was the source of the organisation's funding. It reported that 'a great many dollars are coming from America' or, put more simply, 'there are Yankee dollars behind it'. Conservative sources reported that this US-funded British pressure group intended 'to spend a considerable number of dollars over the years in this country with the purpose of combating communism'.[48]

The British government considered the US connection to Common Cause unsettling, and potentially troublesome. Sources at the FO reported Natalie Paine – the chief American promoter for the creation of a British Common Cause – claimed the group had the direct backing of the US State Department and the approval of her close friend Walter Bedell Smith, the director of the CIA. They also stated she privately confessed that the real objective for Common Cause in the UK had more to do with influencing US politics than fighting domestic communism in the UK. Paine believed 'there is a considerable body of opinion in the US which considers that the UK is only lukewarm in its anti-communist attitude'. Hence, the creation of a well-funded and highly publicised group like Common Cause (UK) would cut 'the ground from under the feet of Americans who retain isolationist prejudices, and also ... weaken the campaign already existing there to reduce American financial help to the UK on the grounds that the UK is using such help in riotous living and not in combating communism'.[49] The British embassy in Washington, DC, supported Paine's objective. It supported her efforts 'to help restore the belief of Americans that we are playing our full part in the struggle for Western values against communism'.[50] Opinions on the benefits of Common Cause were not all as favourable back at Whitehall. In November 1951, Maggie Hamilton of the Information Policy Department wrote to a journalist who had frequent contact with Paine. She warned, 'I think you know that we are officially more than doubtful of the wisdom of anything like a public campaign against communism in this country.' In a confidential letter to the British Information Services, Hamilton reported the FO sought to damage the group. 'We have been occupied here in trying to keep the infant Common Cause England on the rails', she explained; 'in other words to prevent them launching out on anything in the nature of an anti-communist campaign.'[51] Like Hamilton, many in the British government feared that the Americans wished to export (sanctioned by the CIA and the State Department or not) Common Cause not only to improve US public opinion towards the UK but also to spread the McCarthyite anti-communist reaction across the Atlantic.

Her superior, John Peck, the department head of the IRD, overruled Hamilton's fears about the potential dangers of Common Cause. Peck, a dedicated cold warrior in the same vein as IRD's creator Christopher Mayhew, considered the outside organisation as both a worthy ally and a potential tool in the fight against the domestic red enemy – an ally who deserved his department's support. Even before the official launch of Common Cause, on 3 December 1951 Peck wrote to Lord Malcolm Douglas-Hamilton to offer suggestions on the organisation's anti-communist efforts. He recommended it should focus its attacks on the Soviet-sponsored peace campaign: 'We feel, therefore, that it would be a tactical error to concentrate on straight communist propaganda and activities if a large part of the real damage is being done by the peace campaigners.'[52] Such advice and assistance to the group was not an isolated incident. On another occasion, C.A. Smith's secretary contacted the IRD requesting sensitive information to strengthen its 'press battles' supporting West German rearmament, which the IRD then provided.[53]

While Common Cause garnered some limited success from gaining 'unofficial' support from IRD, this did not set the group apart from other anti-communist organisations. Many of the larger pressure groups of the same ilk were also provided a helping hand by the IRD – such as the MRA and the Economic League. Common Cause's basic operations and structural make-up mirrored those of its competitors. It set up a national structure with local branches – in 1954 there were fourteen scattered through England, Scotland and Wales. Like similar pressure groups, its principal function was the production and distribution of anti-communist literature to 'inform' the public of the encroaching 'red menace'. It appeared Common Cause also covertly worked against communist campaigns in officer elections of the Amalgamated Engineering Union.[54]

What differentiated Common Cause from other anti-communist pressure groups were two major themes it emphasised. One was its non-partisan nature; while others also claimed this, none did so more than Common Cause. Common Cause claimed it had a better reputation with the working class than the Economic League, which it privately labelled as appearing reactionary.[55] The second theme was an almost unwaveringly pro-American stance. As an anti-communist force in the UK, Common Cause remained one of the few entities which refused to condemn the excesses of the red scare raging across the US. Even as the Army–McCarthy

PRESSURE GROUPS   159

hearings turned millions of Americans against McCarthyism, the organisation did not openly refute McCarthyite methods:

> For several months there has been a steady trickle of requests from readers of this Bulletin that Common Cause should define its attitude towards McCarthyism. Hitherto we have declined to do so for the reason that much of the frenzied denunciation of the Wisconsin Senator is motivated by the conscious desire to create ill-will between Britain and America. Since the preservation of freedom in the world depends on Anglo-American friendship and co-operation, Common Cause will not assist in playing the game of hate America party-liners.[56]

Although the British Common Cause publicly proclaimed itself as having no ties to its US namesake, its unfalteringly Americanophile stance calls this into question. The only other body which refused to take a harsh line towards McCarthy was the CIA-backed Congress of Cultural Freedom and its magazine *Encounter*.[57] An article appearing in *Encounter*, written by Tosco Fyvel, a founder of the magazine, argued the rise of McCarthy was merely a fad and nothing to worry about. He favourably compared it to the British domestic sentiment after the First World War.[58] The fact the only other anti-communist entity in the UK that openly defended McCarthy was Common Cause gives some credence to the supposition that American interests directed it. Also, if Paine's assertions of having the tacit backing of the CIA and the State Department were accurate, then it takes little guesswork to determine who ultimately defined Common Cause's politics. Regardless of whether it had links to the US government or not, the organisation sought tirelessly to defend American anti-communism, even when this proved wildly unpopular.

In terms of ingratiating itself with the two main political parties in its own country, Common Cause's efforts proved less effective. In 1954, a motion at the Labour Party conference to declare Common Cause a proscribed organisation was put forward. In response, Smith – as general secretary – wrote to Morgan Phillips, defending the group. Smith claimed Common Cause was a target of communist 'smear-campaigns' which 'included we are financed by American interests and are supported by the British government – all of which are lies'.[59] As the records prove, this all turned out to be true. Although the Conservatives never attempted to dissociate officially from Common Cause, the party questioned the effectiveness of the group's anti-communist efforts. In 1956, the Central Office assessed that the group had done a certain amount of work 'within the trade unions by means of propaganda and week-end schools but it is difficult to gauge what success has been achieved'.[60] It recommended that the

Conservatives focus on other more worthwhile endeavours than contributing their time and money towards Common Cause.

By 1953, the IRD began covert discussions on the future of Common Cause. The talks centred on a proposed unofficial 'takeover' of the group by the government. The FO determined that, as a domestic anti-communist propaganda engine, the organisation could potentially 'serve a useful purpose'. However, for this takeover of Common Cause to transpire, a change of leadership needed to occur. Writing on the situation, IRD department head Peck stated:

> The danger is that as at present constituted 'Common Cause' is inclined to employ slightly hysterical methods and its leading spirit Dr C. A. Smith is a fanatic who sometimes comes dangerously near to advocating witch hunts and also appears to be vain and indiscreet ... It looks therefore as if we should discreetly work for the building up of an effective executive committee to run 'Common Cause'.[61]

Peck's point on the fanatical mindset of Smith was evident when reading the material produced by the group. The front page of one of the group's newsletters gives a typical example:

> Democratic rights are for those who accept democratic procedure. Freedom is for those who respect the freedom of others ... So let us treat Stalinist traitors in 1952 as we treated Hitlerite traitors in 1940 and remove them from positions in which their treachery could do most harm. This is not a witch-hunt. It would better termed a rat-hunt – save that this is unfair to the quadrupeds.[62]

The man Peck recommended to officiate the oust of Smith was Major Tufton Beamish, a reactionary Conservative MP who sat on the advisory council of the group. It was recommended that Beamish 'should be pressed to co-operate in finding suitable members who could take effective control of Common Cause'. Beamish rejected the FO request and excused himself from such a role, claiming his duties as an MP left him little time for such an operation. Disagreeing with Peck, Anthony Nutting saw little use for Common Cause. Exclaiming about such groups, Nutting said, 'I doubt very much that they do any serious good.' He added, 'It's always the same story – a bunch of enthusiasm from some well-meaning but not very stable do-gooders and then a gradual run-down, leading to collapse.'[63] Peck remained firm; despite his misgivings towards Smith, he maintained that Common Cause filled 'large gaps in the anti-communist organization particularly in the field of general education'.[64]

Eventually, Nutting's assessment proved correct. In 1956, Common Cause fell apart and split into rival factions. Its trade union members helped found a new group called Industrial Research and Information Services Ltd (IRIS) to continue the struggle against communistic influence in unions.[65] Evidence suggests that the IRD succeeded in having effective control over IRIS, but disavowed the remnants of the Common Cause organisation with which it broke.[66] In 1962 the Committee on Communism (Home) later classified IRIS as the 'most useful of the anti-communist organizations, at least from the point of view of the government'.[67] Although Common Cause continued to exist, by the mid-1960s the government considered it an unusable organisation for its anti-communist purposes:

> Common Cause is a useless, counter-productive, right-wing and irresponsible organization. It suffers from too ample an income, apparently derived from business circles, for which it has no real use ... its progress has been beset by internal schisms and feuds ... by 1959 there was discernible neo-Fascist element inside the organization.[68]

In 1967, when questioned if IRD ever had dealings with Common Cause, departmental officials lied and claimed it did not.[69]

Moral Rearmament or ruin

Of all the anti-communist organisations operating in the UK during the postwar period, one of the most successful was the MRA. In terms of funding, logistics and political influence, the group far surpassed its contemporaries. From 1945 and throughout the next decade it proved one of the most effective anti-communist organisations inside the UK. A self-proclaimed religious movement, it did not spread a specific dogma or an underlying sacred belief, though it constantly sought converts to its cause. The MRA claimed it proselytised a simple choice to the world: either live or govern by the principles mandated by the MRA or become enslaved by the tyranny of godless communism. It preached that the struggle between East and West boiled down to a global plebiscite in which the only correct vote was the adoption of MRA moralities or else Marxist communism conquered. In December 1954, one of the groups' most ardent devotees articulated this point in the House of Commons. 'The moral standards of Moral Rearmament are something above religion', stated Labour MP John McGovern. He continued, 'People can worship God in their own way and yet can unite around the moral and spiritual forces provided by Moral Rearmament and ... present a solid phalanx throughout the world against the communist creed.' McGovern's anti-communism did not result from his conversion to the MRA. As early as 1937, he railed against communist atrocities during the Spanish Civil War, and in 1939 he memorably denounced the 'bloodstained handshake of Stalin and Ribbentrop'.[70] Yet by 1954, McGovern had come to believe that no alternative existed to halt the 'red menace' except the MRA: 'In the struggle which is taking place in the world Moral Rearmament has been the one unifying force presented as a superior ideology ... I believe that if we cannot unite the population on that basis the world is lost and godless communism will take over country after country, step by step.'[71]

The founder of the MRA, and its leader until his death in 1961, was Frank Buchman. Born in Pennsylvania in 1878, Buchman came from a Swiss family which immigrated to the US in the 1700s.[72] Having completed his education, and after undertaking various international study tours, he took up jobs both pastoring and running a home for runaways. In 1918, he undertook a mission trip to China under the auspices of Hartford College. In 1921, Buchman was invited to Oxford, where he soon found friends and followers, especially among the undergraduates attracted by his puritanical outlook. He made use of the experience he had gained as a missionary to gather followers to his teachings. At Oxford, one of the methods he employed was holding house parties as a means of converting people to his spiritual beliefs.

Soon his meetings turned into a formal organisation called the Oxford Group. Buchman laid down its goals in four points known as the 'Four Absolutes'. He defined these tenets as absolute unselfishness, absolute honesty, absolute purity and absolute love on the personal and national plane.[73] Adherents adopting these standards were instructed to take active and conscious steps to ensure that their daily lives were lived entirely in accordance with them. The standard method adopted by his followers was to receive divine guidance by having a quiet time each morning, during which the follower wrote down thoughts on the action to be taken during the day. Buchman maintained that all problems, whether personal or political, were solvable if an individual examined themselves and acknowledged their own moral corruption and dealt with it in an honest fashion. The group, which changed its name to Moral Rearmament in 1938, extended this programme to cover personal, social, industrial, national and supranational fields. It sought, in the words, of Buchman to solve personal, national and international problems by bringing men and women everywhere back to the basic principle of a Christian life, thus enhancing all of their primary loyalties.[74] According to Buchman, the MRA was not an organisation, sect, society or denomination. He claimed it had no membership lists, subscriptions, badges or rules. And he proudly boasted that a large number of persons, members of all the recognised Christian churches throughout the world, representing almost every creed, political party, class and colour, were following in its teachings. According to the founder, its aim was a new social order under the control of the spirit of God, making for better human relationships, for unselfish cooperation, for cleaner business, for cleaner politics, and for the elimination of political, industrial and racial antagonism. In essence, the group preached that the moral redemption of individuals would bring about a spiritual reconstruction of nations.

Buchman sought a wider field of followers than that of mere university students. He targeted the influential and the wealthy. Through Buchman's efforts, the MRA became composed of politicians, industrialists and trade unionists. When international tensions increased during the late 1930s, the MRA's popularity skyrocketed in both the US and UK. The movement promoted the belief that if only world leaders adopted and governed through the philosophy of the four absolutes, peace could be maintained. In the UK, a book published by the group entitled *The Battle for Peace* (1938) sold over half a million copies. In 1939, 240 members of the House of Commons and 25 members of the House of Lords signed messages of greetings and support for the movement.[75] Throughout the US, the group gained powerful allies such as Harry S. Truman.[76] By the end of the 1930s, the MRA had expanded its followers to include those residing in over fifty countries. The advent of the Second World War brought the MRA to the attention of the British government.[77] Both MI5 and MI6 investigated reported links between the group and Nazi Germany. This examination included contacting the FBI for information the American government held concerning the movement.[78] The Home Office requested a police report on the group as well. What concerned British intelligence about the MRA was its anti-war message but also remarks made by Buchman regarding Hitler. As well as a devoted Christian, Buchman was also a devout anti-communist. So much so that he viewed it as the ultimate evil and thus a much greater danger than fascism. Buchman would later regret saying, in an August 1936 interview with the *New York World-Telegram*:

> I thank heavens for a man like Adolf Hitler who built a front line defence against the anti-Christ of communism. My barber in London told me Hitler saved Europe from communism. That's how he felt. Of course, I don't condone everything the Nazis do. Anti-Semitism? Bad, naturally. I suppose Hitler sees a Karl Marx in every Jew.[79]

In the spring of 1941, MI5 reported that 'there is no doubt that Buchman was on terms of friendship with certain of the Nazis leaders' and stated it is 'certainly curious' that the MRA had 'perhaps unconsciously been of assistance to the German cause'.[80] Nevertheless, after a thorough investigation, British intelligence determined that the MRA had no ties with Nazi Germany and was not seeking to impede the war effort in any manner.[81]

The postwar era revitalised the MRA. It brought about a revolutionary shift of its priorities and stated goals. Also, through the generous donations of wealthy supporters, the MRA began to expand its political activities and its outreach programmes. In 1946, Frank Buchman moved its headquarters to Caux, a small town in Switzerland, which his followers essentially purchased. But more importantly, the onset of the Cold War saw the movement's emphasis transform from focusing on individual lives to a much grander narrative. As Buchman stressed, the MRA now provided an ideology for the salvation of the world against the West's greatest menace, communism.[82] Buchman directed MRA chapters to actively attempt to influence and alter the political agendas and civil societies of nations in which they were located. He directed them to push an anti-communist agenda. The two countries where this campaign garnered the most success in Europe was in West Germany and the UK. West German Chancellor Konrad Adenauer stood as one of the movement's most prominent allies. In 1952, Adenauer awarded Buchman his nation's highest honour – the Order of Merit of the Federal Republic of Germany.

According to the movement's numerous critics, the methods the MRA employed were anything but subtle. Through its growing propaganda machine, the MRA put forth a dichotomy of how the future of the world would progress. Simply put, the nations of the world could either embrace the principles of Moral Rearmament or fall to the tyranny of godless communism.[83] Buchman and his followers preached that democracy as an ideology was too vapid and empty for effectively overcoming the strength of Marxist totalitarianism. In 1950, MRA supporter and former wartime director of British naval intelligence Admiral J.H. Godfrey gave a ringing endorsement of this theory:

> We have an urgent need to develop a moral ideology which can effectively answer communism on a world front. We made Fuchs a British subject and gave him a passport, but omitted to provide him with a moral background and he remained a communist at heart ... I believe that Caux offers the following things at this critical moment in history: An ideology strong enough to change communists and make them fight with at least equal vigour for a democratic way of life.[84]

The MRA preached that the world needed something more to fill the void inside the common man in order to stop communism. This void-filling ideology was the central teaching of the MRA – not the allure of capitalism. The MRA propaganda postulated that the conflict between communism and capitalism amounted to a struggle between two forms of materialism. It argued that tired, old capitalistic materialism could not win against the much more aggressive and revolutionary communist ideology. Only the 'revolutionary ideology' of Moral Rearmament, which is superior, can build the coming new world. Although officially non-denominational, the movement addressed its message in American fundamentalist rhetoric. In regards to communist countries, it stated:

> The nations that have forgotten this struggle, have forgotten God, and lost their freedom. Some have remembered this struggle and dis-covered the master of Evil ... An extreme of evil must be met with an extreme of good; a fanatical following of evil by a passionate purist of good. This is why democracy fails time after time in the world today. Only a passion can cure passion.[85]

The dissemination of this message was the primary aim of the MRA. Working with professional advertising agencies and with the assistance of trained journalists such as Peter Howard, its propaganda wing in the UK soon rivalled those of both the Conservative and Labour Parties. Howard, who eventually succeeded Buchman as leader of the MRA after the latter's death in 1961, joined the MRA in the 1930s. While working as a reporter for the *Daily Express*, the newspaper's owner Lord Beaverbrook ordered him to investigate Buchman and his movement. Howard soon fell in with Buchman and worked as the head of the MRA in the UK, as well as becoming its chief propagandist. Like his leader, Howard was a committed anti-communist who sincerely believed communism explic-itly threatened the British way of life.[86] In 1951, he warned Buchman that the UK 'is sick unto death with problems' and thus 'the infiltration of communism into the heart and head of Britain is truly astonishing'.[87] Seeking to curb this 'red menace', the MRA distributed anti-communist literature but also sought more inventive ways to spread its gossip. One of these was the use of performance art. The movement produced and staged plays – and even created feature-length films – in a bid to gen-erate interest for the movement within the larger public.[88] None other than Peter Howard authored a substantial portion of these pro-MRA plays.[89] On numerous occasions, the MRA used these plays in order to specifically bolster its influence inside one segment of the population, the trade union movement. One of its most successful plays was entitled *The Forgotten Factor* – the group later produced an American film ver-sion of it. The plot dealt with industrial unrest and how the principles of the MRA could solve this over those of the communists. The group held showings of *The Forgotten Factor* in coal mining and manufacturing regions. It invited trade union officials and prominent members of the local communities to the play's numerous premieres. Often a spokesperson for the group forestalled the play in order to give a speech promoting the movement's message. At the 1946 premiere of *The Forgotten Factor* performance at Belfast Opera House, Peter Howard was on hand. Before the film, he compared a democratic state without an underlining ideology to 'a crab without a shell – tempting bait and easy meat for the evil birds of totalitarianism'.[90] Praising the play when it showed in his city, the Lord Mayor of Cardiff said: 'Western civilisation is on the verge of a great crisis, and this play holds the unsuspected solution.'[91] Making sure to advertise its positive reaction, the MRA produced literature reprinting praise for the film by a number of trade unionists.

As early as 1947, it began targeting its efforts to converting prominent union officials in the coal mining industry. As an MRA report stated, 'the question of what men and ideals will control 700,000 British miners' was of prime importance to the organisation.[92] The MRA promised an end of all industrial ills if trade unions only adopted its principles and its leaders converted to the movement. It pledged through the guiding hand of MRA leadership industry production would increase, teamwork between management and workers would foster and, most importantly, the subversive forces of communism would wither and die. The MRA ran their own candidates for union offices held by communists.[93] It also paid the expenses of trade union leaders to visit Caux, where the group then attempted to 'convert' these individuals to the movement. Often these conversion methods succeeded. By 1955, the organisation had over 150 full-time agents working to convert trade union members. Through concerted attempts, the MRA sought first to infiltrate and then seize control of the trade union movement. This was the exact same strategy, a number of its critics pointed out, used by the MRA's greatest foe, the communists. In a 1951 memorandum on the group, a government official stated the MRA 'sometimes seems almost to have learnt lessons from the communist technique by ways in which by persistent and steady pressure it gets interested persons into the net'.[94]

Both MI5 and the FO's postwar sentiments towards the MRA were mixed. In particular, the debate broke down to the moral question of means justifying ends. In a number of department correspondences and letters, British officials both praised its anti-communist efforts but in the same breath questioned its methods. Director of MI5 Percy Sillitoe wrote in 1951 that the leadership of the MRA 'have always been strongly opposed to communism'; however, the movement exaggerated its successes in converting communists to its cause.[95] A later MI5 memo to a security liaison officer emphasised that the MRA 'may be doing useful work in this field' against communism. However, it stressed the movement 'must be regarded with a certain amount of caution partly because some of its supporters are of somewhat unstable character and because its methods of obtaining support for the movement are not always entirely above board'.[96] In 1955 a confidential report from the British embassy in Bern to the head of the security department at the FO described a visit by FO diplomats to the movement's headquarters in Caux. The account stated:

> On the whole I think we can claim to have extricated ourselves from the MRA spider's-web spun from Caux without undue hurt ... this personal experience of the methods of the MRA headquarters staff, as it were, leaves, however, a somewhat nasty taste in the mouth and evokes the conclusion that whatever one might think of the purposes of MRA their methods are quite unworthy of respect. It may, of course, be argued that one cannot fight communism with kid gloves and so MRA is obliged to play the Kremlin at its own game (e.g. the ends justify the means). However plausible such a plea may be, this recent example of its application is scarcely calculated to make friends. Having thus been warned of the unscrupulous tactics of these MRA chaps we propose in the future to give them a wide berth.[97]

As the above account demonstrates, by the mid-1950s facets of the British government viewed the MRA as a liability and if not quite dangerous, then a menacing organisation. The Conservative Central Office essentially assessed the MRA along the same lines. The party applauded its successful efforts fighting communism but also did its best not to closely associate with the organisation. But not everyone agreed with this lukewarm stance towards such a potentially powerful ally. In a report to the Conservative Party chairman, the stalwartly anti-communist Marjorie Maxse sought to change the party's attitude towards the group:

> The effect that MRA is having on communists cannot be denied. We have received several reports on this. Luckily for us, MRA have decided that communism is the complete antithesis to their message and are therefore concentrating on infiltration into communist ranks, in some cases with remarkable success ... The gist of this memorandum is that in view of the fight of MRA against communism, should we take a more sympathetic attitude towards it? There is no question of finance as they have all the money they need, but we have consistently kept them off with the proverbial barge-pole.[98]

In a separate memo, Maxse argued that her party should not do anything to impede the movement, stating, 'It is so obviously anti-communist in its action that I feel it can be safely left to its own momentum.'[99] Her colleagues at the Central Office did not hold her zeal for the movement. One labelled it 'as something of a snob version of the Salvation Army.'[100] W.M. Ridwell, the party's publicity organiser, conceded that the MRA did hold a 'number of well-known Conservatives among its active supporters', but still argued 'no useful purpose could be served by our giving official blessing to the movement'.[101] 'Buchman is largely a charlatan', one employee wrote, but callously added, 'one cannot help thinking an organization which fights communism to this extent cannot be a harmful influence ... it would be a pity if it got into socialist hands'.[102] A handwritten note he scrawled on a memo sent by Maxse concerning the MRA reveals Conservative Party chairman Lord Woolton's opinion towards the group. It simply stated, 'I distrust the people who run this movement.'[103] The leadership of the MRA had mutual feelings towards the Conservative chairman. Peter Howard, in a letter to Buchman, branded Woolton a man of 'questionable calibre'.[104]

Many interested and influential parties agreed with Woolton's assessment of the MRA. As the movement grew in size and influence, it garnered a larger number of opponents from a various range of affiliations. The loudest and earliest critic of the movement was future Labour Party chairman Tom Driberg. Early in his career as a journalist, Driberg wrote negatively on the activities of both Frank Buchman and his movement.[105] A career transition to electoral politics by Driberg did not stop him from continuing this endeavour. Like his Labour colleague John McGovern, Driberg loudly voiced his opinion of the MRA – though the two men vehemently disagreed over the supposed merits of the organisation. In 1946, Driberg urged the Home Office to prohibit Buchman from visiting the UK and to deport him if he set foot on British soil. Later in life, he authored a book on the movement entitled *The Mystery of Moral Re-armament* (1964). In it, he criticised the movement thoroughly and in depth. He surmised the MRA worked as an American organisation which sought to promote the goals of its wealthy financial backers. Driberg argued that its anti-communist strategy

> had been adopted because MRA's rich backers – particularly the American industrialists who have contributed so generously to its funds – had seen in it a convenient instrument for anti-communist propaganda, or another 'voice of America' in the Cold War. That would indeed be to confuse means with ends, to use religion and God in a totally impermissible way, and to reduce what had begun, in intention, as a humane and 'life-changing' force to a mere quasi-spiritual McCarthyism.[106]

In September 1953 in a bid to counter the MRA's efforts towards trade unions, the International Confederation of Free Trade Unions (ICFTU) published a critical report on the organisation. It accused the movement of anti-trade union activities, which went as far as to label its efforts as attempts to form 'yellow trade unions'. Mirroring Driberg's later criticism, the report questioned both where the MRA received its financial support and how these unidentified sources likely directed the objectives of the organisation. The ICFTU also labelled Buchman's authoritarian control over the group as a concern: 'His is not the path of a democratic movement, but that of a dictatorship.' The report concluded that the group's motives were 'hardly aimed at the welfare of mankind in general' and argued that the 'MRA should be prevented from encroaching upon trade union preserves'.[107] In November 1956, continued interference of the MRA in industrial matters caused the ICFTU executive board to issue a statement advising trade unionists to sever all connections with the group. Arthur Deakin, the leader of the TGWU, stated his union was 'completely opposed to any interference' by the MRA 'in our industrial organization'. Driberg wrote that: 'These sharp rebuffs by the ICFTU must be among the severest set-backs that MRA has received.' In this case, obviously, the MRA could not indulge in its usual McCarthyite smear and allege that anybody who criticised it was a communist or 'communist-inspired'.[108]

In 1955 the Church of England publicly criticised the MRA through a report issued by the Social and Industrial Council of the Church Assembly. *The Times* quoted it as calling the movement 'psychologically dangerous and gravely defective in its social thinking'.[109] Critiquing its strong anti-communism, the church body wrote that the MRA 'as an ideological warfare against communism is a naïve and irresponsible response, and fails to measure up to the magnitude of the communist challenge to mankind'.[110] In its most damning of statements on the movement, the council's report determined it a form of Christian heresy.[111] Archbishop of Canterbury Geoffrey Fisher found much at fault with the MRA as well. Prior to the issuing of the council's report, the MRA applied to Fisher, as he put it in his own words, the 'strongest possible pressure upon me and upon other people to prevent any report being published'.[112] Privately Fisher described its methods as 'those of American evangelism and high business'. He considered the movement dishonest, saying, 'it gets money from people by what I can only describe as very nearly false pretences'.[113] 'I think some of their methods are unhealthy', Fisher wrote in January 1955, 'and their dominance by Frank Buchman with money and publicity is dangerous.'[114] The archbishop also doubted the threat the MRA claimed to pose against the communist ideology. Replying to pro-MRA correspondence, Fisher wrote:

> You say that communists regard MRA as their most active and dangerous enemies: that requires corrections: the communists undoubtedly regard the Roman Catholic Church as their most active and dangerous enemies ... I have never heard any communist criticism of MRA. It does not reach me.[115]

Speaking 'brutally', Fisher concluded that the MRA did not 'offer any alternative at all' in fighting against red ideology, since 'only the Christian religion does that', and as 'MRA had really ceased to be in any tangible form a Christian movement', he assessed it as a useless tool in the fight against communism.[116] Fisher was quite correct in his 'criticism' of the MRA not remaining a Christian movement. By then, it had begun seeking allies and converts from all world faiths, except the faith of Marxist-Leninism. Disagreeing with the Church of England and the archbishop of Canterbury was Pope Pius XII. In 1950, he christened the movement 'a good thing. We must, above all, give the world peace. We must also abolish communism by giving those people something better and the Church and Moral Rearmament can do this. I give Moral Rearmament my blessing'.[117]

Communists remained another obvious critic of the movement. As early as 1941 the CPGB had opened a file on the group.[118] It labelled the organisation as 'an Anglo-American plot' supported by business interests from both sides of the Atlantic.[119] Although the CPGB was publicly dismissive of the group, MI5 reported in 1950 the party was concerned over the success the MRA was having in converting some of its members. Thus, the CPGB 'is considering placing an agent in the movement to expose the methods by which it works and so nullify its effect'.[120] For its part, *Pravda* termed the MRA a 'pro-fascist international organization ... which is headed by the outspoken Hitlerite, Frank Buchman'.[121]

Routinely countering the onslaught of negative criticism of the group were prominent and influential allies of the MRA. Just as its criticism came from various societal factions – political, governmental, religious and union movements – a number of its defenders arose from these as well. However, during the early Cold War period the MRA could rely on the consistent support of individuals from one group more than any other. Ironically, this particular group also housed its most dogged opponent, Tom Driberg. After Driberg forcefully criticised the MRA during a Commons speech in 1946, fifty Labour MPs wrote an open letter 'dissociating' themselves from their colleague's words. 'Our present wish is to place on record our belief in the principles which MRA stand', the letter stated. It went on to say, 'We believe that civilisation will be submerged in a welter of materialism unless the spirit of MRA ... is understood and practised in all walks of life'.[122] Labour MP Arthur Lewis went so far as to label Driberg's attacks 'a smear campaign'.[123] In response to the ICFTU criticisms of the MRA, six Labour MPs issued a statement voicing their continued support for the movement.[124]

During times of crisis, the MRA relied on Labour Party members to work as a de facto parliamentary lobby for the group. Some in Labour even wished for it fully to align with the movement. As early as 1946, four Labour MPs issued a joint statement, arguing if their party only embraced the 'force and philosophy' of the MRA, 'it would give Labour a new spiritual dynamic and bring unity where there is danger of discord'.[125] In 1955, a member of the party executive, James Haworth, said the only way to 'restore the lost soul' of Labour was the adoption of 'the four absolute standards of MRA'.[126] By far the loudest voice for Moral Rearmament, inside or outside the Labour Party, during the period was John McGovern. Like some trade unionists who visited the MRA headquarters in Caux, McGovern came back from an August 1954 visit a 'converted man' and, in his own words, with 'the beginning of a new life'.[127] In the period from 1955 to 1959, McGovern travelled over 150,000 miles and addressed more than 125,000 people across the globe endorsing the MRA.[128] Despite his zeal, McGovern projected little influence over his colleagues or the government. This was not the case with another Labour MP. Prior to McGovern's conversion, the MRA already had a key ally in the form of a person situated in a strategic position within the Attlee government. Evidence shows that the founder of the IRD, Christopher Mayhew, was both a personal friend of Peter Howard and an ardent advocate of the MRA.

Like McGovern, Mayhew transformed into a vocal supporter of the MRA following time spent at its facilities in Caux. After visiting, he wrote of being 'tremendously impressed with Moral Rearmament' and, despite it not having 'got a very good name in this country [the UK]', he 'hoped and believed the movement will thrive'.[129] Mayhew's conversion to supporting the MRA appeared to be one the group wholeheartedly orchestrated. On two separate occasions, in 1949, Labour MP Arthur Lewis and prominent artist Lawson Wood, both MRA devotees, met with Mayhew to discuss the group and praise its accomplishments.[130]

After his visit, Mayhew sought to influence the government towards a more sympathetic and accepting stance regarding the group. He also went to great lengths to aid the movement, often in ways which bordered, if not entirely crossed into, the illicit. 'You cannot call me a member of the party', Mayhew relayed to his close friend Peter Howard regarding his connection with the MRA, 'but I am an enthusiastic fellow-traveller.' However, he assured Howard, 'If it would help for me to go on the public record how highly I regard the work of Moral Rearmament, I shall be very glad to do so.'[131] Public or not, he worked to promote the cause. Mayhew requested all British ambassadors in Europe to give reports on Moral Rearmament, for what ends Mayhew did not state. When HM Treasury and the FO advised against an MRA application for funds, Mayhew lobbied his superior, Foreign Secretary Ernest Bevin, to support the application, since the MRA would 'forward the purposes of our foreign policy'.[132] He also secretly warned Howard that Bevin's main source of information on the MRA came from 'our old buddy, Tom D[riberg]'.[133] Indeed, Mayhew held no love for Driberg personally. He called him a 'friend of [Guy] Burgess' and 'a fellow traveller'.[134] According to Howard, Mayhew sought to counteract Driberg, sell the movement to Bevin and even 'tackle the prime minister on the subject of Moral Rearmament'. He gleefully reported to Buchman that Mayhew planned to lobby the BBC to produce a favourable television programme on the movement. Howard emphasised, 'These are Mayhew's own convictions and it will be interesting to see how far he gets with them.'[135] With respect to the BBC, Mayhew did not get far. The BBC denied Mayhew's request in airing a show on the group, justifying it by calling the MRA 'highly controversial' and stating 'in spite of the most continued and varied attempts we have never managed to persuade anybody from MRA to discuss or argue it'. 'The group seemed to be prepared to put out propaganda', the BBC response to Mayhew noted, 'but not to discuss.'[136]

Mayhew sought to assist the MRA without foreseeable reservations. After the disappearance of Burgess and Maclean, while the nation collectively wondered about the two missing diplomats, Howard, and by extension Buchman, were given confidential information regarding the situation by Mayhew. Howard informed Buchman that Mayhew 'told us that the Foreign Office have no news of any kind whatever about where the disappearing diplomats have gone to, but added in confidence that another Foreign Office official here has just had his passport withdrawn by the intelligence authorities'. Such leakage of governmental information suggests Mayhew violated the Official Secrets Act. Howard excitedly recounted in summer 1951 that Mayhew 'is known now as an MRA spokesman right through the Labour Party'. He added, 'he talks about us wherever he goes'.[137]

Although the MRA had substantial influence inside the Labour Party, this did not prohibit the organisation from attempting to cultivate prominent Conservative politicians as well. The most committed Conservative in the Commons to the group was Hamilton Kerr, but Howard aimed for higher allies within the party.[138] Two that Howard personally targeted were David Maxwell Fyfe and Quintin Hogg. The MRA's chief propagandist reported that despite Maxwell Fyfe's history as a 'Russophile', the Conservative 'now sees the communist danger' but still 'lacks an ideological answer'. 'God I know he is meant to be a spokesman and statesman of the new [MRA] order', Howard maintained, 'and we are going to fight for him.'[139] Howard also met with Hogg, who he wrote 'understands ideology better than many of the British Conservatives'. Hogg's views of the 'red menace' were those that the MRA also campaigned on. 'The fight to answer communism overrides every other issue in the world today', Hogg told a delighted Howard. He added, 'Until we understand that they are as devoted to their faith as monks we shall never be able to bring the answer.'[140] Evidence is unclear if Hogg and Maxwell Fyfe promoted the MRA's agenda in such a manner as Mayhew, but it appears highly doubtful.

Enthusiasm for the MRA waned after Buchman's death in 1961. Its influence in British politics diminished and its recruitment numbers stalled. These trends escalated and continued after Buchman's handpicked successor Peter Howard died suddenly only four years later. Its former allies, like Christopher Mayhew and Konrad Adenauer, jumped off the movement's bandwagon. Driberg quoted Mayhew admitting having been an MRA 'fellow-traveller' but protested that he 'always resisted' complete involvement with the group and had 'cooled off' on the movement by the 1960s.[141]

Economic League: private McCarthyism

Historian John Jenks characterised the Economic League as the 'granddaddy of anti-communist publicists' inside the UK.[142] The label is quite fitting, since the founding of the group even preceded the creation of its chief enemy, CPGB, by a year. But classifying the league's activities as only publicists merely covers one-half of the organisation's efforts. While the well-financed group did generate a large and steady amount of literature attacking communism – as well as socialism and trade unionism – it also functioned as a private intelligence group for corporate and business interests. Its focus on intelligence gathering makes sense when reviewing the group leadership, which had direct links within British intelligence. The founding fathers of the league were William Reginald Hall and John Baker White. Hall was the head of naval intelligence from 1914 until 1919. Baker White was the league's director-general (1926–39) until taking a post with MI6 in 1940. Also, 'MI5's greatest spymaster' – as his biographer labelled him – Maxwell Knight worked for the league in his earlier days.[143]

The Economic League proudly advertised its 'educational efforts' about the benefits of the market economy and the 'evils' of the Marxist ideology. In 1938, it boasted in the past sixteen months the league had held 12,128 meetings, which addressed close to 2 million people. In the same time period, it distributed over 4.5 million leaflets. Baker White maintained these efforts were necessary just to keep the red threat at bay. Without a 'continual counter-campaign', Baker White argued, 'the menace of communism and its power to do harm would be far greater'. He also claimed that the 'influence of the Communist Party must not be gauged by its numerical strength', since even if the number of CPGB members was small, one had to remember 'each and every member of the party is a danger to the state'.[144]

Unlike its propaganda efforts, the organisation sought to keep its intelligence-gathering activities from the public at large. During the 1930s, the Economic League monitored and infiltrated left-wing political groups, which it considered 'dangerous subversives'. The league then compiled reports on these groups' members and distributed them to companies. One of its initial targets dealt with persons involved with the Young Communist League (YCL). The league in one year alone issued 150 such reports on YCL activists.[145] Throughout the decade, the Economic League collected hundreds of files on 'subversive individuals' which documented their movements and personal activities. Its enquiries into subversive activities led to trouble in 1937. Allegations appeared in the press that Manchester police allowed members of the Economic League access to its files on communists. The *Daily Worker* got hold of league correspondence which stated as much and greatly publicised it, to the embarrassment of the police and the league. After an investigation, the chief constable stated no police information was given to the league. However, he did concede that the police did 'somewhat indiscreetly' tell the group about materials it compiled on certain individuals. The incident caused the Home Office to recommend other departments to 'take care' when dealing with the league and warned 'it had some trouble with the organization'.[146]

Despite the negative press attention that the Manchester affair garnered, by the 1940s MI5 held a favourable opinion of the group. Answering a 1942 Home Office request for information on the league, MI5 called it 'quite a reputable anti-communist (and anti-fascist) [organisation] whose chief function seems to be to act as a kind of private intelligence agency to collect and publish information about communist and other extremist activities'.[147] MI5 did state they had some misgivings about the group:

> It may perhaps be said that the league does on occasions fail to distinguish sufficiently sharply the real communist or agitator from the man who is merely a good trade unionist and generally anxious to improve the working conditions of his fellow men. This failure may, of course, result in the penalisation and ultimate embitterment of useful members of the community. Within these limits the league is regarded as a perfectly reputable concern.[148]

The Cold War brought a renewed vigour to the Economic League's battle against communism. By 1950, the group reported its activities were far exceeding its interwar output.[149] In the summer of that year, the league distributed 700,000 copies of a single leaflet denouncing the Soviet-backed peace campaign. They employed fifty-seven full-time and twenty-six part-time speakers. Only weeks after the invasion of Korea the group had seventy-eight letters denouncing communism and supporting the war published in seventy different newspapers.[150] Its estimated 1951 income amounted to £142,000.[151] Like similar anti-communist groups, it advertised itself as a non-partisan organisation. Through its propaganda, it argued that it was the only British group fighting full-time against the 'red menace':

> The three main political parties, Conservative, Labour and Liberal, are vehemently opposed to communism by the very nature of their constitutions and programmes, but their first concern must be with parliamentary affairs. The Economic League, supported by industry, has the countering of communism as its major task. It exposes the aims and plans of the communists, and counteracts their propaganda by economic education and giving the facts.[152]

Some Conservatives gravitated towards supporting the league because of its right-wing nature. Like Labour's support for Moral Rearmament, the league counted many in the Conservative Party as powerful allies. Both league bigwigs Hall and White represented the Conservative Party in the House of Commons. Unsurprisingly, the group held the enthusiastic support of Waldron Smithers, who also sat on its central council.[153] As a league member, Smithers personally recommended those he knew to support the organisation. In 1939, Smithers joined a delegation of Conservative 1922 Committee members who met with Chancellor of the Exchequer John Simon. Smithers used the opportunity to thrust on Simon 'several voluminous documents' dealing with 'the danger of the menace of communism and communistic tendencies'.[154] Included in these documents was a litany of Economic League literature. This trend of Conservative support for the league continued into the early Cold War. In 1954, again Smithers sought to promote the league, writing to the chief publicity officer of the Conservative Party that he was impressed by the 'remarkable record of work by the Economic League'. He urged the party to 'cooperate with them as much as possible'.[155] In 1949, the league held an 'anti-communist staff course' at Caxton Hall in Westminster. On the itinerary were speakers that included the former military attaché in Moscow, alongside Conservative MPs Christopher Hollis (the brother of MI5 agent Roger Hollis, who later headed the agency) and Tufton Beamish, who was involved with Common

Cause as well.[156] Alongside individual Conservatives, the party's Central Office also gave tangible support to the league's anti-communist efforts. A 1951 Central Office memo from the speakers' department stated the party held no objection to Economic League members speaking at Conservative meetings. It even suggested to local branches the group's 'popular talks' on 'full employment and communism'.[157] In 1950, Marjorie Maxse requested all of the party's Central Office agents to assist in an Economic League survey gauging communist support in English universities.[158] A year earlier, speaking on the party's position, she wrote in definite terms: 'We work very closely with the Economic League.'[159]

Throughout the early Cold War period, the league sought to coordinate its anti-communist efforts with the British government. It largely failed in these attempts. On at least one occasion the IRD did pass on confidential data to the league, but overall the covert FO department did not hold it in high esteem.[160] The IRD considered the league a 'reactionary outfit', which tended to regard 'social democracy as a step in the direction of communism and a pretty long step at that'. In its estimation, the league preached 'only to the converted, and its efforts in the anti-communist field may be reckoned, I think to do us possibly more damage than good'. Since the league was considerably disfavoured in trade unions, it did not reach a prime target audience of the IRD: 'its activities are anathema to those circles about whom we may feel concerned in this country'.[161]

On 13 February 1951, the director of the Economic League, Robert Hoare, met with Home Office Permanent Secretary Frank Newsam to offer direct assistance of the organisation to the government. Hoare asked Newsam whether the league could be of help to the Home Office in fighting the activities of the Communist Party and whether Newsam could express on behalf of the government the best line of anti-communist propaganda for it to take. Hoare told Newsam that he personally thought the league could take a much harsher line towards communism. Newsam said that the 'government could not be in any way associated with the activities of the league' and it would 'be quite inappropriate for the government to express any opinion as to the line which the propaganda of the league should take'. Although not the news Hoare sought, not all of Newsam's reply was negative. The permanent secretary did say the league was 'perfectly entitled to attack communism vigorously' and, in lieu of official support, Newsam proposed an informal arrangement between the league and the Home Office,[162] one in which the league would keep providing information on communist activities and individuals through documents issued by the group directly to the Home Office. Newsam's restrained response to Hoare met the approval of Home Secretary James

Chuter Ede. Familiar with the Economic League's history, the Labourite Ede called it 'an active anti-socialist organization'.[163]

An unsigned Economic League memo dated 2 August 1950 that is located in the Home Office files proposed that in case of a future crisis or war, the British government should elevate the private organisation to an official anti-communist body of the state. The private and confidential document entitled 'The Economic League and the Present Crisis' stated:

> It would be difficult to confine even the 40,000 known members of the [Communist] Party (quite apart from the crypto-communists) to the Isle of Man or elsewhere. It is reasonable, therefore, to assume that the government would have to establish, at the outbreak of any crisis, a strong political warfare organization which would conduct its activities not only externally against the enemy overseas, but also internally to counter the work of enemy agents in our midst. The work of the Economic League already fits into this picture. It is obvious that it should become part of the overall plan of the government's political warfare organization. No existing body is better equipped to fight communism on the home front than the Economic League.[164]

The plan explained the government should exempt league members from any future draft requirements and grant the group 'preferential treatment in regard to the obtaining of transport, petrol, and paper for leaflets and other publications'. Throughout the crisis, the league would 'work in close co-operation with the directorate of the ministry responsible for all matters connected with communism'.[165] How the Home Office viewed this offer from the league remains a mystery, since no response or commentary appears with the unsigned memo. MI5's postwar view of the Economic League is somewhat murky, though it appeared deputy director Guy Liddell had friendly relations with the league or at least some of its leadership. He labelled Hoare 'intelligence' and thought he 'held a fairly balanced view of communist activity in this country'.[166] Liddell also speculated Hoare had ongoing dealings with the IRD.

The Economic League continued its efforts far beyond the 1950s, disseminating its anti-communist propaganda. It also continued its investigations on behalf of private businesses into the political affiliations of their workers. Acting as a form of privatised McCarthyism, such controversial practices endured decades after the 1950s. At the time of its closure in 1993, the Economic League still held thousands of files on left-wing individuals, including large numbers of serving Labour MPs. A file even existed on future prime minister Gordon Brown.[167] Despite this revelation and its controversial legacy, the closing of the Economic League did not halt others from continuing to employ the practices it first began. Its immediate successor, Corporate Asset Protection and Risk Management (CAPRiM), and other comparable businesses such as The Consulting Association (TCA), continued to gather information and place on blacklists individuals who were deemed far left.[168] This form of political discrimination and unofficial vetting only stopped after an act of parliament declared such practices illegal in 1999.

Conclusion

As this chapter has shown, anti-communist pressure groups were both numerous and influential during the early Cold War period. Regrettably, this is a key aspect of British domestic Cold War politics that has been left unexamined. While academic works have focused on both the BHL and the LEL, these writings, which have been cited throughout this chapter, do not explore the fact that a key function of these two organisations was combating communism. Also, the suspected link between Common Cause and the US government has in the past not been raised. Indeed, hardly any scholarly work is available on the Moral Rearmament movement in general – let alone its anti-communist activities.[169] Of particular note is the absence of research on Mayhew's relationship with Peter Howard and by extension the MRA. Speaking to the larger context, what these groups show is that a desire to fight communism transcended the efforts of the British government and the Labour and Conservative Parties. Various concerned individuals and interested groups used these anti-communist organisations as vehicles to promote ancillary agendas which agreed to the fight against Marxism. With respects to the BHL and the LEL, these groups' reasons for organising against communism are obvious. For the BHL and the LEL, their efforts arose from ideological conflicts with Marxism, pure and simple. However, when examining the latter three organisations covered in this chapter, a pattern emerges. The ambitions of these more influential groups speak to a grander narrative of the interests encouraging anti-communism in the UK, namely those of the American and British governments, capitalists, and those who sought to defend the economic and political status quo. Comprising these supplementary aims were the promotion of business and corporate interests, spreading an America-centric worldview to the British citizenry, and the dissemination of quasi-religious dogma.

With Common Cause, the MRA and the Economic League, a dovetailing theme emerges: one of defending and strengthening Anglo-American relations – and in the case of the MRA and Common Cause, defending aspects of US anti-communism which Britons found unpopular and excessive. Although the literature and activities of the Economic League focused on domestic industrial relations, it still promoted a pro-American stance. League speakers and leaflets indicated on a number of occasions that one of the main objectives of communists which needed halting was their attempts to split the UK away from the US. The league also sought to expose supposed communist plots to sabotage Marshall Aid.[170] If Natalie Paine (later Lady Natalie Malcolm Douglas-Hamilton) – founder of Common Cause (US) and the wife of the creator of Common Cause (UK) – is to be believed, then the raison d'être for Common Cause was to transform British views on anti-communism to resemble those of the US public. The ultimate goal was that such a transformation in the UK would result in decreasing isolationist and Anglophobic sentiments that existed across the Atlantic.

Although never stated explicitly, the MRA's overarching objective was quite similar. Tom Driberg, who spent a large amount of his adult life investigating the movement, viewed its aims as such. He charged that after the Second World War, the MRA, beholden to its wealthy backers, became an American-sponsored tool to promote anti-communism and defend US interests. Admiral William Standley, former chief of naval operations and US ambassador to Moscow, and a devoted MRA follower, promoted the same notion.[171] Standley said the objective of the movement was 'to make men and nations incorruptible and therefore a bulwark against the advance of communism' in every 'free country'. 'It is the continuation of the American Revolution on a world scale', he said in a 1959 speech. He assured his US audience, 'With Moral Rearmament America can go on the offensive in the world war of ideas.'[172] Alongside Common Cause, the MRA in the UK refused to denounce American McCarthyism. Writing on the UK in 1951, Peter Howard blamed communist infiltration into 'the thinking of this nation' for the 'anti-Americanism' and 'anti-MacArthur' sentiment.[173] He told Buchman that such ideas were crippling the UK. For Howard to state the public's dislike of Douglas MacArthur, a darling of the American public, was a 'communist inspired' creation is telling. Because of MacArthur's bellicose rhetoric, the majority of Britons approved Truman's decision to fire the general. A UK Gallup Poll conducted in May 1951 showed 55 per cent supported Truman, with only nineteen backing MacArthur.[174] The head of the MRA in the UK classifying British 'Anti-MacArthur' sentiment as communistic shows that his views aligned more with an American standpoint than with the mainstream political sentiment inside his own native country.

The MRA's moral crusade against 'godless' communism never wavered during its lifespan. Yet as the Cold War progressed, the MRA downplayed the movement's religious nature and its Christian roots. Seeking to open new frontiers to the message of the movement, the group opened itself to members of any religious or spiritual creed – including Islam, Shintoism, Buddhism and Sikhism. Eventually, atheists were considered potential allies as well. Speaking in the early 1960s, Howard told a crowd that the MRA would bring the nation back to God, 'or if you don't believe in God, a nation centred on the morality and spirit and character of men'.[175] While the four absolutes of the movement still held the answer to fighting communism and overhauling the world, they no longer exclusively worked as a path to the Christian God. As the Cold War spread from Europe into non-Christian regions of Africa and South-East Asia, the inter-faith and inter-religion stance of the MRA made perfect sense if it sought to promote and safeguard US interests and please its deep-pocketed American donors, in addition to garnering converts to the movement. Such a supposition is based on more than mere speculation. In his memoirs, CIA officer Mile Copeland admitted that 'arrangements we [CIA] made with Moral Rearmament gave us useful secret channels right into the minds of leaders not only in Africa and Asia but also in Europe'.[176] The underlining motives of the MRA give insight into what role religion played in the postwar UK in a Cold War context. The MRA, like Lord Vansittart, considered the promotion of anti-communism as trumping an allegiance to a specific spiritual creed. In the mind of Vansittart, and perhaps in those of Buchman and Howard, the true heresy rested in not forsaking the Christian ethos of 'disarming charity' but in displaying an unwillingness to commit unflinchingly to the battle against the red religion.[177]

All of these outside organisations had varying degrees of collaborative success with the British government and the Labour and Conservative Parties. Although wary of its true intentions, and the true motives of its American backers, the FO still measured Common Cause as a useful organisation, one the IRD sought to control. Despite its dogged efforts to exhibit itself as a non-partisan group, the attempts by Labour members to have the group prohibited by the party show this did not totally succeed. Because of its anti-trade union stance and its surveillance activities against workers, the Economic League had little luck in gaining support in the ranks of the Labour Party. In direct contrast, the MRA could boast that some of its most dedicated and ardent supporters were Labour politicians. Both John McGovern and Christopher Mayhew worked towards the advancement of Buchman's agenda, alongside a large number of other Labour MPs. While other anti-communist organisations were unpalatable to Labourites because of their right-wing ideologies, the MRA's form of anti-communism found a receptive home in certain circles of the British left. Of key interest here is the close working association of the MRA and Mayhew. The extent to which Moral Rearmament and the IRD collaborated can only be guessed at, since no files have yet been released on the subject. But with the personal backing of its founder and leader, it can be safely assumed some form of collaboration did occur.

Interested parties – for ideological, economic and self-serving reasons – wanted a more anti-communist UK. Through pressure groups, they fought for this cause. In this battle, they often found sympathetic allies in various facets inside political institutions, but not in any uniform manner. Although these groups all sought to curb and eliminate supposed communist influence inside the UK, they were received and treated by factions of the establishment in very different ways. Often certain organisations had an almost symbiotic partnership with the government and the Conservative and Labour Parties. Other times it was a relationship of contention and animosity. But the overarching theme which interlinked these groups and the powers-that-be was the promotion of a cause – the central genesis of pressure groups in the first place. When British officials, Conservatives or Labourites named these outside organisations as beneficial in aiding their ongoing war against the ideology of Marxist-Leninism, they readily used them towards this endeavour.

Notes

1. *Treachery!*, Common Cause pamphlet, 1951.

2. Lord Woolton to Marjorie Maxse, 27 September 1950, CPA: CCO 3/2/117.

3. See F. Saunders, *Who Paid the Piper?* (London, 1999).

4. A. Eister, *Drawing-Room Conversion* (Durham, NC, 1950), p. 202.

5. MI5 to Home Office, 21 September 1942, TNA HO 45/25476.

6. For its interwar activities, see A. McIvor, '"A crusade for capitalism": The Economic League, 1919–39', *Journal of Contemporary History*, 23 (1988): 631–55; for the league's activities during the 1980s, see M. Hollingsworth and C. Tremayne, *The Economic League: The Silent McCarthyism* (London, 1989).

7. *The British Housewives League*, pamphlet by Irene Lovelock, 1948.

8. G. Love, 'A "mixture of Britannia and Boadicea": Dorothy Crisp's Conservatism and the limits of right-wing women's political activism, 1927–48', *Twentieth Century British History*, 30 (2019): 174–204, at p. 201.

9. Lord Woolton to Dorothy Crisp, 5 February 1948, CCO 3/1/12.

10. J. Hinton, 'Militant housewives: The British Housewives' League and the Attlee government', *History Workshop Journal*, 38 (1994): 129–56, at p. 140.

11. *Dundee Courier*, 25 June 1947, p. 3; *Gloucester Citizen*, 14 June 1947, p. 1.

12. *Kent and Sussex Courier*, 20 June 1947, p. 5.

13. Report by Kathrine Wilmot, 21 June 1948, CCO 3/1/12, CCP.

14. *Housewives Today*, May/June 1948.

15. *Housewives Today*, March 1951.

16. *Sunderland Daily Echo*, 5 June 1947, p. 8.

17. *Western Morning News*, 7 June 1947, p. 3.

18. London District Communist Party Leaflet, 1947.

19. *Aberdeen Press and Journal*, 7 June 1947, p. 1.

20. *Nottingham Journal*, 7 June 1947, p. 1.

21. *Western Daily Press*, 7 June 1947, p. 6.

22. *Bath Chronicle Weekly Gazette*, 14 June 1947, p. 16.

23. *Kent and Sussex Courier*, 20 June 1947, p. 5.

24. *Housewives Today*, May/June 1948.

25. S. Taylor, *The National Front in English Politics* (London, 1982), p. 11.

26. M. Pitchford, *The Conservative Party and the Extreme Right* (Manchester, 2011), p. 56.

27. D. Sandbrook, *Never Had It So Good* (London, 2005), p. 298.

28. R. Eatwell, *Fascism* (London, 2003), p. 334.

29. *Western Mail*, 19 January 1956, p. 1; *Belfast News-Letter*, 15 December 1956, p. 5.

30. *Coventry Evening Telegraph*, 19 April 1956, p. 17.

31. *Birmingham Daily Post*, 19 April 1956, p. 24.

32. G.E. Higham to Lord Hailsham, 23 June 1958, CCO 3/5/88.

33. Q. Hogg, *A Sparrow's Flight* (London, 1990), p. 316.

34. *Candour*, vol. 5, no. 163, 7 December 1956.

35. *Western Mail*, 24 October 1955, p. 1.

36. *Britain's Graveyard*, pamphlet by League of Empire Loyalists, 1957.

37. C. F. Scott, 'Caring about the British Empire: British imperial activists groups, 1900–1967, with special reference to the Junior Imperial League and the League of Empire Loyalists' (unpublished King's College London PhD thesis, 2013), p. 210.

38. *The Times*, 29 October 1958.

39. Taylor, *National Front*, p. 13.

40. N. Fielding, *The National Front* (London, 1981), p. 19.

41. P. Corthorn, 'Cold War politics in Britain and the contested legacy of the Spanish Civil War', *European History Quarterly*, 44 (2014): 678–702, at p. 683.

42. Christopher Mayhew to C.P.A. Warner, 17 June 1948, Mayhew 4/1/1.

43. D. Atholl, *Working Partnership* (London, 1958), p. 252.

44. *Common Cause (Britain)*, leaflet, CPA: CCO 3/3/57.

45. C.A. Smith to Morgan Phillips, 23 June 1954, LPA/GS/PROS/1-85.

46. 'Common Cause', The CPO, 22 February 1952, CPA: CCO 3/3/57.

47. Gill to Watson, 24 June 1952, CPA: CCO 3/3/57.

48. 'Common Cause', The CPO, 2 April 1952, CPA: CCO 3/3/57.

49. Desmond Morton to John Peck, 28 November 1951, TNA FO 1110/374.

50. Adam Watson to A.C.E. Malcolm, 5 November 1951, TNA FO 1110/374.

51. M.A. Hamilton to D'Arcy Edmondson, 6 December 1951, TNA FO 1110/374.

52. John Peck to Malcolm Douglas Hamilton, 3 December 1951, TNA FO 1110/374.

53. Handwritten note by J.E. Manchip-White on M. Sharman to Manchip-White, 9 July 1954, TNA FO 1110/704.

54. H. Wilford, *The CIA, the British Left and the Cold War* (London, 2003), p. 68.

55. File minutes by J. Manchip White, 16 December 1954, TNA FO 1110/704.

56. *The Catholic Standard*, 23 April 1954, p. 5.

57. Saunders, *Who Paid the Piper?*, pp. 203–4.

58. 'The Broken Dialogue', *Encounter*, August 1954.

59. C.A. Smith to Morgan Phillips, 23 June 1954, LPA/GS/PROS/1-85.

60. Barbara Brooke to Mr Banks, 26 March 1956, CCO 3/5/50.

61. J.H. Peck, 'Paix Et Liberte and Common Cause', 1 March 1953, TNA FO 1110/547.

62. *Common Cause*, no. 2, July 1952.

63. File notes, Anthony Nutting, 3 March 1953, TNA FO 1110/547.

64. File notes, John Peck, 12 March 1953, TNA FO 1110/547.

65. J. Jenks, *British Propaganda and News Media in the Cold War* (Edinburgh, 2006), p. 108.

66. 'Common Cause Bulletin, Spring 1964', J.C. Edmonds, 2 June 1964, TNA FCO 168/1237; L.C. Glass to Burke Trend, 4 June 1964, TNA FCO 168/1237.

67. Official Committee on Communism (Home) meeting notes for November 1962, TNA CAB 134/1347.

68. 'Common Cause', J.E. Tyrer, 17 November 1967, TNA FCO 95/408.

69. Handwritten note by J.S. Champion, 19 November 1967, on 'Common Cause', J.E. Tyrer, 17 November 1967, TNA FCO 95/408.

70. *Terror in Spain* pamphlet by John McGovern, 1937; P Corthorn, *In the Shadow of the Dictators* (London, 2006), p. 215.

71. Hansard, HC, vol. 535, c. 653 (6 December 1954).

72. Eister, *Drawing-Room*, p. 29.

73. Eister, *Drawing-Room*, pp. 167–8.

74. *What Are You Living For?*, MRA pamphlet by Frank Buchman, 1950.

75. F. Buchman, *Remaking the World* (London, 1953), p. 252.

76. *One Hundred Million Listening*, MRA pamphlet, 1939.

77. See DAV/274, Papers of John Campbell Davidson, Westminster Parliamentary Archives. The file contains dossiers of MRA members and full-time workers, some of whom were possible subjects of investigation by MI5.

78. Arthur Thurston to R.D. Gibbs, 15 April 1943, TNA KV 5/66.

79. Quoted in G. Lean, *Frank Buchman* (London, 1985), p. 239.

80. Roger Fulford to name redacted, 23 April 1941, TNA KV 5/66.

81. M.E.D. Cumming to name redacted, 4 May 1953, TNA KV 5/68.

82. T. Driberg, *The Mystery of Moral Re-armament* (London, 1964), p. 150.

83. *A Hurricane of Common Sense*, MRA pamphlet by Frank Buchman.

84. J.H. Godfrey to McGill, 15 August 1950, CPA: CCO 3/2/117.

85. *The Answer to Any 'Ism' Even Materialism*, MRA pamphlet by Frank Buchman.

86. P. Boobbyer, 'The Cold War in the plays of Peter Howard', *Contemporary British History*, 19 (2005): 205–22, at p. 207.

87. Peter Howard to Frank Buchman, 31 January 1951, M.S. Oxford 3/79.

88. Eister, *Drawing-Room*, p. 64.

89. R. Palmer, 'Moral re-armament drama: Right wing theatre in America', *Theatre Journal*, 31 (1979): 172–85, at p. 174.

90. *Belfast Newsletter*, 18 June 1946, p. 2.

91. *Somerset County Herald and Taunton Courier*, 12 June 1948, p. 6.

92. 'Coal – key to recovery' report by the MRA. Copy located in the Norman Kipping Papers, MRC.

93. Allen, V. Allen, *The Russians Are Coming* (Shipley, 1987), p. 289.

94. P.S. Scriverner to G.P. Young, 5 April 1951, with attached untitled memorandum authored by T.S. Tull, TNA KV 5/67.

95. Percy Sillitoe to Chief Constable Pembrokeshire, 4 November 1952, TNA KV 5/67.

96. E. McBarnet to S.L.O. Nigeria, 28 September 1955, TNA KV 5/68.

97. L.H. Lamb to A.J. de la Mare, 9 August 1955, TNA KV 5/68.

98. Marjorie Maxse to Lord Woolton, 25 September 1950, CPA: CCO /3/2/117.

99. Maxse to D.M. Redd, 23 November 1950, CPA: CCO 3/2/117.

100. Branston to Maxse, 20 April 1950, CPA: CCO 3/2/117.

101. W.M. Ridgwell to A.H.P. Nobel M.P., 19 June 1952, CPA: CCO 3/3/97.

102. Brigadier Clarke to Maxse, 4 April 1950, CPA: CCO 3/2/117.

103. Handwritten note by Woolton on memorandum from Maxse, 29 March 1950, CPA: CCO 3/2/117.

104. Peter Howard to Frank Buchman, 30 October 1951, M.S. Oxford 3/79.

105. T. Driberg, *Ruling Passions* (London, 1977), pp. 98–9. In an odd parallel to Peter Howard, Driberg was also working for Beaverbrook's *Daily Express* when he first encountered the MRA.

106. Driberg, *Moral Re-armament*, p. 185.

107. Report on Moral Rearmament, issued by ICFTU, 1–2 July 1953, MSS 292/806/1–5, TUC, MRC.

108. Driberg, *Moral Re-armament*, p. 138.

109. *The Times*, 29 January 1955, p. 1.

110. 'Moral Rearmament: A study of the movement prepared by the Social and Industrial Council of the Church Assembly', C.A. 1129, 1955, MSS 292/806/1–5, MRC.

111. *Guardian*, 29 January 1955, p. 1.

112. Geoffrey Fisher to Gordon Home, 24 February 1955, Fisher vol. 159.

113. Fisher to Lord Luke, 28 July 1953, Fisher vol. 129.

114. Fisher to E.G. Sarsfield-Hall, 31 January 1955, Fisher vol. 159.

115. Fisher to Sarsfield-Hall, 19 January 1955, Fisher vol. 159.

116. Fisher to George West, 10 November 1955, Fisher vol. 159.

117. Quoted in D. Sack, *Moral Re-Armament* (New York, 2009), p. 159.

118. CPGB report, 'Oxford Group', November 1943, CP/CENT/ORG/12/05.

119. 'The world movement for moral re-armament', MI5 report, 27 August 1951, TNA KV 5/67.

120. Name redacted to G.R. Mitchell, memo attached 'The Moral Re-Armament Group', 29 December 1950, TNA KV 5/67.

121. *Pravda*, 7 January 1951, TNA KV 5/67.

122. *Londonderry Sentinel*, 10 August 1946, p. 3.

123. Arthur Lewis to Christopher Mayhew, 6 October 1949, Mayhew 2/1/1.

124. *The Times*, 26 October 1953, p. 5.

125. *Guardian*, 26 August 1946, p. 3.

126. *Valley Times* (California), 14 January 1955, p. 3.

127. J. McGovern, *Neither Fear Nor Favour* (London, 1960), p. 185.

128. McGovern, *Neither Fear*, p. 193.

129. Christopher Mayhew to his father, 28 October 1950, Mayhew 2/1/1.

130. Arthur Lewis to Mayhew, 6 October 1949, Mayhew 2/1/1; Mayhew to Lord Henderson, 25 April 1949, Mayhew 4/2/1.

131. Peter Howard to Frank Buchman, 21 December 1950, M.S. Oxford 3/79.

132. Christopher Mayhew to Ernest Bevin, 10 January 1950, Mayhew 4/1/2.

133. Peter Howard to Frank Buchman, 25 May 1949, M.S. Oxford 3/79.

134. Notes on interview with Georgy Zhukov, undated, Mayhew 4/1/2.

135. Howard to Buchman, 21 December 1950, M.S. Oxford 3/79.

136. Grace Wyndham Goldie to Christopher Mayhew, 23 February 1956, Mayhew 12/2.

137. Howard to Buchman, 29 July 1951, M.S. Oxford 3/79.

138. Tom Driberg to Julian Amery, an enclosure with letter, 24 September 1963, AMEJ 1/6/10, CAC.

139. Howard to Buchman, 14 June 1947, M.S. Oxford 3/79.

140. Howard to Buchman, 22 April 1950, M.S. Oxford 3/79.

141. Driberg, *Mystery of Moral Re-armament*, p. 121.

142. Jenks, *British Propaganda*, p. 108.

143. H. Hemming, *M: MI5's Greatest Spymaster* (London, 2017), pp. 32–3.

144. 'Communism in Britain', memorandum by J. Baker White, June 1938, TNA HO 45/25376.

145. M. Hollingsworth and R. Norton-Taylor, *Blacklist* (London, 1988), p. 149.

146. Frank Newsam to A.I. Tudor, 7 December 1939; Tudor to Newsam, 25 November 1939 – both located at TNA HO 45/25476.

147. File minutes by E.H. Gwynn, 12 September 1942, TNA HO 45/25476.

148. 'The Economic League', MI5 summary for the Home Office, 21 September 1942, TNA HO 45/25476.

149. Economic League Central Council 31st Annual Report, 1950.

150. *Red Octopus*, Economic League booklet, 1950.

151. C. Miller, 'Extraordinary gentlemen: The Economic League, business networks, and organized labour in war planning and rearmament', *Scottish Labour History*, 52 (2017): 120–51, at p. 130.

152. *Red Octopus*, Economic League.

153. Miller, 'Extraordinary gentlemen', p. 137.

154. Q.L. Drute to A.S. Hutchinson, 11 January 1939, HO 45/25467.

155. Waldron Smithers to Mark Chapman Walker, 14 August 1954, CCO 3/4/50.

156. 'Technique of World Communism', 6 October 1949, TNA HO 45/25476.

157. J.H. Constable to J. Dodd, 11 January 1951, CCO 3/3/68.

158. Marjorie Maxse to Central Office Agents, 16 June 1950, CCO 3/2/85.

159. Marjorie Maxse to Greville, 10 October 1949, CCO 3/2/85.

160. File notes by C.M. Kirwan, 22 September 1950, TNA FO 1110/361.

161. File notes by Maclaren Wilkinson, 6 October 1950, TNA FO 1110/361.

162. 'Memorandum of an interview with Col. Hoare', 13 February 1951, TNA HO 45/25476.

163. Handwritten note by Chuter Ede on 'Memorandum of an interview with Col. Hoare', 13 February 1951, TNA HO 45/25476.

164. 'The Economic League and the present crisis', 2 August 1950, TNA HO 45/25476.

165. 'The Economic League and the present crisis', 2 August 1950, TNA HO 45/25476.

166. Liddell diary, 11 December 1952.

167. D. Smith and K. Ewing, 'Blacklisting of trade unionists: What is the point of human rights law?', in *Confronting the Human Rights Act: Contemporary Themes and Perspectives*, ed. N. Kang-Riou (London, 2012), 249–68, at p. 251.

168. M. Hughes, *Spies at Work* (London, 2012), pp. 309–11.

169. An exception is David Belden, 'The origins and development of the Oxford Group (Moral Re-Armament)' (unpublished University of Oxford PhD thesis, 1976). As the name suggests, this work focuses on the MRA's early years and its foundation, so its assistance is quite limited for those seeking to examine the movement's Cold War activities. In addition, the previously cited monograph by Daniel Sack, *Moral Re-armament: The Reinventions of an American Religious Movement*, centres on the MRA in the context of American religious studies.

170. Hughes, *Spies at Work*, p. 74.

171. *Ideology and Co-Existence*, MRA pamphlet, 1960.

172. *San Marino Tribune*, 26 March 1959, p. 2.

173. Peter Howard to Frank Buchman, 24 January 1951, M.S. Oxford 3/79.

174. G. Gallup, *Gallup International Public Opinion Polls: Great Britain 1937–1975* (New York, 1982), p. 248.

175. Sack, *Moral Re-armament*, p. 168.

176. M. Copeland, The *Game Player* (London, 1989), p. 177.

177. Vansittart, *Even Now*, p. 117.

Chapter 5

The trade union movement: a fifth column?

We cannot afford to allow the communists' attempted infiltration into and domination of the trade unions to succeed.[1]

—Arthur Deakin

This was the time of Deakinism, which was strongly McCarthyism.[2]

—Jack Dash, trade union organiser

The trade union movement, categorised by some as the fifth estate for the immense importance and power it wielded, provided the frontline in the domestic struggle for and against communism. Within the movement's ranks and leadership existed publicly committed Marxist-Leninists and open members of the CPGB who commanded significant influence.[3] Since the Second World War, communists in the trade unions had made gains in electing officials to local branches, as well as to the executive councils of national boards. The UK's wartime alliance with the Soviet Union swelled the numbers of communists in union posts. It additionally strengthened internationalist impulses among the rank and file. Such moves universally frightened non-communists in the UK during the postwar era. For those espousing anti-communist sentiments inside the government, political parties, intelligence agencies and trade unions themselves, the stakes were dangerously high. They feared that communist gains could bring about a seizure of the entire movement. Industrial action, sabotage, a Labour Party takeover by Soviet stooges, work stoppages, food shortages, blackouts and even a full-blown revolution were not implausible possibilities. Short of Soviet paratroopers landing throughout the country, the likelihood of a red UK came from the power wielded by the unions. Only two decades had elapsed since the General Strike of 1926. Disturbing images of it continued to resonate both in the government's institutional memory and within the consciousness of those occupying state offices. This degree of alarm became one of the focal points of the Attlee government; it became an obsession which initiated overt and covert campaigns against trade union communists, some of which endured throughout the governments of Winston Churchill and Anthony Eden.

This chapter examines anti-communist activities inside the trade unions, with an emphasis on the political and governmental response in the whole of the trade union movement. Previous historians have argued it was the frontline battle against domestic communism in the early Cold War period:[4] a battle, it was insisted, which both sides considered paramount for their cause to prevail. Similar to previous chapters, this chapter details the efforts made against communism by the principal supporters of the anti-communist cause. These include elements within the British government, the Labour and Conservative Parties, and the leaders in the trade union movement. The chapter shows, as in most instances of the period, that the Labour Party took an increasingly aggressive anti-communist stance. While in power, it set forth the governmental agenda in seeking to halt communist influence inside trade unions. In conjunction with MI5 and Special Branch, they enacted a campaign to both halt and repel communist power inside the movement. These efforts were explicitly ordered to stay 'off the record'; from a moral and legal standpoint, their measures bordered on the unethical to the illicit. Such actions included granting intelligence to sympathetic trade unionists to use against their political opponents, seeking to influence internal union elections and spreading anti-communist propaganda orchestrated by the IRD. In all these measures they found the wholehearted support of a number of trade union leaders. Covert campaigns as such continued from the period of 1948 until the end of the 1950s. Fluctuations of government brought no radical change in such a policy. From the CPGB's perspective, these attacks constituted one of the most serious assaults, since they targeted its primary stronghold of power.[5]

Regarding another area of concern, however, substantial disagreements arose – the Labour government found itself both in conflict with MI5 and questioned by its political opposition. Contention arose because of the purported role communists had in instigating the numerous unofficial strikes which plagued the nation during the era. Here, Labour differentiated itself from the Conservatives and MI5. Contemporarily it is generally accepted that the CPGB did not, as a matter of policy, seek to inspire industrial unrest for political expediency. When summing up the period, Nina Fishman was correct to argue: 'It is difficult to avoid the conclusion that British communists were not disrupting or manipulating anything very much, let alone engaging in sabotage ... The belief that Britain was vulnerable to industrial attacks by communists was never sustained by the facts.'[6] She was not alone in her view. John Callaghan stated that the idea of a 'conscious orchestration' of communists seeking to wreck the UK's economy 'could not be supported with any evidence'.[7] This chapter argues MI5 commonly reported the same assessment made by Fishman and Callaghan to the Labour and Conservative governments. Yet Attlee and his ministers disregarded the reports and publicly blamed communistic agitation for industrial unrest and supposed acts of sabotage. Allying with them and echoing such charges were several key trade union leaders. In a similar case to governmental vetting, MI5 considered these unsubstantiated and largely fabricated accusations of the Labour government disproportionate and highly concerning. Charges as such were engendering an atmosphere where the communist threat was both grossly exaggerated and fabricated. After the handover of power in 1951, strikes continued; however, Churchill's government rarely alleged that an organised conspiracy of communists was the reason for the specific dispute.

Here, one has to believe the guidance and recommendation of the MI5 had a lot to do with this matter. Under the Conservatives, a fundamental shift occurred in governmental thinking. The anxiety over communist infiltration inside trade unions did not abate, but it did become directed towards a realistic assessment of the situation. This alteration began in 1954 and progressed to fruition in 1956 when MI5 produced a confidential report detailing the lack of communist involvement in unofficial strikes. Unlike their Labour predecessors, the Conservatives accepted the security service's evidence as fact.

To provide foundation and context, the first section of this chapter examines the events surrounding the Grimethorpe stint strike. It will assess the extent to which this industrial action altered thinking. Gradually, a new way of thinking gained power inside governmental circles. It was widely believed that communists were seeking to paralyse the government through work stoppages and industrial disruption. Here the lack of evidence did not deter the government from fomenting the idea, which had international repercussions. The second section highlights a series of anti-communist activities promoted by trade union leaders. It emphasises the anti-communist efforts of the most powerful organisations in the movement, namely the TUC and the TGWU. It additionally investigates the contributions of both the US government and the American trade unions in supporting these measures. The subsequent section describes the governmental policy against trade union communists enacted under Labour. The measures used were covert. They continued until the 1960s. Following this is a critical evaluation of Labour's misguided campaign against communist agitation. It is the textbook example of red-baiting in its purest form. The next two sections describe how governmental policy shifted under the premierships of Winston Churchill and Anthony Eden. The election of 1951 resulted in the end of the Labour-induced red scare occurring over industrial actions. Although unofficial strikes and work stoppages persisted, the Conservatives rarely blamed red agitation. The final section examines the continuation of covert anti-communist policies by the state and how an MI5 investigation opened governmental eyes to the true nature of the 'red menace' in trade unions.

Dunkirk or Grimethorpe?

For many, communists and communist agitation were the root of all industrial stoppages, strikes and supply shortages. A notable episode of this type of thinking occurred in 1947 during the five-week Grimethorpe stint strike. The strike began in the aforementioned village in south Yorkshire when, on 11 August 1947, 200 coalminers in a pit walked off the job over an issue resulting from the application of the Five-Day Agreement.[8] This resulted in 2,600 more coming out on strike. Ten days later, miners at neighbouring collieries walked out in sympathy. By 28 August, the strike increased in severity, with the dispute spreading through west Yorkshire. By the first week of September, a third of all Yorkshire's pits were idle.

For various reasons, the events in Grimethorpe alarmed the UK. For Labour Party supporters, the strike came as a dreadful realisation; it was the first instance of industrial action following the nationalisation of the coal industry five months prior. It showed the hollowness of claiming that nationalisation would permanently solve such industrial matters. The National Union of Mineworkers (NUM), the union of which the striking coalminers were members, viewed the unsanctioned strike as a blatant disregard of control over its members and was perplexed about how to regain control of the situation. Concerned over output and economic recovery, the national government found the loss of over 600,000 tons of coal in the five-week shutdown devastating towards its production plans for the British state.[9] Adding to the headache of the situation came the negative press reaction in the US. A *New York Times* editorial on 9 September harshly criticised the British for permitting the prolongation of such an action. It questioned if American foreign aid to the UK should remain a foregone conclusion. It summated with:

Under the Marshall Plan each participating nation will be expected to contribute the goods or services it is best equipped to produce. In the case of England this clearly can mean only one thing – coal. Unless the Labour government can demonstrate its ability to get coal mined it is difficult to believe that the Marshall Plan will produce the enthusiasm and the hope which it merits and which are so essential to its success. Messengers Attlee, Bevin etc. have made much in recent months of 'the spirit of Dunkirk'. Sooner or later they will have to demonstrate, not with figures of speech, but by their own actions, whether it is to be the spirit of Dunkirk or the spirit of Grimethorpe.[10]

The *New York Times* ran a succeeding article three days later. It argued that US Treasury Secretary John Snyder and President of the World Bank John McCloy could not possibly help but 'draw the worst sort of conclusions from the Grimethorpe Strike'. With the British economy dependent on continued American aid, such sentiments were a formidable warning that for the US, industrial actions such as Grimethorpe were intolerable.

The striking miners showed no signs whatsoever of having been fomented by communist agitation; political motivations were not inspiring their actions. Yet one of the nation's most prominent communists was in the middle of the maelstrom regarding Grimethorpe. As general secretary of NUM, Arthur Horner sought a resolution to the industrial action occurring within his union. He refused to back the miners and classified their action as a wildcat strike without any official sanction. Horner, alongside the CPGB and its general secretary Harry Pollitt, were in general agreement with the rest of the UK that the miners were damaging the nation and the situation needed resolving. Addressing a meeting at Hyde Park, Pollitt told the audience he supported the miners but urged them to quit the strike and return to work. Denouncing the strike, Horner warned the 'lack of coal can bring down any government in this country. It is not even the fate of the government which is involved. It is the fate of the country'. Although in complete agreement with the government, public opinion and NUM, Horner and his political party were still suspected of causing the crisis.

The leadership of the newly formed National Coal Board (NCB), the public corporation created to run the nationalised coal mining industry, suspected communists were somehow to blame for the strike. In a meeting with Guy Liddell of MI5, NCB member Charles Ellis stated that with the Grimethorpe situation the communists, and Horner in particular, were 'playing a very tricky double game' and sought to 'bring the whole [coal] industry down in ruins'. From other sources, Liddell had surmised that NCB chairman John Hindley felt the same as Ellis. Liddell and MI5 totally disagreed. They claimed it was in the interests of the Communist Party to get the government over the crisis, otherwise it might bring the Conservatives to power. 'It would be better for them to have a Labour government', Liddell deduced, 'and push it more and more left until they obtained power by constitutional means'. 'The Grimethorpe issue was not a good one' for the communists, since they 'would not gain credit with the public as a whole if they were to aggravate the hardships of the householder.'[11] Disagreeing with the professional assessment of the security service, and voicing aloud the sentiments of NUM, was Labour MP for Wednesbury, Stanley Evans. Like Ellis and Hindley, Evans pointed the finger for Grimethorpe at Horner and the CPGB. Speaking on the situation, Evans accused the 'communist-infiltrated' NUM for the present troubles:

> Never in its history was the coal industry the sport of politics as it was today. The mineworkers' organization was being used as an instrument of ideological political tactics. For those who were Kremlin addicts first and British socialist a bad second, coal in abundance was politically undesirable ... The Miners' Union, a great and influential organization representing a loyal band of Labour supporters, was being used as a pawn on the communist chessboard.[12]

Such accusations occurred against NUM even before Grimethorpe. Alluding to Horner's affiliations, Fred Woods, general secretary of the Clerical and Administrative Workers' Union, referred to 'the sinister propaganda of the Communist Party within the trade union movement' when he opposed an executive motion being argued to allow miners 'to withdraw their labour' if deemed necessary.[13]

Ultimately, on 15 September, the miners agreed to return to work on pre-strike conditions, ending the month-and-a-half-long ordeal. Both the NUB and NUM agreed to set up a commission to sort out the miner grievances which sparked the situation. Shortly after the strike, the search began for culprits to blame for it snowballing into a national crisis. Horner stated the blame lay at the door of the British newspapers. 'The capitalistic press had done everything possible to create confusion', he accused. They sought to 'drive a wedge between the men and National Coal Board, to drive a wedge between the men and the government and to drive a wedge between the men and the union'.[14] The Marxist economist Edgar Hardcastle blamed the lack of leadership of all involved, including Horner: 'Whatever else may come out of the Grimethorpe strike it should teach some miners at least not to put their trust in nationalisation, or in Labour administration of capitalism, or in leaders, communists included.'[15] Although Horner admonished the strikers and came out resolutely against the strike, for many – including Evans, Ellis and Hindley – they suspected the communist Horner of instigating the whole affair – probably on direct orders from the Kremlin.

Although general secretary of the union, Horner's communist affiliation did not sit easily with the rest of the NUM leadership. He had a tense and often rancorous relationship with Will Lawther, the president of NUM. Although close allies in the prewar period, the two had come to exemplify the divide between the communist and the non-communist left inside the trade union movement. Prior to the Second World War, Lawther had been a committed Marxist and worked closely with Horner in coordinating union support for the anti-Franco Republican cause. During the Grimethorpe strike, Lawther broke with Horner and announced the fault directly rested with the striking miners. The NUM president called for the prosecution of the strikers by the coal board. As might be expected, this sentiment did not go down well in the region; in the midst of the strike, a graffitied wall in Grimethorpe read 'Burn Will Lawther' with gallows inscribed beside the words.[16] A year later in 1948, when Horner travelled to France to support a communist-backed miner strike, Lawther condemned his NUM colleague and the French strikers. Horner maintained that Lawther took this position because of American pressure originating from the State Department.[17] In 1949, the NUM national executive appointed a special subcommittee to investigate statements made by Horner in which he argued that right-wingers in the trade union movement were preparing the UK for a war against the Soviet Union. Horner maintained there was a plot to remove him from the secretaryship by these same elements, since it would prove less inconvenient than imprisoning him when the war he was warning of actually started. The subcommittee's report called Horner's assertions 'ridiculous'. It went on to state:

> To suggest that those of us who are regarded by the communist as right wing leaders, because we refuse to accept that party's principles, have prepared for war, is a slander without foundation ... we are satisfied that our abhorrence [towards war] is shared by every member of the socialist government but the government and its supporters would be lacking in foresight and open to severe criticism if they failed to take such precautionary measures as are necessary, so that, if called upon, this country could withstand any attack on this great democracy, no matter from what quarter danger threatened.[18]

The report concluded with a direct swipe at the communist Horner: 'We shall resist any attempt on the part of the communists to use trade union organizations for the sole purpose of advancing their lust for power.' In addition to their perceived ability to foment industrial action, prominent communists in leadership roles of NUM, such as Horner, raised another concern. Both the TUC and Labour politicians, such as Evans, viewed the union as being vulnerable to a full-blown takeover by the Communist Party. Such an occurrence would endanger the Labour Party since at past party conferences NUM had wielded the second largest number of block votes. Although the CPGB had been denied affiliation by Labour, through the control of the voting blocks of the unions, communists could wield substantial influence or even potentially take full control of the party. Writing on the topic, George Orwell stated:

> The British Communist Party appears to have given up, at any rate for the time being, the attempt to become a mass party, and to have concentrated instead on capturing key positions, especially in the trade unions. So long as they are not obviously acting as a sectional group, this gives the communists an influence out of proportion to their numbers. Thus, owing to having won the leadership of several important unions, a handful of communist delegates can swing several million votes at a Labour Party conference. But this results from the undemocratic inner working of the Labour Party, which allows a delegate to speak on behalf of millions of people who have barely heard of him and may be in complete disagreement with him.[19]

Echoing this sentiment, at the height of the Grimethorpe strike, in September 1947 George Gibson, former chairman of the TUC, warned in the *Sunday Times* of infiltration of communists into key positions in various trade unions, trade councils and even the TUC itself. He argued that an insignificant body of communists had succeeded in placing a disproportionate number of their members into positions of national influence throughout trade unionism. Gibson estimated communists were within measurable distance of capturing the entire trade union movement. Warning of the danger, he urged trade unionists to regularly attend their branch meetings to combat those seeking to disseminate 'theories dictated from abroad'.[20]

Grimethorpe educated many in the UK about the power organised labour could wield and, if unleashed, how difficult such a force was to control. If allowed to continue longer, the loss of coal stock caused by the Grimethorpe shutdown directly threatened the jobs of 50,000 Yorkshire industrial workers and endangered the Sheffield steelworks and Lancashire gas companies and cotton mills.[21] In a matter of weeks, the unsanctioned actions of a mere 200 miners turned into a mounting crisis affecting millions of Britons. If it was allowed to progress, the strike had the power to both topple the national government and jeopardise Marshall Plan aid. The peril of future Grimethorpes became a sword of Damocles hanging over the British Isles.

'Defend democracy'

According to Nina Fishman, Morgan Phillips fired the first shot of the 'British domestic Cold War on trade union terrain' in December 1947.[22] In an open declaration of war entitled 'The Communist: We Have Been Warned', the Labour Party chairman described the coming battle and the methods the enemy would use:

> We can expect that a campaign of sabotage against the Labour government and all it stands for will be carried out by the communists and their fellow travellers during the coming months. We can expect communist-inspired attempts to foment discontent in the factories and workshops, which may result in slowing down and hampering the production drive, on which our national prosperity and recovery depends ... We can also expect intensified attempts to continue their efforts to undermine and destroy the Labour movement from within, particularly by activities within the trade union movement in the interests of the Communist Party ... Now is the time for all Labour people to go out on a great campaign against communist intrigue and infiltration inside the Labour movement.[23]

A year later another declaration came, which echoed Phillips's words. The issuing of this additional document could be termed the second shot of the war, since it marked, for many, the time when the industrial side of labour joined the political side in its anti-communist crusade. In 1948, the general council of the TUC issued a six-page, forty-two-paragraph document pledging the TUC to fight communism inside the trade union movement. Entitled *Defend Democracy: Communist Activities Examined*, the pamphlet consisted of two anti-communist policy statements issued by the TUC. In them, the general council claimed it had obtained evidence 'of the ways in which communist influence within and outside the trade unions are seeking deliberately to obstruct economic policy ... and to disrupt the unity of the trade union movement'. Under the direction of the Cominform, the Communist Party had 'been specifically ordered to oppose the Marshall Plan' and 'sabotage' it. It charged the communists also 'promoted political agitation' both to 'magnify industrial grievances' and 'bring about stoppages in industry'. The joint statements urged the executives of all affiliated unions, their district branches and 'responsible officers and loyal members to counter act every manifestation of communist influences within their unions'. The TUC general council beseeched all 'workpeople to open [their] eyes to the dangerous subversive activities which are being engineered' against 'the declared policy of the trade union movement'.[24] Directly after its release, the TUC sent a letter to all of its affiliated organisations urging them to purchase copies of *Defend Democracy* for immediate distribution.[25] 'Glad to act', the assistant national agent of the Labour Party assured the TUC, the party would aid in 'a wide circulation of the pamphlet'.[26] It proved wildly popular; by February 1949, demand for the pamphlet caused it to be on its eighth printing since the preceding ones had all sold out.[27]

Defend Democracy caused a stir throughout the trade union movement. The pamphlet divided unions and brought forth numerous trade council resolutions both condemning and praising its anti-communist stance. TUC archival files in the Modern Records Centre house hundreds of letters from union branches and individual trade unionists which attest to its controversial reception. One unsigned and undated correspondence simply reads: 'Perjurers and Skunk. Our Answer to You!' Another one, written in a sincere fashion, states: 'Wishing you and all concerned success in your "witch-hunting", and trusting that it will not be rigidly confined to professed communists.'[28] In a letter of solidarity, the Congress of Irish Unions General Secretary Leo Crawford wrote to TUC General Secretary Vincent Tewson after the issuing of the statement. Crawford reported: 'the problem is not so great here, although there are still active members of the Communist Party' in unions needing to be dealt with, just as there were in the UK.[29]

Despite the unequivocal language of the statement, the TUC leadership contemplated even stricter measures. Tewson considered issuing a blanket prohibition of communists as delegates at all trade councils associated with the congress. He stopped short, surmising with such a move 'the initiative would then pass again to the communists.' Since every 'Trade Council and Federation would month after month have to deal with resolutions that the ban should be lifted'. Tewson also conceded 'administratively [it would be] impossible for this office to operate the ban'.[30] However, Tewson did recommend that trade councils should be encouraged to exclude communists on a local level. Working off Tewson's playbook, many councils did just that. In early 1949, the Darlington Trade Council voted at its annual meeting to expel all 'known and vowed' communists from its ranks. After the meeting, the council president announced that any communists present must leave forthwith.[31] In an interview afterwards, the member who proposed the resolution stated his reasoning: 'I think as a council we should all play our part in trying to defeat the communist terror.'[32] The Plymouth Trade Council banned all communists from attending future meetings and accordingly notified its branch unions that they should not attempt to send communist delegates.[33] Joining Plymouth, the trade councils of East Ham, Irlam, Cadishead and Wandsworth all began refusing the credentials of affiliated branch delegates who were communists.[34] In August, the general council of the National Society of Painters, in an eleven to four majority, voted to bar known communists from holding office in the society as well.[35]

On 11 July 1949 the UK's largest trade union, the TGWU, banned all Communist Party members from holding office inside the union. The measure, proposed by its general secretary Arthur Deakin, was endorsed at its annual conference by an overwhelming vote of 426 to 208.[36] Several unions, including the General and Municipal Workers and the National Union of Railwaymen, already had such bans in place.[37] The TGWU decision occurred at its biennial conference after members proposed a resolution denouncing *Defend Democracy*. Instead of a resolution denouncing the document, the conference endorsed 'the TUC policy contained in the pamphlet *Defend Democracy*' by a vote of 508 to 123. 'We then went on to discuss the question of eligibility of office on the part of members of the Communist Party', explained Deakin in a press conference announcing the ban.[38] 'We have decided that no member of the Communist Party shall be eligible to hold office within the union', he said.[39] The ban had an immediate impact on the course of the TGWU. It halted nine communist members of the union's national executive (out of thirty-four) from standing for re-election and scores of others in the over 4,000 TGWU local branches. With a membership of 1.5 million, the union's anti-communist action dwarfed Attlee's civil service purge.

Not all of the larger unions followed the TGWU. The Civil Service Clerical Association (CSCA) refused to endorse the TUC proposal. Its general secretary L.C. White remarked: 'The TUC document, *Defend Democracy*, in which it called for action against communists in trade unions, was an attempt by the general council to incite political discrimination in a union which had no political ties.'[40] Speaking in regards to the CSCA, he added: 'We are quite capable of dealing with any people of the left, right or centre who abuse their position. The time has come for the TUC to mind its own business and let us mind ours.'[41] Although the CSCA's central council was not swayed by the TUC's brand of anti-communism, *Defend Democracy* did embolden some in the union to speak out about their fears. A London branch secretary of the CSCA wrote to Tewson, explaining:

Now that the TUC have issued their documents condemning the infiltration and have encouraged trade unions to take positive action to combat such activities we feel that we may officially ask for support. Our association suffers from communist infiltration to a large degree. I speak in confidence when I say that our general secretary [L.C. White] and deputy secretary are believed to be communists – or near-communists – and some 13 members of our present national executive committee support the communist 'line' even if they may not be members of the party. That is the problem we have to face and the battle we have to fight.[42]

A special meeting of the British Actors' Equity Association, chaired by Leslie Banks and attended by fellow film-stars Richard Attenborough, Sheila Sim and Gertrude Lawrence alongside over 700 other union members, voted its support for *Defend Democracy*. But the meeting rejected, by a three to one majority, a resolution that barred communists from holding any office in Equity. Speaking on the significance of the meeting's decisions, an attending actor remarked, 'It means that while keeping in line with the general TUC policy there is not going to be any purge or witch hunt in Equity.'[43]

Effectively, *Defend Democracy* brought with it a declaration of war against communists in the trade union movement. The TUC took its propaganda war against communism international. With the assistance of the IRD of the FO, the TUC disseminated its pamphlets throughout the British colonies. By 1949, the TUC began sending hundreds of copies of its anti-communist pamphlet entitled *The Tactics of Disruption* to Nigeria.[44]

The author of these pamphlets and press releases was future TUC general secretary Victor 'Vic' Feather, who held the post from 1969 to 1973. A dedicated and committed trade unionist, Feather's anti-communist activities began much earlier in his career when he worked as TUC liaison to the individual trade councils. During the interwar period, he advised the council on anything and everything. He gained a reputation as a jack of all trades. Working in this capacity as a de facto trouble-shooter, Feather had his first dealings with the communist 'threat'. In this role, Feather was tasked to strengthen trades councils' resistance to communist pressure and also bring back in line communist-dominated 'heretical councils'. As a natural brawler, he relished the fight; so much so that on one occasion in 1938, the fight turned literal. To the chagrin of his TUC superiors at a trade council meeting in Watford, Feather ejected two communist troublemakers by physically hoisting them through the doors. A communist opponent once described Feather as an individual not to be underestimated. 'We knew Victor', he reflected. 'He was the kind of man who caresses your back looking for the right place to put the knife.'[45] Yet his earlier pre-Cold War undertakings were the mere skirmishes of a junior official. After having risen in the ranks of the TUC in the 1940s, Feather transformed his anti-communist activities into a sustained full-time campaign.

In the battle for the soul of the trade councils, Feather had one ultimate weapon. The trade councils, which represent all the union branches in a town or district, derive their authority from the TUC. If a certain trade council did not conform to the TUC's rules and guidelines, the offending council lost its legitimacy, and the unions were expected to withdraw their branches forthwith. In practice, this sanction was invoked very sparingly. Yet Feather and the TUC employed it to break up the largest trades council in the nation. Their target was the London Trade Council, which worked as both a district federation of local councils and the centre of the district committees of individual unions. By the early 1950s, it held an affiliated membership of over 800,000 trade unionists – including Clement Attlee and Herbert Morrison.[46] What troubled Feather about the council was its leadership. Both its general secretary, Julius Jacobs, and members of the council's executive were communists – a fact they proudly proclaimed. Fearing the London Council was sliding into dangerous hands, anti-communist trade union leaders began withdrawing their district committees from the umbrella organisation.[47] Still unsatisfied with the direction of the council in 1952, the TUC took the bold step of withholding its registration. The TUC justified the action by saying there 'appeared to have been collaboration between some of the council's executive and the Communist Party in arrangements for recent demonstrations, although the affiliated organisation had not agreed to such collaboration which was contrary to the council's rules'. The council refused to accept the validity of the action against it and refused to disband. In response, the TUC formed a new London Trade Council, registered under the title 'London Trade Council (1952)'.

Alongside government support and liaison situated across the Atlantic, the TUC also had powerful international allies in its fight against internal communists. Elements in the American government and the US trade unions both backed the TUC cause. Writing from Moscow in 1945, George Kennan warned that 'communist circles' considered the international labour movement as one of the most promising instruments to promote Soviet foreign policy. Kennan observed, 'it seems now to have been decided in Moscow that political parties especially those bearing the name "communist" are not always the most effective medium for such assertion of influence and emphasis had shifted ... above all to organized labour'.[48] US labour attaché in London Samuel Berger in December 1947 described the situation there as such: 'It is axiomatic, that US financial aid alone cannot defeat the communists. They can only be permanently defeated if their influence in the trade union movements is broken.'[49] Yet policymakers in Washington, DC, understood that a light touch was needed and the US must hide its involvement to halt any type of anti-American blowback. Like their British counterparts, they surmised the war inside UK trade unions needed to be fought from within the union movement. As Hugh Wilford pointed out, attempted direct intercession by agencies of the US government into British labour unions all ended in complete failure.[50] So it fell to the American unions to support their comrades in the UK in taking up the fight against communism.

It is true from their inception that the American trade unions diverged greatly from their British counterparts. Whereas organs like the TUC was strongly associated with socialism from the late 1800s, the American Federation of Labor (AFL), under the leadership of Samuel Gompers, did not seek to involve itself with an ideology. Gompers and the AFL focused on higher wages for skilled workers instead. 'Following on from this denial of a broader, social purpose', Wilford wrote, 'was marked reluctance on the part of the AFL to identify itself with any political party – Gompers believed that political entanglements would lead inevitably to the domination of labour by more powerful economic interests.'[51] This contrasted with the British trade unions' strong association with the Labour Party. Labour – as a party and as a movement – were intrinsically linked. While British labour leaders were on the whole stalwartly anti-communist, prior to the Second World War they still generally avoided a direct confrontation with the communists in their ranks. They preferred to promote instead a policy of improving the poor working conditions on which communism thrived. The same cannot be said about their American counterparts, who were quite aggressive and open in their anti-communist tactics. The early years of the Cold War era saw this divergence between the British and American strategies towards communists narrow considerably.

In October 1945, in an attempt to keep up the spirit of unity and cooperation fostered during the war, a number of international trade unions formed the World Federation of Trade Unions (WFTU). Its mission was to do for organised labour what the newly formed UN did for nation states, which was to create a body where all trade unions could be represented on a global scale. The WFTU brought together major union organisations from the three central allied powers – the Soviet All-Union Central Council of Trade Unions (VTsSPS), the American Congress of Industrial Organizations (CIO) and the British TUC. Its formation marked a key event in international labour history; it represented the only time when the mass workers' organisations of the Soviet Union and the US participated in a union federation. It had a lofty goal: to de-ideologise international labour relations by bringing together trade unions from nations with starkly different economic systems and forms of government.[52]

Not all valued or wished for such international cooperation to thrive. A notable absence of union associations which refused to join the WFTU was the AFL. Being staunchly anti-communist, the AFL thought any cooperation with the Soviet Union was unwise and unpatriotic. The AFL labelled the WFTU a worldwide communist 'controlled Frankenstein' and was determined to 'sabotage it at any cost'.[53] The AFL representative in Europe, Irving Brown, explained to American diplomat Samuel Berger that the WFTU could not be allowed to continue since it lent legitimacy to the communist-controlled trade unions behind the Iron Curtain. He counselled Berger:

> [Their] association with bona fide trade unionists in the WFTU had enabled the communists to parade as bona fide trade unionists. The WFTU has been a mantle of respectability. If the WFTU could be split, the mantle would be torn away and the true character of the communists revealed.[54]

The AFL, through its liaisons with the TUC, sought to impress these sentiments onto their Atlantic cousins. Initially, these attempts proved unsuccessful; although the TUC was decidedly anti-communist, its leadership saw little harm in participating in the WFTU. In 1946, Arthur Deakin was selected as WFTU president; the TUC held no question regarding his anti-communist bona fides.[55] In the early years of the WFTU's existence, the AFL's lobbying against the federation to the TUC did not gain much traction. Part of the difficulty came from having developed an image as a respectable body with a good reputation in international circles.[56] However, the situation rapidly shifted with the introduction of the Marshall Plan.

The vast majority of British trade union leaders considered Marshall Plan funding necessary for the economic life of the UK. Since the Soviet Union and its allies were fundamentally opposed, for political reasons, to US aid to Europe, the plan caused rifts inside the WFTU. For anti-communist opponents of the WFTU, it created the ideal conditions to further their agenda.[57] On the urging of the AFL, the US State Department and the FO attempted to convince the TUC to propose a general European trade union conference on the Marshall Plan independent of the WFTU. Brown applied pressure to the TUC leadership to act urgently, but they demurred, fearing that left-wing elements in the British unions would see this as an obvious ploy to undermine the WFTU. After further consultations with FO and AFL officials, the TUC decided to bring the Marshall Plan debate into the WFTU and have its member organisations vote to endorse it. They brought this action knowing full well it would result in an irrevocable split, since the communists' unions would refuse to come to terms with such a resolution. Instead of coming to a showdown, the situation petered out after the WFTU postponed a meeting scheduled to discuss the issue. At the TUC 1948 annual conference, Arthur Deakin labelled the WFTU as 'nothing more than another platform and instrument for the furthering of Soviet policy'.[58] The conference elected to turn the matter of the WFTU over to the TUC general council. After consulting the CIO leadership, the council decided to push for the suspension of the WFTU for a year. The FO was in full support of such a move. It assessed the Soviets would refuse to accept such a proposal, thus giving the CIO and the TUC a justified reason to break with the international federation.[59]

At the final meeting of the united WFTU in January 1949, Deakin put the TUC motion to a vote. Linking domestic and international events, Deakin claimed the 'machinations and Machiavellian tactics of the agents of communism in Great Britain' forced the TUC to proceed in this manner.[60] Immediately after the call for a vote, pandemonium erupted as members protested Deakin's proposal. In response, Deakin merely stated 'the situation is clear'. He then got up from his chair and brazenly waved goodbye as he walked out of the hall. Exiting with Deakin were the entire delegations of the TUC and CIO. At the next TUC annual conference, a challenge to the TUC's withdrawal from the WFTU was put to a vote. It was overwhelmingly defeated, yet over a million votes still favoured continued affiliation.[61]

Fighting from the shadows: covert anti-communism

Six months after the Grimethorpe strike, the Official Committee on Communism (Home), also known as the Brook Committee, began meeting. Alongside the purging of communists in the civil service, another major priority of the top-secret committee was how to deal with the communist threat inside the trade unions. A working committee report, which reviewed anti-communist security measures, laid out the situation the government faced. It concluded that the CPGB's 'penetration of the trade unions' had one overarching goal – simply, 'the installation of a communist government'. 'Though this goal may at present seem remote', the authors of the report conceded, at present the communists, through the trade unions, could exert pressure 'to modify the policy and composition of the government of the day or to embarrass it in the hope that it will collapse'. The government viewed any communist success achieved inside the trade unions as a step towards this nightmarish outcome. The report warned: 'It has already made considerable progress towards attaining this aim' and claimed 'there is hardly a union in which a [Communist] party member does not hold a position of some prominence'. The report went on to state that since the CPGB wished to 'preserve the air of patriotic respectability', communists had not yet turned to promoting 'unofficial industrial unrest' in case they appear as 'irresponsible agitators'. It concluded that as a whole the matter of communist influence inside trade unions 'is superficially a satisfactory one ... It is, however, a dangerous situation for the future'.[62]

A consensus arose that overt governmental anti-communist actions within the trade union movement were impossible because of the need to appear impartial towards internal trade union affairs. A light, and more importantly a hidden, touch was deemed the best approach. The government did not find it wise to follow in the footsteps of Morgan Phillips and his publicly announced declaration of war on trade union communists. Such a tactic had the potential to ruffle many feathers. A *Times* article on Phillips's methods highlighted such likely criticisms:

> It is an open secret, however, that many trade union leaders are unhappy about Mr. Morgan Phillips's public appeal for a campaign against communists ... We do not wish to see in this country the persecution of any left-wing opinion now common in the United States. If a campaign to remove an enemy within is allowed to develop until it becomes the rigid imposition of the views of those at the top, then the cure will be worse than the disease.[63]

Government officials recommended to Attlee that support and assistance to anti-communists in the trade union movement should be actively promoted but only through covert methods. The committee believed any ham-fisted approach had the potential of backfiring: 'This is not a matter on which the Security Service or government departments as such can be of any direct help. It is one which the responsible elements of the trade unions ought to settle for themselves, helped by publicity and other measures to ensure a healthy and informed state of public opinion.'[64] Working towards such ends, the government influenced the Catholic Church to roll back its anti-communist activities inside unions. In April 1948, the Roman Catholic bishops of the UK issued a statement, saying: 'No Catholic can be a communist, no communist a Catholic.' They urged all Catholic workers to 'join their appropriate trade unions' to influence the unions' activities.[65] A Brook Committee meeting only a few weeks later commented that such Catholic combativeness towards communists in trade unions 'had produced some useful results', but there were warning signs: 'if pressed too far, it would provoke a reaction in the opposite direction'. On the advice of the committee, Nye Bevan visited the Cardinal of Westminster, warning of such a danger.[66] The CPGB responded to the Church's prohibition of all communists a month later. It released a pamphlet entitled *Catholics and Communism: The Communist Case*. Written by MP William Gallacher, it argued that Catholicism and communism were compatible and emphasised the exploitations Catholic coal miners had to endure in the past under capitalism.[67]

The Labour ministry, headed by George Isaacs, was decided as the best department to liaise with the trade unions vis-à-vis anti-communist activities. Like Attlee, Isaacs's aversion to communism bordered on the fanatical. One such example of this occurred in 1950; Attlee and Isaacs ordered MI5 to investigate 'communist influence' over all 'Irishmen in this country'.[68] Alongside their worries over red Irishmen – about which the security service said 'there is no cause for any particular alarm' – both men were obsessed with red agitators in unions. On Isaacs's instructions, the labour ministry held discussions with the TUC over their dissemination of anti-communist propaganda.[69] To the satisfaction of Attlee, the Labour minister reported that by the spring of 1948 the TUC general council was 'now fully alive to the dangers of communist encroachment in the trade unions, and more active steps were now being taken to combat this'. Mirroring the Brook Committee, the TUC formed a small and secret group of 'leading members of the council' to 'watch the problem' and 'ensure that useful information about communism was disseminated to the unions'. Alongside propaganda, another urgent task was halting additional communists from being elected to key union positions. Here the government could be of little direct help, since it feared blowback inside the unionist movement if it got caught attempting to rig elections. The Brook Committee did propose indirect clandestine aid to be given to anti-communist elements. At a committee meeting, the question was raised to what extent trade union leaders were aware of 'which of their officials were communists or crypto-communists'. The committee members agreed 'it would be desirable that they should be enlightened' regarding the information held by MI5 on this subject 'whenever possible'. However, they deemed it too risky to hold regular briefings with trade union leaders over the matter, since the chances of such an arrangement could leak to the public and thus damage the impartial reputation of the government. Instead, a backchannel was set up, in which the ministry of labour would convey MI5-collected information on individual communists 'to completely reliable' union leaders for use against individuals. Although the arrangement between the labour ministry and the trade union leaders remained informal, the information sharing between MI5 and the ministry became compulsory. The committee decided that MI5 reports would be sent to the labour ministry 'as a matter of routine, and any information about communists in important positions in the unions should be provided to the Ministry of Labour'.[70]

Alongside the reporting of MI5 intelligence through the ministry of labour to trade union leaders, the IRD also developed a strong partnership with high officials inside the movement.[71] During Labour's time in office Denis Healey – then just a young party official working at Transport House – conducted liaisons for the IRD. Through Healey, the IRD held frequent communications with Herbert Tracey, the chief TUC publicity officer and editor of *Labour Industrial News*. Neither MI5 nor IRD needed to worry in the slightest with regards to where Tracey's loyalties lay. He wore his aversion to communists as a badge of honour, even going so far as accepting a seat on the grand council of Common Cause.[72] Christopher Mayhew had already sought Tracey's help by offering to fund and revamp Tracey's anti-communist newsletter *Freedom First*.[73] Contact between IRD and the TUC leadership went higher on both ends of the connection than simply Healey and Tracey. As early as January 1949, meetings were being arranged between the aforementioned TUC assistant secretary, Victor Feather, and the director of IRD, Ralph Murray.[74] The relationship between Feather, who rose to the top of the TUC with his election as general secretary in 1969, and the IRD blossomed into a full-blown partnership. During the early 1950s, Feather authored several books warning of the dangers of communism in the trade union movement (*Trade Union – True or False?* and *The Essence of Trade Unionism*). The publisher of these works was a small company (Ampersand Ltd) secretly controlled and funded by the IRD.[75]

Shouting from the rooftops: Labour's reaction to unofficial strikes

A fundamental disagreement arose in both future Brook Committee meetings and correspondences between the Labour government and the security service. The disagreement was regarding how much of a threat communists in the trade union movement posed. By 1947, Attlee and his ministers, most notably Herbert Morrison and George Isaacs, believed that the CPGB had disregarded attempts at 'patriotic respectability' and were undermining the government through industrial action. Labour considered from 1948 until leaving office in 1951 the majority of wildcat strikes as being directed by communist elements inside the trade unions who were following directives from the Soviet Union. Despite scant evidence, the Labour Party and trade union leaders routinely accused communists of directing an assault against the nation's economy and the Attlee government.[76] The allegations were mainly directed towards a number of the nation's dockworkers, who held a series of strikes between 1949 and 1951. These unsubstantiated claims led to the most vicious piece of strikebreaking done by a Labour government.

In solidarity with the Canadian Seamen's Union, dockworkers at Avonmouth refused to unload a cargo ship on 14 May 1949. They contended it was a 'black ship' manned by scab sailors. When management threatened to penalise the workers for the refusal, the unofficial work stoppage turned into a lockout. A few days later, 600 Bristol dockers began striking in support of their Avonmouth brethren. In response, the government sent troops into Avonmouth to unload perishable food goods. The addition of soldiers to the situation only sparked more agitation. On 30 May, 1,400 Liverpool dockworkers joined the strike.[77] By June, the number of dockers on strike had reached 11,000. From its earliest inception, the strike was considered by Attlee and his government as a communist-inspired attack against the nation, even though both MI5 and the local police stated to the cabinet that little indication existed that communist activities were fomenting the various dock strikes.

Without any proof, Isaacs took to the BBC to lay the blame for the strike solely on communist involvement. In the 11 June broadcast, the minister of labour claimed 'the communists in this country are doing their best to mislead the workers'. Appealing directly to the striking dockworkers, he warned them that they were being used by the 'communists in this country to dislocate trade and thus retard our economic recovery'.[78] On 14 June, the Avonmouth dockers returned to work. But the struggle had meanwhile flared up in London. Here employers refused to hire labourers for newly arrived ships unless they agreed to unload two other 'black' Canadian ships. By the beginning of July, over 8,000 London dockworkers had joined this new industrial action. Commenting on this renewed strike, Cabinet Minister Philip Noel-Baker stated: 'Once again our good-hearted dockers have been duped by communist lies.'[79] Speaking in the Commons on 8 July, the home secretary labelled the whole affair a red-instigated threat to the nation:

> The only reason why we are having to deal with the trouble in this country is that the communists see in it a chance of fomenting unrest, injuring our trade and so hampering our recovery and with it the whole process of Marshall Aid on which the recovery of Western Europe depends. The issue with which we are faced is not one of a legitimate industrial dispute. We are faced with a challenge to the whole authority of the state, and it must be met.[80]

An emergency committee created to deal with the strike asserted that 'the effect and timing of these and other industrial troubles clearly demonstrated the existence of a communist attempt to cause industrial trouble and financial damage'.[81] Speaking to a crowd of over 12,000 in Manchester, Attlee denounced such unofficial strikes as 'foolish actions' backed by communists. He urged the exposure 'of these hypocrites' who were 'merely the instruments of a foreign dictatorship'.[82]

On 11 July, the prime minister announced a national state of emergency, declaring 'the situation is such as gravely to injure the economy of this country at a critical period in its history'.[83] Two days later the House of Commons debated the measure. During the debate, frontbenchers in the Liberal and Conservative Parties questioned Attlee's narrative over the communist involvement in the strike. Responding to the prime minister, Anthony Eden wondered aloud how much of the fault laid at the feet of communists. He said it was not a sufficient explanation to say they led the dockers blindly, as Labour argued. 'There is the maximum of communist intrigue and manoeuvre', asked Eden, 'but does the government really feel that that, and nothing but that, is a sufficiently searching diagnosis of this problem?'[84] The leader of the Liberal Party, Clement Davies, echoed Eden's doubts on communist involvement:

> No one dislikes the communists and the totalitarians more than I do, because they would take away the liberties that we regard as safeguards. One dislikes their methods and ideas, but it is wrong to attribute all that goes wrong today to the communists ... The right thing is not to blame the communists but to try to remove the grievance and to cure the sore. In that case, the communists would not have any influence at all. I do not believe that the 13,000 men who are out of work are communists to a man.[85]

Parliamentary criticism and sceptical reports from the intelligence community did little to stymie the governmental belief that communism agitation had brought on the strikes. Joining the chorus against the governmental charges was Major General Robert Neville, an officer commanding the troops who had replaced the striking dockers. Neville told Attlee he had 'over-played' the communist issue and it was backfiring – since the majority of the strikers 'are, of course, not communists, but the amount of emphasis thrown on the fact that they have been duped by the communists tends to make them bloody minded'.[86] Yet, still many inside the Labour Party and the civil service were as adamant about the guilt of communists as Attlee and Isaacs. Writing on the strike, Keith Jeffery and Peter Hennessy stated, 'The government's concern about communist activities was rapidly turning into an obsession.'[87]

Four Labour MPs, who represented the docklands affected by the strike, conducted their own informal investigation into the matter. Once finished, they handed a copy of their report to Home Secretary James Chuter Ede, claiming the dispute 'was riddled with communist activity so serious [a] nature that the facts should be investigated by MI5'.[88] Joining in on the red-hunt, a member of the Labour government took matters into his own hands. Looking for a justification to prosecute the strike leaders, Attorney General Hartley Shawcross searched for signs that communists were directing the industrial action. Guy Liddell stated that Shawcross 'seemed to be searching round for something in the nature of the Zinoviev Letter, which would show that on the direction of Moscow strikes are being started in Canada, Australia and the UK, with the object of wrecking the Marshall Plan'.[89] MI5 took a dim view of this personal scavenger hunt conducted by Shawcross. It believed no such 'Zinoviev Letter'-type document existed, since guidance from Moscow could simply come from the open press.[90] Writing directly to Attlee about the situation, MI5's Graham Mitchell reminded the prime minister 'that the Security Service is really the focal point for information on these matters' and the attorney general had no authority to trample on its 'preserves'. Mitchell also stated that with regards to the strike 'the general picture was fairly clear' the Communist Party had not instigated it. Liddell also considered Shawcross's mission as flawed, since no court case could legally be made against the strikers even if communists had provoked the industrial action. Refusing to let the matter rest, Shawcross requested the Office of Director of Public Prosecutions to ask MI5 and Special Branch for an assurance that they 'were doing all they could in connection with the dock strike'.[91] Also perpetuating the anti-communist frenzy over the strike was Permanent Secretary of the Ministry of Transport Gilmour Jenkins. He delivered an unsigned memorandum entitled 'Communism and the Dock Strikes' to his fellow civil servant, Home Office Permanent Secretary Frank Newsam. The note claimed that 'three weeks of careful investigation have shown the London dock strike ... is under direct control of the Cominform itself'.[92] Newsam passed the memo to MI5. The security service was 'inclined on its face value to doubt its reliability', though it did investigate the memo.[93] MI5 discovered it originated 'from right-wing sources in Europe of dubious reliability'.[94] The co-authors of the note turned out to be Conservative MP John Baker White and Colonel Robert Hoare, both leaders of the Economic League. Angered over the situation, the Home Office reported 'a good deal of time and labour might have been saved if the Ministry of Transport had told us from the start that the information had come from the Economic League'.[95]

Despite governmental efforts, by 20 July over 15,000 men were on strike. They only returned to work on 22 July when the Canadian Seamen's Union, having obtained concessions, withdrew their pickets from certain ships and announced that they were terminating their dispute. The cessation of hostilities did not last long. On 19 April 1950, a strike on the London docks began again. It was in direct succession to the Canadian seamen's strike the year prior. Three of the major figures in the previous year's strike were expelled from the TGWU, thereby threatening the men's livelihood. Six thousand dockers immediately walked out in sympathy.[96] Again, the striking dockers had no grievance about their conditions of work. They struck only in protest against the expulsions. One of the expelled men was Ted Dickens, who was a member of the executive committee of the Communist Party. When the strike began, party action followed immediately. But no evidence existed that the CPGB had planned or wished for this industrial unrest. Attempts were made, however, by the CPGB to arrange an immediate expression of support for the dockers in various provincial ports.[97] Regardless of the lack of evidence, and echoing the same sentiments of the year before, Isaacs laid the blame directly on the 'red menace'. In the House of Commons, he declared:

> The present stoppage is clearly communist-inspired and is nothing else than an attack on the democratic and constitutional rules of the Transport and General Workers' Union ... This stoppage shows once again the lengths to which the communists are prepared to go in their attempt – and I am glad to say in their losing attempt – to gain control of the trade union movement. No consideration of hardship to the workpeople or their families, or the country generally, is allowed to interfere with their plans.[98]

In the estimation of the Labour government, communists were not limiting their attacks only to the nation's docks. It blamed communist incitement as the primary reason for unofficial strikes occurring throughout the industrial and transport sectors of the country. So even after the ending of that specific dock strike, Isaacs's accusations continued. Like the American Joseph McCarthy, Isaacs showed an ever-growing mania over supposed communist infiltration. In September 1950, the minister of labour claimed that the CPGB ran a secret organisation inside the trade union movement, which sought to disrupt essential services and destroy the unions from within.[99] Responding to the allegation, the CPGB issued a statement refuting the charge and daring Isaacs to provide proof to back up his words. 'The fact that he has not done so', the statement read, 'is complete confirmation that his attempt to launch a red scare has no foundation in fact.' It added, 'For a cabinet minister to fool and deceive parliament and people by making allegations which he is unable to back with proof is a scandalous, shameful and cowardly action.'[100] In the House of Commons, Isaacs also faced questions over his claims that such a secret organisation existed. Conservative MP Bernard Braine asked what 'steps have been taken to deal with the subversive organization'. Isaacs awkwardly answered that such activities were being watched. Braine followed up by stating many concerned parties do 'not believe in the existence of such an organization and believe that the government are using the communists as a scapegoat'.[101] MI5 records of the period do not show any evidence of such an organisation ever existing, but the belief was widespread inside the Labour government.[102] Isaacs was not the sole public promoter of such a notion. Speaking of unofficial stoppages, Minister of Agriculture Tom Williams claimed 'inside knowledge that they are mostly inspired by a half dozen members of the Communist Party'.[103]

Any type of industrial unrest occurring after 25 June 1950 was considered by governmental circles as being of an even more sinister nature. With British troops poised to fight in Korea, such actions were seen as impeding the national struggle. With the UK now in open conflict against communist forces, many Britons naturally assumed that their domestic communist compatriots would work to sabotage the country's war effort. Such a belief brought with it more unsubstantiated charges against domestic communists. On the night of 14 July, an explosion of eight fifty-foot ammunition barges occurred at Portsmouth harbour. The blast injured six workers and shattered hundreds of windowpanes of nearby buildings.[104] Accounts stated the aftermath resembled the destruction wrought from wartime air raids conducted by the Luftwaffe. From the onset, many suspected the bombing was a deliberate act of sabotage to disrupt the upcoming British military efforts in Korea. The most prominent purveyor of this view turned out to be the nation's prime minister. Even before an official board of inquiry reported on the cause, Attlee took to the floor of the Commons to declare the explosion a case of sabotage.[105] Although the prime minister refused to speculate on the probable perpetrators, few needed to guess the most likely source of the 'attack'. Attlee's brazen announcement shocked MI5, since, contrary to what the prime minister stated, 'recent evidence seemed to indicate that the explosion was due to faulty construction of a depth charge'. MI5's Deputy Director Guy Liddell speculated that 'political wishful thinking about a communist plot' is what motivated Attlee to make such a charge.[106] The evidence points to Liddell being correct. The nation's press picked up the prime minister's sentiments; the following day, headlines ran declaring 'War on Britain's 5th Column' and warning of 'The Enemy Within'.[107] In a 31 July broadcast to the nation about the situation in Korea, Attlee linked the 'ruthless and unscrupulous' communist 'menace' with the 'outrage at Portsmouth'.[108]

Taking Attlee's lead, right-wing union leaders continued the prime minister's narrative on the Portsmouth incident and widened the charges of sabotage. Writing in his union's journal, Tom Yates, general secretary of the National Union of Seamen, called the Portsmouth explosion 'only one incident of many' of supposed sabotage. 'There have been other cases of mysterious damage to naval vessels by fires, explosions and breakdowns, which could not have occurred by accident', he wrote.[109] Yates went on to warn seafarers against communists who might lure them into causing breakdowns of ships about to leave port and told them to keep an eye on colleagues who acted suspiciously. 'There is only one course to take with them', he wrote about communists' inside unions, 'they must be hunted out, run down, and driven out of our movement.'[110] He also reminded his readers that sabotage could take many forms, not only violent explosions – hinting that unofficial strikes worked as a type of sabotage. Yates's accusations did not go unnoticed or unanswered by the CPGB. In response to Yates's article, Communist MP William Gallacher sent letters to Yates, the director of public prosecutions and General Secretary of TUC Vincent Tewson. The letters all called for Yates to provide proof for his charges. Gallacher argued that by the tone of Yates's words, 'he knows the people responsible' and should make a statement to the police if such was the case.[111] The recipients refused to respond to Gallacher's challenge. Shortly after the Plymouth explosion, TGWU leader Arthur Deakin joined the chorus in blaming communists inside trade unions of sabotage. He also added that they were resorting to threatening violence in achieving their goals within the movement.[112] Deakin considered it his 'duty' to warn trade unionists of the pitfalls into which they are being advised to go. He called the battle against communism an attempt to halt 'a national policy as defined and determined by an agency outside this country' which sought 'to keep alive industrial unrest'.[113] Deakin proposed a simple solution: outlaw and ban the CPGB. When questioned if such a move would only make communists more dangerous, since they would be less easy to detect, Deakin retorted, 'they couldn't be more underground than they already are'.[114]

The security service held a dim and critical opinion of the alarmist assertions made by the government. In a meeting with Brigadier R.F. Johnstone (deputy director of military intelligence at the War Office), Liddell stated MI5 felt the 'attitude on the question of communism' by members at the top level of government had 'rather worried' them. He claimed that high-level officials held the impression that communist conspiracy was 'directing strikes and sabotage over the country'. Liddell explained to

Johnstone these 'were not our views ... our view was that the disturbances in the country were due to a lack of trust by the rank and file in their trade unions leaders, whom they regarded as too much identified with the policy of the government'. These disenfranchised workers 'therefore took matters into their own hands'.[115] Speaking directly about the threat of the communists with regards to strikes, he went on to state they 'were generally a bit slow off the mark ... and hardly initiated anything'. Liddell confided that MI5 felt that regarding the communist threat it was 'somewhat dangerous that they [the government] should be misguided at the top'. By early 1951, it became quite understandable why MI5 felt this way. Time after time, the agency reported that the CPGB had not initiated the vast majority of the unofficial strikes. When party members were involved, it was on an individual and usually isolated basis. While it was true the party did support existing industrial action, its reasoning had more to do with showing solidarity with the strikers than seeking to halt production or topple the government. As well, no evidence existed that communists were engaging in acts of sabotage. For Attlee, his ministers and their allies in the trade union movement to state otherwise was only needlessly stoking public fears. Wholeheartedly agreeing with this warning, Johnstone explained the refusal of MI5's intelligence being accepted by their superiors. Johnstone claimed 'a number in government' felt MI5 'had an enormous job which was overwhelming them', hence the agency was missing the warning signs of communist agitation inside the trade union movement.[116] While not a direct criticism of the security service, such a supposition allowed members of the Labour government to continue to make baseless charges which were not supported by any evidence provided by the intelligence community. Neither Isaacs nor Attlee consulted MI5 before they alleged communistic involvement with strikes and sabotage.[117] MI5 labelled Isaacs's charges of communist conspiracies 'stupid' and said they would be 'likely to recoil on our heads' since Isaacs had 'little or no evidence on which to base' such statements.[118] The only impact they had was a negative one. Since, as Liddell maintained, they 'caused a good deal of anxiety in the US', MI5 needed to assure their American counterparts of 'the real position'.[119] The 'real position' was that such a communist conspiracy was non-existent.

Seeking to curb both sabotage and industrial unrest during the period, the cabinet considered enacting some stricter form of legalisation to make it a criminal offence to impede in any way the measures being taken which affected state security.[120] It appeared a similar action had been contemplated during the 1949 dock strike. Speaking to Deakin on 30 May, Home Secretary James Chuter Ede said a benefit of the strike was that it allowed the government to deal with 'the elements which fomented these continual strikes'. Agreeing with Ede, Norman Brook argued that such a law would only be useful if it covered unofficial strikes, such as ones initiated by the dockworkers. Brook believed if the government failed to act in this matter, it would be 'highly detrimental to the security and efficiency of the country'. Herbert Morrison voiced his agreement with Brook on the matter. Both were overruled after governmental consultations with trade union leaders discovered that these union officials were opposed to such a restrictive measure.[121] In September 1950, the full cabinet approved a small group of three ministers to organise a plan 'to counter communist endeavours to cause industrial unrest'.[122] The trio consisted of Herbert Morrison, George Isaacs and James Chuter Ede. At a cabinet meeting four days later, Attlee instructed Morrison, the head of the unnamed committee, to 'consider whether the criminal law could with advantage be strengthened to counter a communist conspiracy to foment industrial unrest in this country'.[123] As Morrison and his fellow committee members were busy deliberating, Attorney General Harry Shawcross found it necessary to act. He ordered the prosecution of ten leaders of an unofficial London gas workers' strike. The ten were charged with violating the 1875 Conspiracy and Protection of Property Act that made it a crime for utility workers to break their contracts of service. They were initially sentenced to a month's imprisonment.[124] The government believed a communist-controlled union had instigated the strike. When publicly questioned about the prosecutions, Shawcross argued they were necessary because communists were attempting to prolong the strike.[125] In the meantime, the Morrison-headed committee assessed that any new legislation would have to be presented in parliament. Brook argued to Attlee that such a move was politically unwise, since such a proposed bill needed overwhelming public support. Brook stated that Attlee's efforts in claiming sabotage and subversion had not led to a widespread belief that such communist subversion existed. Thus no new legislation was introduced, since it was likely to fail.[126] But this did not stop further prosecutions. In February 1951, Special Branch arrested seven members of a committee of London dockers who were heading an unofficial strike.[127] They had recently been denounced as communists by the TGWU. The arrests placed Deakin on the defensive since a number of the strikers suspected that he masterminded the arrests.[128] No evidence ever came to light to link him directly with the arrests; but Deakin clearly showed sympathy for the police action, stating, 'If it can be proven that these seven men have been engaged since October 1950, in a conspiracy, then they should have been dealt with long ago.'[129]

The government had sanctioned their arrests by the revival of a wartime measure titled the Conditions of Employment and National

Arbitration Order, more commonly known as Order 1305. The order effectively banned strikes and forced any side in a dispute to bring their case to an arbitration panel rather than go on strike. The governmental action boomeranged, since the arrests sparked more than 19,000 dockers to go on strike. Within forty-eight hours, all of the UK's major ports were locked out.[130] These peacetime arrests and prosecutions did not go over well inside the trade union movement. Even the stalwart anti-communist TUC was disturbed by such extreme measures. Fearful of losing key trade union allies, the government agreed to a revision of the Order that deleted the prohibition on strikes and lockouts.

A shift in policy: the Conservatives take power

The results of the October 1951 General Election reinvigorated the threat of communist-inspired strikes and industrial unrest in quarters of the government and political society. Because of the CPGB attitude towards the right-wing Conservative Party, such a shift made perfect sense. Since the party had concentrated much of its propaganda activities in denouncing the Tories since 1945, an attempt to bring down Churchill's new government through industrial action seemed a likely CPGB strategy. Even MI5, which consistently doubted communist involvement in the industrial sector, believed it was something which needing watching. At a July 1952 meeting, Percy Sillitoe warned Home Secretary David Maxwell Fyfe, 'Since the end of 1951 the Communist Party ... instructions to its followers in British industry are that strike action must be achieved where possible.'[131] The fear of communist-inspired strikes gained the Conservatives support from places that they would have found baffling in any other circumstance. A few months after the Conservative victory, the National Council of Labour unanimously passed a resolution condemning any unofficial strikes protesting the new government. The council, a consultative body set up to coordinate the policies and actions of the TUC and the Labour Party, stated in the 'strongest terms its condemnation of the attempts now being made by irresponsible elements to persuade trade unionists to take industrial action in order to achieve political ends'. It went on to argue that any strike 'being organized under the pretext of protesting against the action of the present reactionary government is in fact part and parcel of a world conspiracy to undermine the industrial power of the nation'.[132] Articles in the press kept such a narrative alive as well. G.L. Wilson, the industrial correspondent for the *Yorkshire Post*, blamed unrest growing in northern coalfields on 'the price that is being paid for the sense of power and indispensability which has gone to the heads of an irresponsible minority of workers'. Echoing the same suspicions which accompanied the Grimethorpe shutdown, Wilson maintained 'it is communism which is benefiting from the increasing number of strikes'.[133]

Unlike Attlee and Isaacs, Churchill and his minister of labour, Walter Monckton, were unmoved by these charges of communist unrest in trade union action. A review of the cabinet conclusions attests to the fact. Although oftentimes strikes occurring were discussed, they were very rarely suspected of being caused or instigated by communists. When communists were mentioned during these discussions it was always as a secondary reference. In September 1952, Monckton remarked that a dispute at Park Royal Vehicles had attracted the attention of 'the communists'. He did not argue they were the cause of the unrest, just that they were seeking to capitalise from it.[134] When 2,000 workers at the Austin Motor Works in Birmingham went on strike in 1953, Monckton stated the union calling for the action was 'under communist control'. But he assured the cabinet that since other unions were also involved, 'it seemed likely that different views on the merits of the strike would develop' among the men being affected by it.[135] In 1954, after renewed dock strikes, Monckton told the cabinet he was investigating the part 'played by the communists in organising this series of strikes' but did not accuse them of being involved with starting them.[136] Only in one case did Monckton label a strike 'communist-inspired'. This was in 1955, over one occurring at the Rolls Royce factories in Scotland.[137]

Although the Churchill government did not publicly continue ringing the alarm over communist-inspired strikes, this did not mean the issue was suddenly laid to rest. In 1954, again the dockers of London went on strike. Charges of communist agitation by trade unionist leaders quickly followed – especially by Arthur Deakin. The Churchill government reacted quite differently to its predecessor. During the 1949 and 1950 dock strikes the Labour government issued white papers which blamed 'communist agitation' for their occurrences. In the midst of such a similar strike, the Conservatives refused to follow suit. The lack of a white paper was intentional, done to take the wind out of the sails of Deakin's accusations that communists were again to blame. Although Deakin was a stalwart ally and vocal supporter of Labour's allegations of communist agitation, the Conservatives wished to temper his more bombastic rhetoric; supporting this, no doubt, was MI5. Although a darling of the Labour government, the security service viewed Deakin as problematic. They labelled his 'irresponsible statements about communist interference in industry' as 'damaging' and categorised Deakin as someone 'ready to take any political advantage which presented itself'.[138] In one particular incident, MI5 was alarmed after they discovered Deakin spreading false charges of communist agitation. In February 1951, Deakin called together sixty reporters and distributed a document entitled 'Agent Provocateur' which he alleged the CPGB were dispensing among seamen on merchant ships. After an investigation, MI5 determined 'the document was almost certainly a fake, since the Communist Party would be unlikely to distribute anything of the kind'.[139] However, when police in Cardiff began investigating the document, MI5 did not release this information but cautioned them to be 'circumspect' over the issue. No need to embarrass a prominent trade unionist; though overzealous, Deakin was still on the right side. A similar assessment took place during a meeting of the Brook Committee during a 1954 dock strike. Contrary to what Deakin said in the press, MI5 reported 'the strike had been the product of an industrial grievance, accentuated by inter-union rivalry'. The security service suggested it might be useful 'in dispelling Mr. Deakin's myth of communist instigation'. Although considered by the committee, it was determined there was 'nothing to be gained' by pricking 'Mr. Deakin's bubble', since 'nothing would alter his conviction that the strikes were communist inspired'.[140]

The key factor for this shift of governmental attitudes against the likelihood of communists causing unofficial strikes came through the acceptance of intelligence gathered by MI5. Sillitoe's warning to the home secretary of communist resistance to the new Conservative government proved alarmist. The security service did not uncover any evidence which supported the cautionary counsel. In 1954, MI5 found it safe to report to the Home Office that it was 'generally true to say that the [Communist] party now dares not take the initiative in starting a strike. The most it can, and does, do is to try to cash in on strikes and disturbances started by someone else'.[141] This situational assessment would not diminish over time but strengthened into the late 1950s.

As mentioned previously, governmental concern over communists in trade unions was divided into two main issues: one was their ability to foment unrest and the second was their growing influence inside the hierarchy and apparatuses of the trade union movement. Unlike with the first, when dealing with the latter the Conservatives stayed the course set by Labour. The fundamental blueprint of combating communism inside trade unions did not vary with the changing of power in 1951. Such was the case with the number of anti-communist measures enacted under Labour (governmental vetting, visa restrictions, efforts of the IRD, and so on); the Conservatives kept the anti-communist policy towards trade unions in place. This meant the strategy of a light touch and covert assistance to trusted and reliable anti-communist trade unionists remained unaltered. Here the government did show favourable progress. Despite the natural distrust of trade unionists towards the right-wing Conservatives, the two parties found the hatred of communism as a common ground on which to foster a working relationship. The rapport between the two became so cordial that Harold Macmillan reported to Prime Minister Anthony Eden that several trade union leaders had become very sensitive about the accusation of acting as 'Tory stooges'.[142] Working off intelligence from MI5, the Conservatives grasped the true objective of CPGB inside the trade union movement. The formation of strikes and sabotage did not interest the Churchill and Eden governments. What did was limiting and rolling back the political influence/power communists held through the trade union movement.

Six months into the Churchill government, the ministry of labour produced a memorandum giving its appraisal of communist activities in industry. In it the ministry endorsed the current covert efforts against communists and 'stressed the importance of avoiding any government interference with the unions in this matter'.[143] On that very critical subject, the report went into great detail about the reasoning behind the continued policy:

> It is most important to remember that trade union opinion is extremely sensitive towards any semblance of a threat to its complete freedom and independence. Intervention by the government, however mild in form or benevolent in intention, would set up violent reactions in the trade unions, even in those which have pursued the most strongly of anti-communist policy. It is easy to guess at the political capital which could be made if it became known that the government was passing information or advice to one section of the trade union movement to use against another section of the movement. This would be constructed as an attempt to set one official against another and to split trade union solidarity for what would be described as reactionary purposes, and as an attack upon the democratic procedure by which trade union officials are elected.[144]

It went on to state that on the whole 'relations with the trade unions were good' and that trade union leaders 'were very forthcoming in their efforts to fight communist penetration'.[145] But the ultimate goal should not be forgotten: 'the government must see to it that communist trickery does not capture the trade union movement'. In its final assessment, it stressed continued vigilance against 'signs of communist intervention in the labour field' and a willingness towards counter-action when such opportunities arose. However, it did again warn that governmental agencies 'should not attempt to take a hand in the wider fight against the communist in the unions', since 'that fight is already being waged vigorously and with reasonable success, and the anti-communist forces would not be likely to welcome outside intervention in the struggle which might indeed react to their disadvantage'.[146] At a meeting of the Brook Committee in October 1952, Guy Liddell reaffirmed the passage of MI5's confidential information to the labour ministry for dissemination to trade unionist allies. Speaking of the arrangement, Robert Gould said although it was an informal practice, because of concerns over secrecy, 'this process ... was going on all the time'. Gould went on to say that in respect of its anti-communist activities, 'the Ministry of Labour were already taking more action than was generally known or talked about'. Such actions included directing trade unionists to discredit 'those advocating extreme measures'.[147]

A fundamental problem the government had to deal with was the exuberance and over-eagerness of leaders of the trade union movement. A key facet of the government's plan to fight communism hinged on these anti-communist unionists. MI5 and the ministry of labour both relied on them as the vanguard in the war waging within the trade union movement. But past experiences, particularly with the likes of Deakin, had made them come to the realisation that 'TU leaders could not be trusted where their own interests were concerned'. With this in mind, the security service rebuked a TUC attempt to liaise directly with the agency. 'It would be quite impossible for us to enter into any kind of exchange which might facilitate the task of the TUC in getting rid of their communists', Liddell determined, since 'they would be almost certain to misuse the information that was given to them, with possibly disastrous results'.[148] This wariness about using these trade unionists undoubtedly hindered the efforts by the government in this sector. To this point, by 1954 MI5 had assessed the situation of communists in trade unions as static. Despite covert governmental efforts to roll back communist influence, Dick White dolefully reported, 'in the past six years the communists in the unions have held their ground surprisingly well'. White also acknowledged the CPGB had not been able to widen its power, stating the 'party has broken little new ground and in the unions where its foothold was precarious'.[149] In a complete reversal of what occurred under Labour, the ministry of labour held a more optimistic opinion of the situation than the security service. Its representative on the Brook Committee, Robert Gould, reported communists were suffering 'several severe defeats' in the trade union movement.[150]

In 1956, the security service produced a report that caused an immediate paradigm shift in the relevant governmental departments dealing with trade unions and communism. Descriptively titled 'Industrial Unrest 1953–1955: The Role of the Communist Party', it consisted of an overall assessment of the situation for the purpose of a re-evaluation of governmental policies concerning the topic. In certain governmental circles, its findings were quite shocking and, more than anything else, unexpected. The report began by setting the scene:

> The past two years have seen an increase in industrial unrest in this country. There have been a number of major strikes, and though relations between employers and the unions have remained much the same, relations between the unions themselves have deteriorated. Responsibility for a substantial proportion of this unrest has been attributed to the British Communist Party both by the popular press and by responsible trade union opinion.[151]

After outlining its findings, the report stated in a very definitive and very unequivocal way what it ultimately discovered:

> The examination shows that none of the strikes was directly inspired by the Communist Party and throughout the party's industrial staff, work failed to measure up to its task. In some instances, the party was unaware that trouble was brewing in the particular industry, despite the presence of communists in many of the danger spots, and in other instances where the party had received warning it was slow both to appreciate the depth of feeling involved and to exploit its opportunities.[152]

The authors of the report measured the lack of CPGB involvement as arising from a Machiavellian mindset in which the party operated. The central goal of the party in industrial affairs was to capture and consolidate positions of strength in the trade union movement as a first stage towards 'the attainment of political power in the United Kingdom'. This turned out to be a completely accurate assessment.[153] Involvement with unofficial strikes was considered harmful to this objective because of the negative reactions the instigators of such strikes often received. The report made sure to emphasise that in the minds of the party the fomenting of industrial unrest was no more than a tactical method, not the main objective.

The rest of MI5's findings held in the memorandum were not as sanguine. The report stated influence inside the trade union movement of the CPGB had been routinely underestimated. Although CPGB members averaged less than one in 500 of the entire trade union membership, communists controlled the executive committees of three national unions and held the post of thirteen general secretaries, and with 'thirteen more the holder of this post had exhibited communist sympathies in recent years'. At executive committee level, communists held control over the Electrical Trade Union (a key industrial union with over 200,000 members), the Association of Scientific Workers and the Fire Brigades Union. It was also believed that the CPGB had sufficient members or sympathisers on the national executive bodies of the United Society of Boilermakers, Shipbuilders and Structural Workers, the Constructional Engineering Union and the Association of Building Technicians. Even more frightening was that at least one in eight of all trade union officials could now be classified 'on the basis of recent evidence' as either a communist or communist sympathiser.[154] In summation, the report marked communist penetration of the trade union movement as substantial and a vital security threat. This threat came not from communists' capability to foment industrial unrest but from them accumulating legitimate influence inside the fifth estate.

The report came as a shock to the members of the Brook Committee; no one was more shocked than the committee chairman. During the Attlee years, Norman Brook had been a firm proponent of the belief that communists were behind a large number of unofficial strikes. After reading MI5's assessment, he then proposed that a concerted effort be made to correct this misconception both inside the trade unions and to the public. Too much time had been misspent on the strike issue and not enough on the real danger of the growing communist influence. He declared it was now up to the committee to propose countermeasures to combat it. Speaking to the committee, Brook reminded them of the obvious. For reasons they all knew, and despite the increased threat, 'the government could not take direct action to prevent further communist penetration of the trade unions themselves'.[155]

On the sunnier side, Brook said evidence existed that leaders in the trade union movement felt they could do more to halt the spread of communist influence 'if the rank and file knew which of the leading trade unionist were communists'. If the government gave them the names of communist trade unionists MI5 and Special Branch had collected, the trade unions leaders could disseminate them 'to ensure that non-communist candidates were elected'. The committee suggested that the minister of labour could approach 'certain trade union leaders in confidence' with the information they desired. Alongside the constant eagerness of a number of trade union officials to do more, the committee also noted the 'considerable propaganda' being carried out in the unions by anti-communist organisations. The most notable were the Economic League, Common Cause and Aims of Industry. While the committee believed these bodies were achieving useful results, it understood their impact was limited since many trade unionists considered such groups as 'bosses' organizations'.

The committee then considered a new alternative which sought to bring a bipartisan measure to the problem. It was suggested that the Conservative government approach for assistance 'the other parliamentary parties, in particular the Labour Party', since it 'had a keen interest in preventing the spread of communist influence in the unions'. It hoped the Labour Party 'might be urged to take the communist challenge on a political level'. However, such a plan did have complications, since 'it might lead to jealousy and ill-will between the industrial and political sides of the Labour movement'.[156]

Alongside reinvigorating the Brook Committee, which had been dormant for many months, the MI5 report also spurred Minister of Labour Iain Macleod to gather several trade union leaders together. In July 1956, he met with Vincent Tewson (TUC general secretary), Tom Williamson (National Union of General and Municipal Workers general secretary) and Wilfred Heywood (National Union of Dyers, Bleachers and Textile Workers general secretary) to discuss communist influence in the trade union movement along the lines pointed out in the memorandum by the security service. Macleod described the meeting as 'a very long and rather inconclusive discussion'. Although he classified his guests as 'very fierce anti-communists', he judged their influence as quite limited, only reaching 'unions where communist influence is negligible'. The meeting did not reach a consensus, but the union leaders did express that they did not consider government inference to be the solution, stating 'it was very much their battle' to be fought.[157]

Conclusion

Although more influential than in any other sector of British society, the successes of communists inside the trade union movement were by no means a threat to the UK from an existential standpoint. A comparison with the influence wielded by their compatriots in the Italian and French trade unions points to the fact that CPGB successes in the fourth estate were actually quite limited. The fact they sought to disrupt or topple the government through industrial action also did not hold much credence. But the question still remains: why did Attlee, his ministers and their trade union allies continue to persist in arguing the contrary?

Prior historians contended the realistic fear of the Soviet Union held by Attlee and his ministers gave credence to their behaviour. It was argued the Labour government's actions came not from paranoia but from 'clearheaded suspicions of subversions at home'.[158] Phillip Deery wrote that 'communism, insofar as it was the central to the government's evaluation of the London dock strike of 1949, was not an irrational concoction arising from fevered imaginings'.[159] More recently released governmental files (most notably the Liddell diaries opened to the public in 2002) showed such was not the case. This newer evidence helps to form a more accurate narrative, one showing Attlee and other Labour politicians simply disregarded MI5's intelligence reports on the matter.

It is relatively easy to put a pessimistic spin on their actions. From the perspective of trade union leadership, attacks against internal communism did have their net benefits. Aside from the typical rhetoric against the 'red menace', trade union leaders had another reason to fear communist involvement in their movement. Much more than just the political beliefs of the communists inspired concern in many leaders. They disrupted the status quo and questioned the authority of the union hierarchy. Often communists were articulating the rank-and-file sentiments and grievances of the ordinary worker concerning the undemocratic nature of the union structure. Colin Davis argued that Arthur Deakin embodied this critique by using anti-communism as 'part of a personal crusade to protect his political power within the TGWU'.[160] He used the issue of red infiltration to take the spotlight off the fact that through these unofficial strikes Deakin had lost de facto control over his own members and thus used the issue to request governmental support in reining in these rebels. His pleas for assistance allowed Attlee to despatch troops into the docks as liberators of the national interest, not as strike-breakers of the working man. Another problem that Deakin, and other trade union leaders of his ilk, routinely encountered was CPGB members questioning their close relationship with the state. Communist trade unionists were quick to point out the sycophantic allegiance organs such as the TUC and TGWU displayed towards government policies and directives. Criticising the close relationship, Arthur Horner stated in 1947 that the leaders of the TUC were nothing more than puppets of the current regime. When he reflected on the period, Vic Feather held no regrets for his leading part in the anti-communist campaign. He did not see himself leading a witch hunt but participating in a fair fight against his Marxist-Leninist-inclined compatriots.[161]

With the legislating of nationalisation, frustration fomented inside Labour, since the government's policies received a backlash – not only from the Conservatives but also from one-time supporters inside the industrial sector. To Labour's dismay and outrage, the unofficial strikes which occurred under the past National and Conservative governments continued unabated. It makes perfect sense that when seeking a reason for this continuation, Attlee and his ministers turned to the spectre of the 'red peril'. As Labour was successfully eliminating the social conditions that bred communists and fomented Marxist revolution, these forces would inevitably lose viability. So, as the theory went: to halt the success of social democracy, the CPGB, using conspiratorial means, fomented strikes and work stoppages. If this was not the case, then the Attlee government had no one to blame for the industrial unrest. Speaking about Labour's frustration after the Grimethorpe affair, the left-leaning Aneurin Bevan let loose a tirade:

> It is necessary to tell some of our people in industry that they are beginning to lose heart, and that some of them appear to have achieved material prosperity in excess of their moral status. Some of them have got what they have got too easily, and they are in danger of throwing it away by a few months of dissipating anarchy what we have spent our lifetime in building up. We shall keep faith with the people but the people must keep faith with us.[162]

Especially for the idealist Bevan, the indication that the people were losing faith in the socialist reforms must have come as an unfathomable notion. The belief in sinister forces conspiring against the national interest must have seemed a more plausible scenario. Industrial stoppages in the postwar era brought with them the question of how workers should behave in the newly nationalised industries. Here, Labour governmental attitudes did not reconcile with substantial segments of the trade union movement. Widespread unofficial strikes raised existential questions for Labour politicians 'who believed that they were reconstructing economic and social relationships in a way that required a new morality'.[163] Hence, the use of anti-communist stereotyping by Labour essentially kept the government from admitting structural problems which its new economic reforms could not entirely alleviate.

Although MI5 consistently reported that communists were rarely instigating strikes, the Labour leadership continued to hold a different opinion. The Conservatives, in regards to Labour, took a very different view. Unlike their blindness towards treasonous upper-class penetration, the Conservatives were not shackled to the same societal blinders when examining communists of the working-class variety. That was the case when in government they chose a less confrontational response to the matter than their Labour predecessors. Part of this divergence had to do with a more complacent reliance of the Conservatives on following the guidance of MI5. When the security service reported that communists were not the instigators in industrial unrest, such reports were believed. This was not typically the case with the previous government, which often disregarded the advice of MI5, preferring to place increased emphasis on gut feelings rather than the facts of individual cases. After an examination of the media of the time and governmental documents, one does not find the same sense of urgency of an impending crisis under the leadership of Churchill and Eden. Worrisome industrial action was not less worrisome to the government. But now the communistic threat was shown not to be the cause of the situation. However, the opposite trend in the Labour leadership persisted into the 1960s. In 1966, following the lead of Clement Attlee, Prime Minister Harold Wilson once again blamed communist elements inside the trade union movement for industrial unrest. Angered after months of unconstructive negotiations during a seaworkers' strike, Wilson took to the floor of the Commons to state the leaders of the strike had bowed to undemocratic pressures. Although he did not mention 'communism', the press and the public knew this is what he was alluding to. A few days later Wilson gave a list of eight names of union officials he claimed were communists or under the influence of the CPGB. Breaking with his party leader, Anthony Benn labelled Wilson's actions as McCarthyite.[164]

Starting from a highpoint at the end of the Second World War, communist influence inside the trade union movement remained static because of an onslaught of anti-communist measures, activities and propaganda. While communist membership decreased within the movement, the CPGB influence remained considerable.[165] Effectively, the battle remained a draw; neither side achieved the outright success it struggled to obtain over its foe. Such a stalemate favoured the anti-communist cause. By the late 1950s, communist elements in the trade union movement remained effectively contained, and right-leaning trade union leaders were still firmly at the helm of the movement.

Notes

1. *Daily Herald*, 15 December 1947, p. 1.

2. Audio interview by Fred Lindop with Jack Dash, MSS.371/QD7/Docks 1/10a/ii, MRC.

3. J Callaghan, 'The plan to capture the British Labour Party and its paradoxical results, 1947–91', *Journal of Contemporary History*, 20 (2005): 707–25, at p. 711.

4. A. Deighton, 'Britain and Cold War, 1945–1955', in *Cambridge History of the Cold War* vol. 2, ed. M. Leffler and O. Westad (Cambridge, 2017), 112–32, at p. 124.

5. W. Thompson, 'British communists in the Cold War, 1947–52', *Contemporary British History*, 15 (2001): 105–32, at p. 124.

6. N. Fishman, 'The phoney Cold War in British trade unions', *Contemporary British History*, 15 (2001): 83–104, at p. 96.

7. J. Callaghan, 'Towards isolation: The Communist Party and the Labour government', in *Labour's Promised Land?*, ed. J. Fyrth (London, 1995), p. 108.

8. B. McCormick, *Industrial Relations in the Coal Industry* (London, 1979), pp. 180–1.

9. *Gloucester Citizen*, 29 September 1947, p. 1.

10. *New York Times*, 5 September 1947, p. E10. The editorial made news in the UK as well; see *Liverpool Echo*, 9 September 1947, p. 2.

11. Liddell diary, 1 October 1947.

12. *Daily Herald*, 10 October 1947, p. 3.

13. *Nottingham Evening Post*, 5 April 1947, p. 4.

14. *New York Times*, 15 September 1947, p. 5.

15. 'The Grimethorpe Miners', *Socialist Standard*, October 1947.

16. *Sphere*, 6 September 1947, p. 5.

17. A. Horner, *Incorrigible Rebel* (London, 1960), p. 185.

18. *Yorkshire Post and Leeds Intelligencer*, 14 January 1949, p. 1.

19. G. Orwell, 'Burnham's view of the contemporary world struggle', 29 March 1947, in *The Collected Essays, Journalism and Letters of George Orwell*, vol. 4, 1945–50, ed. S. Orwell and I. Angus (London, 1970), p. 320.

20. *Truth*, 12 September 1947, p. 5.

21. *Coventry Evening Telegraph*, 5 September 1947, p. 1.

22. N. Fishman, 'Phoney Cold War', p. 89.

23. Morgan Phillips, 'The communist: We have been warned', press release, 22 December 1947.

24. *Defend Democracy*, TUC pamphlet, 1948.

25. Vincent Tewson, 'Trade union movement and communism', 24 November 1948, MSS 292-777.5-1, MRC.

26. L. Williams to Vic Feather, 4 January 1949, MSS 292-777.5-1, TUC, MRC.

27. 'Statement on trade unions and communism', 17 February 1949, MSS 292-777.5-1, TUC, MRC.

28. H.W. Andrews to Vincent Tewson, 29 November 1948, MSS 292-777.5-1, TUC, MRC.

29. Leo Crawford to Tewson, 15 November 1948, MSS 292-777.5-1, TUC, MRC.

30. Tewson to Ray Boyfield, 3 February 1949, MSS 292-777.5-2, TUC, MRC.

31. *Yorkshire Post*, 3 February 1949, p. 1.

32. *Northern Despatch*, 3 February 1949, p. 1.

33. P.H. Wadge to Boyfield, 7 April 1949, MSS 292-777.5-2, TUC, MRC.

34. Tewson to Boyfield, 3 February 1949, MSS 292-777.5-2; Ray Boyfield to P.H. Wade, 1 March 1949, MSS 292-777.5-2, TUC, MRC.

35. S. Horsfield to Tewson, 4 August 1949, MSS 292-777.5-5, TUC, MRC.

36. P. Deery and N. Redfern, 'No lasting peace? Labor, communism and the Cominform: Australia and Great Britain, 1945–50', *Labour History*, 38 (2005): 63–86, at p. 78.

37. H. Pelling, *The British Communist Party* (London, 1958), p. 154.

38. For an in-depth analysis for Deakin's anti-communist positions, see V. Allen, *Trade Union Leadership* (London, 1957), pp. 274–88.

39. *Belfast Newsletter*, 12 July 1949, p. 6.

40. *Herald Express*, 24 May 1949, p. 1.

41. *Daily Herald*, 27 May 1949, p. 5.

42. W.E. Brough to Tewson, 3 February 1949, MSS 292-777.5-3, TUC, MRC.

43. *Daily Mirror*, 14 February 1949, p. 1; *Belfast Newsletter*, 14 February 1949, p. 4.

44. C.A. Grossmith to H.B. Kemmis, 26 October 1949, MSS 292-770-5, TUC, MRC.

45. E. Silver, *Victor Feather, TUC* (London, 1973), p. 67.

46. Silver, *Victor Feather*, p. 99.

47. *Daily Herald*, 27 February 1952, p. 2.

48. V. Silverman, *Imagining Internationalism in American and British Labor, 1939–49* (Chicago, IL, 1999), p. 87.

49. A. Brogi, *Confronting America* (Chapel Hill, NC, 2011), p. 100.

50. H. Wilford, 'American labour diplomacy and Cold War Britain', *Journal of Contemporary History*, 37 (2002): 44–65, at p. 64.

51. Wilford, *The CIA, the British Left*, p. 10.

52. D. MacShane, *International Labour and the Origins of the Cold War* (Oxford, 1992), p. 121.

53. P. Weiler, *British Labour and the Cold War* (Stanford, CA, 1988), p. 91.

54. Quoted in Weiler, *British Labour*, p. 112.

55. MacShane, *International Labour*, p. 126.

56. A. Carew, 'The schism within the World Federation of Trade Unions: Government and trade-union diplomacy', *International Review of Social History*, 29 (1984): 297–335, at p. 301.

57. Weiler, *British Labour*, p. 144.

58. Trades Union Congress, *Report of the 1948 Annual Trades Union Congress*, p. 448.

59. Alfred Gee to A. Gordon, 23 November 1948, TNA FO 371/72856.

60. P. Weiler, 'The United States, international labor, and the Cold War: The breakup of the World Federation of Trade Unions', *Diplomatic History*, 5 (1981): 19.

61. M. Harrison, *Trade Unions and the Labour Party since 1945* (London, 1960), p. 221.

62. Working Party report of Gen 226, 'Security measures against the encroachments by communists or fascists in the United Kingdom', 26 May 1948, TNA CAB 130/37.

63. 'Strong influence of active minority', *The Times*, 10 February 1948.

64. Gen 226 report, 'Security measures against encroachments by communists or fascists in the United Kingdom', 26 May 1948, TNA CAB 130/37.

65. *Daily Mirror*, 9 April 1948, p. 3.

66. Gen 226 meeting minutes, 1 June 1948, TNA CAB 130/37.

67. *Catholics and Communism*, CPGB pamphlet by William Gallacher, 1948.

68. George Isaacs to Clement Attlee, 9 August 1950, TNA PREM 8/1276.

69. Committee minutes of GEN 231, 11 May 1948, TNA CAB 130/37.

70. Official Committee on Communism (Home) minutes, 22 June 1951, TNA CAB 134/737.

71. 'The British ministry of propaganda', *Independent*, 26 February 1995.

72. 'Member of the Grand Council and supporters of Common Cause', MSS 292-770-6 part 2, TUC, MRC.

73. 'Origins and establishment of the Foreign Office Information Research Department, 1946–48', report by Library and Records Department, August 1995. Copy located in Mayhew 4/2.

74. John Brunett to Victor Feather, 17 January 1949, MSS 292-770-5, TUC, MRC.

75. L. Smith, 'Covert British propaganda: The Information Research Department: 1947–77', *Millennium: Journal of International Studies*, 9 (1980): 67–83, at pp. 76-7.

76. K. Jeffery and P. Hennessy, *States of Emergency* (London, 1983), p. 196.

77. Cabinet meeting conclusions, 2 June 1949, TNA CAB 128/15.

78. Broadcast talk by the minister of labour, 11 June 1949, TNA LAB 43/150.

79. Quoted in Jeffery and Hennessy, *Emergency*, p. 203.

80. Hansard, HC, vol. 466, c. 2593 (8 July 1949).

81. Jeffery and Hennessy, *Emergency*, p. 204.

82. *Daily Herald*, 4 July 1949, p. 1.

83. Hansard, HC, vol. 467, c. 441 (13 July 1949).

84. Hansard, HC, vol. 467, c. 447 (13 July 1949).

85. Hansard, HC, vol. 467, cc. 452–3 (13 July 1949).

86. Davis, *Waterfront*, p. 191.

87. Jeffery and Hennessy, *Emergency*, p. 205.

88. *Northern Whig*, 4 July 1949, p. 1.

89. Liddell diary, 4 July 1949.

90. Liddell diary, 15 July 1949.

91. Liddell diary, 7 July 1949.

92. 'Communism and the Dock Strikes', undated and unsigned, TNA HO 45/25577.

93. Frank Newsam to Gilmour Jenkins, TNA HO 45/25577.

94. M.J.E. Bagot to S.H.E. Burley, 28 July 1949, TNA HO 45/25577.

95. S.H.E. Burley to M.J.E. Bagot, 2 August 1949, TNA HO 45/25577.

96. *Belfast Telegraph*, 20 April 1950, p. 7.

97. 'Report on British Communist Party', April 1950, TNA HO 45/25577.

98. Hansard, HC, vol. 474, c. 331 (20 April 1950).

99. *Belfast Newsletter*, 28 September 1950, p. 5; Hansard, HC, vol. 478, cc. 1405–8 (15 September 1950).

100. *Northern Whig*, 29 September 1950, p. 1.

101. Hansard, HC, vol. 478, c. 1859 (17 October 1950).

102. Cabinet conclusions, 14 September 1950, TNA CAB 128/18.

103. D. Howell, *Respectable Radicals* (London, 1999), p. 347.

104. *Sheffield Daily Telegraph*, 15 July 1950, p. 1.

105. Hansard, HC, vol. 478, cc. 35–7 (24 July 1950).

106. Liddell diary, 26 July 1950.

107. *Newcastle Journal*, 25 July 1950, p. 1; *Nottingham Journal*, 25 July 1950, p. 4.

108. *Nottingham Journal*, 31 July 1950, p. 1.

109. *Aberdeen Press and Journal*, 2 September 1950, p. 1.

110. *Coventry Evening Telegraph*, 1 September 1950, p. 5.

111. William Gallacher to director of public prosecutions, 11 September 1950; Gallacher to Vincent Tewson, 11 September 1950, MSS 292-770-6 part 1, TUC, MRC.

112. *Gloucester Citizen*, 22 September 1950, 5.

113. *Daily Herald*, 29 September 1948, p. 1.

114. *Sheffield Telegraph*, 19 September 1950, p. 4.

115. Liddell diary, 7 February 1951.

116. Liddell diary, 7 February 1951.

117. Liddell diary, 4 October 1950.

118. Liddell diary, 18 September 1950.

119. Liddell diary, 12 October 1950.

120. G. Bennett, *Six Moments of Crisis* (Oxford, 2013), p. 32.

121. Liddell diary, 27 July 1950; cabinet conclusions, 20 July 1950, TNA CAB 128/18.

122. Cabinet conclusions, 14 September 1950, TNA CAB 128/18.

123. Cabinet conclusions, 18 September 1950, TNA CAB 128/18.

124. *Sheffield Telegraph*, 6 October 1950, p. 5.

125. J.T. McKelvey, 'Legal aspects of compulsory arbitration in Great Britain', *Cornell Law Review*, 7 (1952): 403–18, at p. 413.

126. I. Beesley, *The Official History of the Cabinet Secretaries* (London, 2016), p. 48.

127. H. Clegg, *A History of British Trade Unions since 1889: Volume III* (Oxford, 1994), p. 405.

128. Davis, *Waterfront*, p. 203.

129. Statement by the general secretary to the General Executive Council, 8 March 1951, MSS I26/TG2, TUC, MRC.

130. J. Dash, *Good Morning, Brothers!* (London, 1969), p. 83.

131. C. Andrew, *The Defence of the Realm* (London, 2009), p. 408.

132. *Yorkshire Post*, 26 February 1952, p. 1.

133. *Yorkshire Post*, 17 April 1952, p. 8.

134. Cabinet conclusions, 18 September 1952, TNA CAB 128/25.

135. Cabinet conclusions, 19 February 1953, TNA CAB 128/26.

136. Cabinet conclusions, 20 October 1954, TNA CAB 128/27.

137. Cabinet conclusions, 6 December 1955, TNA CAB 128/129.

138. Minutes of MI5 director general's meeting, 6 February 1951, TNA KV 4/473.

139. Minutes of MI5 director general's meeting, 13 February 1951, TNA KV 4/473.

140. Official Committee on Communism (Home) minutes, 19 January 1954, TNA CAB 134/739.

141. Dick White to Frank Newsam, 28 September 1954, TNA HO 45/25577.

142. P. Dorey and D. Aldcroft, *British Conservatism and Trade Unionism, 1954–1964* (London, 2009), p. 66.

143. Official Committee on Communism (Home) minutes, 24 March 1952, TNA CAB 134/737.

144. Memorandum by the Ministry of Labour and National Service, 'The Communists and Trade Unions', 3 March 1952, TNA CAB 134/737.

145. Official Committee on Communism (Home) minutes, 24 March 1952, TNA CAB 134/737.

146. Memorandum by the Ministry of Labour and National Service, 'The Communists and Trade Unions', 3 March 1952, TNA 134/737.

147. Official Committee on Communism (Home) minutes, 20 October 1952, TNA CAB 134/737.

148. Liddell diary, 27 January 1953.

149. Dick White to Newsam, 28 September 1954, TNA HO 45/25577.

150. Liddell diary, 20 October 1954.

151. MI5 report, 'Industrial unrest 1953–1955: The role of the Communist Party', 27 March 1956, CAB 134/1194.

152. MI5 report, 'Industrial unrest 1953–1955', 27 March 1956, CAB 134/1194.

153. R. Samuel, *The Lost World of British Communism* (London, 2006), p. 204.

154. MI5 report, 'Industrial unrest 1953–1955', 27 March 1956, CAB 134/1194.

155. Official Committee on Communism (Home), minutes, 13 April 1956, TNA CAB 134/1194.

156. Official Committee on Communism (Home), minutes, 13 April 1956, TNA CAB 134/1194.

157. Iain Macleod, 'Communism and trade unions', 5 July 1956, TNA CAB 134/1194.

158. P. Deery, 'A very present menace? Attlee, Communism and the Cold War', *Australian Journal of Government and History*, 44 (1998): 69–93, at p. 70.

159. Deery, 'A very present menace?', p. 88.

160. Davis, *Waterfront*, p. 124.

161. Silver, *Victor Feather, TUC*, pp. 101–2.

162. Quoted in Howell, *Respectable Radicals*, p. 347.

163. Davis, *Waterfront*, p. 347.

164. D. Sandbrook, *White Heat* (London, 2006), p. 282.

165. See R. Stevens, 'Cold War politics: Communism and anti-communism in the trade unions', in *British Trade Unions and Industrial Politics: The Post-War Compromise, 1945–1964*, ed. J. McIlroy, N. Fishman and A. Campbell (London, 1999), pp. 168–91.

Conclusion

In Britain generally, the witch-hunt was more demoralizing than damaging. But bad enough in the worst period, from 1948 to 1956 ... it was a bad time.[1]

—Eric Hobsbawm

The year 1956 has long been used as a demarcation line for British history. The event most cited for this reasoning is the Suez fiasco, which signalled the end of the UK as a great power.[2] Yet it was also a transitional year for domestic anti-communism. It was when the consensus over the issue solidified. In 1956, the public report of the Security Conference of Privy Counsellors was delivered – officially endorsing the anti-communist governmental vetting procedures. That year also saw the production of the top-secret MI5 assessment on 'communism in trade unions' which reassessed the threat industrial communism posed to the nation. Both of these official documents reaffirmed the course set by previous governments in tackling communism, and recommended that the course should not alter.

Indeed, the Cold War did not introduce anti-communism to the UK; it had been an element in the political culture of the country since the Russian Revolution and the formation of the Comintern. Yet it reached its pinnacle during the immediate postwar era when collective governmental anxiety over a communist threat took hold. If taken as a whole, it is shown to be all-encompassing. The main objective of numerous organisational procedures, domestic policies and independent administrative decisions enacted by the government was to safeguard the nation from supposed infiltration or subversion. Although UK policymakers and politicians sought to differentiate their internal anti-communist initiatives from the 'witch-hunt hysteria' occurring in the US, they were often keen to conduct – albeit less publicly – hunts for the 'red witch' as well. The key components which halted the expansion of British governmental anti-communist activities were fear of a negative public reaction, the limited resources of the security services and a parliamentary system which restricted independent and autonomous committees. The individuals occupying the corridors of Whitehall and the rooms of 10 Downing Street regarded communism and its followers as an existential threat to the future not only of the nation but also the whole of Western civilisation. What they feared the most was the indistinct, hidden and insidious nature of the communist danger.

Unlike previous foes, the international facets of classical Marxism made the 'enemy' unclear. Harking back to the time of religious conflict over the secession of the English monarchy, the communist enemy perceivably held loyalty higher than king or country. The nature of battling an ideologically driven opponent left members of the Communist Party open to accusations of treachery just for having such an affiliation. In the early Cold War, suspicion came from association with the theory of Marx. This effectively meant that any communist employed by the government, wishing to seek entrance into the country, active in the trade unions, peacefully protesting or even elected into parliament could be a possible traitor or probable security risk. The British establishment, once they viewed communism 'as a threat to Western civilisation', considered that the barbarians were not just at the city gates but had infiltrated the palace halls.[3] Searches and purges of communists and fellow travellers were conducted in the government, the legislative branch and even private corporations. The Cold War brought a dimension of uncertainty into the minds of those governing the UK, which translated into tangible anti-communist actions that directly focused on the citizens of the nation and which, through their planning and execution, show how sectors of the UK government considered a segment of their own population as effectively an 'enemy within'.

The unified nature of the British state allowed for a comprehensive and controlled anti-communist response.[4] This permitted the government to implement counterinsurgency measures clandestinely and present their overt anti-communist efforts to the public in a more positive light. This was unlike the American experience, where the decentralised US state made it less able to coordinate methods across various jurisdictions and allowed (one might say, even invited) alternative political and governmental reactions to the supposed 'red menace'. A prominent example is the activities of the US legislative branch in which HUAC and Joseph McCarthy were constitutionally permitted to engage in aggressive and intrusive investigations which ultimately harmed the anti-communist cause.[5] These types of public and damaging 'witch hunts' were not permitted in the UK because of the inability of MPs such as Waldron Smithers to independently set up such committees within the Westminster framework. Hence, unlike in the US, no backlash to these non-existent 'star-chambers' ever occurred. The unified governmental structure also allowed it to implement practices homogeneously over the entire country without little to no oversight. Additional restrictive measures did not take the form of new legislation, since this would result in a public Commons debate in which the government would have to justify itself. The British state wanted nothing close to transparency or public accountability. It sought to hide significant portions of its anti-communist campaign.

Uniformity among the public at large also contributed to how the red hunt in the UK played out differently to its counterpart in the US. By and large, Britons held a negative attitude to the publicised excesses in the US over the communist issue. As schoolchildren, all were taught the cautionary and villainous tale of Titus Oates – an Anglican priest who caused the death of innocents with his phoney charges of popish plots and internal dangers to the security of the realm during the seventeenth century. The similarities with McCarthy did not go unnoticed. As Lord Vansittart – as well as other politicians such as Attlee and Churchill – discovered, such highhanded and ruthless tactics were unpalatable to the public. Publicised excesses would not take wing in the UK, as conventional wisdom has stated since: the tolerance-loving people would not allow it. However, what they did accept, without opposition, was the 'othering' of fellow countrymen. The demonisation of communists solely for their political beliefs was commonplace by the press, trade union officials and most leading statesmen. Also, during the early Cold War period, there grew a tendency for increased governmental surveillance and restrictions on civil liberties. These went routinely unchecked and hardly warranted any public opposition. Although officially implemented as a policy to detect potential espionage agents, the purge procedures worked as a proscription of legal political beliefs and lawfully protected associations between individuals. As the collective political establishment routinely harassed British subjects and constructed the founding apparatuses of the modern security state, few batted an eye or counselled a word of warning. Most notably absent was opposition from the British left. Those on the Labour left were themselves purged from the party as 'crypto-communists' or, like Nye Bevan and John Strachey, supported the centre-right Labour leadership in forming an anti-communist consensus. Indeed, organised opposition did not form against increased state powers until 1956 with the formation of the Campaign for Limitation of Secret Police Powers.

Conversely, in the US, throughout the darkest days of McCarthyism, robust public and political opposition existed. Americans of the period inherited a long and cherished tradition of citizens invoking and protecting their inherent rights secured in the nation's constitution and its bill of rights. Like their forefathers, the opponents of McCarthyism vociferously did the same.[6] Because of the lack of a written constitution, Britons who wished to protest their government's increased repressive measures had no document to rally behind. In fact, as British subjects (not citizens), they did not even have a national constitutional guarantee of their rights, as Americans did. While lacking a written constitution, what the UK did possess, which the US lacked, was a more reinforced sense of social cohesiveness especially of a political nature. As in the US, a politicisation of the communist issue occurred in the nation. However, despite Conservative attempts, it did not successfully transpire into a partisan issue. Thus, no major political party sought to halt the increased anti-communism of the period.

Two highly significant determinants that caused this divergence between the British and American red scares were the differing demographics and class structures of the nations. Indeed, any analysis of British politics of the period would be woefully incomplete without tackling the issue of class in society. Not surprisingly, it played a crucial role regarding how anti-communism manifested contrarily between the US and UK. As all the evidence indicates, the real communist threat to the Atlantic world came not from the unwashed masses in the streets but the well-manicured hands in, or close to, the corridors of power. For advantageous motives, a segment of American society readily suspected this to be the truth. In the UK, because of a different societal make-up, the opposite reaction occurred. The discovery of numerous esteemed scientists (Alan Nunn May, Klaus Fuchs and Bruno Pontecorvo) as atomic spies, and the eventual disappearance of two highly placed diplomats (Guy Burgess and Donald Maclean), did little to alter the situation. While all this transpired, Attlee lamented the threat posed by communist waiters, the Conservative Central Office investigated employees of Blackwell Booksellers and MI5 spent its time and public funds on determining whether individuals were members of a legal political party (CPGB). No doubt simultaneously, such trivial investigations were conducted in the US. But a shifting demographic political make-up and a growing disdain for elitism in the US created a conducive atmosphere for hunting traitors in the ruling class as well. Status anxiety and the drive by second- and third-generation immigrants striving for proof of their Americanism contributed to the popularity of seeking out a certain type of traitor in ruling circles.[7] Indeed, certain academics have pushed this supposition as far as to state it functioned as the central catalyst of the American red scare. Historian Peter Viereck called McCarthyism 'the revenge of noses that for twenty years of fancy parties were pressed against the outside window pane'.[8]

In the US, the waning social-economic dominance of WASPs (White Anglo-Saxon Protestants) combined with the rising political power of more recently arrived ethnic minorities (Irish, Italians, German and other European nationalities) caused societal upheaval. By the late 1940s, with the zeitgeist of the nation firmly rooted in a Cold War mentality, to differentiate themselves, these status-conscious groups found it necessary to radicalise their anti-communist standpoints in order to make the case that they were as American as the WASP elite, or even more so.[9] For this reason, Joseph McCarthy – an Irish Catholic and son of immigrants – came to prominence as the champion of these interest groups, and this is also why his less than gentle style did not instinctually bother these now newly minted patriots.[10] Naturally wary of the WASP establishment, the McCarthyites were delighted to be handed by circumstance a cudgel to beat their enemies. Their leader and figurehead said it best:

> It has not been the less fortunate or members of minority groups who have been selling this nation out, but rather those who have had all the benefits that the wealthiest nation on earth has had to offer – the finest homes, the finest college education, and the finest jobs in government we can give ... the bright young men who are born with silver spoons in their mouths are the ones who have been the worst.[11]

In the UK, the situation was starkly different. Unlike in the US where large demographic changes and populism were ever present in its history, in the UK these factors were absent. Although Labour's victory in the 1945 General Election did cause a transformation of the economic policies of the country, the political and cultural norms stayed relatively unaffected. In the UK there was not a burgeoning immigrant base seeking to integrate into the status quo or disrupt the class system. Thus critics, such as Marc Silverston, were completely correct in stating that, unlike in the US, there was an 'absence of a comparable British grassroots anti-communist lobby' due to a lack of 'a more populist and participatory ethos' in British politics, 'as well as to the structural elements of the respective political systems'. In addition, he was accurate in stating that 'in the end, McCarthyism simply could not take root in British soil'.[12] Indeed, what transpired in the UK was a different form of anti-communist political repression. From a purely utilitarian standpoint, it was perhaps less effective, since it did not seek to disrupt or thoroughly investigate the upper class.

The times saw a British government at war with a specific political ideology and willing to use a variety of measures to either disrupt or eradicate its influence inside the nation. When looking for the instigators of this witch hunt, one is likely first to consider the loudest voices that thundered against communism. As Chapter 1 illustrates, the likes of Lord Vansittart and Waldron Smithers could be labelled the prime suspects. They were the quintessential red-baiters. Like frightened children pointing to monsters in the dark, they saw communists everywhere. Their language was McCarthyite. Yet their demagoguery failed to garner them the public support McCarthy was able to achieve. Nor did this type of outlandish anti-communism gain much traction; Vansittartism did not take hold. The unitary form of government halted rogue politicians such as Vansittart and Smithers from setting up formal hearings such as were conducted by HUAC and McCarthy's senatorial committee. Although they were the brashest and most extreme, they were not alone. When mainstream leaders of the British establishment deemed it politically expedient to smear an opponent as a communist, then they routinely made such a charge.

As Paul Addison and a number of other historians have attested, the end of the Second World War brought a postwar consensus in British politics.[13] A key pillar of this new era of cooperation was the acceptance and spread of the ideology of anti-communism throughout the nation's institutions. While conventional wisdom has judged the emergence of this postwar consensus as a positive development, the restrictive and punitive measures to combat communism enacted by Labour under Clement Attlee and continued by the successive Conservative governments of Winston Churchill and Anthony Eden call into question the universal approval of this cooperation. Collaboration against domestic communism gestated outwards from the core belief asserted by Ernest Bevin, in which he categorised the spread of communism as an existential threat not only to the UK but also to the whole of Western civilisation. The consensus functioned by seeking to minimise and eliminate communism inside the nation. As this study demonstrates, a myriad of methods were employed. One recurring theme which needs emphasising is that the legal status of the CPGB and the civil liberties of individual communists did not factor significantly in the implementation of anti-communist measures. The ways and means used to achieve this goal were often hidden and concealed from the public. Moreover, this was for a good reason, since oftentimes they mirrored the conspiratorial techniques which the opponents of communists claimed their foe employed.

As the British red hunt played out, an ever-present spectre influenced its direction: pressures originating across the ocean from the US. US impact on UK domestic anti-communism came in conflicting components.

First was the US government, which sought to pull the UK towards a more anti-communist stance. Here, security matters, especially dealing with atomic secrets, were the fundamental concern of the US. Attlee's decision in implementing the civil service purge and introducing stringent vetting procedures can be directly linked to a bid seeking to satisfy Washington, DC. In the larger arena of British politics, the US played a key role as well. Through clandestine efforts involving pressure groups such as Common Cause and the MRA, and through exerting influence inside British trade unions, the US promoted a harsher anti-communist agenda on the whole of British society.

A significant factor affecting the formation of the government's counterinsurgency strategies and methods used by political institutions in combating communism in the UK was the acceptance of these measures by the general public. Coverage of the American anti-communist response played a key role. The British populace took a dim view of the situation across the Atlantic as McCarthyism took hold in the US. The fear that the witch hunts of the new world would arise in the old permeated throughout the political discourse in the British Isles. During the period, certain politicians and segments of the popular press routinely labelled government ministers, MPs and even prime ministers as acting in McCarthyite fashion or attempting to institute McCarthyism inside the borders of the UK. Cognisance of this criticism led policymakers in Whitehall and non-state actors to push a more clandestine anti-communist agenda. A direct result of this state of affairs was a secretive and less overt form of anti-communism when it involved repressive and interventionist methods. Hence, grand and sweeping laws introduced of an anti-communistic nature were not needed. However, the absence of new statutes should not be misconstrued as a sign of tolerance towards communism. The governmental make-up of the UK allowed the prime minister and his cabinet to enact policies with little oversight from the legislative and especially the judicial branches of government.[14] In contrast to the US, where the battles over governmental anti-communist measures were publicly fought in the courts and the chambers of congress, the political process of the UK permitted the nation's domestic anti-communist activities to remain in the shadows.

Notes

1. Eric Hobsbawm to Peter Hennessy, undated, Papers of Eric Hobsbawm, 9937/2/133, MRC.

2. D. Reynolds, *Britannia Overruled* (London, 1991), p. 205.

3. 'Threat to Western civilisation' is the actual title of a memo authored by Ernest Bevin outlining his fears of the Soviet Union and its external support of domestic communism. 'The threat to Western civilisation: Memorandum by the secretary of state for foreign affairs', 3 March 1948, TNA CAB/129/25.

4. Vernon Bogdanor once quipped, though not entirely in jest, that the British constitution can be summed up in eight words: 'Whatever the Queen in Parliament decides is law.' *The British Constitution*, ed. M. Qvortrup (London, 2013), p. 2.

5. R. Powers, *Not without Honor* (New York, 1995), p. 272.

6. P. Wander, 'Political rhetoric and the un-American tradition', in *Cold War Rhetoric*, ed. M. Medhurst, R. Ivie, P. Wander and R. Scott (East Lansing, MI, 1990), 185–200, at pp. 192–3.

7. L. Storrs, *The Second Red Scare and the Unmaking of the New Deal Left* (Princeton, NJ, 2012), pp. 98–9.

8. P. Viereck, 'The revolt against the elite', in *The Radical Right*, ed. Daniel Bell (New York, 1964), p. 136.

9. D. Presland, *The Red Flag* (London, 2009), p. 231.

10. M. Gerth, 'The sinews of war: McCarthyism crosses the Atlantic', *Australian Journal of Politics and History*, 68 (2022): 90–108, at p. 94.

11. Quoted in R. Hofstader, *Anti-Intellectualism in American Life* (New York, 1962), p. 13.

12. M. Seleverston, *Constructing the Monolith* (Cambridge, MA, 2009), p. 203.

13. Addison was the most prominent advocate of the postwar consensus theory. It argued after the Second World War both Conservative and Labour Parties supported a mixed economic model, limited nationalisation, Keynesianism and the creation of a welfare state. Such a consensus on these ideas held until the late 1970s. P. Addison, *The Road to 1945* (London, 1975), pp. 164–5, 276–7. A historiographic debate arose in the late 1980s over the validity of the consensus thesis, most notably in the pages of *Contemporary Record* between historian Ben Pimlott and political scientists Peter Morris and Dennis Kavanagh. While Morris and Kavanagh defended the thesis, Pimlott called postwar consensus 'a mirage, an illusion that rapidly fades the closer one gets to it'. B. Pimlott, D. Kavanagh and P. Morris, 'Is the "postwar consensus" a myth?', *Contemporary Record*, 2 (1989): 12–15, at p. 13. Addison would again defend the theory in a book review on a revisionist monograph on the topic. P. Addison, 'Consensus revisited', *Twentieth Century British History*, 4 (1993): 91–4.

14. K. Ewing, J. Mahoney and A. Moretta, *MI5, Cold War, and the Rule of Law* (Oxford, 2020), p. 469.

Bibliography

Archives

Bodleian Library and Archives, Oxford University, Oxford:
    Archive of the Oxford Group (MS Oxford)
    Conservative Party Archive (CPA)
    Papers of Clement Richard Attlee, 1st Earl Attlee
    Papers of Harold Macmillan, 1st Earl of Stockton
Churchill Archive Centre, Churchill College, Cambridge:
    Churchill Papers (CHUR) (CHUN)
    Papers of 1st Viscount Chandos
    Papers of Julian Amery
    Papers of Lord Vansittart of Denham (VNST)
Lambeth Palace Library, London:
    Council on Foreign Relations Papers (CFG)
    Geoffrey Fisher Papers (Fisher)
Liddell Hart Military Archives, Kings College, London:
    Christopher Mayhew Papers (Mayhew)
Modern Records Centre, Warwick University, Coventry (MRC):
    Norman Kipping Papers
    Papers of Arthur Deakin
    Papers of Eric Hobsbawm
    Papers of Ernest Bevin
    Papers of Richard Crossman
    Records of Trade Union Congress (TUC)
    Transport and General Workers' Union Archive
    Union of Communication Workers Archive
People's History Museum, Manchester:
    Communist Party Archives (CP)
    Labour Party Archives (LPA)
    Morgan Phillips Papers
Public Record Office of Northern Ireland (PRONI), Belfast:
    7th Marquess of Londonderry Papers
The National Archives (TNA), Kew, London:
    Records of Dominions Office and Commonwealth Relations Office (DO)
    Records of Ministry of Labour (LAB)

Records of the Cabinet Office (CAB)
Records of the Foreign and Commonwealth Office (FCO)
Records of the Foreign Office (FO)
Records of the Home Office (HO)
Records of the Prime Minister's Office (PREM)
Records of the Security Service (KV)
Westminster Parliamentary Archive, London:
Beaverbrook Papers (BBK)
Papers of John Campbell Davidson
Papers of William Wedgwood Benn, 1st Viscount Stansgate (ST)
Records of the Leader of the House of Lords

Governmental papers

Report concerning the disappearance of two former office officials,
September 1955, Cmd. 9577
Statement on the Findings of the Conference of Privy Councillors on
Security volume 9715 of Cmd. (HM Stationery Office, 1956)

Hansard

House of Commons (HC) debates: 1946, 1947, 1948, 1949, 1950, 1952,
1954, 1955
House of Lords (HL) debates: 1944, 1950

Newspapers and periodicals

Aberdeen Press and Journal
Bath Chronicle Weekly Gazette
BBC News Magazine
Belfast Newsletter
Belfast Telegraph
Birmingham Daily Gazette
Blyth News
Bucks Herald
Canberra Times
Catholic Herald
Catholic Standard
Chelmsford Chronicle

Chicago Daily Tribune
Coventry Evening Telegraph
Daily Derby Telegraph
Daily Herald
Daily Mail
Daily Mirror
Daily News (New York)
Daily Worker
Donegal News
Dundee Courier
Encounter
Everybody's
Falkirk Herald
Fife Free Press
Forward (Glasgow)
Gazette of the John Lewis Partnership
Globe and Mail
Gloucester Citizen
Gloucestershire Echo
Guardian
Hartlepool Northern Daily Mail
Herald Express
Huffington Post
Independent
Intelligence Digest
Kent and Sussex Courier
Lincolnshire Echo
Liverpool Echo
Londonderry Sentinel
New Europe
New Statesman and Nation
New York Times
Newcastle Journal
Newcastle Sun
Northern Dispatch
Northern Whig
Nottingham Evening Post
Nottingham Journal
Observer
Pall Mall Gazette
People
Perth Daily News

Pravda
Salisbury Times
San Marino Tribune
Scotsman
Sheffield Daily Telegraph
Socialist Commentary
Socialist Standard
Somerset County Herald and Taunton Courier
Spectator
Sphere
Sunday Dispatch
Sunday Mirror
Sunderland Daily Echo
The Times
Time
Tribune
U.S. News and World Report
Valley Times (California)
Vital Speeches of the Day
Western Daily Press
Western Mail
Western Morning News
York Diocesan Leaflet
Yorkshire Evening Post
Yorkshire Post and Leeds Intelligencer

Pamphlets

The Answer to Any 'Ism' Even Materialism: A World Broadcast by Frank
   Buchman (Los Angeles, CA, 1948).
The Answer to Communism by D. Hyde (London, 1949).
The British Housewives' League: Your First Questions Answered by
   British Housewives' League (London, 1947).
British Labour and Communism by National Council of Labour
   (London, 1948).
British Socialism Is Destroying British Freedom by C. Palmer
   (London, 1949).
Catholics and Communism: The Communist Case by W. Gallacher
   (London, 1948).
Christians in the Class Struggle by G. Cope (Birmingham, 1942).

From Communism Towards Catholicism by D. Hyde (London, 1948).

Communism in Great Britain: A Short History of the British Communist Party by H.A. Taylor (London, 1951).

Communism: The Enemy Within Our Gates by Young Citizens Challenge to Communism (London, 1949).

The Communists: We Have Been Warned by M. Phillips (London, 1947).

Defend Democracy: Communist Activities Examined by Trade Union Congress General Council (London, 1948).

Don't Be Misled by the Housewives League! by London District Communist Party (London, 1947).

Economic League Central Council 31 Annual Report 1950 (London, 1950).

The Economic League: Points of Policy of an Organization by the Economic League (London, 1954).

A Hurricane of Common Sense by F. Buchman (London, 1960).

Ideology and Co-Existence by Moral Rearmament Movement (London, 1960).

Labour and Communist: Achieve It Together by London District Communist Party (London, 1946).

Let Us Face the Future: A Declaration of Labour Policy for the Consideration of the Nation by Labour Party Executive Committee (London, 1945).

Moral Rearmament: A Study of the Movement Prepared by the Social and Industrial Council of the Church Assembly (Westminster, 1955).

One Hundred Million Listening: Re-makers of the World, a World Broadcast on Moral Re-Armament by Moral Rearmament (London, 1939).

The Pound and You by W. Smithers (London, 1945).

Red Octopus by the Economic League Central Council (London, 1950).

Reds and Our Churches by J.B. Matthews (New York, 1953).

The Secret Battalion: An Examination of the Communist Attitude to the Labour Party by H. Laski (London, 1946).

The Secret Police and You by The Campaign for the Limitation of Secret Police Powers (Teddington, 1956).

Socialism Offers Slavery by W. Smithers (London, 1945).

Spearhead of an Answer: A Report of Two Months in S. Wales with 'The Forgotten Factor' by Moral Rearmament (Watford, 1948).

Strike and Subversive Movements: How Defeatists Exploit Disputes by the Economic League Central Council (London, 1943).

The Tactics of Disruption: Communist Methods Exposed by Trade Union Congress (London, 1948).

Terror in Spain: How the Communist International Has Destroyed Working Class Unity, Undermined the Fight against Franco,

and Suppressed the Social Revolution by John McGovern
(London, 1937).

Treachery! by Common Cause (London, 1951).

The Trojan Horse: An Open Letter from Mr. Tufton Beamish to Mr. Herbert Morrison by T. Beamish (Kent, 1953).

The Truth about the Reds by the Economic League (London, 1932).

The TUC and Communism by Trade Union Congress (London, 1955).

What Are You Living For? by F. Buchman (Caux, 1950).

Who Controls British Industry? by the Economic League (London, 1936).

Work and Play under Capitalism by the Economic League (London, 1932).

Published primary sources

Atholl, D., *Working Partnership* (London, 1958).

Attlee, C., *As It Happened* (London, 1954).

Attlee, C., *The Labour Party in Perspective* (London, 1937).

Boyd-Carpenter, J., *Way of Life: The Memoirs of John Boyd-Carpenter* (London, 1980).

Browne, A.M., *Long Sunset: Memoirs of Winston Churchill's Last Private Secretary* (London, 1995).

Buchman, F. *Remaking the World: The Speeches of Frank N. D. Buchman* (London, 1953).

Churchill, W., *Churchill Speaks, 1897–1963: Collected Speeches in Peace and War*, ed. R. James (Leicester, 1982).

Churchill, W., *In the Balance: The Speeches of Great Britain's Prime Minister in the Crucial Pre-Election Days of 1949 and 1950* (New York, 1952).

Churchill, W., *Victory: War Speeches by the Right Hon. Winston Churchill*, ed. C. Eade (London, 1946).

Cooper, D., *The Duff Cooper Diaries, 1915–1951*, ed. J.J. Norwich (London, 2005).

Copeland, M., *The Game Player: Confessions of the CIA's Original Political Operative* (London, 1989).

Crosland, A., *The Future of Socialism* (London, 1956).

Crossman, R., *The Backbench Diaries of Richard Crossman*, ed. J. Morgan (London, 1981).

Dalton, H., *The Second World War Diary of Hugh Dalton 1940–45*, ed. B. Pimlott (London, 1986).

Darke, B., *The Communist Technique in Britain* (London, 1952).

Dash, J., *Good Morning, Brothers!* (London, 1969).

Driberg, T., *Ruling Passions* (London, 1977).

Eden, A., *Days for Decision: Selected Speeches* (London, 1950).

Eister, A., *Drawing-Room Conversion: A Sociological Account of the Oxford Group Movement* (Durham, NC, 1950).

Gaitskell, H., *The Diary of Hugh Gaitskell*, ed. P. Williams (London, 1983).

Hayek, F., *Hayek on Hayek: An Autobiographical Dialogue*, ed. S. Kresge and L. Wenar (Chicago, IL, 1994).

Hobsbawm, E., *Interesting Times: A Twentieth-Century Life* (London, 2002).

Hogg, Q., *A Sparrow's Flight: The Memoirs of Lord Hailsham* (London, 1990).

Horner, A., *Incorrigible Rebel* (London, 1960).

Hyde, D., *I Believed: The Autobiography of a Former British Communist* (London, 1951).

Koestler, A., *Darkness at Noon* (London, 1940).

Labour Party Annual Report 1946 (London, 1946).

Macmillan, H., *Macmillan Diaries: The Cabinet Years, 1950–1957*, ed. P. Catterall (London, 2003).

Macmillan, H., *Tides of Fortune 1945–1955* (London, 1969).

Mayhew, C., *Time to Explain* (London, 1987).

McGovern, J., *Neither Fear nor Favour* (London, 1960).

Milne, T., *Kim Philby: A Story of Friendship and Betrayal* (London, 2014).

Morrison, H., *An Autobiography* (London, 1960).

Muggeridge, M., *Like It Was: The Diaries of Malcolm Muggeridge*, ed. J. Bright-Holmes (London, 1981).

Nicholas, H.G., *The British General Election of 1950* (London, 1951).

Nicolson, H., *Diaries and Letters 1945–1962*, ed. N. Nicolson (London, 1968).

Petrov, V. and E. Petrov, *Empire of Fear* (London, 1956).

Philby, K., *My Secret War: The Autobiography of a Spy* (London, 1968).

Shils, E., *The Torment of Secrecy: The Background and Consequences of American Security Policies* (Chicago, IL, 1956).

Strachey, J. *The Coming Struggle for Power* (London, 1933).

Vansittart, R., *Black Record: Germans Past and Present* (London, 1941).

Vansittart, R., *Bones of Contention* (London, 1945).

Vansittart, R., *Even Now* (London, 1949).

Vansittart, R., *Events and Shadows: A Policy for the Remnants of a Century* (London, 1947).

Vansittart, R., *Lessons of My Life* (London, 1943).

Vansittart, R., *The Mist Procession: The Autobiography of Lord Vansittart* (London, 1958).

Secondary sources

Addison, P., *Churchill on the Home Front: 1900–1955* (London, 1992).

Addison, P., 'Consensus revisited', *Twentieth Century British History*, 4 (1993): 91–4.

Addison, P., *The Road to 1945: British Politics and the Second World War* (London, 1975).

Aldrich, R., *GCHQ: The Uncensored Story of Britain's Most Secret Intelligence Agency* (London, 2010)

Aldrich, R., 'Secret intelligence for a post-war world: Reshaping the British intelligence community, 1944–51', in *British Intelligence Strategy and the Cold War, 1945–51*, ed. R. Aldrich (London, 1992), pp. 14–49.

Aldrich, R., *The Hidden Hand: Britain, America and Cold War Secret Intelligence* (London, 2001).

Aldrich, R. and R. Cormac, *The Black Door: Spies, Secret Intelligence and British Prime Ministers* (London, 2016).

Allen, V.L., *The Russians Are Coming: The Politics of Anti-Sovietism* (Shipley, 1987).

Allen, V.L., *Trade Union Leadership: Based on a study of Arthur Deakin* (London, 1957).

Anderson, S., *The Quiet Americans: Four CIA Spies at the Dawn of the Cold War* (New York, 2020).

Andrew, C., *Secret Service: The Making of the British Intelligence Community* (London, 1985).

Andrew, C., 'The British Secret Service and Anglo-Soviet relations in the 1920s part I: From the trade negotiations to the Zinoviev letter', *Historical Journal*, 20 (1977): 673–706.

Andrew, C., *The Defence of the Realm: The Authorised History of MI5* (London, 2009).

Barber, J., 'The War of the Worlds broadcast: Fake news or engaging storytelling?', in *Radio's Second Century: Past, Present, and Future Perspectives*, ed. J.A. Hendrick (Newark, NJ, 2020), pp. 96–118.

Barnett, C., *The Lost Victory: British Dreams, British Realities 1945–1950* (London, 1995).

Beckett, F., *Clem Attlee* (London, 1997).

Beesley, I., *The Official History of the Cabinet Secretaries* (London, 2016).

Belden, D., 'The origins and development of the Oxford Group (Moral Re-Armament)' (University of Oxford, 1976).

Bennett, G., *Six Moments of Crisis: Inside British Foreign Policy* (Oxford, 2013).

Bennett, G., *The Zinoviev Letter: The Conspiracy That Never Dies* (Oxford, 2018).

Bogdanor, V., 'Winston Churchill, 1951–1955', in *From New Jerusalem to New Labour: British Prime Ministers from Attlee to Blair*, ed. V. Bogdanor (London, 2010), pp. 23–41.

Boobbyer, P., 'The Cold War in the plays of Peter Howard', *Contemporary British History*, 19 (2005): 205–22.

Bothwell, R., ed., *The Gouzenko Transcripts* (London, 1982).

Bower, T., *The Perfect English Spy: Sir Dick White and the Secret War 1935–90* (London, 1995).

Boyle, A., *The Climate of Treason* (London, 1979).

Brogi, A., *Confronting America: The Cold War between the United States and the Communists in France and Italy* (Chapel Hill, NC, 2011).

Brotherton, R., *Suspicious Minds: Why We Believe Conspiracy Theories* (London, 2015).

Bullock, A., *Ernest Bevin: Foreign Secretary 1945–1951* (London, 1983).

Burridge, T., *Clement Attlee: A Political Biography* (London, 1985).

Butler, J., *The Red Dean of Canterbury: The Public and Private Faces of Hewlett Johnson* (London, 2011).

Callaghan, J., *Cold War, Crisis and Conflict: The History of the Communist Party of Great Britain 1951–68* (London, 2003).

Callaghan, J., 'The plan to capture the British Labour Party and its paradoxical results, 1947–91', *Journal of Contemporary History*, 20 (2005): 707–25.

Callaghan, J., *Rajani Palme Dutt: A Study in British Stalinism* (London, 1993).

Callaghan, J., 'Towards isolation: The Communist Party and the Labour government', in *Labour's Promised Land? Culture and Society in Labour Britain 1945–51*, ed. J. Fyrth (London, 1995), pp. 88–99.

Carew, A., 'The schism within the World Federation of Trade Unions: Government and trade-union diplomacy', *International Review of Social History*, 29 (1984): 297–335.

Carlton, D., 'Anthony Eden, 1955–1957', in *From New Jerusalem to New Labour: British Prime Ministers from Attlee to Blair*, ed. V. Bogdanor (London, 2010), pp. 42–59.

Carlton, D., *Anthony Eden: A Biography* (London, 1981).

Carter, M., *Anthony Blunt: His Lives* (London, 2001).

Caute, D., *Fellow-Travellers: A Postscript to the Enlightenment* (London, 1977).

Caute, D., *The Great Fear: The Anti-Communist Purge under Truman and Eisenhower* (New York, 1978).

Charmley, J., *Chamberlain and the Lost Peace* (London, 1989).

Clarke, P., *Hope and Glory: Britain 1900–2000* (London, 2004).

Clegg, H.A., *A History of British Trade Unions since 1889: Volume III 1934–1951* (Oxford, 1994).

Cockett, R., *Thinking the Unthinkable: Think-Tanks and the Economic Counter-Revolution 1931–1983* (London, 1995).

Colvin, I., *Vansittart in Office: An Historical Survey of the Origins of the Second World War Based on the Papers of Sir Robert Vansittart* (London, 1965).

Corthorn, P., 'Cold War politics in Britain and the contested legacy of the Spanish Civil War'. *European History Quarterly*, 44 (2014): 678–702.

Corthorn, P., *In the Shadows of the Dictators: The British Left in the 1930s* (London, 2006).

Corthorn, P., 'Labour, the left, and the Stalinist purges of the late 1930s', *The Historical Journal*, 48 (2005): 179–207.

Cosgrave, P., *The Strange Death of Socialist Britain: Post War British Politics* (London, 1992).

Costello, M.J., *Secret Identity Crisis: Comic Books and the Unmasking of Cold War America* (New York, 2009).

Courtois, S., ed., *The Black Book of Communism: Crimes, Terror, Repression* (Cambridge, MA, 1997).

Cradock, P., *Know Your Enemy: How the Joint Intelligence Committee Saw the World* (London, 2002).

Davenport-Hines, R., *Enemies Within: Communists, the Cambridge Spies and the Making of Modern Britain* (London, 2018).

Davies, N., *Rising '44: The Battle for Warsaw* (London, 2003).

Davis, C., *Waterfront Revolts: New York and London Dockworkers, 1946–61* (Champaign, IL, 2003).

Deery, P., 'A very present menace? Attlee, communism and the Cold War', *Australian Journal of Government and History*, 44 (1998): 69–93.

Deery, P. and N. Redfern, 'No lasting peace? Labor, communism and the Cominform: Australia and Great Britain, 1945–50', *Labour History*, 38 (2005): 63–86.

Defty, A., *Britain, America and Anti-Communist Propaganda 1945–53* (London, 2004).

Deighton, A. 'Britain and Cold War, 1945–1955', in *Cambridge History of the Cold War*, vol. 2, ed. M. Leffler and O. A. Westad (Cambridge, 2017), pp. 112–32.

Doherty, T., *Cold War, Cool Medium: Television, McCarthyism, and American Culture* (New York, 2003).

Donoughue, B. and G.W. Jones, *Herbert Morrison: Portrait of a Politician* (London, 1973).

Dorey, P. and D. Aldcroft, *British Conservatism and Trade Unionism, 1954–1964* (London, 2009).

Dorril S., *MI6: Inside the Covert World of Her Majesty's Secret Intelligence Service* (New York, 2000).

Driberg, T., *The Mystery of Moral Re-armament: A Study of Frank Buchman and His Movement* (London, 1964).

Dutton, D., *Anthony Eden: A Life and Reputation* (London, 1996).

Eatwell, R., *Fascism: A History* (London, 2003).

Ewing, K., J. Mahoney and A. Moretta, *MI5, Cold War, and the Rule of Law* (Oxford, 2020).

Farrant, A. and N. Tynan, 'The control of engagement order: Attlee's road to serfdom?', in *F.A. Hayek and the Modern Economy: Economic Organization and Activity*, ed. S. Peart and D. Levy (London, 2013), pp. 157–80.

Farrant, A. and N. Tynan, 'Sir Waldron Smithers and the long walk to Finchley', *Economic Affairs*, 32 (2012): 43–7.

Farrant, A. and N. Tynan, 'Sir Waldron Smithers and the muddle of the Tory middle', *Economic Affairs*, 32 (2012): 63–7.

Fayet, J., 'Reflections on writing the history of anti-communism', *Twentieth Century Communism*, 6 (2014): 8–21.

Ferris, F., 'Indulged in all too little? Vansittart, intelligence and appeasement', *Diplomacy and Statecraft*, 10 (1995): 122–75.

Fieldhouse, R., *Adult Education and the Cold War: Liberal Values Under Siege, 1946–1951* (Leeds, 1985).

Fielding, N., *The National Front* (London, 1981).

Fishman, N., 'The phoney Cold War in British trade unions', *Contemporary British History*, 15 (2001): 83–104.

Fleming, J., *The Anti-Communist Manifestos: Four Books That Shaped the Cold War* (New York, 2009).

Foote, G., *The Labour Party's Political Thought: A History* (London, 1997).

Gallup, G., *The Gallup International Public Opinion Polls: Great Britain 1937–1975* (New York, 1982).

Gerstle, G., *American Crucible: Race and Nation in the Twentieth Century* (Princeton, NJ, 2002).

Gerth, M., 'The sinews of war: McCarthyism crosses the Atlantic', *Australian Journal of Politics and History*, 68 (2022): 90–108.

Gilbert, M., *Winston S. Churchill: Never Despair, 1945–1965* (London, 1988).

Glees, A., *The Secrets of the Service: British Intelligence and Communist Subversion 1939–51* (London, 1987).

Goldberg, A., 'The atomic origins of the British nuclear deterrent', *International Affairs*, 20 (1964): 409–29.

Goldberg, A., 'Germans and Nazis: The controversy over "Vansittartism" in Britain during the Second World', *Journal of Contemporary History*, 14 (1979): 155–91.

Goodman, G., 'The British government and the challenge of McCarthyism in the early Cold War', *Journal of Cold War Studies*, 12 (2010): 62–97.

Goodman, G., '"Who is anti-American?": The British left and the United States, 1945–1956' (University College London, 1996).

Harmer, H., *The Longman Companion to the Labour Party, 1900–1998* (London, 1999).

Harris, K., *Attlee* (London, 1982)

Harrison, E., *The Young Kim Philby* (Exeter, 2012).

Harrison, M., *Trade Unions and the Labour Party since 1945* (London, 1960).

Haseler, S., *The Tragedy of Labour* (Oxford, 1980).

Haynes, J.E., *Red Scare or Red Menace: American Communism and Anticommunism in the Cold War Era* (Chicago, IL, 1996).

Hemming, H., *M: MI5's Greatest Spymaster* (London, 2017).

Hennessy, P., *Having It So Good: Britain in the Fifties* (London, 2006).

Hennessy, P., *Never Again: Britain 1945–1951* (London, 1994).

Hennessy, P., *The Secret State: Preparing for the Worst 1945–2010* (London, 2010).

Hennessy, P. and G. Brownfeld, 'Britain's Cold War security purge: The origins of positive vetting', *Historical Journal*, 15 (1982): 965–74.

Hinton, J., 'Militant housewives: The British Housewives' League and the Attlee government', *History Workshop Journal*, 38 (1994): 129–56.

Hinton, J., 'Self-help and socialism the squatters' movement of 1946', *History Workshop*, 25 (1988): 100–26.

Hofstader, R., *Anti-Intellectualism in American Life* (New York, 1962).

Hollingsworth, M. and R. Norton-Taylor, *Blacklist: The Inside Story of Political Vetting* (London, 1988).

Hollingsworth, M. and C. Tremayne, *The Economic League: The Silent McCarthyism* (London, 1989).

Holzman, M., *The Language of Anti-Communism* (Briarcliff Manor, NY, 2017).

Horne, A., *Macmillan 1894–1956* (London, 1988).

Howell, D., *Respectable Radicals: Studies in the Politics of Railway Trade Unionism* (London, 1999)

Hughes, M., *Spies at Work: The Rise and Fall of the Economic League* (London, 1995).

Hyman, H., 'England and America: Climates of tolerance and intolerance', in *The Radical Right*, ed. D. Bell (New York, 1962), pp. 269–306.

Jackson, I., 'Waging the economic Cold War: Britain and Cocom, 1948–54', in *Cold War Britain, 1954–1964*, ed. M. Hopkins, M. Kandiah and G. Staerack (New York, 2003), pp. 41–54.

Jago, M., *Clement Attlee: The Inevitable Prime Minister* (London, 2017).

Jeffery, K., *MI6: The History of the Secret Intelligence Service 1909–1949* (London, 2010).

Jeffery, K. and P. Hennessy, *States of Emergency: British Government and Strikebreaking since 1919* (London, 1983).

Jeffreys-Jones, R., *We Know All about You: The Story of Surveillance in Britain and America* (Oxford, 2017).

Jenkinson, J., *Black 1919: Riots, Racism and Resistance in Imperial Britain* (Liverpool, 2008).

Jenks, J., *British Propaganda and News Media in the Cold War* (Edinburgh, 2006).

Jones, B., *The Russia Complex: The British Labour Party and the Soviet Union* (Manchester, 1977).

Jones, H., 'The impact of the Cold War', in *A Companion to Contemporary Britain 1939–2000*, ed. J. Addison and H. Jones (Oxford, 2005), pp. 23–41.

Jones, I., 'The clergy, Cold War and the mission of the local church: England ca. 1945–60', in *Religion and the Cold War*, ed. D. Kirby (London, 2002), pp. 188–99.

Judt, T., *Postwar: A History of Europe since 1945* (London, 2005).

Kandiah, M., 'The Conservative Party and the early Cold War: Construction of "New Conservatism"', in *Cold War Britain, 1954–1964*, ed. M. Hopkins, M. Kandiah and G. Stareck (London, 2003), pp. 30–8.

Kazin, M. *The Populist Persuasion: An American History* (Ithaca, NY, 2017).

Kerr, S., 'British Cold War defectors: The versatile durable toys of propagandists', in *British Intelligence Strategy and the Cold War, 1945–51*, ed. R. Aldrich (London, 1992), pp. 110–39.

Kirby, D., 'Ecclesiastical McCarthyism: Cold War repression in the Church of England', *Contemporary British History*, 19 (2005): 187–203.

Kirby, D., 'The Anglican Church in the period of the Cold War 1945–55' (Hull University, 1990).

Knightley, P., *Philby, KGB Master Spy* (London, 1988).

Kovel, J., *Red Hunting in the Promise Land: Anticommunism and the Making of America* (London, 1994).

Kundnani, A., *The Muslims Are Coming! Islamophobia, Extremism, and the Domestic War on Terror* (New York, 2014).

Lacey, K., 'Assassination, insurrection and alien invasion: Interwar wireless scares in cross-national comparison', in *War of the Worlds to Social Media: Mediated Communication in Times of Crisis*, ed. E. Hayes, K. Battles and W. Hilton-Morrow (New York, 2013), pp. 57–82.

Larres, K., *Churchill's Cold War* (New Haven, CT, 2002).

Laybourn, K. and D. Murphy, *The Rise of Socialism in Britain* (Stroud, 1997).

Laybourn, K. and D. Murphy, *Under the Red Flag: A History of Communism in Britain* (Stroud, 1999).

Lean, G., *Frank Buchman: A Life* (London, 1985).

Leigh, D., *The Wilson Plot: How the Spycatchers and Their American Allies Tried to Overthrow the British Government* (New York, 1988).

Lewin, M., *The Soviet Century* (New York, 2005).

Lilleker, D., *Against the Cold War: The History and Political Traditions of Pro-Sovietism in the British Labour Party, 1945–89* (London, 2004).

Lomas, D., *Intelligence, Security and the Attlee Governments, 1945–51: An Uneasy Relationship?* (Manchester, 2016).

Lomas, D., 'Labour ministers, intelligence and domestic anti-communism, 1945–1951', *Journal of Intelligence History*, 12 (2013): 113–33.

Love, G., 'A "mixture of Britannia and Boadicea": Dorothy Crisp's conservatism and the limits of right-wing women's political activism, 1927–48', *Twentieth Century British History*, 30 (2019): 174–204.

Luff, J., *Commonsense Anticommunism: Labor and Civil Liberties between the World Wars* (Chapel Hill, NC, 2012).

Luff, J., 'Covert and overt operations: Interwar political policing in the United States and the United Kingdom', *American Historical Review*, 122 (2017): 727–57.

Luff, J., 'Labor anticommunism in the United States of America and the United Kingdom, 1920–49', *Journal of Contemporary History*, 53 (2018): 109–33.

Macintyre, S., *A Proletarian Science: Marxism in Britain 1917–1933* (Cambridge, 1980).

MacShane, D., *International Labour and the Origins of the Cold War* (Oxford, 1992).

Mahoney, J., 'Civil liberties in Britain during the Cold War: The role of the central government', *The American Journal of Legal History*, 33 (1989): 53–100.

Mahoney, J., 'Constitutionalism, the rule of law, and the Cold War', in *The Legal Protection of Human Rights: Sceptical Essays*, ed. T. Campbell, K.D. Ewing and A. Tomkins (Oxford, 2011), pp. 127–47.

Marchetti, V. and J. Marks, *The CIA and the Cult of Intelligence* (New York, 1974).

McCormick, B.J., *Industrial Relations in the Coal Industry* (London, 1979).

McFarland, E.W. and R. J. Johnston, 'The Church of Scotland's special commission on communism, 1949–1954: Tackling "Christianity's most serious competitor"', *Contemporary British History*, 23 (2009): 337–61.

McIvor, A., '"A crusade for capitalism": The Economic League, 1919–39', *Journal of Contemporary History*, 23 (1988): 631–65.

McKelvey, J.T., 'Legal aspects of compulsory arbitration in Great Britain', *Cornell Law Review*, 7 (1952): 403–18.

Miliband, R. and M. Liebman, 'Reflections on anti-communism', in
Soviet Register 1984: The Uses of Anti-Communism, ed. R. Miliband
and M. Liebman (London, 1984), pp. 1–22.

Miller, C., 'Extraordinary gentlemen: The Economic League, business
networks, and organized labour in war planning and rearmament',
Scottish Labour History, 52 (2017): 120–51.

Mills, S., 'Be prepared: Communism and the politics of scouting in 1950s
Britain', *Contemporary British History*, 25 (2011): 429–50.

Mitrokhin, V. and C. Andrew, *The Mitrokhin Archives* (London, 1999).

Moore, R., *The Emergence of the Labour Party 1880–1924* (London, 1978).

Moran, C., *Classified: Secrecy and the State in Modern Britain*
(Cambridge, 2013).

Mullin, C., *A Very British Coup* (London, 1982).

Orwell, G., 'Burnham's view of the contemporary world struggle', *New
Leader*, 29 March 1947 in *The Collected Essays, Journalism and Letters of
George Orwell*, ed. S. Orwell and I. Angus (London, 1970), pp. 313–25.

Qvortrup, Matt, 'Introduction', in *The British Constitution: Continuity
and Change – A Festschrift for Vernon Bogdanor*, ed. Matt Qvortrup
(London, 2013), pp. 1–7.

Palmer, R., 'Moral re-armament drama: Right wing theatre in America',
Theatre Journal, 31 (1979): 172–85.

Parsons, S., 'British McCarthyism and the intellectuals', in *Labour's
Promised Land? Culture and Society in Labour Britain 1945–51*, ed.
J. Fyrth (London, 1995), pp. 224–45.

Payne, K., 'Winning the battle of ideas: Propaganda, ideology, and terror', *Studies in Conflict and Terrorism*, 32 (2009): 109–28.

Pelling, H., *The British Communist Party: A Historical Profile* (London, 1958).

Pelling, H., *Churchill's Peacetime Ministry, 1951–55* (London, 1997).

Phillips, T., *The Secret Twenties: British Intelligence, the Russians and
the Jazz Age* (London, 2017).

Pimlott, B., D. Kavanagh and P. Morris, 'Is the "postwar consensus" a
myth?', *Contemporary Record*, 2 (1989): 12–15.

Pincher, C., *Their Trade Is Treachery* (London, 1981).

Pincher, C., *Treachery Betrayals, Blunders and Cover-Ups: Six Decades of
Espionage* (London, 2011).

Pitchford, M., *The Conservative Party and the Extreme Right, 1945–1975*
(Manchester, 2011).

Porter, B., *Plots and Paranoia: A History of Political Espionage in Britain
1790–1988* (London, 1989).

Potter, K., 'British McCarthyism', in *North American Spies: New
Revisionist Essays*, ed. R. Jefferys-Jones and A. Lownie (London, 2013),
pp. 167–83.

Powers, R.G., *Not Without Honor: The History of American Anticommunism* (New York, 1995).

Presland, D., *The Red Flag: Communism and the Making of the Modern World* (London, 2009).

Ramsden, J., *Man of the Century: Winston Churchill and His Legend since 1945* (London, 2002).

Read, A., *The World on Fire: 1919 and the Battle with Bolshevism* (London, 2008).

Reynolds, D., *Britannia Overruled: British Policy and World Power in the Twentieth Century* (London, 1991).

Robinson, N., *Live from Downing Street: The Inside Story of Politics and the Media* (London, 2012).

Roi, M., *Alternative to Appeasement: Sir Robert Vansittart and Alliance Diplomacy, 1934–1937* (London, 1997).

Romero, F., 'Cold War anti-communism and the impact of communism on the West', in *Cambridge History of the Cold War Part 1: Expansion and Conflict*, ed. N. Naimark, S. Pons and S. Quinn-Judge (Cambridge, 2017), pp. 291–314.

Rose, N., *Vansittart: Study of a Diplomat* (London, 1978).

Sack, D., *Moral Re-Armament: The Reinventions of an American Religious Movement* (New York, 2009).

Samuel, R., *The Lost World of British Communism* (London, 2006).

Sandbrook, D., *Never Had It So Good: A History of Britain from Suez to the Beatles* (London, 2005).

Sandbrook, D., *White Heat: A History of Britain in the Swinging Sixties* (London, 2006).

Saunders, F. S., *Who Paid the Piper? The CIA and the Cultural Cold War* (London, 1999).

Scott, C.F., 'Caring about the British Empire: British imperial activist groups, 1990–1967, with special reference to the Junior Imperial League and the League of Empire Loyalists' (King's College London, 2013).

Seldon, A., *Churchill's Indian Summer: The Conservative Government, 1951–55* (London, 1981).

Selverstone, M.J., *Constructing the Monolith: The United States, Great Britain, and International Communism, 1945–1950* (Cambridge, MA, 2009).

Shaw, T., *British Cinema and the Cold War: The State, Propaganda and the Consensus* (London, 2001).

Shepherd, R., *Iain Macleod: A Biography* (London, 1994).

Silver, E., *Victor Feather, TUC* (London, 1973).

Silverman, V., *Imagining Internationalism in American and British Labor, 1939–49* (Chicago, IL, 1999).

Smith, D. and K. Ewing, 'Blacklisting of trade unionists: What is the point of human rights law?', in *Confronting the Human Rights Act: Contemporary*, ed. N. Kang-Riou (London, 2012), pp. 249–68.

Smith, L., 'Covert British propaganda: The Information Research Department, 1947–77', *Millennium: Journal of International Studies*, 9 (1980): 67–83.

Smyth, J., *Cold War Culture: Intellectuals, the Media and the Practice of History* (London, 2016).

Stafford, D., *Churchill and Secret Service* (London, 1997).

Stevens, R., 'Cold War politics: Communism and anti-communism in the trade unions', in *British Trade Unions and Industrial Politics: The Post-War Compromise, 1945–1964*, ed. J. McIlroy, N. Fishman and A. Campbell (London, 1999), pp. 168–91.

Storrs, L., *The Second Red Scare and the Unmaking of the New Deal Left* (Princeton, NJ, 2012).

Swift, J., *Labour in Crisis: Clement Attlee and the Labour Party in Opposition, 1931–40* (New York, 2001).

Tate, S., *A Special Relationship? British Foreign Policy in the Era of American Hegemony* (Manchester, 2012).

Taylor, S., *The National Front in English Politics* (London, 1982).

Thomas, H., *John Strachey* (London, 1973).

Thompson, W., 'British communists in the Cold War, 1947–52', *Contemporary British History*, 15 (2001): 105–32.

Thorpe, A., *A History of the British Labour Party* (London, 1997).

Thorpe, A., '"The only effective bulwark against reaction and revolution": Labour and the frustration of the extreme left', in *The Failure of Political Extremism in Inter-War Britain*, ed. A. Thorpe (Exeter, 1988), pp. 11–28.

Thorpe, D.R., *Supermac: The Life of Harold Macmillan* (London, 2010).

Thurlow, R., *The Secret State: British Internal Security in the Twentieth Century* (Oxford, 1994).

Tombs, I., 'The victory of socialist "Vansittartism": Labour and the German question, 1941–5', *Twentieth Century British History*, 7 (1996): 287–309.

Toye, R., *Churchill's Empire: The World That Made Him and the World He Made* (London, 2010).

Toye, R., *The Labour Party and the Planned Economy, 1931–1951* (Woodbridge, 2003).

Toye, R., *The Roar of the Lion: The Untold Story of Churchill's World War II Speeches* (Oxford, 2013).

Toye, R., 'Winston Churchill's "crazy broadcast": Party, nation, and the 1945 Gestapo speech', *Journal of British Studies*, 49 (2010): 655–80.

Turchetti, S., *The Pontecorvo Affair: A Cold War Defection and Nuclear Physics* (Chicago, IL, 2012).

Twigge, S., E. Hampshire and G. Macklin, *British Intelligence: Secrets, Spies and Sources* (Kew, 2008).

Viereck, P., 'The revolt against the elite', in *The Radical Right*, ed. Daniel Bell (New York, 1964), pp. 135–54.

Ullrich, W., 'Preventing "peace": The British government and the second world peace congress', *Cold War History*, 11 (2011): 341–62.

Vogel, S., *Betrayal in Berlin: George Blake, the Berlin Tunnel and the Greatest Conspiracy of the Cold War* (London, 2019).

Wander, P., 'Political rhetoric and the un-American tradition', in *Cold War Rhetoric: Strategy, Metaphor, and Ideology*, ed. M. Medhurst, R. Ivie, P. Wander and R. Scott (East Lansing, MI, 1990), pp. 185–200.

Weiler, P., *British Labour and the Cold War* (Stanford, CA, 1988).

Weiler, P., 'The United States, international labor, and the Cold War: The breakup of the World Federation of Trade Unions', *Diplomatic History*, 5 (1981): 1–22.

Weiner, T., *Legacy of Ashes: The History of the CIA* (New York, 2007).

West, N., *Cold War Spymaster: The Legacy of Guy Liddell, Deputy Director of MI5* (Barnsley, 2018).

West, N., *Mole-Hunt: The Full Story of the Soviet Spy in MI5* (London, 1987).

West, N., *The A to Z of British Intelligence* (Plymouth, 2005).

West, N., *The Circus: MI5 Operations 1945–1972* (New York, 1983).

Whitaker, R., 'Fighting the Cold War on the home front: America, Britain, Australia and Canada', in *Socialist Register 1984: The Uses of Anti-Communism*, ed. R. Miliband, J. Saville and M. Libman (London, 1984), pp. 23–67.

White, P., *Our Supreme Task: How Winston Churchill's Iron Curtain Speech Defined the Cold War Alliance* (New York, 2012).

Wilford, H., 'American labour diplomacy and Cold War Britain', *Journal of Contemporary History*, 37 (2002): 44–65.

Wilford, H., *The CIA, the British Left and the Cold War: Calling the Tune?* (London, 2003).

Wilford, H., 'The Information Research Department: Britain's secret Cold War weapon revealed', *Review of International Studies*, 24 (1998): 353–69.

William, F., *Ernest Bevin: Portrait of a Great Englishman* (London, 1952).

Wood, J., 'A "third way"? The Labour left, democratic socialism and the Cold War', in *Labour's Promised Land? Culture and Society in Labour Britain 1945–51*, ed. J. Fyrth (London, 1995), pp. 73–87.

Young. J., *Winston Churchill's Last Campaign 1951–5* (Oxford, 1996).

Young, K., 'Cold War insecurities and the curious case of John Strachey', *Intelligence and National Security*, 29 (2014): 901–25.

Index

A

Adenauer, Konrad, 164, 173
America. *See* United States
American Federation of Labor (AFL), 202–4
Anglican Church, 9, 29, 32–7, 47–8, 169–70, 235
anti-socialism, 8, 28, 38, 49, 109–16, 138, 150, 173, 177
Attlee, Clement, 58, 69–70, 79, 92, 110–12, 115, 120, 137, 191, 214–15, 236, 239
  atomic weapons, 78
  criticism of, 28, 39, 66, 82,
  deputy leader, 61–2, 64
  foreign policy, 63, 71, 74
  government, 13, 60, 108–9, 140, 190, 225, 238
  House of Commons, 38, 43, 57, 81, 85, 212
  Marxism, 7–8
  red-baiting, 59
  relationship with MI5, 65–6, 67–8, 82–3, 91, 136, 206, 208, 210, 212, 224
  religion, 47
  Second World War, 63
  Trade Unions Congress, 201, 205–6

B

Baker White, John, 41, 173–4
Beamish, Tufton, 72, 160, 175
Beaverbrook, Lord, 40–43, 80, 165
Bellenger, Frederick, 67–8
Benn, Anthony, 31, 226
Bevan, Aneurin 'Nye', 64, 72, 206, 225, 235
  Bevanites, 71
Bevin, Ernest, 66, 98, 139, 193, 238
  Christopher Mayhew, 94, 98, 172
  foreign secretary, 8, 26, 61, 64, 70–71, 74, 91, 136
  Transport and General Workers Union, 61, 62–3
Bing, Geoffrey, 39, 67–8
Blake, George, 140
Blunt, Anthony, 129, 140
Bobrinskoy, Alexis, 44–5
Boy Scouts, 49
Braddock, Elizabeth, 68, 72
British Broadcasting Company (BBC), 10, 20, 24, 29, 32, 37, 44–6, 48, 95, 138, 172, 208
British Legion, 29, 116–17
British Union of Fascists, 153

Brook, Norman, 86, 88, 93–4, 96, 108, 120, 215, 222
Brooman-White, Richard, 126, 131
Brown, Gordon, 177
Buchman, Frank, 162–9, 172–3, 179–80
Burgess, Guy, 15, 126, 127, 128, 129, 133–5, 172, 236
  debate and investigation over disappearance, 74–5, 88, 107–8, 119–20, 121, 125–6, 130, 132, 136–7

C

Cairncross, John, 140
Cambridge University, 126, 129, 133
Campaign for Limitation of Secret Police Powers, 123, 235
Canada, 25–6, 77–8, 88, 208, 210
Catholic Church, 9, 26, 33–6, 47, 170, 205–6
Central Intelligence Agency (CIA), 97, 128, 148–9, 157–9, 180
Chapman-Walker, Mark, 113–14
China, 24–5, 27, 86, 162
Church of England. *See* Anglican Church
Churchill, Winston, 7–8, 20, 25, 38, 69, 111, 139–41, 235
  BBC, 45–6
  counterintelligence, 127
  government, 89, 108, 190–2, 216–17, 219, 238
  red-baiting, 109–10, 113
  religion, 47–8
  vetting, 75–7, 89, 98, 120
Colville, John, 21, 127
Common Cause, 147–50, 155–61, 178–80, 207, 222, 239
Common Wealth Party, 155–6
Communist Party of Great Britain (CPGB), 71, 91, 93, 111, 194, 196, 212
  interwar period, 11–12, 40, 78
  labelled a threat, 7, 67, 80–81, 97, 112, 122, 156, 174, 212, 234
  membership in, 41, 75, 79, 84, 90, 123, 129, 177, 211
  MI5, 2–3, 216, 218, 220–1
  squatter's movement, 57–9
  trade unions, 194, 196–7, 198–9, 201, 205, 210, 216
Congress of Cultural Freedom (CCF), 148–9, 159
Congress of Industrial Organizations (CIO), 202, 204
Conquest, Robert, 94, 95

260 INDEX

Cooper, Duff, 75, 125, 136
Cope, Gilbert, 33
Cordeaux, John, 134–5
Craigavon, Lord, 45
Crisp, Dorothy, 150–3
Crosland, Anthony, 8
Crossman, Richard, 7, 66, 137

D

Daily Worker, 1, 30–31, 34, 63, 73, 174
Dalton, Hugh, 70
Davies, Clement, 209
Deakin, Arthur, 169, 189, 199, 203–4,
    213–15, 217–18, 220, 224
de Courcy, Kenneth, 20, 25–8, 42, 49
Driberg, Tom, 168–9, 170–73
Dukes, Paul, 111
Dutt, R. Palme, 24

E

Economic League, 38, 41, 148–50, 158,
    173–80, 210, 222
Ede, James Chuter, 58, 92, 176–7, 210,
    214–15
Eden, Anthony, 27, 69, 109, 121, 131, 151,
    153–5, 209, 225
    compared to Churchill, 138–40
    foreign secretary, 121
    government, 108–9, 129, 190, 219, 238
    opinion of Socialism, 113
Eisenhower, Dwight, 120, 154
Eliot, T.S., 37

F

fascism, 6, 7, 13, 23, 63, 65, 79, 81, 112,
    153, 161
Feather, Victor 'Vic', 200–201, 207, 224
Federal Bureau of Investigation (FBI), 30,
    87, 120, 141, 163
Fisher, Geoffrey, 9, 32–7, 47, 169–70
France, 23, 35, 60, 129, 195, 223
Franco, Francisco, 26, 36, 195
Fuchs, Klaus, 87–8, 138, 164, 236

G

Gaitskell, Hugh, 70, 72
    Gaitskellites, 71
Gallacher, William 'Willie', 39, 65, 71, 81,
    206, 213
General Election
    1924, 11
    1945, 14, 59, 109–10, 147, 237
    1950, 14, 28, 40, 71, 94, 113–16, 118–19, 138
    1951, 28, 45, 89, 116, 138, 216
    1955, 72
    1964, 73

Germany, 60, 63, 124, 158, 164
    Berlin, 62, 73, 128
    Nazi, 21–3, 38, 63, 115, 163–4
Gouzenko, Igor, 74, 77–8
Gunn, Herbert, 41, 42

H

Hayek, Friedrich, 38, 110
Hiss, Alger, 125, 140
Hitler, Adolf, 20, 21, 22, 26, 34, 38, 39
HMS Amethyst, 24, 48
Hoare, Robert, 176–7, 210
Hogg, Quintin, 154, 172–3
Hollis, Roger, 77, 83, 102n109,
    140, 175
Home Guard, 140
homosexuality, 120–2
Horner, Arthur, 193–6, 224
House Un-American Activities
    Committee (HUCA), 39, 57, 84, 90,
    126, 234, 238
Housewives' League, 148, 150–3, 178
Howard, Peter, 165–6, 171–3, 178–80
Hutchinson, Lester, 68, 71, 114
Hyde, Douglas, 34, 41, 73

I

Information Research Department (IRD),
    37, 92, 94–8, 112, 156, 158, 160–1, 171,
    176–7, 180–1, 190, 200, 207, 218
Intelligence Digest, 25
International Confederation of Free
    Trade Unions (ICFTU), 169, 171
Isaacs, George, 39, 206–9, 211–12, 214–15,
    217
Italy, 69, 85, 223

J

Jacob, Ian, 37
John Birch Society, 154
John Lewis Partnership, 49
Johnson, Hewlett, 32–3, 39, 48
Johnson, Louis, 27, 42–3

K

Kell, Vernon, 12
Knight, Maxwell, 68, 173
Korean War, 27, 35, 44, 92, 107–8, 175,
    212–13

L

League of Empire Loyalists, 148, 153–5,
    178
Liddell, Guy, 82, 83, 84, 91, 140, 177, 212,
    220
    concerns over Soviet threat, 86, 87

diaries, 16n5, 223
hunt for communists in Labour Party, 65, 66, 67–9
investigations into strikes, 193–4, 210, 212–14
Kim Philby, 12–19, 136
opinion of Waldron Smithers, 38
relationships with Anthony Blunt and Guy Burgess, 129
Lipton, Marcus, 126, 127, 128, 129–30, 131, 135, 137
Listeners' Association, 45

M

MacArthur, Douglas, 179
MacDonald, Ramsay, 7, 11
Maclean, Donald, 15, 119, 126, 127, 129, 132–3, 172, 236
debate and investigation over disappearance, 74–5, 88, 107–8, 119–20, 121, 125–6, 130, 132, 136–7
Macmillan, Harold, 15, 37, 111, 113, 126–8, 130–5, 138, 140, 144n89, 155, 219
Makins, Roger, 78
Marshall Plan, 35, 193, 197, 203, 210
Marx, Karl, 7–8, 59–60, 163
Maxse, Marjorie, 111, 116–17, 118, 119, 167, 176
Maxwell Fyfe, David, 119, 120, 123–4, 136, 137–8, 139, 150, 152, 172–3, 216
Mayhew, Christopher, 70, 94, 95, 96, 98, 112, 158, 171–3, 178, 180–1, 207
McCarran Act, 90
McCarthy, Joseph, 29–30, 49, 57, 107, 140, 159, 237–8
comparisons to, 1, 20, 29–30, 47, 48–9, 58, 123, 211, 234–5
McCarthyism, 3–4, 47, 108, 159, 177, 179, 235–6
McGovern, John, 36, 72–3, 161–2, 168, 171, 180
McMahon Act (1947), 78, 88
Menzies, Stewart, 128–9
MI5. *See* Security Service
MI6. *See* Secret Intelligence Service
Mitchell, Graham, 129, 140, 210
'mole' hunt, 140
Monckton, Walter, 217
Montgomery, Bernard, 108
Moral Rearmament, 48, 72–3, 147–50, 161–73, 178–81, 239
Morrison, Herbert, 39, 58, 61, 69–70, 72, 84–5, 110, 137, 201, 215
attacks on Soviet Union, 62
BBC, 45
election campaigning, 110, 111, 114, 115–16

foreign secretary, 71, 127, 132, 207
home secretary, 63–4, 75, 76
House of Commons, 57, 98, 132, 133–4
nationalisation, 60
religion, 47

N

National Coal Board (NCB), 193–4
National Front, 155
National Union of Mineworkers (NUM), 191, 193–6
NATO, 42, 71, 74, 91
Newsam, Frank, 176, 210
New York Times, 25, 42, 85, 192–3
Nicolson, Harold, 21, 64
Nixon, Richard, 140
Noel-Baker, Philip, 208
Northern Ireland, 35, 45, 68, 84
Belfast, 36, 166
Londonderry, 35
Nunn May, Anthony, 77–9, 80, 236
Nutting, Anthony, 160

O

Oates, Titus, 46, 235
Official Secrets Act, 78, 120, 172
Orwell, George, 62, 65, 95, 99n27, 196
Orwell's List, 95

P

Petrov, Vladimir, 127
Philby, Kim, 15, 124–33, 135–8, 140
Phillips, Morgan, 8, 66–8, 70, 72–3, 139, 159, 197, 205
Piratin, Phillip, 65, 71
Platts-Mills, John, 68–71, 81, 114
Pollitt, Harry, 63, 66, 85, 193
Pontecorvo, Bruno, 88, 236
populism, 2, 130, 140, 146n142, 237

Q

Queen Elizabeth, 91

R

red scare. *See* United States
Reilly, Patrick, 131, 138
revolution
American, 179
Chinese, 86
fear of in Britain, 10, 12, 63, 189, 224
Russian, 10, 149, 233
Rothschild, Lord, 140

S

sabotage, 64, 69, 179, 189, 191, 197, 203, 212–15, 219

262 INDEX

Scotland, 37, 72, 118, 158, 217
Secret Intelligence Service (MI6), 2,
    3, 11–12, 64, 111, 128, 131, 137, 156,
    163
  membership in, 116, 119, 126, 135
Security Service (MI5), 2, 3, 73, 79, 82–3,
    91, 206–7, 210, 212
  BBC, 45–6
  Economic League, 149, 173–5, 177
  Herbert Morrison, 71, 85
  interwar period, 11–12
  investigations, 45–6, 48, 58, 67–8,
    217–18, 236
  Kenneth de Courcy, 25, 27
  Kim Philby, 128, 131, 138
  Labour Party, 64–5
  Moral Rearmament, 163–4, 166–7,
    170
  surveillance, 77, 80, 87, 129
  trade unions, 191, 193, 214, 216, 220–5,
    233
  vetting, 75, 76–7, 83–4, 86, 88–9,
    120–1
  Winston Churchill, 127
Shawcross, Hartley, 41, 58, 210, 215
Shinwell, Emanuel 'Manny', 42–3, 47,
    151
Sillitoe, Percy, 84, 136, 166, 216, 218
Smith, C.A., 155–6, 158
Smith, Walter Bedell, 128, 157, 159, 160
Smithers, Waldron, 13–14, 19–20, 37–49,
    57–9, 69, 80, 85, 97–8, 151, 175, 234,
    238
social democracy, 8, 49, 61, 70, 113–15,
    176, 224–5
Soviet All-Union Central Council of
    Trade Unions, 202
Spain, 36, 62
Special Branch, 15, 58, 65, 88, 190, 210,
    215, 222
Springhall, Douglas Frank, 75–6, 79
Stalin, Joseph, 12, 39–40, 62–3, 94, 111,
    162
Stansgate, Lord, 31–2, 49
Strachey, John, 20, 40–4, 47–8, 64, 80,
    82, 151, 235
strikes
  Atlantic Fleet (1931), 11
  Austin Motor Works (1953), 217
  dockworkers, 96, 208–11, 214, 215–16,
    217–18, 223, 226
  General Strike (1926), 11, 12, 190
  Glasgow (1919), 10
  Grimethorpe (1947), 191–7
  London gas workers (1950), 215
  Savoy Hotel (1947), 91
Suez Crisis, 154, 233

T
Tacitus, 21
Tewson, Vincent, 198–200, 213, 223
Thatcher, Margaret, 7, 97
Tomney, Frank, 134
Trade Unions Congress (TUC), 66, 74,
    82–3, 95, 191, 196–204, 206–7, 213,
    216, 220, 223–4
Transport and General Workers' Union
    (TGWU), 61, 62–3, 169, 191, 199, 211,
    213, 215, 224
treason, 90, 107, 125, 131, 135, 138, 140, 225
Truman, Harry, 78, 107, 163, 179

U
UFOs, 127
United States
  Anglo-American relations, 41–2, 75, 128,
    154, 192–3
  atomic weapons, 25, 78, 86–8, 141
  Common Cause, 156–9, 178–9, 180
  compared to Britain, 2–4, 9, 57, 84, 97,
    205
  influence on Britain, 1, 10, 13, 88,
    119–22, 127, 149, 195, 202–3, 239
  Moral Rearmament, 168, 178–9, 180
  pro-American feeling in Britain, 34–5,
    39
  red scare 2–4, 9, 19, 49, 97, 158–9, 179,
    235–8
Unity Theatre, 85
University of London, 48

V
Vansittart, Lord, 20–37, 43, 44–5, 46–8,
    49, 58, 121, 180, 235, 238
  Vansittartism, 20–3, 28, 31, 46–7, 49
Venona, 87

W
Waitrose, 49
White, Dick, 127, 131, 220
Wilson, Harold, 96, 140, 226
Wilson, Woodrow, 10
Winnifrith, John, 87–8
World Federations of Trade Unions
    (WFTU), 202–4
World Peace Council (WPC), 91–2, 123

Y
Youth Peace Festival, 124

Z
Zilliacus, Konni, 24, 68, 70–1
Zinoviev Letter, 11–12, 64, 136, 210
Zuckerman, Solomon 'Solly', 83–4

Printed in the USA
CPSIA information can be obtained
at www.ICGtesting.com
JSHW070958220324
59626JS00009B/51